CAPTAIN MEDWIN

Friend of Byron and Shelley

CAPTAIN
MEDWIN

Friend of Byron and Shelley

ERNEST J. LOVELL, JR.

UNIVERSITY OF TEXAS PRESS, AUSTIN

Library of Congress Catalog Card No. 62–9788

Printed in the United States of America
by The R. L. Bryan Company

*Published with the assistance of a grant from the Ford
Foundation under its program for the support of
publications in the humanities and social sciences*

THIS BOOK

is for

ANNE and JIM

ACKNOWLEDGMENTS

This, the first full-length biography of Thomas Medwin, is based solidly upon Medwin's published books, articles, tales, sketches, poems, and translations. Sixty of these have never before been listed in any bibliography. However, this biography would have been impossible to write without the generous aid of the following persons, to whom I here give my particular thanks, in grateful appreciation, chiefly for their help in providing important unpublished materials: Sir John Murray, K.C.V.O., D.S.O., of London, for the contents of a large box file of papers dealing with Medwin, including Medwin's letters to Byron; Mrs. Doris L. Moore of London, for a lengthy transcript of unpublished portions of John Cam Hobhouse's diary and for other important aid; Mrs. Joan St. George Saunders, my friend and representative in London, for a copy of the will of Medwin's father and for other important and extended aid; Mr. D. W. King, O.B.E., F.L.A., Librarian of the British War Office at Whitehall, for lengthy summaries of Medwin's military records; Mr. Ivan Roe of London, for a transcript of the christening record of Medwin's daughter; Mr. T. C. Skeat of the Department of Manuscripts, British Museum, for one Medwin letter; Mr. Thomas G. Stedman of Horsham, Sussex, for photographs of Medwin's tombstone and for other aid; Dr. Herbert Derwein of Heidelberg, for transcripts of articles from the *Badische Post*; Dr. Cino Corti of Florence, for transcripts of court records naming Medwin in the state archives of Florence; Signorina Rosella Masetti of Pisa, for directing me to Medwin's sole living descendant; Count Paolo Mancini and Countess Patricia Mancini of Lausanne and Cortona, for permission to publish Medwin's letters; Signorina Elsa Dallolio and the Marchesa Iris Origo of Rome; Professor Lewis Patton of Duke University and Mr. B. E. Powell of the Duke Uni-

versity Library, for a microfilm in twenty-six reels of the great
Lord Abinger Collection of nineteenth century letters and
diaries; The Carl and Lily Pforzheimer Foundation, Inc., for
permission to quote from thirteen unpublished Medwin letters,
all in The Carl H. Pforzheimer Library; Professor Leslie A.
Marchand of Rutgers University, for photographs of pages from
Teresa Guiccioli's unpublished "Vie de Lord Byron en Italie"
and for a list of Medwin's anonymous contributions to *The
Athenaeum*, which Professor Marchand copied from the marked
file in London; Professor William H. Marshall of the University
of Pennsylvania, for a list of Medwin's signed contributions to
Ainsworth's Magazine, not otherwise available to me; Professor
William A. Jackson of the Houghton Library, for microfilm
copies of Medwin's *Conversations of Byron* with autographic
annotations by Medwin, Trelawny, and General Sir Charles
Napier; Mr. Herbert Cahoon of the Pierpont Morgan Library,
for microfilm of Medwin letters and of a copy of Medwin's *Life
of Shelley*, revised for a new edition and differing from the copy
used by H. Buxton Forman; Mr. Robert F. Metzdorf of the
Yale University Library, for a copy of Medwin's *Conversations
of Byron* annotated by John Cam Hobhouse; Mr. Seymour
Adelman of Philadelphia, for bibliographical details of the very
rare Baltimore edition (1825) of Medwin's *Conversations of
Byron* and for a letter of Heinrich Heine, mentioning Medwin;
Mr. John D. Gordan, Curator of the Berg Collection, New York
Public Library, for one Medwin letter; the Librarian of the
University of Pennsylvania, for Medwin's marked copies of *The
New Anti-Jacobin*, identifying his own contributions; Professor
Warren Roberts, Director of the Humanities Research Center,
University of Texas, for Medwin's unpublished manuscript
play, *Prometheus the Fire-bearer*, for a unique interleaved copy
of Medwin's *Memoir of Shelley*, presented by the author to
Caroline de Crespigny, for letters of Lady Caroline Lamb, and
for other aid; Professor Willis Pratt and the late Professor David
L. Clark of the University of Texas, for a typescript of the unpublished diary of Claire Clairmont, photostats of which are at

Acknowledgments ix

the University of Texas; Professor C. L. Cline, of the University
of Texas, for transcripts of letters of Medwin and Trelawny;
Professor William B. Todd, of the University of Texas, for a
transcript of a letter of Charles Armitage Brown; and Miss Ruth
Hale and others of the University of Texas Library, for their
unfailing courtesy and highly informed assistance.

I am also greatly indebted to Mr. Alexander Moffit, Librarian
of the University of Texas, for aid in securing photographic
reproductions of unpublished material. The University of Texas
Research Institute was kind enough to give to me a leave of
absence and several very generous grants.

ERNEST J. LOVELL, JR.

The University of Texas

CONTENTS

CAPTAIN MEDWIN

Friend of Byron and Shelley

1
English Origins

Thomas Medwin is perhaps one of the most outrageously misrepresented men in all literary history—and also, at times, one of the most exasperating. It is this quality which explains much of his later treatment by Byron and Shelley biographers, who, without important exception, beginning with Sir Egerton Brydges in 1825, Leigh Hunt in 1828, and John Galt and Thomas Moore in 1830, have plundered his books as primary sources of knowledge concerning Byron and Shelley.

Why has he so angered those who followed him? It is true that in Medwin's *Conversations of Byron* and elsewhere he sometimes named persons, places, and dates with a lordly unconcern for what turned out later to be the facts; but one should remember that he, unlike his later critics, was a pioneer who wrote his books about Byron and Shelley without benefit of an adequate library or sufficient letters. Furthermore, charges of carelessness similar to those levelled at Medwin are seldom brought against Lady Blessington, who also reported the conversations of Byron at book length. Her relative immunity to such charges points up a chief difference between the minds and styles of the two writers and explains much. For Medwin had an instinctive affinity for the specific, concrete (and colorful) detail; thus his pages are much more easily proved wrong than those of Lady Blessington, with their smooth generalities and the relative absence of names and dates.

Medwin has continued to suffer also from the judgments of some of his contemporaries—notably, of Mary Shelley, ill and unhappily married, under whose roof Medwin was too long a house guest; of E. J. Trelawny, now proved a liar of monstrous proportions; of Byron's Claire Clairmont, the unwed mother who feared Medwin; of John Murray, Byron's publisher; and of John Cam Hobhouse (later Lord Broughton), Byron's friend and the self-appointed official protector of Byron's reputation. These two men hated the author of the *Conversations of Byron* for what the book, through the mouth of the dead Byron, said about them. And so Medwin was attacked, viciously and variously, down through the years, new critics echoing old.

But Byron and Shelley took him in, gave him many long hours of friendship, and neither has left behind an unkind word about him.

To be sure, so great was his disappointment at arriving late, by a matter of hours, for the cremation of the body of his beloved Shelley that he was capable of implying his own presence at that dramatic event, avoiding an outright lie only by the thinnest line, if avoid it he did. But later in print he twice admitted his absence at the cremation of Shelley's body, and he was quite incapable of altering Shelley's letters, as T. J. Hogg did, or burning some of Keats's letters, as Sir Charles Dilke did,[1] or turning upon Byron after his death as Trelawny and Leigh Hunt did. His love of the two great poets in his life and continuing devotion to their poetry were greater than those of many who belabored him.

And finally, before it was all over, he was a man of no small achievements—friend of Byron, Shelley, Washington Irving, and others less centrally located in the stream of literature; a poet of some competence himself, although never able to escape the established poetic idiom of his day; journalist, editor, and traveler extraordinary; novelist, short story writer, essayist, playwright, and biographer; translator of Aeschylus and lesser poets, Latin, Italian, Spanish, Portuguese, and German; and a most important influence in determining the early English, American, and European reputation of Byron and Shelley.

[1] Joanna Richardson, *Fanny Brawne; A Biography* (London, 1952), p. 169. The burning was witnessed by Sir Charles's private secretary.

Who exactly was Thomas Medwin, and what had made him at the time when he associated intimately in Pisa with two of the greatest poets of the age, in 1820, 1821, and 1822? To answer this question, we must go back to Horsham, Sussex, an ancient little town of about 4,000 people, where on March 20, 1788, Thomas Medwin was born, the son of Thomas Charles and Mary Pilfold Medwin.[2] Here in Horsham Medwin passed his early life among scenes quite familiar to the poet Shelley, his second cousin, who lived two miles away at Field Place.

The town of Horsham is so old that the origin of its very name is lost in the mists of antiquity, one opinion being that it was founded and named by Horsa, brother of Hengist. However that may be, the manor of Horsham, with its forty-one farms, was given by William the Conqueror to one of his Norman knights, William de Braose, and continued in his family until a female descendant, Olivia,

. . . carried it by marriage in 1298 to John de Mowbray, . . . whose descendant, Thomas, was created Duke of Norfolk in 1391. His granddaughter Margaret marrying Sir Robert Howard, Knt., and becoming coheiress of the de Mowbray property, their son John Howard, K. G., was in 1483 created Duke of Norfolk by Richard III, and from him . . . the estates, including the lordship of Horsham, have lineally descended to the present head of that illustrious house.[3]

The head of that illustrious house when Thomas Medwin lived in Horsham was the immensely wealthy and eccentric Charles Howard, the eleventh Duke of Norfolk, to whom Medwin's father, "an expert on Manorial Law and Custom," was steward.[4] It was Norfolk who attempted to achieve a reconciliation between Shelley and his father and to persuade the young poet

[2] Birth dates and parentage of Medwin are from the records of the Horsham Parish Church. The sketch of Horsham which follows is taken largely from D. Hurst, *Horsham: Its History and Antiquities* (London, 1868), published the year before Medwin's death.

[3] Hurst, *Horsham,* pp. 2–3.

[4] William Albery, *Parliamentary History of the Ancient Borough of Horsham* (London, 1927), p. 123, quoted by Kenneth Neill Cameron, *The Young Shelley* (New York, 1950), p. 39.

to enter upon a political career, for which he was so eminently unsuited.

Although Horsham is only thirty-five miles from London, a distance that the local coach took four hours to traverse, many ancient customs persisted in Medwin's day, and certain living conditions were quite primitive. May day was still celebrated with garlands and flowers, and flowers were strewn before a bride and bridegroom when they left the church.

"Gooding" on St. Thomas' Day [was] still kept up . . . The curfew . . . regularly tolled at 8 o'clock in the evening from Michaelmas to Lady-day; . . . and the practice of ringing the old year out and the new year in [was] invariably observed, a full peal of eight bells being rung with various changes for nearly an hour at midnight.

Bull baiting in the open space called the Carfax persisted until after 1812,[5] the year when Thomas Medwin sailed for India.

Not until 1835 was the town lighted by gas, which replaced the dingy oil lamps that Medwin knew. There were no police; a few watchmen patrolled the streets with lanterns, calling out the hour at intervals, according to ancient custom. Water, supplied from wells and the River Arun, was conveyed in wooden pipes, through which it was forced by pumps worked by a great water wheel at the town mill.[6]

The business of the town was law, marketing, and divine worship. Spring assizes for the county were held in the town hall, a massive old stone building, with arches and towers, on which the Duke of Norfolk spent £8,000 in 1812. The assizes were held in the upper rooms, prisoners were kept in the cellar, and that part of the building on ground level, with its open arches, served regularly on each Monday as a market for poultry. The "corn" or grain market (which had been granted by Henry VI to the Archbishop of Canterbury) was held on Saturdays. Running east and west through this oldest and central part of town was "Butcher's Row," a medieval street so narrow

---

[5] Hurst, *Horsham*, pp. 26–27.
[6] *Ibid.*, pp. 31, 33, 42.

that two vehicles could not pass abreast. The scene was enlivened by five annual fairs, two of them chartered in 1461, and also by "balls and society, along with good hunting of geese and teal," as Shelley observed in 1808.[7]

If the town hall and ancient market place dominated the center of town—the parish church, St. Mary the Virgin, endowed in 1231, dominated the extreme southern portion of the town, its warped wooden spire of 230 feet rising high above the River Arun below. Here, in this ancient, spacious church, erected about the year 1247, its interior containing massive Norman columns and lofty arches, worshipped Thomas Medwin and the poet Shelley, in boyhood and young manhood. Here are buried Medwin's father and brothers; here are buried Shelley's father, mother, grandfather Sir Bysshe and his wife Mary Catherine, the poet's grandmother. It was this church, specifically, and its curate of thirty-five years, the Rev. George Marshall, that provided the irritant which was eventually to produce *Queen Mab* and Shelley's other attacks upon organized Christianity.

Thomas Medwin, however, may well have acquired the beginnings of a sense of history from his attendance at the Church of St. Mary the Virgin. For its tower, "adorned with grotesquely carved heads" and supported by massive buttresses, is in the Anglo-Norman style; and within the church, beneath its panelled oak ceiling decorated with colored bosses of "wonderful variety of design," were three very impressive monuments out of the past. Above the tomb of Thomas, Lord Braose (died 1395), descended from the Conqueror's knight, so richly rewarded in land, is his recumbent effigy, carved to represent him wearing full battle armor. Another canopied and elaborately carved tomb, its testern supported with marble pillars, is that of Thomas Hoo (died 1486), brother of Lord Hoo. And on an altar-tomb is the recumbent effigy, in white marble, of

---

[7] *The Journal of Harriet Grove*, ed. Roger Ingpen (London, 1932, Privately Printed), p. xii, a letter from Shelley to a schoolfellow, Jan. 10, 1808.

"a lady in the dress of the 17th century, with her right hand on her breast, and her left resting on a book. This figure, which is quite perfect, is elaborately and beautifully executed . . ." It commemorates Elizabeth Delves, who died in 1654.[8] Among the old tablets in memory of Medwin's ancestors (and Shelley's) is one naming John Michell, "gent.," who died in 1610, and another naming John Pilfold, who died in 1759.[9] In 1585 Henry Pilfold, whose name was borne by Medwin's mother, had established a charitable foundation for the parish poor, setting aside certain lands for its support.[10]

But Thomas Medwin's sense of kinship with the past, its mystery and beauty, was nourished also by the ruins of a number of ancient great houses or castles in Horsham parish or its immediate area. The remains of the moated baronial mansion of Chesworth, where Edward I and Edward II had been guests, still stood, although much dilapidated. There were strange stories told about the ancient house, once the residence of the Dukes of Norfolk—stories of bells strangely rung, harrowing shrieks, blood that could not be removed from the stones, midnight warriors on horseback. "When the moat was cleaned out . . ., a considerable number of human bones were discovered." These local stories could not have been without effect upon the early literary compositions of Thomas Medwin.

The mansion called Denne (Dane), built in the time of the Stuarts, is close to Picts Hill, where Medwin's brother John was killed at the age of twenty-one, and suggests the ancient warlike inhabitants of the area. The tradition is that Alfred the Great attacked the Danes here. And two and a half miles east of Horsham, Medwin could visit the circular, moated ruins of Sedgewick Castle, built in the time of Henry III.

Within Horsham, there were still many gabled houses of the sixteenth century, plaster filling up a framework of timber. Causeway House was one of the best examples of this style, with its "overhanging floors supported with carved brackets;

[8] Hurst, *Horsham*, pp. 63–76.
[9] *Ibid.*, pp. 77, 82.   [10] *Ibid.*, p. 88.

the eaves projecting over the sides of the house; and the apex
. . . surmounted by decorated pinnacles." [11] And there were at
least six other houses of great age and beauty in the vicinity,
among them the "Old House" of Stammerham, in Horsham
parish, residence since the sixteenth century of the Michell
family, to whom Medwin was related.

But the most splendid house of all was Hills Place, sometimes known as St. Irving's Hills, purchased by the Duke of
Norfolk in 1811 and used by him as a residence. Medwin without doubt knew its interior. Located between Horsham and
Field Place (two miles apart) and erected in the reign of
Elizabeth, it had been built of brick, with stone mullions and
groins. The grounds had been laid out by the famous "Capa-
bility" Brown, the shaded walks extending around them a mile
in circumference and the Arun running through the garden.
Thomas Jefferson Hogg, Shelley's early friend and biographer,
remembered it as "a beautiful place . . . full of magnificent
forest trees, waterfalls, and rustic seats." [12]

Thomas Medwin, dedicated to beauty in all its forms all his
life, remembered that "the country around Horsham is one of
exceeding beauty," [13] and he made this statement after he had
seen a good part of India and Europe. St. Leonard's Forest,
described by Bede and once a royal preserve, was in Medwin's
boyhood still a "famous resort of smugglers," operating in bands
on their way from the coastal area around Brighton to London.
One legend of the place told the story of the noted smuggler
Mike Mills, who literally outraced Old Nick, the prize being
his freedom from "his Satanic Majesty" [14] forever. Medwin's
imagination must also have been stimulated, as Shelley's was,

[11] *Ibid.*, pp. 133–140.

[12] *Ibid.*, pp. 137–139; T. J. Hogg's *Life of Shelley*, quoted by John C.
Jeaffreson, *The Real Shelley* (London, 1885), I, 146.

[13] Medwin, *The Life of Percy Bysshe Shelley* (London, 1847), I, 91,
hereafter referred to as *Shelley* and distinguished from the 1913 edition
of H. Buxton Forman, in one volume, by the use of a Roman numeral
designating the volume number.

[14] Hurst, *Horsham*, pp. 162–163.

by the local legends that peopled St. Leonard's with a "horrible decapitated spectre" and a "famous . . . dragon or serpent."[15]

In this countryside of varied scenery and fertile land, watered by the River Arun, Medwin pursued the usual sports available to the son of a man of some means, and he later became a professionally skilled horseman, an authority on angling, an enthusiastic huntsman and marksman. With the young Shelley he fished in Cinder Banks, then an excellent trout stream, and also in Warnham Pond, on the Shelley property.[16] Thomas Medwin was a man of the outdoors, from the first.

It was a good house that he grew up in, located in the Carfax, the northwest portion of town which included part of the village green, and standing, it seems, on the corner of West Street and the present Carfax. In 1816, when Medwin's father made his will, the house contained "plate, pictures, prints, china, glass, linen, wines and other liquors," to be left to his heirs, along with such other articles specifically named as books and bookcases, library tables, a "fine voiced pianoforte," and "most of the approved and new [musical] publications and compositions." Medwin grew up, then, surrounded by books, paintings, and music; and he himself possessed "some talent for drawing," which was undoubtedly encouraged by his father, who in his will exhorted his daughter "to keep up her music" and left her the pianoforte "as an encouragement and incitement for her so to do."[17]

But good was to turn to ill for the son in the very year, ironically, of the father's death. For Thomas Medwin's interest in the visual arts, fostered in a home in which the oil paintings and prints were of sufficient value to be listed in his father's

---

[15] Medwin, *Shelley*, I, 63–64.

[16] Medwin's obituary, signed W. H. S., in *Albery's Horsham Journal*, Sept., 1869, the only existing file of which, it seems, is located in Horsham, in the house of Mrs. Albery, wife of the descendant of the stationer who printed the paper.

[17] The will of Thomas Charles Medwin, written in his own hand on Sept. 20, 1816, and proved at London, Jan. 1, 1830; Medwin's obituary in *Albery's Horsham Journal*.

will immediately after the plate, was eventually to lead him to ruin. The financial debacle which overtook him in 1829 in Florence, leaving him nearly penniless and destroying his marriage, was the result of mistaken speculation in old Italian oil paintings.

It would have been better for him if he could have forced himself to admire one of the pictures which hung in his father's library. It was a portrait of Sir Edward Coke, author of the famous commentary upon Littleton. But Coke, the father's idol, was so abhorrent to the son that he later confused him with Lord Jeffreys of the Bloody Assizes, although he remembered the appearance of the portrait thirty years after he had left his father's house. It was, he recalled, "a portrait of that cold-blooded old lawyer, Lord [*sic*] Coke. I have it before me now. It was a ferret-like phiz hard as iron, with long eye-lashes, and a beard of formal cut, thin and sharp—every hair almost separate from its fellows: one of those shrewd, cold, inanimate, saffron-hued faces—in short, such as might have belonged to the man . . . who sentenced Algernon Sidney to the block [*i. e.*, Lord Jeffreys]." [18] This difference of opinion about a portrait is a significant index of the larger differences which were to develop between father and son.

None of this is to imply, however, that the elder Medwin was not a generous and affectionate father to his five children. Following his marriage in 1778, he had waited nearly eight years for the birth of his first child, John, born in 1786, and then he had seen this eldest son killed, as the tablet erected in his memory records, "by a fall from a gig near the foot of Picts Hill" in 1806. The bereaved father specified in his will, evidence of his affection and sense of loss even ten years later, "It is my particular desire and request that my Remains may be buried at Horsham Church under my pew beneath the pulpit as near as may be to the Coffin of my Son John Medwin . . ." This son, John, and his third son, Lieutenant Henry Clough

[18] Medwin, "A Short Chapter on Beards," *Ainsworth's Magazine*, I (1842), 113.

Medwin (1790–1815), an officer in the 25th Regiment of the Bengal Native Infantry, who had died at Bhangwanpore, the father described as his "dear and ever lamented children," and to them both he erected tablets in the Horsham Church.

Pilfold, his youngest child, born in 1794, he had made his law partner at the age of twenty-one. His only daughter, Mary Catherine, born in 1793, was clearly a favorite of his, and to her he left his nonprofessional books and an annuity of £50 during the life of her mother, upon whose death the annuity would be doubled, carefully protected from the "debts, engagements, power, or controul of any husband she may . . . marry." She would also receive at this time certain property originally enjoyed by her mother.

But by 1816, when the will was made, his oldest surviving son, Thomas Medwin, had become a bitter disappointment to him. He wrote, in his carefully exact legal hand,

In the Name of God Amen. I Thomas Charles Medwin of Horsham in the County of Sussex Gentleman being at present in tolerable good health and always considering the uncertain duration of life do hereby make publish and sweare this to be my last will and testament whereby I dispose of such worldly Estate and property as it has pleased Almighty God to bestow upon me in manner and form following. Whereas my eldest son Thomas Medwin disliking the profession of the Law to which he was bred and being desirous of entering into the Army I in compliance with such his desire purchased him first a Cornetcy and since a Lieutenancy in His Majesty's twenty-fourth Regiment of Light Dragoons on Service in Bengal whither he sailed to join his regiment on the first day of August 1812 and is now on duty with such regiment at Cawnpoor and having equip'd him out at great expense incurring on those and other occasions an expenditure of about four thousand five hundred pounds in my lifetime I feel that I ought not in Justice to the other parts of my Family to make any further provision for him by this my will but in token of my remaining affection towards my said son I give him ten guineas for a ring . . .

"Remaining affection . . ." Ten guineas for a memorial ring. It was the same sum, directed to be used for the same purpose, that he left to his sister-in-law.

To his younger son Pilfold, however, named in his will his sole executor, he left his professional library and his office furniture; his gold watch, with its chain and seals, "requesting my said son to preserve and keep the same in respect" to him and his uncle, who had given it to him; his dwelling in the Carfax and the clerk's office; his "pews and sitting places in Horsham Church"; all his household goods and effects not specifically disposed of elsewhere; and, following the death of his wife, his "Farm and Lands called Dorks in Horsham . . . and also my meadows called the Town Meads in Horsham . . . with the buildings and gardens thereto belonging . . ."

To his wife, for her lifetime, he willed his "freehold messuage and garden at Tanbridge in Horsham and . . . the furniture and effects therein," all of which was to go to his daughter upon the death of her mother.

And to Thomas, named after himself, like himself "bred" to the law, his elder surviving son, ten guineas. Their quarrel must have been a bitter one indeed.

Although Thomas Medwin was never enrolled in any of the Inns of Court, he has left a caustic description of student life at Lincoln's Inn and of the legal profession that his father wished him to enter:

There were at that time only 800 students *eating* their way to the bar, or, in other words, qualifying themselves for Barristers-at-law, by dining a certain number of days during the Term, in Hall . . . Of these 800, scarcely eight were ever heard of, even by name. Many, it is true, paraded up and down Westminster Hall, and darkened the courts, after the manner of hungry crows that hover about carcasses which the vultures have got to themselves; till, in despair of a brief, they tried their hand as Chamber Council, and gave opinions.

One would suppose that these opinions ought to be sound, and that there was a great responsibility attached to giving them. Never could be formed a grosser mistake. They always found, from the multitude of conflicting reports, one favourable to the views of their employer, the attorney, and the bearing of his client's case; and accordingly discovered a loophole for a lawsuit.[19]

For years the father must have cherished the hope that Thomas would take his place as the leading solicitor in Horsham. Very probably Thomas, working as clerk or apprentice in his father's law office, had believed himself, for a while, that he would become an attorney. It is possible that he was reading law independently as late as March, 1811, when he lived in Garden Court, in the Temple.

But Thomas disliked the profession to which his father thought he had been "bred." He had in fact been bred a gentleman, with no taste for long, regular hours of office work; little talent, we may assume, for pleading a case before a court; and small sense of the very serious importance of money, deeds, titles, and contracts. As a gentleman he lived, and on the certificate of his death, 1869, in the column reserved for the occupation of the deceased, there is written the one word, "Gentleman." The dusty hours of the law were not for him. And not liking the church, he had only one place to go—the Army.

Both his younger brother, Henry Clough, and his paternal great-uncle, George Dolbon, had been in India; and he did not need his brother to tell him that a commission in the cavalry was superior to one in the infantry, both in terms of status and of ease. And so his father purchased for him a Cornetcy in the 24th Light Dragoons, which at the time had been stationed for fifteen years in India. The regulation price for the Cornetcy purchased by the elder Medwin in 1812 was £735, that for the Lieutenancy purchased in the next year was £997; however, "it is, in fact, almost certain that he would have paid much in excess of the regulation price, although this practice was not

[19] Medwin, *Lady Singleton; or, The World as It Is* (London, 1843), II, 33–34.

officially allowed."[20] Assuming that no money was lost on the resale of the Cornetcy and that the cost of uniforms, passage to India, incidentals, and the Lieutenancy amounted to as much as £1,500 (difficult to believe), what had the young Thomas Medwin done with the remaining £3,000—the equivalent of seventy-five thousand 1962 American dollars—which his father had given to him?[21]

If, at Oxford and at London, Thomas Medwin had lived with reasonable economy, he could not possibly have spent the immense sum of £3,000 or more, at a time when it was possible for an unmarried man to live decently, if frugally, on £100 a year. The only conclusion is that Medwin lived very unreasonably indeed, spending with the very greatest extravagance. We know from his own confession that shortly before sailing for India he "mixed in London life" in circles that included some of the friends and acquaintances of Byron, among them Lord Blessington, and that he regretted the experience.[22] We know from the same source that he belonged to the Racket's Club at Brighton: this demanded expensive clothes, and there was also gambling. It is a rather singular coincidence that in Medwin's novel, *Lady Singleton*, which shows a remarkable knowledge of gambling, Maxwell the inexperienced young Englishman, a student, should lose in a game of faro his entire inheritance from his father, exactly £4,500, the sum named in the elder Medwin's will. Thus ruined the young Maxwell commits suicide. But whatever the exact nature of the young Medwin's extravagance, he had lost a very generous friend indeed in his father, and at a time too, as it turned out, when he needed his help most, in 1829. Long before that year, how-

[20] Letter to the author from Mr. D. W. King, Librarian of the British War Office Library, Whitehall.

[21] A rough but reasonable formula for converting the English pound of 1810–1820 into 1962 American dollars would seem to be one to twenty-five. See R. H. Inglis Palgrave, *Dictionary of Political Economy* (London, 1899), III, 634–647.

[22] Medwin's unpublished marginalia in his revised copy of *The Conversations of Lord Byron* (London, 1824, A New Edition), p. 4, in the Houghton Library. For gambling in *Lady Singleton*, see III, 184, 194, 205.

ever, Medwin had acquired expensive tastes and habits which were difficult for him to gratify later.

The social and economic position to which Medwin was born, then, is one of some interest, for it determined a fundamental bias within him and finally led him in fact to ruin. He was not only a member of a very well-to-do family. He was also related, through his mother, to some of the best and oldest families in the county, the Michells, the Pilfolds, and the Shelleys. But Thomas Charles Medwin, the father, was a newcomer, an outsider, the son of a draper (Luke Medwin) from Berkshire, and the Medwin name does not appear in the parish records before 1778, when he married Mary Pilfold. He had been articled to a solicitor in Chichester, and as a solicitor, not a barrister, he had little more status among the old gentry than a mere medical doctor. Thus was born in Thomas Medwin, the son, the need to assert repeatedly and publicly his family connections and later to proclaim his relationship with Shelley and his intimacy with Byron.

Furthermore, although the elder Medwin was wealthy enough, there were other houses that his son Thomas entered which were far richer and finer than his own. There were the several residences of his father's employer, the Duke of Norfolk, who lived in great splendor either at Norfolk House in London, at Arundel Castle, one of the most splendid baronial mansions in England, less than half a day's journey from Horsham, or at St. Irving's Hills, within Horsham parish. The early image of the Duke of Norfolk (known as "Jockey of Norfolk"), bon vivant, friend of the Prince Regent, Colonel in the Sussex militia, art collector on the grand scale, may well have been an abiding influence in the life of Thomas Medwin. Even Shelley's own Field Place was better than the house in the Carfax, and Medwin very probably also visited in the Welsh home of his very wealthy relative, Thomas Grove. But before the Duke of Norfolk he was clearly an inferior, the son of the Duke's servant; and Shelley's father, a member of Parliament, just as clearly occupied a position superior to that of the elder

Medwin, who had to work for a living and who had, in fact, worked to get Shelley's father elected to Parliament.[23] The repeated sight of this greater wealth and this greater leisure, falling upon some native weakness in the character of Thomas Medwin, surely explains much of his lifelong search for status, his need to live beyond his income, which drove him finally to run through his wife's sizable fortune in four years.

And so Medwin published himself the friend of Byron (inserting as the frontispiece of his *Conversations of Byron* a fine copper-plate facsimile of the poet's letter recommending him to Hobhouse); and so he advertised himself the cousin of Shelley. The relationship, he explained in later years, was somewhat complicated:

. . . Miss [Mary Catherine] Michell, Sir Bysshe's first wife [Sir Bysshe Shelley was the poet's grandfather], was my grandfather's first cousin; and . . . my mother [Mary Pilfold Medwin] bore the same degree of consanguinity to Miss [Elizabeth] Pilfold [Shelley, mother of the poet], their fathers being brothers; which circumstances I mention in order to account for the intimacy of our families, and mine with Bysshe [the poet], as he was always called.[24]

(He added that Shelley's mother, "daughter of Charles Pilfold, Esq., of Effingham Place, . . . had been brought up by her aunt, Lady Ferdinand Pool, the wife of the well-known father of the turf, and owner of 'Potoooooooo,' and the equally celebrated 'Waxy' and 'Mealy.'") Medwin and Shelley, then, were double cousins, but at closest they were second cousins.

Thomas Medwin was four years and four months older than Shelley. If he entered Syon House Academy at Isleworth, near Brentford, at the same age that Shelley entered, the age of ten, Medwin would have enrolled in 1798. There he followed the same course of study that Shelley did, but presumably he got along better with the other sixty boys. The subjects of study

[23] This amusing story is told in Albery's *Parliamentary History of Horsham*, pp. 123–191.
[24] Medwin, *Shelley*, pp. 13–14.

were "reading and writing, arithmetic, Latin, French, geography, and astronomy." [25] Although Medwin remembered the master, Dr. Greenlaw, unfavorably ("not wanting in good qualities, but very capricious in his temper"),[26] it was here at Syon House that he laid the foundation for his enthusiastic and lifelong interest in languages and literature.

The two cousins were at Syon House together between 1802 and 1804, Medwin leaving to attend a public school for a year at some time in 1804 prior to Shelley's departure.

Shelley's earliest letter, preserved and first published by Medwin, was addressed to Medwin's aunt, Catherine Pilfold. Dated July 18, 1803, it establishes beyond doubt the boyhood intimacy and the affection that Shelley had for his cousin. "Dear Kate," he wrote impudently,

We have proposed a day at the pond next Wednesday; and, if you will come to-morrow evening, I would be much obliged to you; and, if you could any how bring Tom over to stay all the night, I would thank you. We are to have a cold dinner over at the pond, and come home to eat a bit of roast chicken and peas at about nine o'clock. Mama depends upon your bringing Tom over to-morrow, and, if you don't we shall be very much disappointed . . . I am not Your obedient servant, P. B. Shelley.[27]

The bond between the boys is suggested also by the fact that Shelley at Syon House walked in his sleep to Medwin's room, in another dormitory—a breach of the rules, the full implication of which he probably did not understand.[28] Medwin says further of this period, revealing his own early love of natural beauty and his interest in the theatre, which he was to share later with Byron, ". . . at Brentford we had more than once played the truant, and rowed to Kew [Gardens, across the Thames], and once to Richmond, where we saw Mrs. Jordan

[25] Newman I. White, *Shelley* (New York, 1940), I, 19.

[26] Medwin, *Shelley*, p. 19.

[27] *The Complete Works of Percy Bysshe Shelley*, ed. Roger Ingpen and Walter E. Peck (London, 1926), VIII, 3; hereafter referred to as *Works*.

[28] Medwin, *Shelley*, p. 27.

in *The Country Girl,* at that theatre, the first Shelley had ever visited. It was an era in my life." [29] Medwin was about fifteen or sixteen years old, and he recalled the period as an "era" in his life not only because the world of maturity was beginning to open up for him, seen in the bright, golden light of adolescence, but also because at this time, one of the last times in his life, he was the leader, the older boy introducing Shelley into exciting new areas. Later, less sure of his own talents, he was to follow Shelley, and follow him he did, with devotion.

After a year in a public school, Medwin matriculated at Oxford, on December 2, 1805, but he left without taking his degree, at some time before October, 1810, when Shelley entered. According to Medwin, however, the two saw much of each other during the vacations of 1804–1810 and "constantly corresponded." [30] If Medwin may have exaggerated the extent of his association with Shelley during this period, what is clear is that Medwin's own literary and intellectual tastes were developing rapidly at the time, and nothing would be more natural for him than to seek out the young genius, his cousin, and share with him his literary interests. Such people were rare in Horsham. In 1808 Medwin subscribed to the *Poems* of Felicia Dorothea Browne, later Mrs. Hemans, whom he had met when visiting relatives in North Wales, and he talked so enthusiastically about "the beauty (for beautiful she was), the grace, and charming simplicity and *naiveté* of this interesting girl" of fourteen years that Shelley wrote to her. [31] It was during this year also that Medwin's father lent Shelley a book on chemistry, forbidden at Eton. [32] Shelley and Medwin had both heard Adam Walker lecture at Syon House on the wonders of science, Shelley had been "entranced," and Medwin remembered the lectures with "considerable fidelity" decades later, when writing his *Life of Shelley.* [33]

[29] *Ibid.,* p. 39.
[30] *Ibid.,* p. 39.
[31] *Ibid.,* p. 58; White, *Shelley,* I, 61.
[32] Medwin, *Shelley,* p. 34.
[33] White, *Shelley,* I, 22.

Medwin had been studying German, under a tutor,[34] and it may have been this interest, nourished further by the cheap Gothic novels of the day, that led him in the winter of 1809–1810, he says, to collaborate with Shelley, writing alternate chapters "of a wild and extravagant romance, where a hideous witch played the principal part, and whose portrait—not a very inviting one—is given in *The Wandering Jew* . . . , almost versified from a passage in our *Nightmare.*"[35] Unfortunately, no trace of this prose romance remains, except Medwin's description. His accounts of his collaboration with Shelley on *The Wandering Jew* are contradictory in detail, but they agree on the essential point that Medwin wrote some part of the poem, and this, it seems, no one has ever denied.[36]

Meanwhile, Medwin and Shelley were also hunting during this winter and taking walks together around Field Place. These Medwin vividly remembered. "There is something in a frosty day, when the sun is bright, the sky clear, and the air rarefied, which acts like a sort of intoxication. On such days Shelley's spirits used to run riot, his 'sweet and subtle talk' was to me inebriating and electric."[37]

When spring came, Shelley's infatuation for his (and Medwin's) cousin Harriet Grove reached its climax and its end, when Shelley and his mother visited the Groves at Lincoln's Inn Fields. The two families decided that the young romance had gone far enough and that any idea of marriage must be given up. Medwin dined with them all on May 3, 1810, and they afterwards went to an opera. He had met Harriet when she had visited at Field Place, and he wrote of her, nearly forty years later, "I still remember Miss Harriet Grove, and when I call to mind all the women I have ever seen, I know of none that surpassed, or that could compete with her. She

[34] Medwin, *Shelley,* p. 489.
[35] *Ibid.,* p. 39.
[36] For a summary of the vexed question of the authorship of *The Wandering Jew,* probably begun in January or February, 1810, see Cameron, *The Young Shelley,* pp. 307–310.
[37] Medwin, *Shelley,* p. 39.

was like one of Shakespeare's women—like some Madonna of Raphael."[38] Without doubt, Shelley talked to Medwin about her, delighting in his admiration of her.

Medwin visited Shelley only once when the latter was at Oxford, one day in November, 1810, the month after Shelley had matriculated, and they discussed, it would seem, "the mysteries of chemistry," German horror tales, and Shelley's "controversies . . . with learned divines," carried on under an assumed name.[39]

Meanwhile, Thomas C. Medwin was involved in the publication of Shelley's *Original Poetry by Victor and Cazire*. On December 10, 1810, James Phillips wrote to the elder Medwin, "stating that money was due to him from Shelley for printing carried out at Worthing, and asking for a loan until he could secure payment from the poet himself."[40] This seems to be the earliest instance of the elder Medwin's being financially or professionally involved in the life of Shelley. There is no record that Shelley sent to his second cousin Thomas a copy of this book, but on December 18, 1810, he ordered his publisher, the infamous Stockdale, to send one of three gift copies of *St. Irvyne*, his Gothic romance, to "T. Medwin, Esq., Horsham," and Medwin says that Shelley also sent him a copy of the *Posthumous Fragments of Margaret Nicholson*, published in November, 1810.[41]

In March, 1811, when Shelley was expelled from Oxford in connection with *The Necessity of Atheism*, a copy of which he sent to Medwin (one who did not see that necessity), Medwin was living in London, in Garden Court, the Temple. Here Shelley visited him, at four o'clock in the morning, to tell him of his expulsion, an event which Medwin remembered "as if it occurred yesterday." In early April, after Shelley had taken lodgings with Hogg in Poland Street (chosen because of its

[38] *The Journal of Harriet Grove*, p. 58; Medwin, *Shelley*, p. 47.
[39] Medwin, *Shelley*, pp. 67, 69, 73.
[40] Samuel J. Looker, *Shelley, Trelawny, and Henley* (Worthing, Sussex, n. d.), p. 25.
[41] Shelley, *Works*, VIII, 22; Medwin, *Shelley*, p. 88.

inspiring, revolutionary name), Medwin visited him, and in the spring of the year they took "frequent walks in the Parks and on the banks of the Serpentine," two highly verbal, sensitive young men, with problems.[42] Their association and similar literary interests in 1811 are further suggested by the fact that both Medwin and Shelley subscribed to the *Poems* of Janetta Philipps, Shelley enthusiastically taking six copies. One day, when they were walking the streets of London together, Shelley suddenly said to him, "Medwin, I will make you a present of a book," and entering a circulating library and book store, asked for a copy of M. G. Lewis's lurid Gothic romance, *The Monk*, which Shelley greatly admired. It had been published in an expurgated edition in 1798. The bookseller denied having the disgraceful book in stock, and it was only after going from store to store that they found a copy. But Medwin, after reading it, cut it up and tried to burn it.[43] This early prudery, attested by the single incident, he was to overcome.

But there was one part of Shelley's life into which Shelley did not admit Medwin at this time—his elopement with Harriet Westbrook, although in August, 1811, he borrowed £25 from Medwin's father in Horsham to finance the trip and saw Thomas Medwin there on the day before his departure for Gretna Green with Harriet.[44] That Medwin very shortly became acquainted with the details of the marriage, however, is highly probable, for in October, back in Horsham, Shelley consulted the elder Medwin on the legality of Scotch marriages and from this date until mid-summer 1813 regularly employed him as his lawyer. The details of this relationship are set forth in Shelley's letters to T. C. Medwin and need not be spelled out here. It is of interest that one of these letters, that of March 20, 1812, closes, "My kindest regards to all your family. Be assured I shall not forget you or them." The important fact for

---

[42] Medwin, *Shelley*, pp. 87–88, 90.
[43] Shelley, *Works*, VIII, 88, note; Medwin's unpublished marginalia in his *Conversations*, p. 229.
[44] Shelley, *Works*, VIII, 171; Medwin, *Shelley*, p. 109.

the history of the relations between Shelley and Thomas Medwin is that the elder Medwin was very closely associated, in Shelley's mind, with the happy early years of his first marriage. There is no evidence that the two young men ever saw each other in England again after the autumn of 1811.

But the young man that Shelley remembered he liked—one, he recalled, who painted "very well" and was "remarkable, if I do not mistake, for a peculiar taste in, and knowledge of the *belle arti*—Italy is the place for you," he wrote, January 17, 1820, "the very place—the Paradise of exiles . . . If you will be glad to see an old friend, who will be very glad to see you . . . come to Italy."[45]

Exactly how Thomas Medwin was occupied in 1811–1812 is not wholly clear. In 1812 he "mixed in London life," as noted earlier, and at this time he was acquainted with Martin Hawke (son of Baron Hawke of Towton), Captain John Hay, Lord Powerscourt, and Lord Blessington, all known to Byron, who as a young man had made £50 bets with the first two on the chances of matrimony and the turn of events in the Peninsula War.[46] Martin Hawke, a man of "much bonhommie," of whom Medwin was "very fond," introduced him at the Racket's Club in Brighton, to which Byron also belonged. This was heady company for the son of the Horsham solicitor. It was probably at this time also that he knew Sir Godfrey Vassal Webster, son of Lady Holland by her first marriage, and Bryan Waller Procter ("Barry Cornwall"), a friend from whose *Dramatic Scenes* Medwin quoted on the title page of his *Oswald and Edwin,* along with lines by Shelley. Sir Godfrey, M. P. for Sussex from 1812 to 1820, impressed Medwin chiefly by his "elegant taste," his gambling, and wild extravagance,[47] Procter by his literary talents. It was a glittering circle.

[45] Shelley, *Works,* X, 141.

[46] Medwin's unpublished marginalia in his *Conversations,* p. 4; C. L. Cline, *Byron, Shelley and their Pisan Circle* (Cambridge, Massachusetts, 1952), pp. 87–88.

[47] Medwin's unpublished marginalia in his *Conversations,* p. 5.

But Medwin looked back on this period of his life as one of bitter "regrets which poisoned" his life.[48] Perhaps the unknown disappointment was romantic. He wrote of Shelley, without suggesting a date, "He knew I was much attached to a young person whom prudential motives prevented my marrying. To do away with this obstacle, he earnestly proposed (which of course I declined) to raise a sum of money on a post obit and settle it on the lady." [49] Disappointment in love, a dislike for the law, a quarrel with his father, extravagant expenditures—whatever the motive, it was on June 18, 1812, that Medwin was gazetted as a Cornet in the 24th Light Dragoons.[50] Without military training of any kind, he sailed on August 1, 1812, to join his regiment in India.

A new world awaited him.

[48] *Ibid.*, p. 4.
[49] Medwin, *The Shelley Papers; Memoir of Percy Bysshe Shelley* (London, 1833), p. 21.
[50] Letter to the author from Mr. D. W. King, Librarian of the British War Office Library.

2
His Majesty's
24th Light Dragoons

Medwin sailed as a Cornet. He joined his regiment, on November 12, 1813, as a Lieutenant, two months in grade. The regiment, under the command of Lieutenant-General William Loftus, was temporarily in camp near Aligarh (Koil) in the river plain between the Jumna and the Ganges in the state of Uttar Pradesh, formerly the Meerut division of the United Provinces, about 250 miles northwest of Cawnpore, the regiment's usual station.[1] To the north, the United Provinces bordered on Kashmir, Tibet, and Nepal. Ten years earlier, Aligarh, with its polygonal fort, surrounded by a great ditch, had been the headquarters of Sindia's troops, defeated by Governor-General Wellesley in 1803 and faced again by Medwin's regiment in 1817.

The trip to Aligarh had not been a short one. After rounding the Cape of Good Hope, Medwin's vessel put in at Port Louis, capital of the Mauritius, in 1810 captured from the French. Here he dined with Governor Robert Farquhar, whose nephew, the celebrated wit and *improvisatore* Theodore Hook, had recently been appointed accountant-general and treasurer of the island—despite his total ignorance of accounting. Medwin recalled that Hook at this time improvised a song, "giving a Verse

---

[1] The Monthly Returns or Muster Rolls of the 24th Light Dragoons, on file in the Public Record Office, London. Medwin was gazetted as a Lieutenant by purchase on Sept. 16, 1813. Unless otherwise indicated, dates relating to Medwin's military career are taken from the Monthly Returns or Muster Rolls of his regiment; hereafter referred to as Regimental Muster Rolls.

to every one present at the Governor's Table—and not even sparing his uncle Farquhar, which offended him mortally." [2] In 1818 Hook was returned to England because of an unexplained deficit of £12,000 in his accounts—or, as he put it, "on account of a disorder in his chest," a celebrated witticism that Medwin was to hear and quote years later. Here at Port Louis Medwin also saw slaves for the first time: "The isle of France would have seemed a paradise, but for the sights and sounds of horror every day brought under my observation— slaves, the finest men I ever saw, yoked to carts and driven like oxen—the streets echoing with the lashes of those punished at the caprice of their masters for offences, or no offences." [3] Once in India, he would repeatedly see soldiers flogged, a sight he was never able to witness "without shuddering." [4]

Leaving Port Louis and sailing across the Indian Ocean and up the east coast of India, Medwin landed on April 5, 1813, at Calcutta—eight months after his departure from England. This had been a very slow voyage indeed, undoubtedly involving long delays in ports along the way; a troop transport could make the voyage in less than six months, and a quick passage was one of fifteen weeks. [5]

When Medwin landed at the Presidency, he failed to report himself officially present and was listed as absent without leave. But he was there: he went almost at once to a ball given at the Governor's House by Lord Minto, [6] who would very shortly be replaced by Hastings as Governor General, and it may well have been at this time that he passed a pleasant month at Puri, hunting and drinking. However, in July he started the "long

---

[2] Medwin's unpublished marginalia in his *Conversations*, p. 165.

[3] Medwin, *The Angler in Wales, or Days and Nights of Sportsmen* (London, 1834), II, 22.

[4] Medwin, "A Bengal Yarn," *Ainsworth's Magazine*, II (1842), 58.

[5] On the length of a voyage between London and Bombay, see "India Shipping Intelligence," *The Asiatic Journal*, VII (June, 1819), 674, hereafter referred to as *AJ*, and "Home Intelligence," *AJ*, VIII (Dec., 1819), 620.

[6] Medwin, "A Short Chapter on Beards," *Ainsworth's Magazine*, I (1842), 113.

and tedious" voyage of 1,200 miles up the Ganges to Cawn-pore,[7] a trip which might be made in two months but more often required three,[8] and Medwin did not arrive at Cawnpore until October, 1813. He very probably made the river voyage (paying his own expenses) as he described the journey in *The Angler in Wales*, travelling in an eighteen-oared "budgerow," alternately rowed or towed through the alligator infested waters, depending on the current and the depth.[9] It was during the early stages of this trip, perhaps, that he saw Bengalese women washing clothes in tanks full of sacred alligators and later, presumably, shot the beasts with his three-ounce rifle.

At Murshidabad he saw another wonder: tame fish that came at the sound of a bell from all parts of their pond, to be fed by hand and petted. Here he may also have paused to hunt the dangerous Bengalese boar, his weapon a spear, his mount a small Arab horse.[10] If Medwin lingered at all in this city, which was the last Mohammedan capital of Bengal, he would not have missed seeing the great numbers of palaces, mosques, tombs, and gardens which it contains, for his interest in Indian architecture and civilization was to become very great.

Moving on up the river in its northwest course, Medwin would have passed Monghyr. Julian, who is the voice of Med-win in *The Angler in Wales* (and who "had just arrived on furlough from Bengal, with the brevet rank of Captain, and half a liver") says that not far from Monghyr, at "a place called Seetacomb," he saw a marvelous, sacred spring, the water of which may reach a temperature of 150 degrees Fahrenheit during the eight cool months of the year but which is cold dur-

---

[7] Medwin, *Angler*, I, 197.

[8] Henry T. Prinsep, *A Narrative of the Political and Military Trans-actions of British India, Under the Administration of the Marquess of Hastings, 1813 to 1818* (London, 1820), pp. 215–216; hereafter referred to as Prinsep, *British India;* John Shipp, *Memoirs of the Extraordinary Military Career of John Shipp* (London, 1894, Second Edition), p. 143. Shipp served for a time in the 24th Light Dragoons and was at Cawnpore with Medwin.

[9] Medwin, *Angler*, II, 50.

[10] *Ibid.*, I, 56, 108–112.

ing the four hottest months. Here, Julian continues, pilgrims come, understandably, from all over India, and he says he witnessed beside the spring Hindu religious rites, complete with Sanskrit prayers, a finger ring made from a shrub, and a baptism in the sacred waters.[11]

Near this place, Julian says, when he "had not been in India many weeks," he nearly lost his life in the Ganges. "Tired of the monotony and tedium of the voyage," after being towed for days of slow progress against wind and current, he had taken his Joe Manton gun and gone hunting along the banks for hares and black partridges. Trying to cross a rivulet that flowed into the Ganges, he was swept into the great river and was saved only by the quick action of two of his "dandies" or sailors.

Medwin remembered the junction, at Allahabad, of the two great rivers of the area, both sacred, the Ganges and the Jumna, and recalled that the former is "pure as crystal," while the latter is "thick" and "troubled," even though both rivers take their rise in the snow and for many miles flow through similar soil in lines almost parallel.[12] If Medwin spent only a single day at Allahabad, capital of the United Provinces of Agra and Oudh, he would have seen the great fort which commanded the banks of the two rivers, within it the ruins of a splendid palace. Nor would he have missed the serai and gardens of Khasru, son of an emperor, and the Jama Masjid or Great Mosque, desecrated by British officers and used at one time by them as a residence and later as an assembly room.

Finally, on the south bank of the Ganges, more than a mile wide at this point, he saw Cawnpore, where he was to spend most of his Indian years. Far removed from the scene of the Gurkha or Nepal War of 1814–1816, in which Medwin's regiment did not participate, Cawnpore was the chief British frontier station and one of the largest military stations in India, with a highly organized social life and stores that were well

[11] *Ibid.*, I, 70–72.
[12] *Ibid.*, I, 237.

stocked with European goods.[13] Life could be very gay at Cawnpore, and the 24th Light Dragoons was noted for its hospitality. Following the siege of Hathras, in 1817, in which Medwin participated, "nothing but parties, dinners, balls, suppers, &c., were the order of the day" at Cawnpore, a seat of such "festivity and splendour," upon occasion, that its social round could completely exhaust a strong man in ten days. This was the mighty John Shipp, in 1815 an officer in Medwin's regiment.[14]

The officers, who had to provide their own quarters, had built brick bungalows of two or three stories, each with its own "garden and plantation," the whole surrounded by a high mud wall against thieves and wandering livestock. Medwin was impressed: he recalled years later,

No contrast can be greater than between English quarters and an Indian station. Instead of barracks, or lodgings, I found my brother officers inhabiting spacious bungalows, with their thatched roofs, verandahs, and Venetians, surrounded, for the most part, by extensive paddocks, and these belted by Parkinsonia. Each of these compounds (a corruption of campagnes,) presents, on entering it, a scene not destitute of beauty: fields of lucerne, continually irrigated, form a refreshment and relief to the eyes, aching with the dust and glare of the cantonment: gardens, kept in the nicest order, contain most of our vegetables, and some of our fruits, in addition to those of tropical climes—such as plantains, loquats, custard apples; the jack, the guava, the orange, and lime, and trellised vines, form a delightful walk and shelter from the sun.[15]

There were servants in plenty. No English gentleman could exist in India without them, and the English officers were gentlemen all. They dispelled their hangovers by tiger-shooting, pig-sticking, or chasing anything else that crossed their path and then returned again, in the evening, to immerse themselves

[13] See the article on "Cawnpoore" in *The Penny Encyclopædia of the Society for the Diffusion of Useful Knowledge* (London, 1836), III, 339.
[14] Shipp, *Memoirs*, pp. 237, 322.
[15] Medwin, "A Bengal Yarn," *Ainsworth's Magazine*, II (1842), 57.

once more in immense quantities of claret. For skill in field sports and the ability to hold one's drink were the distinguishing marks of the gentleman-officer.[16]

Englishmen lived with the dust as best they could, fought the suffocating heat, the insects, and innumerable duels, which flourished wonderfully in a hot officers' mess, where men often had little more than their honor to protect (after buying a commission) and where the wine flowed freely. But no gentleman ever fought a duel with a tradesman, of course. And the dust was so bad that at one time officers in the field were provided with "a frame of glass which they fix[ed] in the door of their tents."[17] They might take along their own mutton, on the hoof, or their own chosen bottled water, brought from as far away as Monghyr.

In Cawnpore, officers rode about in their own buggies, played with their pets (Julian says in *The Angler* that he had a tame leopard), and "had ample time for study, but the conditions were soporific . . . At the height of summer the day began at five and ended before eleven, when the heat forced all into the stifling, shaded gloom of quarters. There they stayed till near sundown . . . Only the dedicated few forced themselves to study during the day, instead of sleeping."[18] Lieutenant Thomas Medwin was one of those dedicated few.

But he also hunted, and if we may judge from *The Angler*, he was one of the most enthusiastic sportsmen in India. Even here, however, his interest expressed itself in literary terms. It is said of Julian that he kept "very voluminous journals" recording the "wild sports of the East"[19] (parts of which probably appear in *The Angler*), and we know that Medwin read aloud to Shelley an Indian journal of some kind. Even after allowing for substantial exaggeration, one is convinced that only a man with a genuine affection for the outdoor life could have written

[16] E. S. Turner, *Gallant Gentlemen: A Portrait of the British Officer, 1600–1956* (London, 1956), p. 113.

[17] *Ibid.*, p. 181; *The Penny Encyclopædia*, III, 339.

[18] Turner, *Gallant Gentlemen*, p. 251.

[19] Medwin, *Angler*, I, 187.

the following account[20] of the "manly and spirit-stirring sports" of India, and their associated pleasures:

Nothing can be more delightful than the migratory life we lead in India. The little camp, which daily changes its ground, and is pitched in some majestic evergreen tope, or mango grove—the care of our elephants, dogs, and favourite Arabs that know their masters, and follow us to be fed, like dogs—fresh ground to beat every day, perhaps untrodden by man—a line of elephants, the interspace filled up by beaters—our howdahs, furnished with three or four Joe Mantons [*i.e.*, rifles made by that famous gunsmith of London]—game of all sorts, from the florikan to the quail, and the tiger to the antelope, continually sprung—and then, after gun-fire, good cheer!—that brotherhood, which our exile creates, and for which my soul yearns!

Julian, it is said in *The Angler,* "is never happy, or animated, but when his fancy turns back to India."[21] The days were not all spent on duty, as light as this ordinarily was. The most demanding duty of the young subaltern in garrison, after the drill sergeant had given him "a complete knowledge of every part of the firelock, and . . . made [him] master of the manual" of arms, was to take his infrequent turn as regimental officer of the day, inspecting the men's messes and kitchens, the barracks, the hospital, the guardhouse, the farrier's shop, the stables. In addition, it may be said, each troop had its own weekly weapons and equipment inspection and its own monthly inspection of uniforms and clothing. It was also assumed that every young officer, after two years, should be "capable of commanding and exercising a troop or company in every situation, and shall be perfectly acquainted with its interior management, œconomy, and discipline . . ."[22]

But there were also leaves of absence, and during the slightly more than five years between the time when Medwin joined

[20] *Ibid.,* I, 187–188.
[21] *Ibid.,* I, 255.
[22] Charles James, *The Regimental Companion; Containing the Pay, Allowances and Relative Duties of Every Officer in the British Service* (London, 1811, Seventh Edition), I, 84, 88, 119–122.

his regiment in late 1813 and the time when it sailed at the end of 1818, he was on leave for a total of twelve months.[23] These periods, we may believe, Medwin enjoyed very greatly. Julian tells a story in *The Angler* of passing a month at Juggernaut (Puri) on the coast below Calcutta, "with Colonel G—— and a party, among which were two ladies." [24] Here, he says, he saw the famous Hindu Car festival, with thousands of pilgrims vying for the honor of dragging the god on his great wagon, with its seven foot wheels, through the sand. "We passed our time," Julian says, "in hunting all day near the ruins of the Black Pagoda, eating and drinking afterwards till twelve, and then bathing by moonlight in the surf . . ." At the end of this chapter, which contains recollections of Edward E. Williams's account of a lion hunt, upon which Medwin's poem *Oswald and Edwin* is based, Julian cries out, "But . . . the spell is broken—it was a protracted dream . . . Call it exile—call it what you will, India was *my* country. There I had friends, a home, congenial employments—pursuits to rouse the mind to energy: here all is torpor—stagnation . . ."

This was written by the Medwin of 1834, whose prospects had dimmed considerably since the great days when he had known Byron and Shelley and had gone on to marry a countess and heiress. But there are also pages in *The Angler*, "Julian's Journal," [25] which demonstrate, if they have the least foundation in fact, that Medwin was by no means always happy in the 24th Light Dragoons. And that the "Journal" is founded on fact is suggested by its date, 1817, and by the four places where it was supposedly written, Barwa-Sagar, Jhansi, Datia, and Sonari—places where, we know from Medwin's military record, he in that year actually was, as a part of the Grand Army of

---

[23] The Regimental Muster Rolls also show that Medwin was absent on leave from July 3, 1815, for four months, perhaps in connection with his brother's death on June 3, and from May 8, 1818, for eighteen months' terminal leave. A part of his regiment sailed for England on Dec. 16, 1818; the remainder sailed on Dec. 26, to arrive at Gravesend on May 13, 1819 ("India Shipping Intelligence," *AJ*, VII [June, 1819], 674).

[24] Medwin, *Angler*, I, 255.   [25] *Ibid.*, II, 64–85.

Lord Hastings. The "Journal" is the record of a deep and persistent despondency, caused by "too keen a sensibility to the opinion of the world, a want of self-esteem." Twice in the course of it, the writer cries out against indolence and despair—"Activity, I will deify thee!"[26]

If the date of the "Journal," 1817, has any autobiographical authority, Medwin's desire for action should have been satisfied in February and March, 1817, when his regiment, under the command of Major General Marshall, besieged the fort of Hathras and its fortified town or kutra.[27] The 8th Light Dragoons, the regiment of Medwin's friend Edward E. Williams, who was drowned with Shelley, was also present and saw action.

This is not the place to go into great detail concerning the background and origins of the Mahratta and Pindari War of 1817–1818. It may be said, however, that this war marked an end, not a beginning. After 1818 India was a unity, united under the British, the period of internal struggles for supremacy ended. The white man's burden was neither a cliché nor a joke, and part of that burden was to put down the Pindaris, who specialized in looting, burning, enslaving women and children, and collecting protection money from the minor Indian princes, but who maintained intricate relations, nevertheless, with the Mahratta states and were frequently protected by them.

In March, 1816, the Gurkha or Nepal War had been successfully concluded, and Hastings turned his attention to central India, where the Pindaris were active. In the winter of 1814–1815 they had "plundered portions of the Madras Presidency and returned unscathed with £100,000 of booty . . ."[28] Conditions were tense and all India was waiting the next British move, hoping for a show of weakness. Hastings was in the process of assembling the greatest British army that India had

[26] *Ibid.*, II, 74, 81.
[27] "Asiatic Intelligence," *AJ*, IV (Nov., 1817), 524–525; Prinsep, *British India*, pp. 177–180, with picture of Hathras fort.
[28] Vincent A. Smith, *The Oxford History of India* (London, 1958, Third Edition), pp. 566–568.

ever seen, for the purpose of surrounding the elusive Pindaris in their own country.

At this critical point Dya-Ram, the chieftain who controlled Hathras but merely rented land in the district of Aligarh from Sindia, one of the most powerful of the Mahratta princes, showed unmistakable signs of insubordination. The British were forced to strike.

Hathras, kept in perfect repair at the time and incorporating the latest improvements (including a glacis), copied from the neighboring British fortress at Aligarh, "was reckoned one of the strongest forts in India."[29] The purpose, to achieve the reduction of the fort with some "éclat," was brilliantly—or perhaps luckily—achieved.

The fort, measuring 1,600 yards around the glacis and surrounded by a ditch said to be 120 feet wide and 85 feet deep, with 5 feet of water, had 20 circular bastions, "very high and strong," and was defended by 2,500 regular soldiers and 45 pieces of artillery.[30]

After the British had invested the place on all sides, Dya-Ram was offered the opportunity of surrendering the fort and allowing it to be dismantled.[31] He deliberated for several days, in the course of which Lt. White, of Medwin's regiment, was wounded by the inhabitants of a nearby village, which was "immediately burnt."[32]

Dya-Ram still vacillating, General Marshall ordered down the gallopers of the 24th Light Dragoons and fired a shot into the fort, to indicate the end of peaceful negotiations.

Medwin's regiment was stationed between the fort and the fortified town, which were separated by about 700 yards, Edward E. Williams's regiment being stationed nearby, with native cavalry, irregular horse, horse artillery, a mortar battery, and a rocket brigade which could fire Congreve rockets,[33] the

[29] Prinsep, *British India*, p. 177.
[30] "Asiatic Intelligence," *AJ*, IV (Sept., 1817), 304–305.
[31] Prinsep, *British India*, p. 178.
[32] "Asiatic Intelligence," *AJ*, IV (Sept., 1817), 305.
[33] *Ibid.*, IV (Nov., 1817), 524.

latter of such interest to Byron some years later. The British used 71 mortars and howitzers and 34 battering guns (18- and 24-pounders), exclusive of 12-pounders for enfilading.[34] "It was by no means extraordinary to see twenty" shells in the air in the course of a single minute.[35] "Such powerful means had never yet been employed against any fortified place in India."[36] The kutra fell on February 23, and the dragoons were active in preventing the attempted escape of 800 enemy horsemen, who were "terribly cut up."

The bombardment of the fort continued until, on March 2, a little before sunset, a British shell or rocket made a direct hit on the enemy's magazine, said to contain 320,000 pounds of gunpowder. The explosion was heard fifty miles away, the ground shook as if by an earthquake, and dirt and dust rose to an "immense height"—but the defenders kept firing, although the destruction within had been bloody indeed, for many of the women and children had taken refuge in the underground stone magazines, and half the garrison was killed.[37] At midnight, Dya-Ram with about 150 horsemen, dressed in armor beneath their clothes, made good their escape, but he had to fight his way through a detachment of dragoons, at which time a captain was killed, the only English death during the siege of Hathras. Other parties of Indian horse now attempted to escape, but the dragoons, it seems, "literally cut them to pieces."[38]

The fort then surrendered, its interior reduced to "a scene of perfect desolation," and "the impression of the utter futility of resistance spread far and wide through Hindoostan, even through the remote Dukhun, where it materially influenced the

---

[34] *Ibid.*, IV (Dec., 1817), 620.
[35] Shipp, *Memoirs*, p. 222 (Shipp was an eyewitness).
[36] Prinsep, *British India*, p. 178.
[37] William Hough, *A History of British Military Exploits and Political Events in India, Afghanistan, and China, from 1757 to 1849* (London, 1853), II, 43; Shipp, *Memoirs*, p. 226; Prinsep, *British India*, p. 178.
[38] "Asiatic Intelligence," *AJ*, IV (Dec., 1817), 619.

subsequent conduct of the Mahratta chiefs and kuladars."[39]
From the first, the show had promised to be such a good one
that a party of ladies had come from Agra, thirty miles away,
to watch it.[40]

The Pindaris, under the protection of Sindia and Holkar, the
two strongest Mahratta princes, still had to be dealt with. To
do so, and guard against the consequent possibility of war with
the Mahratta states, Hastings assembled the largest British
army that had ever taken the field in India, reportedly of 116,-
000 men in five divisions. The First or Centre Division of the
Grand Army was under Hastings himself, with Major-General
Brown of the cavalry under him as second in command. This
division included the 8th and 24th Light Dragoons (with two
regiments of native cavalry constituting the 1st Brigade of
Cavalry, commanded by Lieutenant-Colonel Philpot of the
24th), three troops of horse artillery, the Dromedary Corps,
the Pioneer Corps, the 87th Regiment of Foot, the European
Flank Brigade, and three brigades of native infantry. This force
was to be in position by October 10, 1817, to move against
Sindia. On September 27 the 24th Light Dragoons had been
ordered to take the field as part of the 1st Brigade of Cavalry.

The Centre Division had left Cawnpore on October 16 and
on the 20th arrived at Sekundra, where other troops joined it,
to bring the Division up to full strength, and where Hastings
reviewed the entire Division, "drawn out on the plain in one
single column."[41] On October 26, the Division left Shergurh
at 3 A.M., one of its members recorded, marched over "a very
narrow road leading through deep ravines, the sides of which
were lined with high craggy rocks, and at six A.M. we passed
over a bridge of boats thrown across the river Jumna."[42] In
passing through this country, Hastings received state visits from
several rajahs, who brought rich gifts, including elephants and
horses, and accepted rich robes of honor in return. On No-

---

[39] Prinsep, *British India*, p. 179.   [40] Shipp, *Memoirs*, p. 219.
[41] "Asiatic Intelligence," *AJ*, V (June, 1818), 567.
[42] *Ibid.*, p. 568.

vember 5, Sindia, properly impressed by this show, signed a treaty of concert or enforced mutual aid, military and political.

This happy conclusion was followed almost at once by an epidemic outbreak of cholera in Hasting's army, which struck fiercely on November 14, as he was moving eastward through Bundelkhand from the Sindh River. In ten days, it was estimated, one-tenth of the entire force died, and the "whole camp was a hospital," wrote Henry T. Prinsep, an eyewitness. He said, "the whole camp continued for some days to move eastward, in the hope of finding a better climate, as soon as it should reach the Betwa; but each day of march many dead and dying were abandoned on the route, and many more fell down on the road, for whom it was impossible to furnish the means of transport . . . Such indeed was the general distress that, so long as the epidemic raged, even the healthy were broken in spirit, and incapable of labour or fatigue . . ."[43] Another observer, author of a "Journal of the Centre Division of the Army from Cawnpore," reported on November 19, a week after the first appearance of cholera, when the division had arrived at Eritch on the Betwa, that 3,753 persons had died. Among other treatments tried was "rubbing the pit of the stomach with opium warmed over the fire."[44] At least two officers in the 24th Light Dragoons died at this time.[45]

Without question this is the epidemic that Medwin recalled and described in *The Angler*, in "Julian's Notes"[46] to the poem there called "Julian and Gizele," which is merely a revision of "The Pindarees," published in 1821.

One march I shall never forget, it has haunted me to-day. I was in the rear-guard, and did not get to my new ground till night, and then left eight hundred men, at least, dead and dying, on the road. Such a scene of horror was perhaps never witnessed. The disease

---

[43] Prinsep, *British India*, pp. 279–280.

[44] "Journal of the Centre Division of the Army from Cawnpore," *AJ*, VI (July, 1818), 7–8.

[45] "Asiatic Intelligence," *AJ*, V (June, 1818), 604.

[46] Medwin, *Angler*, II, 346–347. The poem is also attributed to Julian, clear evidence of the identity of Medwin and that character.

first made its appearance among the coolies, next our servants were affected, afterwards the Sp'hees, then the European soldiers, and last the officers . . . We lost a whole troop. During the first few days, every man who went into hospital fell a martyr to the epidemic . . . What is very remarkable, only one battalian in General Marshall's division suffered, and that lost nearly half its strength.

The 24th Light Dragoons, under Colonel Philpot, was stationed at Barwa-Sagar, so as to connect the Centre Division at Eritch on the Betwa and the Third or Left Division under General Marshall. Medwin has left a description of "Boorwa Saugor," as he spelled the name.[47]

I arose before gun-fire, and made a pedestrian circuit of the place, which occupied me about three hours. The lake of the bluest and most crystalline purity is formed artificially by a "bund" or embankment being thrown across, to confine the water collected from a number of small streams which flow from the neighbouring heights. The "bund" is a colossal piece of masonry, consisting of massy walls, the interspace filled up by earth, in which trees are planted, and which from their size would show the whole to be of no recent date. At the west end rises a large pile, the fortress of the place. Below, is a beautiful botanical garden, composed of the choicest plants and shrubs, from all parts of the Eastern, and some from the Western world, and laid out in the European manner. I could not help reflecting, that we are exotics in the animal, as many of them are in the vegetable kingdom, and sighed and exulted over the concluding paragraph from Gibbon, whilst speaking of the overthrow of the Mogul Empire. "Since the reign of Aurungzebe, their empire has been dissolved—their treasures of Delhi rifled by a Persian robber, and the richest of their kingdoms are now possessed by a company of Christian merchants, of a remote isle in the Northern ocean." The train of thought gendered by the recollection of this remarkable sentence, threw a gloom over my mind, that had till then been pretty tranquil. I sate down for some time in the garden. The air was filled with the odours of the aromatic blooms, and the branches were full of "bulbools," but neither had any sweets or music for me.

[47] *Ibid.*, II, 72–73; Prinsep, *British India*, p. 281, establishes the location of Medwin's regiment.

This is clearly no state of mind for a soldier to be in. The epidemic had hardly subsided when news arrived that a Pindari force of 10,000 was moving northward towards Gwalior. Hastings moved in a northwesterly direction with the Centre Division from the Betwa, hoping to intercept the enemy, and ordered the 24th Light Dragoons, at Barwa-Sagar, to move through Datia, cross the Sindh, and cut the enemy off at Gwalior.

Medwin was thinking of other things. He was delighted to find that the area between Barwa-Sagar and Datia abounded "with temples of the Hindoo deities, and the sculpture is in many . . . singularly minute and delicate—the walls covered with figures of human beings in various postures . . ." some of them erotic. The small town of Jhansi, seen from a distance, he found "very picturesque," and its inhabitants handsome and fair. "The masonry of the place is substantial, and the architecture is, if I may say so, Gothic in miniature."[48]

It is difficult to believe that this man ever became a dedicated military officer of professional calibre. His interests were elsewhere. As his brigade, in pursuit of the Pindaris, approached Datia, he noticed that the fields, as in Europe, were "hedged in. The houses covered with red tiles, and the palace, built on rock, is a handsome and regular pile, bearing a nearer resemblance to a European landscape than any I have yet seen in this country."

Meanwhile, more military minds were at work. Hastings reached Sonari on the banks of the Sindh about thirty miles southeast of Gwalior, on December 11, 1817, thus giving massive support to Colonel Philpot, who, with the 24th Light Dragoons and a regiment of native cavalry, was "posted in advance between Gwalior and Narwar, the Pindaris being in the neighbourhood of the latter place. Having correct information of their movements he marched against them, but as he approached they fled back in a south west direction. It is

48 Medwin, *Angler*, II, 74.

however very improbable that they can escape." [49] But escape they did, temporarily, by abandoning their baggage and families, and the greatest danger that Medwin suffered at this time was probably that which he has described: [50]

We are encamped [at Sonari] very closely together on the edge of the ravines which intersect the country on the banks of the river Sind. It is an extensive, uncultivated plain, compared with that of the Phooj. I have felt a flightiness to-day that reminded me of crossing that river, which I have never thought of without shuddering.

Being on general duty at head quarters, when we were first detached on this "Dour" after the Pindarees, I was not relieved till a late hour, and the regiment had already marched. But the camp followers, an army of themselves, indicated the way. After a time, however, I lost it, and wandered about all day, and found myself, near sunset, on the banks of the river. The approach of night—a new ally's country, and a deep jungle on all sides, I thought it best to ford the stream. It was broad, and rushing swiftly over a broken, black, rocky bed, as slippery as glass. I had on my full uniform, and did not even take the precaution of unstrapping my sword, but let it dangle in the water, so that if my horse had come down, I could have had no chance of getting out by swimming. Sometimes he was up to his knees, sometimes to the girths, and stood occasionally . . . for five minutes, shivering and trembling with terror, after sliding for a yard or two. At last, after sometimes swimming, sometimes skating, he reached the middle, and sank with me at once to the saddle bow, and passed (it fortunately being deep enough) the rest of the way *à la nage* . . .

Medwin was considerably shaken, but it does not appear that the 24th Light Dragoons saw further action, and by January 21, 1818, a British officer, exulting that the war was over, could write, "The whole continent of Hindustan is now in our possession." [51] In February, 1818, the 24th, still with Lieutenant-Colonel Philpot, was "under eventual orders to return to Europe," [52] and in March the regiment was safely back at Cawn-

---

[49] "Asiatic Intelligence," *AJ*, VI (July, 1818), 77.
[50] Medwin, *Angler*, II, 77–78.
[51] "Asiatic Intelligence," *AJ*, VI (Sept., 1818), 303.
[52] *Ibid.*, VI (August, 1818), 181.

pore, Medwin with it. On October 10, the regiment embarked at Cawnpore for the Presidency, at which time Major-General Marshall, "who had served with this regiment nearly eighteen years, emphatically notices its strict discipline, exemplary conduct, love of justice, and humane treatment of the natives, and the consequent regret of the inhabitants at its departure." The General Orders issued at the time of the regiment's embarkation at Calcutta paid tribute to the "undaunted valour" and the "exalted reputation" of "that gallant corps." [53]

How had Medwin conducted himself—in this war in which the enemy defended great mud forts, might wear chain link armor or fight with shields and bamboo spears, along with matchlocks, and in which a British force of 8,000 fighting men would enclose like a great glittering, moving membrane 80,000 camp followers of all legal and illegal occupations, 11,000 bullocks and horses, 650 camels and elephants, great flocks of sheep and goats, and 250 vehicles; an army in which "lawful prize" captured from the enemy was divided among the capturing men and officers "according to the rules and usages of his Majesty's services," in which firing a rifle at an enemy from within a hole or from behind a wall could be debated as unfair, and in which an officer disgraced himself if he removed the insignia of his rank upon entering combat? [54]

Medwin did not distinguish himself. There is no record that he was ever decorated or commended, nor was he ever promoted on the basis of merit. That he was a competent officer, however, is suggested by several facts, the first being that he remained in the Army for about seven years. Sensitive and introspective as he was, if he had felt himself to be incompetent as an officer, he would have sold his commission. Instead, he

[53] *Ibid.*, VII (May, 1819), 550, and VIII (July, 1819), 82.

[54] *Ibid.*, VI (August, 1818), 180; VII (March, 1819), 314; IX (April, 1820), 384; Shipp, *Memoirs*, pp. 123–124, 192, 231, 246–247, 294–297. As a Lieutenant, Medwin received seventy rupees (about seven pounds) in prize money at Hathras; the commanding General received 6,173 rupees, one-sixteenth of the whole. One thousand rupees was the approximate equivalent of one hundred pounds.

went on half pay only when his regiment was disbanded. In addition, in 1815 he was placed in charge of recruits at Buxar, being thus given a position of some responsibility; and in 1817–1818 he was on two occasions placed, presumably, in command of his troop, he being the senior officer present and on duty.[55] But in all these years, finally, he saw very little military action, and it is significant that Julian, who tells in *The Angler* some very tall tales of hunting and fishing, makes no greater claim for his military prowess than that he has been "at the storming of several posts."[56]

Apart from his military and hunting and fishing activities, how did he spend his time in India, what was he aware of, and what did he learn about the country and its people? He was a discriminating observer, it is pleasant to note, and his remarks, for example, on Bundelkhand, an area nearly one hundred miles square between the United and the Central Provinces, are accurate, observant, and appreciative. The Bundelas he considered "the finest race of men in the Upper Provinces." Recognizing their military virtues, for which they are famous, he was astonished and delighted that they had become peaceable, industrious, and prosperous subjects, although he had no sympathy with a Hindu mendicant priest or holy man who had stationed himself on a hill in the area and "vowed to remain there fasting till a certain sum was collected for him . . . A levy of this kind," Medwin concluded, "can scarcely be called gratuitous, from its being strictly enjoined by their religion, and falls much more heavily on the people than any systematic contribution could do." He had had an unpleasant experience at Cawnpore with a naked Hindu ascetic, who had vowed to spend five years making circles in the sand beside the Ganges, with a rude compass. Medwin accidentally stepped inside one of the circles and was soundly cursed by the holy man. This was superstition.[57]

[55] Regimental Muster Rolls.
[56] Medwin, *Angler*, I, 187.
[57] *Ibid.*, II, 333, 342–344.

As for the annexation of Bundelkhand by the Company, he was impressed by the economic benefits of British administration and contrasted the condition of the Bundelas under the tyrannous Mahratta rule. He saw the war against the Pindaris as a very large-scale police action against hordes of bandits, as indeed it was.

He was quite aware of the richness of the soil in Bundelkhand, much of it recently reclaimed and "brought into the highest state of cultivation," and he understood the method of diamond mining at Panna, as well as the declining production of the mines there.

None of this would be noteworthy if Medwin had not been a man interested also in matters much less prosaic or utilitarian—the architecture, religion, literature, language, and customs of the people of India, which he described at length. In addition, he was writing tolerable verse, keeping a journal, studying Spanish and Portuguese. He was by no means just another hard-drinking, indolent cavalry officer.

When his regiment sailed from Calcutta in December, 1818, Medwin was not aboard. There was something he wished to see—India, more of it, and particularly the famous cave temples of Ellora. On May 8, 1818, he had left his regiment at Cawnpore, with an eighteen months' leave of absence and permission to proceed to England by way of Bombay.

Medwin's exact route from Cawnpore to Bombay is not clear. However, Julian in *The Angler* mentions an overland route, instead of one by sea, although not in any very helpful detail. It was possible to travel by dawk, in a palanquin carried by eight bearers relieved every ten miles, at the rate of one hundred miles every twenty-four hours.[58]

The most probable route supported by details in *The Angler* is one that would have taken Medwin south from Cawnpore, using the rivers when possible, to the Nerbudda River, which flows into the Gulf of Cambay north of Bombay by somewhat more than two hundred miles. In the expanded notes to the

[58] Shipp, *Memoirs*, p. 235, note.

poem "Julian and Gizele" (a revised version of "The Pindarees," 1821), where the Julian disguise drops off, we read a
leisurely description of a suttee at "Mundelah" (Mandla) on
the Nerbudda which seems to be an eyewitness report and
which suggests in no way that the witness was on duty with
a military unit at the time.[59] Following the Nerbudda, furthermore, would place Medwin in the vicinity of Ellora, seat of the
famous cave temples (which he described in the *Bibliothèque
universelle*) and in the vicinity of Aurangabad, with the splendid mausoleum built by Aurangzeb for his wife, described in
The Angler as the tomb of his daughter Lalla Rookh.[60] Julian
also says that on his way to Bombay he crossed the "Gauts"
(the Western Ghats) from the "Dukkin" (Deccan),[61] the great
tableland, south of the Vindhya Mountains, through which the
Nerbudda flows.

Following this route, Medwin would have left the Nerbudda
before it empties into the Gulf of Cambay, travelled south by
land to Ellora, then dropped down a few miles to Aurangabad,
crossed the Western Ghats through the pass at "Bore Gaut"
(Bhor Ghat), after deviating from the usual route to see an
old fortress of "Sivagee" (Sivaji) used in his wars with Aurangzeb, and finally followed the valley of the "Concan" (Konkan)
nothward to Panwel, only a few miles from Bombay.

As Medwin describes the Western Ghats, he is quite the
equal of any of the acknowledged masters of picturesque description, Mary Shelley included.

Accounts have reached you of the Gauts. They cannot, perhaps,
be compared with the snow-capped majesty of the Alps, the solemn
grandeur of the giant Andes [which Medwin had never seen], or
the still more stupendous sublimity of the Himalayas, but, in wild
picturesqueness and beauty, are surpassed by neither of the three.
I remember, as though it were yesterday, crossing them from the

[59] Medwin, *Angler*, II, 336–338. Medwin also asserted in "A Bengal
Yarn" (*Ainsworth's Magazine*, II [1842], 59) that he had witnessed a
suttee.
[60] Medwin, *Angler*, II, 60–62.
[61] *Ibid.*, II, 30–36.

Dukkin, in my way to Bombay. One while their inaccessible summits were covered with a vast expanse of vapour; now slowly sailing away, it rendered their fantastic heights distinct in the full blaze of a tropical sun, whilst between their openings the eye caught an occasional glimpse of the sparkling ocean. The long sinuous valley of the Concan, watered by innumerable streams, and rich in pasture and cultivation, was in another direction contrasted with rugged and deep ravines, apparently formed by the subsiding of the waters of some vast deluge. In one place a roaring torrent crossed the road; in another you might count no less than ten cascades, flashing from rock to rock in a continuation of silver falls, or tumbling head-long several hundred feet, into an abyss, where they were still half hid in a sombre precipice of wood.

The luxuriance of verdure from the tropical productions, with which the Gauts are clothed, heightens the effect of the picture. The long waving tresses of the wild plantain—the darker green of the umbrageous mango—the elegant and plum-like gracefulness of the different kinds of palms—the lofty cocoa-nut—the slender and tapering hill bamboo—the broad and fibrous leaves of the teak— the pensile foliage of the sissoo, together with the variety of tints displayed by the flowers of a multitude of creepers, amongst which I noticed the sweet-pea, clambering among the rocks, or hanging in festoons from the branches, combined to make the scene a sort of enchantment. Nature there puts on a different creation, vests the surface of the soil with a new "Flora," a world of plants . . .[62]

Before reaching Bombay, Medwin spent six days at Ellora and its vicinity, and there he wrote the account of its cave temples that in 1821 appeared in the Genevan journal, *Bibliothèque universelle,* translated into French by an unknown hand, "extraits d'un journal inédit, par le Capit. Medwin." The English title that he, presumably, gave to his article was "Some Account of the Cave Temples of Ellora," in three installments.[63] The article is of the very greatest biographical importance, for its thirty-seven pages provide us with the clearest evidence of the kind of man he was very shortly before his reunion with

[62] *Ibid.,* II, 30–31.
[63] *Bibliothèque universelle des Sciences, Belles-Lettres, et des Arts,* XVI (April, 1821), 344–357; XVIII (Sept., 1821), 3–13, 111–122.

Shelley and his meeting with Byron. It is his only extended prose written before that period when he was on intimate terms with the two great poets in his life.

Already he was a man of some discrimination, capable of plotting the strategy of a long article. He will not attempt a minute description of all the cave temples of Ellora, he tells us, but will describe only those that are particularly interesting, beginning with Kailas, "peut-être le monument le plus splendide du bon goût et de l'habilité des anciens Indous."[64] Built in the eighth century, it is indeed the most splendid and perfect of all these temples cut into the side of a hill for a mile and more, and it has been described (not by Medwin) as "one of the most wonderful and interesting monuments of architectural art in India." It is remarkable because in its construction, "first the great sunken court measuring 276 by 154 ft. was hewn out of the solid trap-rock of the hillside, leaving the rock mass of the temple wholly detached in a cloistered court like a colossal boulder," from which the elaborately carved temple was then cut, in one piece.[65]

As Medwin writes of Indian gods and achitecture, those of Greece repeatedly come to his mind, and he uses the Greek architectural term *pronaos* to refer to the outer porch or porch of approach. Its general effect, he observes, cut out of solid rock as it is, suggests the entrance of an Indian fortress. "The facade, however, has the lightness and elegance of Greek construction."[66] Durga, a statue of whom stands in the vestibule, is interpreted as the Greek Minerva. The statue of Ganesa, symbolizing strength allied to prudence, to combat the evils of life, has the body of a man with the head and trunk of an elephant. "La combinaison des figures d'animaux avec la figure humaine, se retrouve souvent dans ces statues de haute antiquité; et c'est un trait frappant de resemblance entre cette

---

[64] *Ibid.*, XVI, 344.
[65] *Encyclopædia Britannica* (New York, 1911, Eleventh Edition), article on Ellora.
[66] *Bibliothèque universelle*, XVI, 345.

mythologie de l'Inde et celle des Egyptiens." Medwin, we see, was already interested in the historical study of comparative religions. As he takes us into the vast interior portico, he points out that the statue of Sri is a statue of the Indian "Cérès Multimmama," seated on her lotus throne. Within the temple proper, he notices a superb bas-relief representing a two-wheeled shell-shaped chariot. He uses the word *quadriga* to refer to it, and he is reminded of those Homer describes, which he says it exactly or perfectly resembles. Siva, represented in the same relief, is slightly bent over, as if he had just hurled a spear, and has nearly the same attitude as the Apollo Belvedere.[67] Such comparisons as these, all drawn from Medwin's first three pages, occur throughout his long article.

He conducts the reader on an orderly tour through the rock temple, moving clearly through its parts, his esthetic sense sharply perceptive, his descriptive powers at their highly visual best, and his interest in intercultural relationships spicing the discussion. He occasionally condemns the excessive multiplication of ornaments and figures, the harmony of the whole thus losing somewhat, but he feels, nevertheless, that "the purest and most classical taste should be fully satisfied by the total effect." [68] He thinks that the classical caryatides and termini may have had an oriental origin, and he notices that the conical tiara of a statue of Siva is similar to a Phrygian or Etruscan cap.

Medwin's clear, straightforward, and highly effective descriptive power may be illustrated by the following passage: [69]

Let us pass now to the second portico. I notice among its decorations a colossal statue of Rajah-Bajh, father of Purwatee, the wife of Siva during her second transformation. The statue is seated, and its pedestal rests on three lions. The figure has a great deal of majesty. The crown is pyramidal, very high, and heavily decorated with ornaments. On both sides are to be seen small, grotesque figures, but they play different musical instruments, almost like those

[67] *Ibid.*, XVI, 346.
[68] *Ibid.*, XVI, 348.
[69] *Ibid.*, XVI, 348–350.

the Indians use today. These figures, without grace, represent de-
formed creatures. Similar ones are to be found among all the
attendants on beautiful statues or elaborate reliefs: it seems that it
was the practice to heighten the beauty of the principal figures
by contrast.

Below Rajah-Bajh one sees the eight spirits who preside over the
eight points of the compass or the principal winds . . . Indra is
mounted on an elephant, Jama on a buffalo, Nirut on a man, Yaruna
on an alligator, Vaya on an antelope, Kuveru on a horse, and Isana
on a bull. The whole composition is admirably grouped.

Medwin, it will be noted, has disappeared. He is not describing himself, his own emotional reaction, but the thing itself,
before him and us, which is simply and clearly pictured without
pretentiousness. It is good soldier's prose in the service of art.

It is also interesting to notice that Medwin was aware of and
seems to have read portions, at least, of the great epic poems,
the *Mahabharata* and the *Ramayana*.[70] How much Sanskrit he
knew is uncertain. He writes, "It is not impossible that the
Hermes of the Greeks has taken his name from the Dhermé of
India, for the *D* is a demonstrative article in Sanscrit, as it was
in the Chaldaic and Syriac languages. That explains why the
triangular busts, surmounted by a head and sometimes having
the form of Egyptian mummies, are called Ermaes."[71] At least
he was interested in the history of languages and their relationships, however shallow his show of knowledge may be. Later,
he informs us that Yama is the Pluto of India, that Yama is also
the name of an Egyptian deity, and that the word in Coptic
means "force."[72] He was probably the only officer stationed at
Cawnpore capable of such an observation.

Curious and learned bits of strange information or misinfor-
mation always interested him. He notes, for example, that the
Hindus supposed their gods to be able to change sex at will
and goes on to observe that there is evidence of a similar belief
among ancient Greeks and Egyptians. Aeschylus, he says, gives

[70] *Ibid.*, XVI, 350–351.
[71] *Ibid.*, XVI, 353.
[72] *Ibid.*, XVIII, 8.

the Cyprian Venus a masculine sex in *Agamemnon*; and the
Egyptian "sphinx was now male, now female." [73] He informs us
that "one of the attributes of Vishnu in his various transforma-
tions is the wheel, inscribed with a triangle. It is the symbol
of the endless succession of generation and destruction in the
universe, for the conservation of all." He then observes that
the disciples of Pythagoras also held the wheel and the triangle
to be sacred. Curiosity, intellectual and otherwise, was one of
his dominant traits. He was driven to explore new fields of
knowledge, foreign lands and literatures, the most minute details in the private lives of people he knew.

Spare soldierly descriptive prose he can write, but he is also
capable of immense enthusiasm, heightened by a sense of
drama. When he has concluded his detailed tour of the Kailas
temple, the reader may feel the need to shift the focus away
from the individual parts and view the whole, as Medwin did.
He gives us that larger view, but not without making us climb
a mountain for it. His short sentences at the beginning of the
description suggest the breathlessness of the ascent, and they
are admirably contrasted with the increasing complexity of the
last sentences. [74]

A path was before me. I followed it. It went up into the mountain.
A stream cut across it at a certain height. During the rains, the
stream became a torrent. It dropped into a basin and then flowed
around the mountain . . . The view was exquisite. I saw the village
of Ellora, with its numerous pagodas, surrounded by groves of rich
foliage. Beyond, extended an immense plain which bounded, in a
semi-circle, the mountains, green up to the summit. On the right,
in a valley extending as far as the eye could reach, I discovered
an isolated mass of boulders which seemed to have been moved
from its primeval position by some great convulsion of nature.

I continued to climb, with difficulty, until suddenly, I found myself on the edge of a precipice. Never shall I forget the impression
that I had, as the eye swept downward over the whole of the
magnificent structures, the details of which I had come to admire.

[73] *Ibid.*, XVI, 354.
[74] *Ibid.*, XVIII, 6–7.

The temples, the pagodas, the galleries, the obelisks, the spacious courts cut into the depths of a mountain of solid stone, which the hand of man has detached from it by removing all that was super-fluous—one can hardly believe his eyes and has to persuade himself that these are human works. All that one had read in fairy stories offered itself to the imagination and troubled the judgment. When one has the most sublime and imposing works of nature before his eyes, the wonder that they were created is lost in the sense of the infinite power of the Architect of the universe; but here the contrast added to the effect: the works are sublime, durable as those of nature, and yet what weak and perishable creatures have executed them!

The vaguely deistic echoes of the paragraph above should not obscure the fact that Medwin's point of view here is primarily esthetic, that of the connoisseur of landscapes. He is fully aware of the importance of choosing the proper position before an architectural work, and he chooses his point of view only after deliberation.[75]

The three great temple excavations which I am about to describe, have a simple beauty which is truly classical, whether one examines them from nearby or places himself at a certain distance to consider them. The spot most advantageous for its point of view is at the foot of a banyan tree of huge dimensions, surrounded by banks of turf and located some hundreds of yards from the front of the excavations. It was here that I pitched my tent, in order to enjoy fully the total effect. I have passed hours here in a sort of ecstasy of wonder . . . The pagodas, the Kailas, and temples were now completely visible. The temples of Dus Atar and of Do Jom were before me, with their elegant galleries, and to complete the effect of the whole, three large waterfalls, formed by the recent rains, rushed down from crag to crag.

Here is the completely experienced picturesque tourist, familiar with all the accepted techniques of viewing. He had almost certainly studied with care William Gilpin's *Three Essays: On Picturesque Beauty; On Picturesque Travel; and On Sketching*

[75] *Ibid.*, XVIII, 9–10.

Landscape: To which is added a poem, On Landscape Painting (1792) or one of the innumerable books spawned by it or written within the same tradition. Medwin had absolutely no need to hear the lecture on the picturesque which Henry Tilney delivered to Catherine in *Northanger Abbey* (1818), leading her at once to reject voluntarily "the whole city of Bath, as unworthy to make part of a landscape." [76]

As Medwin moved on to describe the magnificent temple called by the Indians the Cabana of the Carpenter, that is, of Visvakarman, identified by Medwin as the Indian Vulcan, his style became so polished that the editor of the *Bibliothèque universelle* felt called upon in a footnote to inform the reader that the author had assured him "not one word" of the original journal had been changed. The sentences footnoted were these: "The dimensions of the edifice and the most minute description of its details could give only a very imperfect idea of its total effect. The impression that I have received from the whole, from the unity and the harmony of its proportions, is greater than that I have ever experienced from the aspect of the most magnificent structures." [77]

It is very probably untrue that Medwin did not change a word of what he first wrote in India, but it also seems clear that he was not keeping an ordinary journal. He was writing a very carefully plotted account, with an eye on eventual publication. Nor was that account written by a man seeing his first ancient ruins. He tells us, "I have visited different ruins of religious edifices from Madras to Delhi, the ruins of Gaur, ancient Palibothra, and those of the black pagoda of Juggernaut, of an antiquity even more remote, and in all these I have not found the least trace of arched or vaulted construction. That which I saw in the Cabin of the Carpenter is a unique exception." [78] He was a practiced amateur of the architectural arts, as his article proves, and after he got to Bombay he also made an excursion to the cave temple at the village of Karli,

[76] Chapter XIV.   [77] *Bibliothèque universelle*, XVIII, 10.
[78] *Ibid.*, XVIII, 11.

near Poona.[79] This is said to be (not by Medwin) "without exception the largest and finest *chaitya* cave in India; it was excavated at a time when the style was in its greatest purity, and is splendidly preserved." [80]

By far the greater part of Medwin's article is descriptive. The closing pages, however, are analytical or argumentative in character and thus are of particular interest because they demonstrate the quality of Medwin's power of consecutive reasoning, and it was quite respectable indeed. Here is, then, another important aspect of the man who knew Shelley and Byron and who saw them, furthermore, with some clarity.

"In taking leave of the masterpieces of Ellora," he writes in conclusion,[81]

I should like to present certain observations on their date . . . The Brahmins shrouded in fable the early history of India. They distinguished divine and human epochs, and from the former they derived the races of their kings and heroes, which they made to descend from the sun and the stars. The chronology of India is thus rendered completely uncertain, and it is difficult to form anything more than conjectures concerning the epoch to which the subterranean structures of Ellora belong.

Some have pretended that their age does not exceed nine hundred years, and refer to the schism between the Buddhists and Brahmins, which led to the expulsion of the latter and their withdrawal to the west and to Java. The persecuted schismatics, they argue, and those still separated in opinion from them agreed finally to adopt a middle or compromise system of doctrine and to adhere to the same opinions and to the same worship.

That event, if in reality it took place, is a unique example of its kind. It constitutes an exception to that exclusive and intolerant spirit of priests of all religions; but, above all, it is hardly in accord with the blind and persistent obstinacy of the Hindus, in their attachment to the least important religious observances.

The point in question is not only contrary to all analogies and probabilities; it is not upheld by any historical account. Another

[79] *Ibid.*, XVIII, 12, note.
[80] *Britannica,* edition cited, article on Karli.
[81] *Bibliothèque universelle,* XVIII, 116–118.

opinion expressed concerning the monuments of Ellora appears to be equally devoid of plausibility and proofs. It is pretended that before the epoch of construction of these monuments, the Hindus had no other religion than a pure deism, but that their priests then adopted all the mythological fables of which allegories are found in the temples.

That opinion has been founded upon the silence of the Vedas with respect to the allegorical representations of which the temples of Ellora are full, but that silence appears to be easily explained. The sublime doctrine of the Vedas was no more made for the minds of the vulgar than the ideas of Plato or Aristotle. The laws of Manu established great precautions to keep a knowledge of the Vedas from the people. The Brahmins of our day still take the same care, and in that they act like the priests of Egypt and the disciples of Pythagoras.

It seems probable that the adoration of idols was a concession to the weakness of the vulgar and a compensation for the individual whose limited understanding prevented him from rising to the concept of a pure intelligence. Can one in reality suppose with any likelihood that the Hindus preserved, over a long course of centuries, a religion pure and free of all grosser alloys, then in the ninth century of our era to fall suddenly into a bizarre polytheism and the adoration of a countless number of divinities, under forms often monstrous?

One wonders upon what authority this strange supposition rests, of a pure religion, free of all grosser symbolism, which prevailed among the Hindus over a long succession of centuries. The numerous contradictions which one finds in the Vedas and the puerile observances recommended by the laws of Manu did not lead to the adoption of that system; and above all, it is in opposition to such historians as Arrian, Strabo, Plutarch, and Clement of Alexandria, who represent the peoples of India divided into castes and religiously submissive to the gymnosophists (Brahmins), whose revenues were considerable and who pretended to a lofty antiquity.

Everything was as in our time; and the probabilities are absolutely contrary to the supposition of a total change in the religious system during the ninth century.

That Medwin was more than once mistaken in this argument, which continues for four and a half more pages, should not be allowed to obscure the fact that he can reason in a fairly straight line, at length, upon a difficult and controversial subject, concerning which accurate information was not easy to obtain. It is interesting to notice also his attitude toward priestcraft, which would recommend him to Shelley and Byron, his acquaintance with the ancient historians named, and his generally enlightened view of religious development.

After he had finally arrived at Bombay, he "collected from an old resident there much information respecting that singular and interesting people, who compose the most intelligent and active part of its population—the Parsees,"[82] and he wrote an informed and enthusiastic note of eight pages on them—their origins in Persepolis, their religion and morality, the relation of their language to Sanskrit, their cemetery near the Malabar Point road, the nearby building containing their sacred fire, said to have been brought from Persia, their genius for business, their great charity, and their dress. Medwin, in short, before he left India, was a seasoned and cultured traveller who had read widely and with profit, an educated man of the world quite familiar with a civilization very different from his own and appreciative of it.

For what he had gained, he had paid a price. The monthly muster rolls of his regiment list him as "sick present" during eleven different months between June, 1814, and April, 1818, and he was in ill health also at the time of his Ellora tour. Julian in *The Angler* complains repeatedly of "attacks of liver," and it is said of him that he has gone to Cheltenham for his health, after returning from Bengal "with half a liver."[83] We know from an unpublished letter of Medwin to Jane Williams that in 1823, probably, he went for the sake of his health to Cheltenham, whose waters were famous as a stimulant to the liver, and there are also other references to his ill health after returning from India. There he may very well have suffered from amoebic dysentery, one of the severest complications of which

[82] Medwin, *Angler*, II, 322.
[83] *Ibid.*, II, 4.

was known as "tropical abscesses of the liver." Part of the treatment is removal from a hot climate, and "recovery may be imperfect, the disease continuing in a chronic form . . ." [84] One of its symptoms is extreme nervous depression, "and the state of prostration to which the patient is reduced can scarcely be exceeded." All of this is consistent with the details in "Julian's Journal," as well as with Medwin's own medical history, insofar as that can be established, and later recurrences of the disease would explain much in his later life.

But before he sailed from Bombay in October, 1818, there was an unexpected benefit, which was to influence his entire life. On the eve of his departure, he rediscovered the poetry of Shelley, finding in a Parsee book stall a copy of *The Revolt of Islam,* and was "astonished at the greatness of his genius." [85] He never overcame his astonishment. Shelley was to provide the central experience and the focal point of his life.

[84] *Britannica,* edition cited, article on dysentery.
[85] Medwin, *Shelley,* p. 231.

3

Reunion with Shelley

After leaving Bombay and rounding the Cape
of Good Hope, Medwin's vessel put in at St. Helena, where,
it seems, he caught a glimpse of the Great Exile himself. He
writes in *The Angler*,[1]

Napoleon had not then been long under jailorship; and, speaking
of that modern Prometheus, chained to his lone rock by the sea-
shore, one anecdote I can vouch for. During my stay I was a
pensionnaire at a shopkeeper's, who showed me some of the plate
the Ex-Emperor had sold him to defray the expense of the funeral
of his *cuisinier!* This par parenthèse. I had long been acquainted
with the officers of one of the regiments in that odious place, employed in a still more odious service, and, dining at the mess, was
invited by two brother subs to accompany them the next day on a
fishing excursion. They called for me at an early hour in a boat, and
we were rowed to an isolated rock at the back of the island.

You have heard of rolling down from the Cape to St. Helena;
almost at all seasons of the year, it blows from the same quarter
very nearly a gale of wind, by which Napoleon's *delightful* abode
was swept, whilst the government-house, which ought to have been
given up to him, has the advantage of being completely *abrité*. The
morning was unusually calm, scarcely a ripple broke against the
base of the desolate crag—a fit foreground to the still more desolate
prospect that the land presented; where—appropriate figure for such
a landscape!—we could perceive the illustrious Exile, with his arms
folded, taking his accustomed walk among the stunted shrubs dignified by the name of an avenue. Being soon tired of the dull sport,
and animated with the desire of getting a nearer view of the great
man, I soon took leave of the anglers, who gave orders to the
boatmen to fetch them before parade-time.

[1] Medwin, *Angler*, II, 18–21.

On my return to James Town I procured a passport, and mounting a horse, proceeded on my projected tour. I made the best of my way to Longwood, and esteemed myself fortunate in catching a glimpse of the *General's* profile, as he was entering the door of his crazy hut . . .

Nothing can be more dreary and desolate than St. Helena in the distance: what, then, is it when the eye can examine in detail its savage, herbless, volcanic rocks piled above rocks? To the weather-beaten mariner the sight of almost any land is agreeable; but this waif of the sea, this wreck of nature, this fragment of a demolished world, cannot be viewed with any sensation importing pleasure, with any desire to set foot there: what, then, must have been the horror of Napoleon when he first descried it? I am told that for many hours he did not speak, overcome with the horror of the scene, and with a presentiment that his prison was fated to be his sepulchre. As a light breeze wafted us slowly away, and the island appeared a dim cloud on the horizon, I sat down on the deck, and . . . blushed to be an Englishman . . .

This sympathy with Napoleon would also recommend Medwin, eventually, to Byron.

After Medwin landed at Liverpool, he certainly returned to Horsham, despite the quarrel with his father, and there, perhaps, put on for his family's admiration his uniform of French gray, with its sash and sabre, its yellow facings, its gold lace, and the honorary badge of his regiment, the figure of an elephant circumscribed "Hindoostan." It also appears that he wore a splendid military moustache, lubricated with bear's grease and Macassar oil.[2]

Proud indeed he must have been when, on June 3, 1819, he was presented to the Prince Regent. We read in *The Asiatic Journal*,[3]

His Royal Highness the Prince Regent held a levee at Carlton-house, which was numerously attended by the representatives of

[2] H. M. Chichester and George Burges-Short, *Records and Badges of the British Army* (London, n. d), p. 139; Medwin, "A Short Chapter on Beards," *Ainsworth's Magazine*, I (1842), 114.

[3] "Home Intelligence," *AJ*, VIII (July, 1819), 98.

foreign powers, and splendid circles of individuals from all the ranks of the clergy, nobility, and gentry, and other persons honorably distinguished. The Persian ambassador had the honor of a private audience.

Among the presentations were: Gov. Farquhar [of the Mauritius]; Lieut. Medwin, 24th drag . . .

Here, then, was the more than fitting climax to Thomas Medwin's military career. Present also were a general, three colonels, a Companion of the Bath, and the chief justice of Ceylon, along with Lieutenant George Jervis of the engineers, who is without question Trelawny's "George Jervoice," with whom Medwin was shortly to reside at Geneva. Jervis had sailed from Bombay on December 4, 1818, and Medwin may well have come to know him there. The Geneva Chambre des Étrangers, more accurate than Trelawny, spelled his name correctly, as did Medwin in a letter to Edward E. Williams.[4]

The 24th Light Dragoons had been disbanded at Chatham on May 24, 1819; in July Medwin was placed on the Half Pay List in the rank of Lieutenant (receiving four shillings and eight pence a day), and on September 20, 1819, he arrived in Geneva.[5]

There, with Jane and Edward E. Williams, another half-pay lieutenant returned from India, he rented a house, the Maison Petit (also called the Maison aux Grenades), on the same side of the lake as the Villa Diodati, hallowed for Medwin by the presence of Byron and its supposed association with Milton.[6] Medwin may also have known of the tradition that Rousseau had lived in the Maison Petit in 1754. Here, as well as else-

---

[4] "Asiatic Intelligence," *AJ*, VII (May, 1819), 560; H. W. Häusermann, *The Genevese Background* (London, 1952), p. 11; unpublished letter from Medwin to E. E. Williams, March 28, 1821, in the collection of Lord Abinger, Clees Hall, Bures, Suffolk; hereafter referred to as the Abinger Collection.

[5] Letters to the author from Mr. D. W. King, the Librarian of the British War Office Library; Häusermann, *Genevese Background*, p. 10.

[6] Häusermann, *Genevese Background*, pp. 10–11; Medwin, *Shelley*, p. 145.

where in years to come, he tried to live like a gentleman, on his pay of £85 a year. It was not easy.

On February 7, 1820, was born the first child, a son, of Edward E. Williams and Jane, accepted as his wife, although she never secured a divorce from her brutal husband, to whom she had been married in India. The child was named Edward Medwin Williams, and for some years he was called Medwin.

This fact is of some biographical importance. Thus far, the chief sources for Medwin's biography have been military accounts or records and his own published works. He is now, for the first time, to emerge in the bright and sometimes glaring light of complex human relationships, to be loved or disliked, admired, enjoyed, or rejected by people around him, his words and actions recorded by those who knew him.

The name of Williams's son is the clearest possible evidence of Medwin's ability to evoke strong friendship and affection in others, both men and women. Such evidence is particularly valuable, for after the publication of his *Conversations of Byron* there would be many who would turn against him, to blacken his name and nature.

It is significant that Williams was later approved, accepted, and liked by almost all the critical Pisan circle of Byron and Shelley. Williams became at this time Shelley's closest friend, perhaps. Trelawny described him as the perfect playmate for Shelley and liked and admired him. He even won the complete and unqualified affection of Mary Shelley—and few did at this time. She wrote to T. J. Hogg, September 9, 1822, introducing Jane Williams to him,

You will find in her the dear friend whom he [Shelley] saw daily for nearly two years, to whom he was affectionately attached . . . You did not know Edward, & cannot tell what she has lost in losing him. They were enthusiastically attached to each other, and he by his talents, angelic disposition, his gentle, brave, & generous nature fully merited all the tenderness which she, the model of all gentleness and grace, bore him.[7]

[7] Unpublished letter from Mary Shelley to T. J. Hogg, Sept. 9, 1822, in the Abinger Collection.

As Professor F. L. Jones, editor of Williams's *Journal*, sum-marizes the relation, "suffice it to say that both Shelley and Mary liked Edward Williams from the start and that he was the most satisfactory friend they ever had."[8] After Williams and Shelley were drowned together, Jane and Mary continued for many years to be the most intimate friends.

This was the couple who named their son for Medwin. After sharing the same house with Medwin for a year, Williams wrote in the initial entry in his journal, after recording the birth of his son Edward Medwin, "I pass over the details of this year; it was passed in as much enjoyment, as I believe, is permitted to mortals, or this life to bestow."[9] Of this period in his life, Medwin wrote that he "revived a friendship such as I have never felt for any other individual. A more noble, unworldly being never existed than Williams," Shelley always excepted, of course.[10] They had known each other in India, where they had hunted together and had been drawn to each other by their intellectual interests, unusual among young cavalry officers.

Although Medwin had been ill, he had not been idle in Geneva, for in February, 1820, he had finished his first pub-lished poem, *Oswald and Edwin, An Oriental Sketch*, dedi-cated to Williams, "as a slight memorial of a long and uninter-rupted intimacy, commenced amid the scenes it attempts to revive, . . . by His Affectionate Friend, T. Medwin." This poem of forty-two pages, with a preface of two pages and twelve pages of notes, bore on its title page melancholy quotations from Bryan Waller Procter's *Dramatic Scenes* and from Shelley, who did not admire Procter's poem. Medwin may have known Procter as early as 1811 or 1812, before going into the Army, and had probably seen him when passing through London in 1819.

[8] *Maria Gisborne & Edward E. Williams, Shelley's Friends: Their Journals and Letters,* ed. F. L. Jones (Norman, Oklahoma, 1951), p. 13. Hereafter referred to as Williams, *Journal.*
[9] *Ibid.,* p. 102.
[10] Medwin, *Shelley,* p. 311.

Williams deserved the dedication, for he had supplied notes on a lion hunt for the poem. The preface, dated February 10, 1820, informed the reader,

The scene of the following little Sketch is laid in the Lion plains of Hurryana, or the green desert, bordering on that of Bikaneer: those who are familiar with the features of that highly interesting country, will not accuse me of having embellished the landscape in order to heighten the interest of the picture.

Of the tale (if it deserves the name) little need be said; one remark however is necessary, that the characters are not altogether imaginary: though, it must be confessed, they have been introduced for the purpose of delineating more faithfully, as well as naturally, the incidents of an Eastern Hunt.

I have been frequently present at such encounters, but am much indebted for the materials of this, (such as it actually occurred), to the notes of the friend to whom I have dedicated the work.[11]

Medwin liked the poem well enough to revise it as "The Lion Hunt" for *Sketches in Hindoostan,* published in 1821, and Shelley thought well enough of it to help with the revision of some of the lines. He wrote to Medwin, May 1, 1820, "The poem is certainly very beautiful. I think the conclusion rather morbid; that a man should kill himself is one thing, but that he should live on in the dismal way that poor Oswald does is too much. But it is the spirit of the age, and we are all infected with it."[12] The most that can be said of the poem, perhaps, is that it reveals the author's familiarity with India and a respectable competence in writing the closed couplet, along with a knowledge of the principles of picturesque composition and an enthusiasm for scenes of natural beauty (the purity of which is associated with the presence of Deity and contrasted with the degradation of man). Essentially it is a narrative celebration of a friendship between two young men, one of whom is killed. I quote the opening lines:

[11] Although Medwin omitted this preface when he revised the poem as "The Lion Hunt" for *Sketches in Hindoostan* (1821), he again acknowledged his debt to Williams in the *Angler,* I, 260.

[12] Shelley, *Works,* X, 165.

There is a joy to vulgar souls unknown,
There is a magic in that word—*Alone*!
Though never in the fulness of its power
Owned I its influence till this solemn hour.
Is it—that in these wilds by Man untrod,
More deep is felt the presence of a God?
Or, that on Nature's sacred solitude,
Sprung from the world, its fiends cannot intrude?
Or is it—that amid such scenes as these
The spirit feels enfranchised—more at ease—
Breathes purer air—and deems the Arab clan,
That scorns all commerce with its fellow man,
More wise and happy, in a state thus free,
Than slaves to Cities, Kings, and Luxury.

This, of course, is only our old friend the Noble Savage in another guise.

When, during this period in Geneva, Medwin revised[13] *Oswald and Edwin,* as "The Lion Hunt," he omitted altogether

[13] The greater part, by far, of *Oswald and Edwin* reappeared essentially or wholly unchanged as "The Lion Hunt." However, the nature of the revision performed on those passages rather thoroughly rewritten is suggested by the following parallel lines, the first from *Oswald and Edwin,* IV, 5–16, the last from "The Lion Hunt," IV, 5–15:

> . . . virgin wildernesses
> Of beauties all their own—to deck whose tresses
> Spring with her sister Summer interweaves
> A never-fading garland of green leaves
> From Nature's inexhaustive stores; whose hand—
> As with the magic of Enchantment's wand—
> A prodigality of fruits and flowers
> Of richest taste and fragrance ever showers
> On the lone tracts of that so favoured land;
> Where like rich pearls on some deserted strand
> Cast by the impetuous surge—they waste their bloom,
> The roses of a long-abandoned tomb.

> . . . virgin wildernesses
> Of beauties all their own; with sunny tresses
> By sister seasons ever decked, whose hands,
> As with the magic of Enchanter's wands,
> A prodigality of fruit and flower
> Of richest taste and fragrance ever shower

section XXIII, which was a needlessly distracting and unneces-
sary element in the narrative. It is an account of a Pindari
attack on "Seta's favorite village," and thus it became the germ
of "The Pindarees," the second long poem of *Sketches in
Hindoostan, with Other Poems*, published by Ollier. In the later
poem Medwin retained the feminine character Seta, who is
again the beloved of Oswald, and also kept certain lines from
Oswald and Edwin, part XXIII. He was from the first an eco-
nomical writer, ever ready to revise and republish, down to the
last years of his life.

Shelley also helped with the revision of "The Pindarees," in
manuscript, and liked it even better than *Oswald and Edwin*.
He wrote to Medwin, April 16, 1820, "That poem is highly fit
for popularity, considered in its subject; there being a strong
demand in the imagination of our contemporaries for the scenery and situations which you have studied. I admire equally
the richness and variety of the imagery with the ease and
profusion of language in which it is expressed." [14] Shelley went
on to object to "the employment of Indian words, in the body
of the piece, and the relegation of the meaning to the notes . . .
[But] then you have Moore and Byron on your side, . . . much
better poets than I am . . ." [15]

"The Pindarees," a poem of thirty-eight pages, with sixty-five
notes occupying fourteen pages, is composed chiefly of closed
couplets and is a tale of love and revenge so leisurely that at
times it seems hardly to move at all. Once more we meet Oswald, again he performs deeds of valour, again he loses one
dear to him, this time his beloved, who dies shortly after hearing false news of Oswald's death, and at the end, once more,
he is left alone to mourn.

On the lone tracts of that so favoured land:
Where, like rich pearls on some deserted strand,
Reckless of human blindness, they expand,
Their charms renewing ever with fresh bloom,
To mock creation's lord with his contrasted doom.

[14] Shelley, *Works*, X, 156.
[15] *Ibid.*, X, 157.

Estranged from man, henceforth he ran his race;
And all employment shunned, but most the chase.
To him of love, the light of life, bereft,
How worthless seemed the empty spark that's left!
Oh none can tell, save those who this have known,
The sickness of the heart—that feels alone;
To find the world contains not ought beside,
A blank—a vacuum not to be supplied.
Music—the dance—the banquet and the bowl,
Have their oblivious potions; but a soul
That once on love's ethereal food has fed,
Spurns at all joys of grosser matter bred.

Medwin's proud and disdainful hero, solitary and suffering, is by no means unrelated to the heroes of Byron.

Despite the fact that he was a published poet, Medwin was unable, it would seem, to effect an entrance into the Genevan society that he aspired to. "Nowhere did at that time castes prevail to such an extent," he recalled, and he thought that the Genevans, who had "at least a dozen different grades" or ranks of citizens, worshipped "rank and riches." [16] Perhaps it was at this time that he met Mrs. Siddons at John Kemble's house in Lausanne and thought her affected and pompous. He was later cut by her at Lydia White's, in London. [17]

At this time, however, he was on friendly terms, it seems, with Charles Pictet-de Rochemont, who with his brother, Professor Marc-Auguste Pictet, had founded the *Bibliothèque universelle*. Medwin wrote to Williams, March 28, 1821, from Rome, in a letter that implies a personal acquaintance with Pictet,

I have had a long and kind letter from Pictet containing lots of compliments, etc., & telling me that the whole of the paper is to appear in his next. He says, "I hope my Brother, Sister, nephews & nieces, who visited at Florence, have had the benefit of your acquaintance & that of Capt. & Mrs. Williams; if not, I desire you to carry this Letter to my Brother."

[16] Medwin, *Shelley*, pp. 152–153; Medwin, *Lady Singleton*, II, 9–10.
[17] Medwin's unpublished marginalia in his *Conversations*, p. 167.

Medwin concluded by observing, "His nephew is Consul—M. Anar, who gives the finest parties in Florence. I shall make acquaintance with them on my way back."[18]

Medwin was later to discuss Professor Pictet with Byron. In 1816 Byron's physician Polidori had invited the professor, along with Bonstetten, to dinner at the Villa Diodati. They came, but Byron did not appear, explaining later that since the invitation was Polidori's, he left the guests to be entertained by his young physician. However, he told Medwin that he had gone sailing earlier in the day and that the wind prevented him from being present.[19] But Medwin also heard another story. "Lord Byron," he wrote in the margin of his copy of *The Conversations of Byron,* "went to a soirée at M. Pictet's and thought himself bound to return the civility. This Dinner without Amphytrion gave great umbrage to the Savant . . . I have this from one of the Professor's family."[20]

This period of Medwin's life in Geneva ended very pleasantly, despite the general coolness of the Genevese, for by the summer of 1820, he was one of a small circle of English that included George Jervis, who had moved into the Maison Petit on May 30;[21] Trelawny, who had arrived at Lausanne in time to be introduced to Wordsworth by Captain Daniel Roberts, the artistic naval officer who was later to build Shelley's ill-fated *Don Juan*; and the wealthy and delightful Sir John St. Aubyn, an acquaintance of Byron, with an annual income said to be £76,000.

Born in 1758 and thus substantially older than Medwin or his other friends, Sir John had fifteen illegitimate children and borrowed £130,000 on the town of Devonport, which he owned, in order to pay the marriage portions of thirteen of the

[18] Unpublished letter from Medwin to E. E. Williams, March 28, 1821, in the Abinger Collection.

[19] *The Works of Lord Byron: Letters and Journals,* ed. R. E. Prothero (London, 1898–1901), III, 340, hereafter referred to as Byron's *Letters and Journals*; Medwin, *Conversations,* p. 12.

[20] Medwin's unpublished marginalia in his *Conversations,* p. 12.

[21] Häusermann, *Genevese Background,* p. 11.

fifteen. In 1816 he was still keeping a mistress, and in 1822 he married, well past sixty years of age. Of one of his sons, whom Medwin knew and liked, Washington Irving wrote, . . . "Mr. Edward St. Aubyn [is] a very amiable young man of one of the most ancient, respectable, & wealthy families of Cornwall. His father, Sir John St. Aubyn, Bart. is one of the very few that are left of the classical old English gentleman of Addison's day . . . A model of the primitive, courteous old gentleman—full of worth and of the most amiable manners." He powdered his hair, Irving noted in his journal, wore a pigtail and silver buckles, had a fine ruddy complexion, and was surrounded by his sons and their wives.[22] Trelawny described him in similar terms. "In the largest country house (Plangeau) near that city [Geneva] lived a friend of mine, a Cornish baronet, a good specimen of the old school; well read, and polished by long intercourse with intelligent men of many nations. He retained a custom of the old barons, now obsolete—his dining hall was open to all his friends; you were welcomed at his table as often as it suited you to go there, without the ceremony of inconvenient invitations." Sir John St. Aubyn, wealthy lover of the arts and sciences, former Whig M.P., was one of Medwin's most cherished friends, and it was at Sir John's house that Trelawny met Medwin, Williams, and Jervis.[23]

In view of Trelawny's later change of heart toward Medwin—as toward Byron—it is good to come again upon his enthusiastic account of Medwin as he was in the summer of 1820, shortly before joining Shelley in October. It was Medwin, we see, who was chiefly responsible for the English membership of the Pisan circle as it was finally gathered around Shelley and Byron. No other contributed so many: Edward E. Williams, Jane, and

---

[22] *Dictionary of National Biography,* article on Sir John St. Aubyn; *Letters of Washington Irving to Henry Brevoort,* ed. George S. Hellman (New York, 1918), p. 404; *The Journals of Washington Irving,* ed. William P. Trent and George S. Hellman (Boston, 1919), II, 107.

[23] E. J. Trelawny, *Recollections of the Last Days of Shelley and Byron,* reprinted in *The Life of Percy Bysshe Shelley,* ed. Humbert Wolfe (London, 1933), II, 167.

Trelawny, who wrote, "Medwin was the chief medium [and probably the only one] that impressed us with a desire to know Shelley; he had known him from childhood; he talked of nothing but the inspired boy, his virtues and his sufferings, so that, irrespective of his genius, we all longed to know him. From all I could gather from him, Shelley lived as he wrote, the life of a true poet, loving solitude, but by no means a cynic." This is the only appearance that Medwin makes in Trelawny's *Recollections of the Last Days of Shelley and Byron*.[24] It is an impressive tribute to Medwin's charm and his disinterested love of Shelley, written by a man who had become his enemy.

Meanwhile, Medwin had been writing to Shelley, from Geneva, and Shelley's earliest extant letter to him, January 17, 1820, is clear evidence of their earlier intimacy and of Shelley's continued liking for him. Its primary theme is Italy, "Paradise of exiles," the famous phrase that was to reappear in *Julian and Maddalo*, and its purpose is to persuade Medwin to come to Italy. "Take up your abode with me," Shelley wrote.[25] This letter should, once and for all, dispose of the common assertion that Medwin magnified his early association with Shelley, even though the standard biographies rely heavily on his accounts of the young Shelley.

An entry in the unpublished diary of Claire Clairmont records that Shelley received a letter on March 19, 1820, from "Captain Medwin," the earliest known use that Medwin made of that rank. That he was in fact ever awarded the brevet rank of Captain now seems impossible to establish. That he had a right to it, however, seems quite as probable as that he had not. Although the rank of Captain never appeared on the title page of any of his books, it does appear below the title of many articles and stories that he contributed to periodicals, and his *Conversations of Lord Byron* was advertised as written by "Captain Medwin." Although the rank of Captain does not appear in the notices of his marriage in *The Examiner* and *The*

[24] Chapter II.
[25] Shelley, *Works*, X, 140–141.

London Magazine, that rank does appear on the christening record of his first daughter. Although Mary Shelley, ambiguously, informed Hobhouse during his furiously raging controversy with Medwin that the latter was a "Captain by courtesy only," Hobhouse, nevertheless, regularly gave him this title, as did Byron, Murray, and Moore, among others. Mary Shelley asked, "is it courtesy to *print* a Lieutenant a Captain? I am not aware of the etiquette on this point." [26] Was it uncommon for young English officers on the Continent to take to themselves the rank of Captain, as did Edward E. Williams and George Jervis? [27] There were advantages, for as mere Lieutenants their only title would be "Mr." However all this may be, it is Captain Medwin that we frequently hear of from now on, and the entry in Claire Clairmont's diary shows that Shelley thought of him as a Captain.

Shelley wrote again to Medwin on April 16, 1820, criticizing "The Pindarees," as noted above, and going on to say, "I am printing some things which I am vain enough to wish you to see. Not that they will sell . . . But there is every reason to hope better things for you," that is, the popular sale of "The Pindarees." [28] Shelley's unsaleable volume, then being printed, was *Prometheus Unbound.*

Shelley, in short, had accepted Medwin as very nearly his intellectual equal and as his superior in potential poetic popu-

[26] Unpublished letter from Mary Shelley to John Cam Hobhouse, Nov. 10, 1824, in the possession of Sir John Murray.

[27] Häusermann, *Genevese Background,* pp. 10, 11. Mr. D. W. King, the Librarian of the British War Office Library informs me that he "can find no mention of his [Medwin's] ever having been granted the honorary or brevet rank of Captain . . ." On June 3, 1819, at his presentation to the Prince Regent, his rank was reported as Lieutenant, but it was by no means always customary to give both actual and brevet rank. An order had been recently issued advancing all Lieutenants of fifteen years' service to the brevet rank of Captain, but Medwin did not meet the requirement. Furthermore, following the coronation of George IV, all field officers were advanced one brevet rank, but Medwin was not a field officer, although he had, upon occasion, it seems, commanded his troop in the absence of his Captain, on special duty elsewhere.

[28] Shelley, *Works,* X, 157.

larity. The letter closes, "Courage! when we meet we will sit upon our melancholy and disorders, bind them like an evil genius and bury them in the Tyrrhene sea, nine fathoms deep.— Adieu. Affectionately yours, P. B. S."

In his letter of May 1, criticizing "The Lion Hunt," Shelley informed Medwin,

I have just published a tragedy called "The Cenci" . . . I don't think very much of it, but it is for you to judge.

Particularly, my dear friend, write to me an account of your emotions, and when and where we may expect to see you. Are you not tempted by the Baths of Lucca? [29]

This letter also closes with the phrase "Affectionately yours," a form (or some variant of it) that Shelley used in 1820 only when writing to his closest intimates—Henry Reveley, the Hunts, the Gisbornes, Peacock, Mary Shelley, and Claire.

Shelley sent to Medwin an early copy of *The Cenci*, which he "received in Switzerland at the Baths of Louche overhung by the frightful precipices and Glaciers of the Gemmi." This was the setting of Werner's "harrowing Domestic Tragedy," *Der Vierundzwanzigste Februar,* which Medwin had been reading amid the scenes it describes. This he "laid down to devour [*The Cenci*] with an all absorbing interest." [30]

Shelley was "delighted" with Medwin's enthusiastic reception of *The Cenci*, felt "encouraged to wish to present you with my 'Prometheus Unbound,'" explained his purposes in writing the latter play, being uncertain of his success in achieving them, and concluded, "But you will judge . . ." [31] This, once more, is the letter of a man who thinks he is writing to an intellectual equal, and Shelley was not one to suffer fools gladly, gentle though he was and kind. Medwin had also sent criticisms of particular passages, and to these Shelley replied. The invitation to come to Pisa was repeated.

[29] *Ibid.,* X, 165–166.
[30] Medwin, *Shelley,* p. 220.
[31] Shelley, *Works,* X, 191–192.

Despite Shelley's repeated invitations, Medwin waited two more months, until the summer was over, and then in October left Geneva to meet Shelley at Pisa, on October 21, 1820, after "nearly seven years." It was the most momentous day of his life, and determined much of the rest of it.

Shelley was returning from Florence, where he had accompanied Claire. Medwin, upon inquiring for Shelley at Pisa, had been referred to Lady Mount Cashell ("Mrs. Mason"), who gave him the necessary information. He found her an "interesting and amiable person," and she thought well enough of him, more than two years later, following the death of Shelley, to suggest to Mary that she employ Medwin as her agent in the delicate negotiations with Sir Timothy Shelley.[32]

On October 22, the end of the season, the two cousins arrived at the Baths of San Giuliano, four miles from Pisa. It was raining the day they arrived, and on October 25 the banks of the Serchio broke, to flood Shelley's house with four feet of water. They retreated upstairs, and Medwin wrote[33] years later, "Well do I remember the scene, which I stood with Shelley at the window to admire. The Contadine bore torches, and the groups of cattle, and the shouts of the drivers, the picturesque dress of their wives, half immersed in the water, and carrying their children, and the dark mountains in the background, standing out in bold relief, formed a singular spectacle, well worthy of a painter's study. Shelley wished me to sketch it, but it was far beyond my powers of delineation . . ."

The day before, Medwin and Shelley had gone to Pisa, presumably to make final arrangements for a house, and on October 29 they all moved into the Casa Galetti, large enough for Medwin to have one of the two rooms on the fourth floor for his own and for Shelley to have the other as a study. Thus the two men had frequent opportunities to converse apart from

---

[32] Medwin, *Shelley,* p. 233; *Shelley and Mary,* ed. Lady Jane Shelley (For Private Circulation Only, 1882), p. 919.

[33] Medwin, *Shelley,* p. 234.

the presence of Mary. The view from his room Medwin never forgot.

More than once . . . we stood watching from my open window in the upper part of the house, the sunsets of Pisa, which are gorgeous beyond any I have ever witnessed; when the waters, the sky, and the marble palaces that line the magnificent crescent of the Lung' Arno, were glowing with crimson—the river a flood of molten gold,—and I seem now to follow its course towards the *Ponte al Mare*, till the eye rested on the *Torre del Fame*, that frowned in dark relievo on the horizon.[34]

Medwin, not in good health himself and in the potentially difficult situation of occupying the house of a sick genius and his critical wife, with problems of her own, got off to a very good start. Less than a week after his arrival, Shelley wrote to Marianne Hunt, "An old friend and fellow townsman of mine Captain Medwin is on a visit to us at present, and we anxiously expect Keats . . . ,"[35] whom Medwin was later to champion as the third member of his poetical trinity, rising up out of his generation.

On October 29, writing to Claire at Florence, Shelley referred to Medwin as one whose influence might be exerted helpfully on her behalf, and it seems that the Williamses were already expected. Medwin was beginning to assemble the Pisan circle. Shelley confessed that he himself had been ill, but Medwin's "cheerful conversation" had been of some "use" to him. Medwin, he continued, "relates wonderful and interesting things of the interior of India. We have also been talking of a plan to be accomplished with a friend of his [Sir John St. Aubyn?], a man of large fortune, who will be at Leghorn next spring, and who designs to visit Greece, Syria, and Egypt in his own ship. This man has conceived a great admiration for my verses, and wishes above all things that I could be induced to join his

[34] Medwin, *Shelley*, II, 7.
[35] Shelley, *Works*, X, 212.

expedition. How far all this is practicable, considering the state of my finances, I know not yet. I know that if it were it would give me the greatest pleasure . . ." [36] It would seem that Medwin had discussed this plan with Shelley before the former had left Geneva, for on September 17 Shelley had asked Byron, "If I were to go to the Levant and Greece, could you be of any service to me?" [37]

Meanwhile, all this was to be kept secret from Mary, [38] and in this there may be a partial explanation of her animosity to Medwin. How Shelley would explain his new interest in Arabic, which he intended to study with Medwin, is not clear.

If Shelley was turning his thought to the East, Medwin was delighted with Pisa, especially "the Campo Santo, which with the Battisteria and the Hanging Tower constitute perhaps one of the most picturesque groups in the world.—They are the more striking," he continued, "from their Solitude and standing as they do in an enclosure of the finest turf, ever verdant and starred with the flowers which never set in Italy, the daisies." [39] It is no diminishment of Medwin's good taste and enthusiasm, by any means, that his closing words echo Shelley's "The Question."

Greece, Syria, Egypt, the Italian scene at hand—but there was also India, in the person of Medwin, and on November 1 and November 6 he read aloud to Shelley and Mary from his Indian journal. [40] On November 10, Shelley recommended *Sketches in Hindoostan* to Ollier, who published it in the next year: "My friend Capt. Medwin is with me, and has shown me a poem on Indian hunting, which he has sent to you to publish. It is certainly a very elegant and classical composition, and, even if it does not belong to the highest style of poetry, I should be surprised if it did not succeed." [41] Meanwhile, Shelley ex-

[36] *Ibid.*, X, 214–215.   [37] *Ibid.*, X, 209.
[38] *Ibid.*, X, 215.
[39] Medwin, *Shelley*, p. 238.
[40] *Mary Shelley's Journal*, ed. F. L. Jones (Norman, Oklahoma, 1947), p. 140.
[41] Shelley, *Works*, X, 220.

pressed his fear that "very few will understand or like" *Prometheus Unbound,* recently published by Ollier. Medwin was much less confident of his book's success than Shelley was and wrote anxiously to Ollier following its publication. "I should like to hear from you whether my Sketches are likely to have any success and what the opinion is regarding them."[42] He asked that two copies be sent to Shelley, whose *Adonais* he had just seen. The latter poem he thought would "produce a great effect." It did, but not during Shelley's lifetime. Medwin was a better judge of greatness than of popular taste.

By mid-November Medwin and Shelley had started to study Arabic together, and Medwin continued to be "very agreeable," Shelley wrote. "He plays at chess, and falls into our habits of reading in the evening, and Mary likes him well enough."[43]

On November 23, however, Medwin became ill, perhaps with a recurrence of amoebic dysentery, and Shelley, he says, cared for him tenderly during his long and "severe" illness.[44] Mary entertained him by reading Spanish with him.[45] Confined to his room, Medwin read all Shelley's works, published and unpublished. "The delight they afforded me," he recalled, "often disarmed pain," and it may have been during his convalescence that he formed the habit of copying unpublished poems and translations from Shelley's commonplace books.[46]

[42] H. B. Forman, "Medwin to Ollier," *Keats-Shelley Memorial Bulletin,* II (1913), 101. Medwin's letter is postmarked Aug. 25, 1821.

[43] Shelley, *Works,* X, 223, 226.

[44] Medwin, *Shelley,* p. 235; Mary Shelley's autograph journal (in the Abinger Collection), Nov. 23, 1820, the only entry referring to Medwin's illness. Both White's *Shelley* and Jones's edition of Mary's *Journal* are in error when they understand other entries as referring to Medwin's illness, and there was of course no Mrs. Medwin at this time. The entries for Nov. 5 and 6, 1820, almost certainly refer to Mrs. Mason; the entry for Jan. 4, 1821, refers to the illness of Shelley.

[45] Mary Shelley's autograph journal, Nov. 24, 1820.

[46] Medwin, *Shelley,* p. 236; Medwin's unpublished marginalia in his interleaved copy of his *Shelley,* facing II, 16 (in the Pierpont Morgan Library) states that he "carefully copied" Shelley's translation from the *Purgatorio* ("And earnest to explore within—around"), altering the incomplete ninth line as printed in his *Shelley,* p. 245, where he states that Shelley gave him a copy of this translation, first published in the *Angler.*

We hear no more of Arabic studies, but Medwin continued to be highly sensitive to Shelley's moods, and together they read Calderón and Dante.[47] By December 5 he was well enough to call, with Shelley and Mary, upon Emilia Viviani, who Medwin thought resembled the statue of the Greek Muse in the Uffizi Gallery at Florence, her features possessing "a rare faultlessness, and an almost Grecian contour."[48] This classical and mistreated beauty, who inspired Shelley's *Epipsychidion* and with reason aroused Mary's jealousy, was also religious. Claire recorded in her journal, July 23, 1821, "Emilia says that she prays always to a saint, and every time she changes her lover, she changes her saint, adopting the one of her lover."

Death, cholera, and the dust of India had little place in this atmosphere, charged Platonically and otherwise. Medwin, it seems, made the mistake of introducing such topics, on the evening of December 7, before an unsympathetic listener—Claire, suspicious of all English strangers and fearful that the secret of her liaison with Byron would reach Medwin's ears. She recorded the topics of his conversation in her diary: "1st Toast at the Indian mess. A bloody war, a sickly season and a field officer's Corpse." Medwin's name is not mentioned, but the entry, it appears, could refer only to him. She then proceeded to analyze his character and predict his future. "There is a strength in truth for everyone but you . . ." This she marked out and started again. "There is a strength in truth that forces conviction, and men are happy to have arrived at a first point from which they act securely, but the dullness of your senses has forbidden this ever to be known to you, and I fear that your constant companions will be as they have been, evil and error." If this is Medwin, it would seem that he had embellished his story to some degree, become increasingly uncertain of his critical audience and, perhaps, finally embarrassed. He may not

[47] Medwin, *Shelley*, pp. 237–238, 243–244.

[48] Unpublished journal of Claire Clairmont, the original of which is in the British Museum and a photostatic copy at the University of Texas; Medwin, *Shelley*, p. 279.

have known at this time that she was the mother of Byron's child,[49] and she took care that he should remain unaware of her true feelings toward him, with the result that he called on her later in Florence a number of times.

On December 15, Claire recorded in her journal, "Shelley is magnetised—he begs them not to ask him more questions because he shall say what he ought not." Although Claire does not name the hypnotist, Medwin stated repeatedly that he had hypnotized Shelley, at the poet's request. He had, he said, seen hypnosis practiced in India and at Paris, benefitted himself from it at Geneva, and compiled some kind of treatise on it. He writes of one session with Shelley, "Mesmer himself could not have hoped for more complete success. The imposition of my hand on his forehead instantaneously put a stop to the spasm, and threw him into a magnetic sleep . . . Mrs. Shelley and another lady were present. The experiment was repeated more than once."[50] The experiment led to a discussion of the relation between body and soul, and Shelley regarded the success of it as proof of immortality.

For the first two months of 1821, both Medwin and Mary record a continued and vigorous intellectual life, in which Medwin participated with Shelley, Mary, and sometimes Prince Mavrocordato. (Professor Francesco Pacchiani, "Il Diavolo" of Pisa, whom Claire thought indecent, Medwin also came to know well and enjoyed his brilliant conversation, but he had no respect for his character. There is no evidence that the two ever read or studied together.) During these months, Shelley translated *Prometheus* aloud to Medwin, and Medwin acknowledged a debt to a recollection of Shelley's words in his own later translations of the plays of Aeschylus. These very probably owed their existence, in important part, to Shelley's enthusiasm for the Greek poet.

[49] Medwin, *The Shelley Papers; Memoir of Percy Bysshe Shelley*, pp. 29–30.

[50] *Ibid.*, p. 64; see also Medwin, *Shelley*, II, 48–49, and Medwin, *Shelley*, pp. 269–270.

Together, Medwin recalled, they also read Schiller's *Maid of Orleans* and Cervantes's *Little Novels*.[51] There were discussions of Petrarch, Milton, Keats, Byron, Hunt, Moore, Rogers, Campbell, Peacock, and others.[52] Medwin was writing poetry, translating selected portions of the *Inferno,* and had already completed the Ugolino canto.[53] In February he sent to the *Bibliothèque universelle,* perhaps prompted by E. E. Williams's earlier appearance in that journal, his long three-part paper on the Indian cave temples at Ellora.[54] This journal, it has been said, was "certainly the most important cultural link existing between England and the Continent."[55] In the two volumes in 1821 that Medwin appeared in, there were extracts from Belzoni's *Narrative of the Operations and Recent Discoveries in Egypt and Nubia,* a book Byron owned; a review of Parry's *Journal of a Voyage for the Discovery of a North-West Passage,* translated from the November, 1820, issue of *Blackwood's;* extracts from Maturin's *Melmoth the Wanderer,* a novel to which Byron was indebted; a prose translation of Scott's *Lay of the Last Minstrel;* and a review of Godwin's book *On Population.* Medwin was in distinguished company.

Edward E. Williams and Jane, long awaited, arrived in Pisa on January 15 or 16, and Medwin introduced them at once to the Shelleys.[56] Medwin had "allured" them to Pisa, he says, to "chase Shelley's melancholy," and he is quite correct in thinking that he conferred "a mutual benefit on both" men,[57] by bringing them together. Shelley required only a little while to appreciate Williams, but Mary's first comments on Jane are characteristically critical and disparaging: "Jane is certainly very pretty but she wants animation and sense; her conver-

---

[51] Medwin, *Shelley,* p. 256.

[52] *Ibid.,* pp. 257–262.

[53] *The Letters of Mary W. Shelley,* ed. Frederick L. Jones (Norman, Oklahoma, 1944), I, 129.

[54] Williams had published an "Extract from a Sporting Journal, par le Capit. Williams" in 1820 (*Bibliothèque universelle,* XIII, 387–391).

[55] Häusermann, *Genevese Background,* p. 31.

[56] Williams, *Journal,* p. 103.

[57] Medwin, *Shelley,* p. 310.

sation is *nothing particular,* and she speaks in a slow monotonous voice: but she appears good tempered and tolerant." [58]

A week before, writing to Claire on January 15, she had delivered herself of one of the most blistering attacks on Medwin she ever made, and it may be said with certainty that she had been making his existence in the house as difficult as possible. In her letter she calls him a *seccatura,* criticizes him for interrupting, "be one reading or writing," damns his understanding of Dante, whom he is translating, says that Shelley is painfully bored with his company, and concludes that "he is Common Place personified."

She protests too much, one feels, and there is no evidence other than hers that Shelley was ever unhappy or discontented with Medwin. But Medwin was becoming increasingly uncomfortable in her presence, and on January 21, writing again to Claire, she complained not that he talked too much; he had become "silent as a fireskreen but not half so useful; except that he sometimes mends a pen." Carried away by the bite of her own satire, she decided that he "had no sympathy with our tastes or conversation—he is infinitely commonplace . . ." [59] This is in striking contrast to the statements of Shelley.

Medwin, for his part, did not think that Mary was very "handsome or even what may be denominated pretty," and she was delighted to be rid of what she called his "seca presenza," [60] when he left Pisa on February 27. "Medwin goes," she recorded laconically in her journal. Mavrocordato, whom Shelley did not care for, was more to her taste; and her Greek Platonics with him neatly balanced Shelley's "Italian Platonics" with Emilia Viviani at the time. Neither Medwin nor any other male house guest could exist gracefully in such a sensitive situation, and Mary contrasted the English Captain quite unfavorably with the Greek Prince.[61] Her evidence against Medwin must be heavily discounted.

[58] *Letters of Mary Shelley,* I, 130.
[59] *Ibid.,* I, 131.
[60] Medwin, *Shelley,* p. 121; *Letters of Mary Shelley,* I, 133.
[61] *Letters of Mary Shelley,* I, 133.

He spent the first week or more of March in Florence and lost no time in calling on Claire, who had made the journey of eight and a half hours from Pisa on December 23, 1820, accompanied by Pacchiani. ("Il Diavolo," sensing a possible prey, perhaps, found her so attractive that he called on her the next six days in succession after they had arrived in Florence.)[62] Medwin called on March 2, 1821, and she saw him again on March 6, the last day of Carnival, when she went to the Veglióne or public masked ball. "Meet Mr. Medwin there," she wrote in her diary, "& the Signor Tempestini also Marchese Riccardi & Colonel Ricci. Return at three in the morning." Medwin called again on March 8, and this time she recorded a visit from "Captain Medwin." He remembered her at the time, "living *en pension* at Florence, then twenty-six or twenty-seven years of age."[63] She was, in fact, only twenty-three. He continued,

She might have been mistaken for an Italian, for she was a *brunette* with very dark hair and eyes . . . As she possessed considerable accomplishments—spoke French and Italian, particularly the latter, with all its *nuances* and niceties—she was much courted by the Russian coterie, a numerous and fashionable one in that city. Though not strictly handsome at that time, for she had had much to struggle with, . . . she was engaging and pleasing, and possessed an *esprit de société* rare among our countrywomen.

It was a slightly worn young woman that Medwin saw, but "strikingly handsome" he thought she must have been when she was Byron's mistress.

But Medwin was touring, and he gave most of his attention to the beauties and riches of Florence, where he chose later to settle, following his marriage. Here he, too, must have "luxuriated in the divine creations of Grecian art,"[64] as he described Shelley doing, and he writes with the greatest enthusiasm of the treasures of the Uffizi Gallery and others.

[62] Unpublished journal of Claire Clairmont, Dec. 24–29, 1820.
[63] Medwin, *Shelley*, p. 169.
[64] *Ibid.*, p. 222.

But he had not yet seen Rome, and he hastened on to arrive there, where Shelley wrote to him on April 4, "happy to hear of [his] safe arrival" and sending him news of the Greek uprising against the Turks.[65] Evidently the two men were still considering a trip to Greece together, for Shelley wrote, "This is a sufficient objection to our Grecian project even if other circumstances would permit my being one of the party.—There is nothing I so earnestly desire as to visit Greece; but the fates do not seem propitious to my desire." Are these sentences slightly formal or evasively circumlocutious? Had Shelley changed his mind about wishing to see Greece with Medwin? One cannot be certain.

"Our friend here," Prince Mavrocordato, was returning to Greece, he informed Medwin; and he directed Medwin, if he would call upon Keats, "dangerously ill" at Rome, to "say every thing that is kind from me to him, & entreat to know if I can in any manner be of any service to him . . . Mrs. S. desires to be remembered kind."[66] *Kind* for *kindly*—here surely was a Freudian slip of the pen. Shelley knew very well that Mary had not been kind to Medwin and could only hope that Medwin would remember her as kind, that Medwin had not been cruelly hurt by Mary, for Medwin was as capable of suffering as Shelley himself. "It is something to have contributed to the happiness of one human being."[67] The sentiment is not Shelley's; it is Medwin's.

Medwin confessed later, "In the whirl and confusion consequent on a first sight of Rome, I did not, for some time make inquiries about Keats . . ."[68] But Keats had died on February

---

[65] Häusermann, *Genevese Background*, pp. 8–9.

[66] Years later, writing his *Life of Shelley*, after Medwin's enthusiasm for Keats had become fully developed, he was so chagrined at not meeting Keats that he invented, it seems, a "large packet of letters or MSS.," supposedly entrusted to him by Shelley, to be delivered to Keats in Rome, and Medwin generally exaggerated the degree of intimacy that existed between the two great poets. See Häuserman, *Genevese Background*, pp. 22–23.

[67] Medwin, *Shelley*, p. 195.

[68] *Ibid.*, p. 302.

23, before Medwin had parted from Shelley at Pisa. In addition to sending him a message for Keats, Shelley had also written, "I hope the recollections of antiquity [in Rome] have consoled you for the melancholy news that awaited you there"—the recent defeat of the Neapolitan army by the Austrians. (Shelley obviously thought that the news of the Greek rebellion would console him even more.) But Medwin viewed the Neapolitan fiasco realistically. Writing to "Ned" Williams from Rome on March 28, in a letter which crossed that of Shelley in the mails, he said, "The Neapolitan business is well over. I have no pity for those Poltroons. The Gendarmes firing upon the populace for upbraiding them for their cowardice was the *comble* to their Villainy."[69] On March 7 the army of General Pepe had faced the Austrians and, almost before a shot was fired, had fled. Medwin's view of the matter quite coincided with that of Byron, who wrote, "The Neapolitans have betrayed themselves and all the World . . ."[70] But Medwin, knowing Shelley, changed his tone toward the end of his letter and directed Williams to "tell Shelley that ill news travels fast enough & that I had not the heart to communicate the disasters of the Neapolitans."

He considered going, along with "all the world here," to Naples, which Austrian troops had occupied on March 23, but here, here before him, was Rome the Eternal. "There is something inspiring in the very atmosphere of Rome," he wrote later. "Is it fanciful, that being encircled with images of beauty—that in contemplating works of beauty, such as Rome and the Vatican can only boast—that by gazing on the scattered limbs of that mighty Colossus, whose shadow eclipsed the world,—we should catch a portion of the sublime—become a portion of that around us?"[71] Surely it does not reduce the enthusiasm of these sentences that the thought may be indebted to Schiller's

[69] Unpublished letter from Medwin to E. E. Williams, March 28, 1821, in the Abinger Collection.
[70] Byron's *Letters and Journals*, V, 403.
[71] Medwin, *Shelley*, p. 211.

Don Carlos, which Medwin quotes on the same page, or to *Childe Harold,* which he does not quote.

It was on this trip to Rome or some later one that Medwin's pleasure was increased by the associations that the city had with Shelley. The Baths of Caracalla, he knew, was a place beloved by Shelley, who had told him that two acts of *Prometheus Unbound* were written here.[72] "But the Praxitelean shapes of the Vatican and the Capitol, were alike sources whence he drew his inspiration in this truly classical drama," Medwin writes, and he read Shelley's prose fragment "The Coliseum," which Shelley had allowed him to copy, in the great arena itself.[73] This was worth more, he thought, than all that "Nibbi," Hobhouse, and Eustace ever wrote on the subject. Medwin knew also that Shelley had written *The Cenci* at Rome, "the greatest tragedy of modern times."[74] If he refers only to tragedy written in English during the eighteenth and nineteenth centuries, he is correct.

While at Rome, Medwin visited Tivoli, site of Hadrian's Villa, and there he wrote nine Spenserian stanzas descriptive of the place.[75] These he sent to Shelley, who at once pronounced them "elegant," no doubt recognizing their debt to *Childe Harold:*

> It is a spot where Dian might resort
> At noontide with her nymphs, "its crystal flood
> Their mirror," and its fount their bath—or sport
> The Fauns and sylvan deities, no more
> Fabled in song. But fancy still may store
> Memory of those creations, and, above,
> A column'd temple may revive the lore
> Of elder worship—worship that may prove
> Worthier a scene like this, where all that live and move,

[72] *Ibid.,* p. 212.
[73] *Ibid.,* p. 216.
[74] *Ibid.,* p. 217.
[75] Medwin, *Angler,* II, 102.

All we behold, breathes, feels, and glows with love.
This cataract is a far more fitting shrine
To wake the spirit's homage; all above,
Around this stream, must ever be divine;
It flows in classic lore, and must entwine
With the heart's best devotions; nor can Time,
With its obliterating hand consign
To cold forgetfulness one lyric rhyme,
That bids thy bard and thee live on through every clime.

Medwin, lover of beauty in all its forms, left Rome in pursuit, it seems, of the daughter of Sir E. Dolbin. On June 22 Shelley reported that Medwin was "in full chase to Venice" and that he was "going to be married" to the girl, reportedly only fifteen years old.[76] But "the lady had left Venice 24 hours before my arrival," Medwin informed Jane Williams.[77] He had met Miss Dolbin and her sister at Rome, where he had written on March 28 to Edward Williams, "I have found some delightful acquaintances in my Cousins the Miss Dolbins—two most charming and amiable girls—and pass many evenings there. The old gentleman who is now 80 is a wonderful man. Tho' a little flighty—and antiquarian—he is one of the ablest members of that venerable society."[78] Which one of the daughters Medwin chose is not clear, nor does it seem likely that she was only fifteen years old, as Shelley thought.

But he found Venice to be of the very greatest interest, lady or no, and from the city he wrote to Jane Williams a long letter about it.[79] He began with a quotation:

[76] Shelley, *Works*, X, 279. Shelley's "Dalbyn" and Medwin's "Dolbin" are unquestionably the same; the name is spelled "Dolbon" in the will of Medwin's father.

[77] Unpublished letter from Medwin to Jane Williams, no date, written in Venice, in the Abinger Collection.

[78] Unpublished letter from Medwin to E. E. Williams, March 28, 1821, in the Abinger Collection.

[79] Unpublished letter from Medwin to Jane Williams (the same as that described in footnote 77). Medwin had been reading Joseph Forsyth, *On Antiquities, Arts, Letters in Italy* (1813).

"With every thing to make life agreeable," says Forsyth, "Venice is the last town in Italy I would choose for a residence." Perhaps I was more inclined to agree with this reflection from the influence of the . . . Sirocco that today weighed heavily on my frame and spirits . . . The Sirocco of Naples or Rome is not to be compared with that of this place—where so much more mephitic air combines with it.

The first view of Venice gave me the idea of a city half swallowed up by a [? lengthy] inundation; the nearer we approached I could distinguish its Domes and palaces: it seemed a work of enchantment. We landed at the Piazetta [*sic*]. The Doge's Palace, St. Mark's Church, the Museum Library, the Mint, and the square containing the Casinos form of St. Mark's Place the finest thing in the world. Thronged as its harbour was with ships and this Piazza with crowds of all nations in [?] of the proud republic—of the former scarcely a Vessel was seen and a few military individuals only loitered about the Caffés, with which the town abounds.

Venice is a body without a soul. The French dominion was light compared to that of the Germans, who are infinitely more detested. It is the cruel policy of Austria to ruin the commerce of Venice for the aggrandisement of Trieste, and the excess of the imports and duties effectually shut this Port. The French spent the money they extorted & left everywhere memorials of themselves here; for instance, they made a delightful public garden, supplied the greater part of the convents, gave the women more liberty, promoted amusements of all kinds. These dull and lethargic Germans are the death of all festivity, are more gripping and avaricious than the former tyrants, and spend nothing. Can you conceive their sending their *old shoes* to be mended at home?

You can form no conception of the inconvenience to which travelers are put here. From the Brenta to Venice we had no less than 4 Police Ships & Officers to have our passports examined. All the heads of departments are Tedeschis, and brutality and a stupid and undeviating compliance with orders are their characteristics.

Austria is now in quiet possession of all Italy—having both extremes. What a disgrace to England to permit it! What had we not in our power at the peace? But we have been hated and are now despised. Truly, however, we are not so impotent as to permit the quiet occupation of Sicily. We have nothing, however, to hope under Lord C[astlereag]h. What was the literal construction of the British declaration? That the King was heartily sorry that the Constitution of Gr. Britain did not permit him to interfere with measures that had his hearty concurrence. This part of the letter is forbid.

Miserable as she is, Venice is daily becoming more so. She is like a spend-thrift living on his Capital.

You may form some notion of her present poverty when gold is at a discount of 3 per Cent, so scarce is other specie.

The sight of her Trophies, of this Winged Lion and the Horses recalled forcibly to my mind the remembrance of Dandolo's Victories. The taking of Constantinople and the glorious siege of Candia. That period when her victorious gallies had almost the command of the Seas, when she resembled England before the *battle of Waterloo,* and I could not help anticipating a similar fate for ourselves.

The Dogeless City no longer weds the Adriatic.

The Bucentaur has sunk & [is] rotting in the Arsenal. Her Palaces, the monuments of Palladio's genius, are fast crumbling to decay— 35 within a few years have been sold by their indifferent nobles as a poor resource and pulled down for their costly materials. Many of their best pictures are still in the Louvre, and their blanks on the walls melancholy records. Still there is enough left to make her proud in her Tintorettos, Paul Veroneses, Palmas, and Titians. The assumption of the Virgin by the latter may justly challenge comparison with the Transfiguration of Raphael, who stands alone. It was in an old church and so black with smoke and age as to be almost indistinguishable in the time of the French and fortunately missed their observation.

Its colors are now as brilliant as they were the first day. This is the case with almost all the pictures here.

The Venetian school does not however please me half as well as that of Bologna. There I saw some five Domenichinos and Guidos, my favorite painters after Raphael. The pageant loving and portrait painting school of Venice pleases me little—indeed I have seen few things that have left much impression on my memory. The architecture of Venice is neither Gothic nor Saracenic nor Mussulman, but a strange mixture and jumble of all—but this singularity . . . contrasts well with the Lightness and regularity of the Grecian orders . . .

Nothing can be more Elegant than the form of their boats, nothing more delightful than to be at full length within, to read or write & to be shot rapidly along almost without motion thro' rows of palaces and Casinos, which are almost innumerable & intersect the city in all directions. So intricate is the navigation by sea & land that it would take several months—nay, years—for a foreigner to find his way. No four footed animal but a Dog is seen here . . .

You will expect to hear something of my private affairs. The lady had left Venice 24 hours before my arrival. Every day makes me *more of an Optimist*. The only thing I cannot reconcile with my system is not hearing from you. My movements have been & are—I came here Post & mean to post it to Geneva on Tuesday. There I shall stay till the middle of September & then return to pass the winter at Florence. Mrs. Shelley's letter relieved me from much anxiety on your accounts.

Tell her to write to me at Geneva so that I may get a line on my arrival—let me know how you are getting on. I shall expect as long a letter as this and a more detailed account of yourselves. Adieu, my dear Jane,

Affectionately yours,
T. Medwin

P. S. I wish to have the Leghorn Post Office searched for Letters, having directed some to be addressed there under the idea of a sea trip. Let we know how the little one is getting on and my little namesake. In three months I shall see you all again, when I shall hope to see Ned's play finished. We mean to *mount* again. This is a shabby letter but forced to be written after seeing the finest Opera in the world . . . It is now 2. Again Adieu.

This letter, written after seeing an opera and finished at 2 A.M., tells much of Thomas Medwin—his sensitivity to beauty, his serious amateur's interest in painting, his hatred of tyranny, the unsettled, rootless character of his life, his normal human need to know that someone (even Mary Shelley) was paying a little attention to him. But he was seeing Italy, and he was reading its history as he looked. With the tone and substance of the political views expressed, Byron would have agreed. England had won the war and lost the peace.

What he remembered about Venice, years later, was "the contrast of its former greatness with its present state of degradation and decay, its once proud independence, . . . and now abject slavery to the Goth . . ." *Julian and Maddalo,* with its portraits of Byron and Shelley, he regarded as

> . . . a faithful picture of Venice. We seem to sail with the two friends in their gondola—to view with them that gorgeous sunset, from the Lido, when—
>
> > They turned, and saw the city, and could mark,
> > How from its many isles in the broad gleam,
> > Its temples and its palaces did seem
> > Like fabrics of enchantment piled to heaven.[80]

When Shelley wrote to Medwin again, on August 22, 1821, Medwin was in Geneva, and there is no further mention of the "most charming and amiable" Miss Dolbin, whose absence from Venice, if we may judge by his letter, hardly seems to have marred the surface of his visit. That Medwin was emotionally now poised for marriage, however, is clearly suggested by later events and by the contents of *Sketches in Hindoostan* (1821), which may here be considered for its romantic elements. Following the first poem, "The Lion Hunt," comes "The Pindarees," with a romantic love story central to its plot and a beautiful heroine who dies for love, mistakenly thinking her lover dead. Each of the shorter poems and translations, with the exception of the Ugolino stanzas from Dante, also celebrates love in some form, personal or philosophic. The stanzas beginning, "Oh, I am blind with gazing . . . ," Shelley thought the best Medwin had ever written.[81] Parts of the poem are derivative, but they derive chiefly from one of the best poems of the day, Byron's *Childe Harold,* III, specifically from the Lake Leman stanzas and from their Shelleyean-inspired pantheistic view of a universe shot through with love, a universe with which the indi-

[80] Medwin, *Shelley,* pp. 200–201. The first two words of the quotation are probably Medwin's own and not a true variant. The accepted text (1. 89) reads, "I leaned, and saw the city, and could mark."

[81] Shelley, *Works,* X, 316.

vidual can merge or mingle in Rousseauistic revery. All of this reveals, of course, the common intellectual milieu of the time, shared by Shelley, Byron, and Medwin and shows that his poetic orientation was Romantically forward looking. (The poem reveals in addition Medwin's mastery of the Spenserian stanza, although occasionally a rhyme is forced, chiming imperfectly, as *lake, peak; still, heal; feel, still; hour, o'er.* It is difficult to believe that these examples represent a deliberate experiment in slant rhyme or consonance.) Because of Shelley's praise of the poem, I quote the opening stanzas, to suggest the flavor of the whole.

Oh, I am blind with gazing! I have seen
A glimpse of opening heaven, streak blend with streak
Of living light, carnation, crimson, green:
Once I have seen a sunset, vain and weak
My verse to tell its wonders, when the lake
Blazed like a sapphire, melting from the view,
As sunk his orb beneath the furthest peak
Of pine-clad Jura, into one deep blue,
Than all but woman's eye more exquisite of hue.

Wooed by the Autumn's breath whose kisses sere
The leaves that to his honied flatteries
Listen, as some fond maiden lends an ear
To whispered accents and impassioned sighs
Of one she loves, trusting his treacheries,
Leman! what gorgeous vesture clothes thy woods
And sloping vines with many tissued dyes,
The whilst an amethystine vapor broods
Over the calm expanse of thy marmoreal floods.

It was a sea of glory, such as man
Must dip his brush in heaven to paint; no dream,
Visioned amid the enchantments that the brain
Of wizard fancy, fevered by the stream
Of Inspiration, conjures, could redeem
Its splendours, or recall from out the bier
That shrouds them, their intolerable beam,
Reflected in the lake, whose mirror clear
Imaged a giant camp, whose snowy tops appear.

Deepens the shade to purple; still the eye
Of golden day smiles on those heights of snow,
Those everlasting glaciers, that defy
His feeble radiance, and, whilst all below
Is wrapt in gloom, are burnished with a glow
Fresher than childhood's cheek, and rosier dyes;
And now dissolves that passing beauteous show,
And their vast outline fades at length, and dies
In mists of night away, mingling with earth, lake, skies.

The southern breeze is on her cradling breast
As if enamoured of its beauty, sleeping,
Hushed like an infant in its innocent rest,
Save where confused and floating murmurs creeping
Along the shore, in balmy opiate steeping
The inebriate sense, o'er all my pulses steal
A magic influence, o'er my bosom sweeping,
Of momentary power almost to still
Its throbs, and staunch those wounds that nought can ever heal.

Nor I alone! all nature seems to feel
The soothing silentness of this sweet hour;
Breathless as if for joy, the lake so still,
That heard the buzz of insects, fluttering o'er
Its glassy surface. Lower now and lower,
List to a watch-dog's bark! succeeds anon
A mule's dull tinkling, whilst from off the shore
Is borne at intervals the sullen moan,
As if of grief at parting, of the filial Rhone.

Moveless the little boat, and seated high
A sylph-like form; the heaven of her clear brow
Images peace, and in her eloquent eye,
Of deeper, softer azure than the glow
Of skies, and brighter than the star that now
In single loveliness, the deity
Of twilight and of silence, smiles below
On this his world of beauty. I read that he
Is most the object of her soul's idolatry.

A girl alone in a boat on the Lake of Geneva, in love with
the night. We can see what is coming. The stanzas in ottava

rima from the Spanish of Calderón, "I saw her once in Paris
. . . ," are a celebration of love gained and thus happiness.[82]
The other translation from Calderón, "The Azure and the Green,
A Dialogue," in an uncommon ten-line stanza, ends on the
following note.

> To him who lives while hope inspires,
> His mistress owes but little favour,
> But one who loves with jealous fires
> Inscribes his love on bronze for ever,
> By the same token, clearly proving
> The jealous know the most of loving:
> A stronger proof of this we see
> In favours that their torments boast,
> And this same hell of jealousy,
> In hoping least oft gains the most.

"Spring," a pantheistic effusion which follows, in terza rima,
informs us,

> All, all is love! so deep, so spirit-steeping,
> What wonder if the bird, stream, wind, fount, flower,
> Felt each a pulse, like that voluptuous sweeping
> O'er my full bosom?

And the poem ends with the assurance, "Effusing love, deep
love—worship there else is none."

The last poem, from the Portuguese of Camoëns, relates the
sad tale of "sweet Inez" (Ines de Castro), who dared to love
a prince and lost her head, cut off by the cruel King Alfonso IV
of Portugal. Medwin makes the most of the pathos of the situation, and the poem shows no sign that he was aware of the
lady's true character.

Medwin, whose only settled home since leaving that of his
father had been the Army, was thirty-three years old. He had
wandered over a good part of the world. It was time for him
to marry and settle down. He had also formed expensive habits,

---

[82] Medwin states that Shelley corrected five lines of this poem, and
these he prints in italics in *Shelley*, p. 244.

and he needed a wife who could help support them. From now on we hear increasingly of his romantic pursuits, which would end in three years with marriage to a rich countess.

Despite some good lines and short passages in *Sketches in Hindoostan,* it is a relief to turn to Shelley's delightful and important letter to Medwin, August 22, 1821.[83]

It opens playfully to imply the most attractive relations between the two men—the democratic free state of masculine humor. "How do you know that there are not seven distinct letters, patiently waiting with the Williams's, seven lost letters, in the seven distinct post offices of Italy, whose contents you have never unveiled?—To write to you hitherto would have been such an enterprise as if the oyster might undertake a correspondence with the eagle, with orders that the billets should be left until called for on every promontory, thunder cloud, or mountain, where the imperial bird might chance to pass."

After stating that he had "read with pleasure" Medwin's "elegant stanzas on Tivoli," which Medwin had sent to him in manuscript, and after inquiring about "the fate of the stanzas on the lake of Geneva, which seemed to me the best you ever wrote," Shelley admitted Medwin into the brotherhood of serious poets, or those who might be with the proper discipline. "Have you any idea, according to my counsel, of disciplining your powers to any more serious undertaking? It might at once contribute to your happiness and your success; but consider that Poetry, although its source is native and involuntary, requires in its development severe attention." Shelley, it is clear, thought that Medwin had poetic talents of some promise.

Any suspicion that Medwin may have had that his presence in Shelley's house had been unwelcome, during the latter part of his long visit, or that he would not be welcomed again, Shelley is at some pains to dispel.

[83] Shelley, *Works,* X, 316–317, corrected from the autograph letter in Keats Memorial House.

Whilst you were with me, that is during the latter period, and after you went away, I was harassed by some severe disquietudes, the causes of which are now I hope almost at an end. What were the speculations which you say disturbed you? My mind is at peace respecting nothing so much as the constitution and mysteries of the great system of things . . . We are undecided for Florence or Pisa this winter, but in either of these places I confidently expect that we shall see you. Mary unites with me in her best regards, and I remain, my dear Medwin, Faithfully and affectionately yours . . .

Medwin, we learn from the letter, had "entirely recovered" his health, which Shelley had despaired of during the winter before, and had been "pleased" with *Adonais,* which he had discussed with Sir John St. Aubyn.

Shelley sent Medwin the news that Williams's play had been completed and stated that his own regard for Edward and Jane "is every day increased; I hardly know which I like best, but I know that Jane is your favourite."

Then came a casual paragraph that must have burned like gold before the eyes of Medwin. Shelley wrote, "I am just returned from a visit to Lord Byron at Ravenna . . . I believe he is about to migrate to this part of the world." Byron—whose poems Medwin had read, with all the world—that magic name. Medwin left Geneva on October 23, to arrive in Pisa again on November 14.[84]

[84] Williams, *Journal*, p. 112.

4

Lord Byron and
the Death of Shelley

Shelley introduced Medwin to Byron on November 20, 1821,[1] Whom did Byron see before him? Medwin had hunted the lion and tiger in India, had fought in one (or two) wars, narrowly escaped death in the Ganges, was a cavalry officer trained in horsemanship and the use of the pistol, rifle, and sabre, a weapon Byron favored; he had travelled in parts of the world as little known to most Englishmen as those Byron had visited; he had two volumes of verse to his credit and a three-part article; read with various degrees of skill Greek, Latin, Spanish, Italian, Portuguese, French, and German; had attended Oxford, had been presented to the Prince Regent, and had known some of Byron's friends of old as well as others shortly to be met—the Duke of Norfolk, Lord Blessington, Lord Powerscourt, Martin Hawke (son of the second Baron Hawke), Captain John Hay, Captain Daniel Roberts, Sir John St. Aubyn, Lady Mount Cashell ("Mrs. Mason"), Mrs. Beauclerc, daughter of the Duchess of Leinster, and others. Born in the same year that Byron was, Medwin was Shelley's cousin, and Shelley had introduced him. Byron took him seriously, as a man of some connections and accomplishments, presented to him an autographed copy of the first issue of the first edition of *Marino Faliero*, recommended him to Hobhouse as "my friend Capt. T. Medwin," a military man who considered offering his services to the Greeks, and took the trouble to write a letter congratulating him (prematurely) on his marriage.

[1] Medwin, *Conversations,* p. 2.

They talked of everything from Shelley's *atheos* to a dose of Wordsworth physic (Wordsworthian pantheism), everything from a rumored auto-da-fé to Byron's *Werner*. Surveying the topics of their conversation, one has the impression that Medwin was excluded from only one important and sensitive area, understandably—that of the X of Byron's letters to Lady Melbourne, and we hear nothing of Y and Z. But from Ada and Annabella, Beau Brummell, Byron, and Barry Cornwall, Coleridge, Cain, Claire Clairmont, and Caroline Lamb, they moved on through the conversational alphabet, Byron telling him of Caroline Lamb, for example, that "she offered young Grattan her favours if he would call me out."[2] They also discussed missionary societies, Napoleon's opinion of women, Swedenborg's disciples, cook books, and the English cathedral service. But chiefly they talked about Byron and the literature and literary figures of the day.

Within less than a month after his arrival, Medwin's place was secure, and an enviable one it was. As Edward Williams wrote to Trelawny,

I will swear that yesterday was Christmas Day, for I celebrated it at a splendid feast given by Lord Byron to what I call his Pistol Club—*i. e.*, Shelley, Medwin, a Mr. Taaffe, and myself, and was scarcely awake from the vision of it when your letter was put in my hands . . . Lord Byron is the very spirit of this place—that is, to those few to whom, like Mokannah, he has lifted his veil . . . He sees none of the numerous English who are here, excepting those I have named.[3]

Byron's male acquaintances at the time, then, were limited to four, and one of them was taking notes on his most intimate conversation.

Medwin, of course, was seeing others as well, and he dined with friends almost every evening. Between the letters and

[2] Medwin's letter to Edward Bulwer, quoted by Michael Sadleir, *Bulwer: A Panorama* (Boston, 1931), p. 54.
[3] Williams, *Journal*, pp. 159–160.

journals of Shelley, Mary, and Williams, there are few days
without some reference to him. His life was very full.

Within his first week in Pisa, he had secured his lodgings,
read to Williams some of his poetry, given Williams a new
poem by St. Aubyn, *Magya,* gone calling with the secretary of
the Greek Prince Argiropoli, practiced pistol shooting with
Byron, and listened to Shelley read to him his recently written
Defence of Poetry.[4] Mary invited him frequently to dinner, and
in the last week of November he helped Williams revise his
new play and with Shelley and Williams read "different works."

By December 11, Shelley was able to write to Claire (about
whom Byron was to tell Medwin "everything infamous"),[5]
"Medwin rides almost constantly with Lord B. and the party
sometimes consists of Gamba, Taafe, Medwin and the Exotic
[Shelley] who . . . thrives ill in so large a society." Shelley confessed that he himself was drooping in "a frost both moral and
physical—a solitude of the heart . . . I cannot endure the company of many persons, and the society of one is either great
pleasure or great pain . . . I am employed in nothing . . . I have
no confidence . . ."[6] Shelley in 1820 had found "great pleasure"
in Medwin's company, but he did not flourish in this strictly
masculine atmosphere of 1821, in which Medwin breathed
easily enough. It is impossible to imagine Shelley participating
in the kind of off-color male conversation suggested by Medwin's letters to Byron. But Medwin could live in both worlds.

Shelley could not escape Byron's presence; their lives were
intertwined, had been since 1816; and it was on the day following Shelley's melancholy letter that Medwin heard at the
bookseller Moloni's that a man had "been condemned to be
burnt alive for sacrilege."[7] A priest told Medwin that the man
had strewn the consecrated wafers about the church and that
he should be burned at the stake. Medwin "left him with

[4] *Ibid.,* pp. 112–113.
[5] Claire Clairmont to Mary Shelley, April 9, 1822, in the Abinger
Collection.
[6] Shelley, *Works,* X, 338.
[7] Medwin, *Shelley,* p. 364.

abhorrence" and hastened to Byron. That night Medwin and Shelley, who had suggested riding armed to Lucca and rescuing the prisoner by force, sat up with Byron at the Lanfranchi palace until two o'clock, talking of the threatened auto-da-fé.[8] A day or so later they learned that the story of the burning was false, and their righteous indignation, well exercised, subsided.

On December 16 Medwin dined with Mrs. Beauclerc,[9] whom he must have known since his Horsham days and whose house in Pisa was a frequent refuge for him. She was, he informs us, "a neighbour of Shelley's family in Sussex . . . and half-sister to Lord Edward Fitzgerald," the Irish patriot. ". . . No one, from her intercourse with the great world, and the leading personages of her time, had a more copious fund of anecdote. She was indeed a person of first-rate talents and acquirements, possessed an *esprit de société* quite unique, and her house, which she opened every evening, was a never-failing resource."[10]

Williams informed Trelawny that she had a "litter of seven daughters: she is the gayest lady, and the only one who gives dances, for the young squaws are arriving at the age when, as Lord Byron says, they must waltz for their livelihood."[11] Medwin introduced her to Byron[12] and probably enjoyed the company of the daughters along with that of the accomplished mother. She and Medwin must have got along very well indeed: Claire paired them as "the two great conductors of gossip through the town."[13] It was this talent for gossip and anecdote, of course, which helped to produce *The Conversations of Byron.*

Medwin was a regular guest at Byron's weekly stag dinners, where the great poet, surrounded by his circle, was at his most charming. The other guests usually left about midnight, but Medwin would often remain, "talking and drinking with his

[8] Williams, *Journal*, p. 117.
[9] *Mary Shelley's Journal*, p. 163.
[10] Medwin, *Shelley*, pp. 367–368.
[11] Williams, *Journal*, p. 160.
[12] Medwin, *Shelley*, p. 368.
[13] Claire Clairmont to Mary Shelley, April 9, 1822, *Shelley and Mary*, pp. 777–778.

noble host till far into the morning . . ."[14] The drinking undoubtedly explains much about *The Conversations,* as Mary
Shelley suggested.[15] It was at Byron's dinner party on Christmas
Day, 1821, that Medwin heard Byron offer Shelley a bet of
£1,000 that Lady Noel would outlive Sir Timothy Shelley,
"which wager Shelley at once accepted."[16] As Williams recorded
the terms of the wager in his journal, however, "Lord B. and S.
proposed to give a thousand pounds to the other who first came
to their estate." Medwin was later indignant when Byron did
not pay, but he did not know, presumably, that the estate of
Lady Noel was not settled until after Shelley's death and that
Byron generously waived a bequest of £2,000 left to him in
Shelley's will.

Trelawny, the last of the Pisan circle drawn to Shelley by
Medwin, arrived on January 14, and two days later he was
invited to one of Byron's dinner parties, introduced by Medwin's friend Williams.[17] Trelawny was never properly grateful
to Medwin for introducing him to Shelley, and in Medwin's
Life of Shelley Trelawny is mentioned by name in connection
with one event only—the cremation of Shelley's body. It is as
if Medwin did not recognize that Trelawny had known the poet
alive. That these two men, in whose minds Shelley lived on
long after his death, each writing two books about the poet,
worshipping at his shrine—that these two should not have been
drawn strongly to each other may seem strange, but it is not
unexplainable. Trelawny may well have felt some of the jealous,
competitive spirit toward Medwin that he felt finally toward
Byron. Both men had travelled widely—Trelawny had also
been to India—both had had adventures, and both could tell
time "by Shrewsbury clock." But Byron applied this phrase to
Trelawny, not to Medwin, and said of the former that he "could

[14] *His Very Self and Voice: Collected Conversations of Lord Byron,*
ed. E. J. Lovell, Jr. (New York, 1954), p. 261.
[15] *Letters of Mary Shelley,* I, 308.
[16] Medwin, *Shelley,* p. 375.
[17] Williams, *Journal,* p. 125.

not, even to save his life, tell the truth."[18] No one, however, had ever questioned Medwin's veracity, before the publication of the *Conversations,* which named important names, and then the charges came thick.

It has been recently discovered that Trelawny's *Adventures of a Younger Son* (1831) contains "no more than one-tenth" truth—the rest is fiction.[19] This is the book that Trelawny declared to be "not a novel," but "my life, . . . my true story."[20] He was writing to Mary Shelley, who believed him. Medwin has never been discovered in a lie equal to this one, and the reader of his *Angler,* which mixes fact and fiction also, is warned clearly in the preface by the thinly disguised "editor": "I disclaim all responsibilities as to . . . the genuineness of the facts . . ." In addition, there are warnings scattered throughout the book that many of the conversations described are fictitious.

But these books came years after the death of Byron and Shelley. How did Trelawny present himself to the Pisan circle in 1822? He told "strange stories of himself, horrific ones . . . I believe them now I see the man," wrote Mary Shelley in her diary, shortly after meeting him.[21] His friends at the time referred to him as "the pirate," and his *Adventures* relate piratical activities, but they are pure fiction.

Byron saw through him, and Medwin was better equipped with knowledge of the East than Byron. He too may have questioned some of Trelawny's stories in 1822. But the failure of a warm friendship to develop between them may be explained on other, less speculative grounds. Trelawny "hated what is called society" and convention;[22] Medwin married a countess. In addition, Medwin was already a published poet

[18] Julius Millingen, *Memoirs of the Affairs of Greece, with Various Anecdotes of Lord Byron* (London, 1831), p. 153.

[19] Anne Hill, "Trelawny's Family Background and Naval Career," *Keats-Shelley Journal,* V (1956), 26.

[20] *The Letters of Edward John Trelawny,* ed. H. Buxton Forman (London, 1910), p. 141.

[21] *Mary Shelley's Journal,* p. 165.

[22] Hill, "Trelawny's Family Background," p. 28.

and a cultured man, who had attended Oxford; Trelawny at
this time "was still a semi-literate, ignorant, and almost barbarous sailor . . . ,"[23] a midshipman who had never held a commission. Medwin was an officer, who also knew as much about
horses and pistols as Trelawny did.

But none of this is to imply that any open animosity necessarily existed between them at the time. Trelawny's only reference in 1822 to Medwin is in a letter to Claire. There he
casually describes Medwin as a companion of Sir John St.
Aubyn in Paris and expresses the wish that Jane Williams had
found one or both of them when she paused briefly in the city.[24]
If Trelawny had at this time thought Medwin to be the
"scoundrel" that he was later to call him, behind his back, he
would surely not have wanted the widow of his dear friend
Williams to find Medwin in Paris. The tone of this earlier
reference is quite unlike that of Trelawny's later allusions to
Medwin. Years after the publication of the *Conversations,* he
wrote to Murray that Medwin "is a mesureless [*sic*] & unprin-
cipled liar—which you do know."[25] Among other matters this
refers presumably to Medwin's unauthorized and misleading
use of one of Trelawny's "ten separate narratives, all different
in some details, of the drowning and cremation of Shelley and
Williams."[26] This account, Trelawny indignantly noted on page
306 of a copy of the *Conversations* which he was reading, is
"an extract from my letter—written to Mrs. Shelley . . ."[27]
Whether he was pleased or displeased at not being named at
all in Medwin's book, we do not know.

It was perhaps in 1829 that Trelawny in some way secured
from Medwin the five letters from Shelley to Medwin that were

[23] *Ibid.*

[24] *Letters of Trelawny,* p. 26.

[25] Trelawny to John Murray, Jan. 15, 1833, a letter in the possession
of Sir John Murray.

[26] Leslie A. Marchand, *Byron: A Biography* (New York, 1957), note
to p. 1021, l. 32.

[27] This annotated copy of Medwin's *Conversations,* with marginal notes
by Trelawny and Sir Charles Napier, who knew Byron in Cephalonia, is
now in the Houghton Library.

finally published in Trelawny's *Records of Shelley, Byron, and
the Author* (1878), after Medwin was long dead. In 1861
Medwin wrote in his unpublished preface for a new edition of
his *Life of Shelley,* "I could have wished to have included in
it many Letters, and most interesting ones, from Shelley to me
after my return from India. They were lent to Mr. Trelawny,
who, tho' often applied to, by a species of Literary larceny
retains them." [28] Trelawny may have thought that these letters
were a fair exchange for Medwin's use of the account of the
cremation. If so, Trelawny did not lose on the transaction. Perhaps he felt that a man he described in 1829 as "a coward, a
liar, and a scoundrel" [29] did not deserve to own five letters from
Shelley—when he had only three.

Liar that Trelawny was, however, he always tried in his
accounts to remain true, it would seem, to the spirit of persons
and events, as he had seen or understood them at the time;
and the three descriptions of Medwin at Pisa which appear in
his *Records* do not reveal open hostility. They do not appear
in his earlier *Recollections.* It was Trelawny, we are told, who
informed Byron that Medwin was "taking notes of your talk."
Byron replied, supposedly, "So many lies are told about me
that Medwin won't be believed." Trelawny answered, "Medwin
has no design to lie about you; he is credulous and will note
your idle words." Byron then stated, "If he publishes lies about
me, you can say they are lies." [30] But Trelawny never said so
publicly, never reviewed Medwin's book; he merely talked or
wrote behind Medwin's back. When Trelawny repeated this
conversation to Mary Shelley, she commented, "That won't
restrain, it will stimulate Byron; he will blab the more" for
knowing that Medwin was taking notes on his conversation
with an eye to publishing. Did Byron really know? Had he

---

[28] When H. Buxton Forman edited Medwin's revised *Shelley* in 1913,
he was unaware of this preface, now in the Morgan Library.

[29] Unpublished letter from Trelawny to Mary Shelley, Oct. 20, 1829,
in the Abinger Collection.

[30] E. J. Trelawny, *Records of Shelley, Byron and the Author* (London,
1878), I, 34–35.

chosen Medwin as the biographer of his Pisan sojourn? Why would he direct Mary Shelley to send to Medwin a long account of the affair with the Italian dragoon in March, along with copies of the depositions made by the principals and a witness?

But "blab" he did, of course, as Mary had predicted, confiding to Medwin details of his life as intimate as most he ever revealed to Hobhouse, Moore, or Lady Byron.

This takes us to the heart of Byron's relations with Medwin. We have seen that by December 11 Medwin was riding "almost constantly" with Byron and that he used to remain at the Palazzo Lanfranchi "till far into the morning," after Byron's other guests had left. The concise style of Williams's journal did not admit of his listing the names of everyone present at every shooting or riding party that he attended, but he made it clear that Medwin was a regular member of Byron's "Pistol Club," and his journal refers to parties, dinners, or other gatherings on thirty-two distinct occasions when it is certain or very probable that Medwin and Byron were together, and Williams was not present, of course, upon all the occasions when Medwin and Byron met.

There is no doubt, in short, that Medwin had the most frequent opportunities for conversing with Byron. Nor is there any doubt that he took notes at the time on Byron's conversation. Did Byron "hum" Medwin, as has been charged more than once? If we understand the term to refer to deliberate efforts to mislead Medwin for the purpose of discrediting his testimony, it is impossible to believe the charge. The evidence is too slight, and Byron's liking and respect for Medwin is too clear. Nor is there any supporting evidence that dates from the time when Medwin was seeing Byron. On September 28, 1832, when Lady Blessington's *Conversations of Byron* was appearing in installments in the *New Monthly Magazine*, she told Henry Crabb Robinson that "Lord Byron was aware that Medwin meant to print what he said and purposely *hummed* him." [31]

---

[31] *Henry Crabb Robinson on Books and Their Writers*, ed. E. J. Morley (London, 1938), I, 413.

It will be noted that Lady Blessington is not reported as saying that Byron told her this. The charge is not said to be based on first-hand knowledge. And earlier she had spoken to Robinson of Byron's "habitual insincerity." Robinson commented, "I shall be very curious now to read what *she* has printed" (italics mine). Byron on occasion was most certainly "insincere" when talking with Lady Blessington, and it is much more likely that he "hummed" her than that he "hummed" Medwin, who was not a pretty bluestocking.

"Bamming" was something quite different. As defined by J. C. Jeaffreson,

"to bam" was to hoax with a humorous fiction . . . The Prince Regent, a consummate master of the elegant art, made "bamming" a favourite pastime with the gentlemen of his entourage. When George the Fourth entertained a dinner-table by describing gravely how he commanded-in-chief at Waterloo, he was not mad or tipsy; he was telling a "bam" for the fun of seeing how it would be received by one of his guests, the Duke of Wellington. "Bamming" was "lying with a difference." It was necessary for a "bam" to be humorous; it might not be uttered for the teller's pecuniary benefit or for his material advantage in any way . . .[32]

Byron was "bamming" when he told William Harness "that his father was insane and killed himself. I shall never forget the manner in which he first told me this," Harness wrote. "While washing his hands, and singing a gay Neapolitan air, he stopped, looked round at me, and said, 'There always was a madness in the family.' Then after continuing his washing and his song, as if speaking of a matter of the slightest indifference, 'My father cut his throat.'"[33] There is nothing like this in Medwin's *Conversations*. Byron was "bamming" Hobhouse on September 20, 1822, when, "Amongst other *scherzi* he said that Cain was right to kill Abel, that he might not have the bore of passing 200 years with him."[34] Medwin heard Byron deliver

[32] J. C. Jeaffreson, *The Real Lord Byron* (London, 1883), I, 287.
[33] *His Very Self and Voice*, p. 45.
[34] *Ibid.*, p. 316.

a variant of this same remark, but there is no hint of "bamming." "When I was a boy," he told Medwin, "I studied German, which I have now entirely forgotten. It was very little I ever knew of it. [Solomon Gessner's] *Abel* was one of the first books my German master read to me: and whilst he was crying his eyes out over its pages, I thought that any other than Cain had hardly committed a crime in ridding the world of so dull a fellow as Gessner made brother Abel." [35]

As the *Conversations* demonstrate, Byron talked at length of literary matters with Medwin, whose level of cultural achievement was second only to his own and Shelley's, among the men in the small group; but in addition he also assumed the character of a man of the world, talking freely to another man of the world. Medwin was thus a bridge for Byron between the unworldly literary genius of Shelley and the semiliteracy of Trelawny, whose later accounts of Byron's conversation agree perfectly with those in Medwin's book depicting Byron's worldly side. Trelawny wrote, years later, of Byron,

> His conversation was anything but literary except when Shelley was near him [we may add Medwin at the same time that we subtract the malice from what follows]. The character he most frequently appeared in [before Trelawny] was of the free and easy sort, such as had been in vogue when he was in London, and George IV was Regent; and his talk was seasoned with anecdotes of the great actors on and off the stage, boxers, gamblers, duelists, drunkards, &c., &c., appropriately garnished with the slang and scandal of the day. Such things had all been in fashion, and were at that time considered accomplishments by gentlemen; and of this tribe of Mohawks the Prince Regent was the chief, and allowed to be the most perfect specimen. Byron, not knowing the tribe was extinct, still prided himself on having belonged to it; at nothing was he more indignant than at being treated as a man of letters, instead of as a Lord and a man of fashion . . . [36]

Of course Byron refused to discuss literature seriously with Trelawny, whether his own work or anyone else's. This was

[35] Medwin, *Conversations*, p. 150.
[36] Trelawny, *Records*, I, 39.

Byron's way of protecting himself from the nearly barbarous "pirate," who had come expecting to see Childe Harold or the Corsair and had met Byron instead. And so Trelawny was "disenchanted," as he wrote, but Medwin had "never met with a man who shines so much in conversation." [37]

Nevertheless, Byron proved himself capable on at least one occasion, it would seem, of "mystifying" Medwin, as he called it—that is, of putting on an outrageously cynical face for the purpose of shocking him. For Medwin, beneath his worldliness, could be very sentimental. And sometimes, uncertain of himself, he could be betrayed into asserting his own attractions. The Countess Teresa Guiccioli told a story years afterward, in which the principals could only be Medwin and Mrs. Beauclerc, a daughter of the Duchess of Leinster and half-sister to Lord Edward Fitzgerald. Teresa, whose country was the most prolific of counts of all European nations, seemingly thought that Mrs. Beauclerc deserved the title of "Lady." All the other identifying details fit. Byron's state of mind must have been similar to that described by Trelawny: "Byron, in his splenetic moods, if any one uttered moral or sentimental commonplace twaddle, sneered and scoffed, and denounced it as cant . . . Under the same provocation, I and others have done the same." [38] The story that Teresa told was this:

When Lord Byron was at Pisa a friend of Shelley's, whom he sometimes saw, had formed a close intimacy with Lady B[eauclerc], a woman of middle age but of high birth. The tie between them was evidently the result of vanity on Mr. M[edwin]'s side, and, as she was the mother of a large family, it was doubly imperative on her to be respectable. But that did not prevent Mr. M[edwin] from boasting of his success, and even (that he might be believed) from going into disgusting details in his eagerness for praise.

One day that Mr. M[edwin] was in the same *salon* (at Mrs. Sh[elley]'s house) with Lord Byron and the Countess G[uiccioli], the conversation turned upon women and love in general, whereupon Mr. M[edwin] lauded to the skies the devotedness, constancy,

[37] Medwin, *Conversations*, p. 334.
[38] Trelawny, *Records*, I, 55.

and truth of the sex. When he had finished his sentimental "tirade," Lord Byron took up the opposite side, going on as Don Juan . . . might. It was easy to see that he was playing a part, and that his words, partly in jest, partly ironical, did not express his thoughts. Nevertheless they gave pain to Mme. G[uiccioli], and, as soon as they were alone, Lord Byron having asked her why she was sad, she told him the cause.

"I am very sorry to have grieved you," said he, "but how could you think that I was talking seriously?"

"I did not think it," she said, "but those who do not know you will believe all; M[edwin] will not fail to repeat your words as if they were your real opinions . . ."

"Very probably," said Lord Byron; "and that will be another true page to add to M[edwin]'s note-book. I can't help it. I couldn't resist the temptation of punishing M[edwin] for his vanity. All those eulogiums and sentimentalities about women were to make us believe how charming they had always been toward him, how they had always appreciated his merits, and how passionately in love with him Lady B[eauclerc] is now. My words were meant to throw water on his imaginary fire." [39]

One need not assume that Teresa wrote up this conversation at the time, and allowances must be made for her point of view (the conversation probably took place at her house, for example, not that of Shelley, which Byron never entered, it seems, during the time when he and Medwin were at Pisa). But if the identification of Medwin and Mrs. Beauclerc is correct— and there are no other candidates in the circle, which was described at such length by its members—then Teresa's account throws some light on a mystery left by Mary Shelley. "Did I uphold and laud Medwin?" she asked Trelawny. ". . . To be sure, we did not desire a duel nor an horsewhipping—and Lord Byron and Mrs. Beauclerk worked hard to promote peace." [40]

[39] Teresa G. Guiccioli, *My Recollections of Lord Byron,* trans. Hubert E. H. Jerningham (New York, 1869), pp. 333–334.

[40] *Letters of Mary Shelley,* II, 24, corrected from the autograph letter in the Abinger Collection. It is barely possible that Mary refers to this averted duel in her journal for Feb. 15, 1822: "The tigers are tamed . . ."

Had some protector of Mrs. Beauclerc come forth to defend her reputation, and, to avoid a spectacle, had both she and Byron tried to hush the matter up? It is not impossible. But it is clear that Byron was sufficiently interested in Medwin to come to his aid at a time when he needed it, as he also did later.

Byron, however, did not wholly trust Medwin with Teresa, it seems—if we can accept the testimony of her unpublished "Vie de Lord Byron en Italie."[41] She described Medwin as an intelligent and agreeable man but one of lax principles, and she wished that Shelley had written the *Conversations of Byron,* in which she discovered nine errors of fact, she said. Noting that Medwin was a regular guest at Byron's stag dinners, lasting late into the evening, she considered the implications of the situation:

One can easily understand that the milieu, material and moral, was not very favorable to exactitude and truth. Without even accusing Medwin of having lied, often—without saying that between men the conversation after dinner takes a certain turn— that these conversations took place between two glasses on the part of Byron (always sober) and ten glasses, probably, on Medwin's part—one must add above all that Byron, talking to amuse himself, not suspecting that his words would be recorded, loving and giving way to mystification all too often, was enjoying himself with a man whose conduct he knew and who exalted women to insinuate that he was fortunate with them. It was this that made Lord Byron take the opposite view to confound him.

In general, it may be said that Lord Byron amused himself with the light and congenial company of the Captain in the hours he wanted to give to diversion and the table. But because he never thought that Medwin was without delicacy and truth [*i. e.,* that Medwin would publish], he boasted of his success equaling the actual one [enjoyed by Medwin] with an English woman, mother

[41] Teresa Guiccioli's unpublished "Vie de Lord Byron en Italie," pp. 904–907, photographs of which were kindly supplied to me by Professor Leslie Marchand of Rutgers University. The original is in the Biblioteca Classense in Ravenna.

of a fine large family and to whom, consequently, respect was owed above all.

Teresa saved the best until last in her account. Medwin, she wrote, discovering one night that her carriage was late in picking her up at the Shelleys's, offered her his arm. She accepted, and they returned to her house on the Lungarno. When Byron learned of this, he "disapproved severely" and told her that "Medwin was not a man with whom a young woman could afford to be seen in public." When she wrote this, she had read, in an otherwise flattering account, Medwin's judgment of herself: "Lord Byron is certainly very much attached to her, without being actually in love."

Meanwhile, the surface of Medwin's life in 1822 continued to be richly varied. In January he watched Bartolini make and remake clay models for Byron's bust, attended the opera with Williams, Jane, and Mary, dined at Shelley's, dined at Williams's, received a call from Williams and Trelawny, dined at Trelawny's with Shelley and Williams, dined, fired pistols, and rode with Byron, and translated a passage from Petrarch's *Africa* for him.[42] Medwin was hearing some of the most delightful and stimulating conversation of all times and hearing it day after day.

A letter written by Mary Shelley on January 18, 1822, vividly conveys, from her somewhat jaundiced and envious point of view, the gaiety and excitement of the world through which Medwin moved.

Pisa today *ha cambiato viso;* all was allegrezza, the Court here, balls &c.—when a brother of the Dutchess, a promising young man, has suddenly died of a *mal maligno,* so the Court has left us. The ladies look in despair at their new gowns, the gentlemen, among them Medwin, sigh to think of the wal[t]zing they might have had.—Oh plaisir! one long adieu!—You know us too well not to know that we have not lost any thing by this change—I had thought

[42] Byron's *Letters and Journals,* VI, 7; Medwin's *Conversations,* p. 113. Medwin's translation appeared in Ugo Foscolo's *Essays on Petrarch* (London, 1823), pp. 215, 217.

of being presented, mais j'ai beau faire—Shelley would not take the necessary steps, and so we go on in our obscure way—the Williams's lead the same life as us, and without a sigh we see Medwin depart for his evening assemblies—Yet though I go not to the house of feasting, I have gone to the house of prayer—In the piano sotto di nos there is a Reverend Divine [Dr. George F. Nott] who preaches and prays, and sent us so many messages that I now make one of his congregation, and that from a truly Christian motive—Vaccá reported that this Doctͬ Nott said in Society that Shelley was a *scelerato*. We told Taaffe and the little gossip reported it to all the world. Doctͬ Nott heard of it, and sent a message by Medwin to deny it, and put our absence from Church on the score of this report, so to prove that I forgave or disbelieved, I went once, and then that I might not appear to despise his preaching, I went again and again.[43]

Mary is posturing again, not very successfully. She ridicules the Court of the Grand Duchess, with its balls, which Medwin enjoyed; but she had tried in vain to be presented: Shelley would not go. She goes to hear the fashionable Dr. Nott preach, former prebendary of Winchester and subpreceptor to the Princess Charlotte, his reputation now tarnished by scandal— Mary goes to hear him only, she says, because he had called Shelley a *scelerato* (at Mrs. Beauclerc's), but she returned at least three more times, possibly five more. Medwin disliked the man, as did Shelley, and recalled that he had earned the name of "Slip-knot," because he had slipped out of so many matrimonial engagements. Byron discussed with Medwin the scandalous gossip about the relations between the Princess Charlotte and Dr. Nott, who had already preached against Byron's *Cain*. When Byron heard that Nott was preaching against atheism in the very house in which Shelley lived, meanwhile, as Medwin recalled, directing significant glances at Mary Shelley in the congregation of fourteen or fifteen, he was outraged and said dryly to Medwin that "the preacher read some of the commandments affirmatively and not negatively, as 'Thou shalt,

[43] F. L. Jones, "Mary Shelley to Maria Gisborne: New Letters, 1818– 1822," *Studies in Philology*, LII (Jan., 1955), 70–71.

Nott! bear false witness against thy neighbour.'" The next day Byron wrote the biting little satire, "Do you know Doctor Nott." Medwin was allowed to copy it and in 1824 wished to include it in his *Conversations,* but Colburn his publisher thought it "*trop fort.*" [44]

Byron's poetry was an "everflowing stream," Mary observed in her letter of January 18, but Shelley was laboring at *Charles the First*. Medwin had secured for him, from the library of the elder Medwin, a pamphlet defending regicide, *Killing No Murder,* but Medwin understood Shelley and Shelley's subject well enough to realize why the play would never be completed. Shelley hated the Puritans and their excesses, he explained, lacked the necessary knowledge of the period, and had lost confidence in his ability to attract readers.[45]

Medwin as a critic is not always to be condemned, by any means. Shelley showed to him the heavily interlined manuscript of *Charles the First,* took serious note of his opinions of such works as *The Cenci* and *Prometheus Unbound*; and Medwin's knowledge of the classics allowed him to see that Shelley was capable of that rare feat, writing an English ode founded on classical models,[46] for Medwin knew what an ode was. As for Byron's poetry, he was the first, perhaps, to realize that *Don Juan* was indebted to Casti's *La Diavolessa,* which Byron first read in 1816, and Medwin later wrote a long account of the relationship between the two poems.[47] He was essentially a critic and scholar, with a passion for poetry greater than that of any other member of the Pisan circle, except for the two master spirits of it, Byron and Shelley.

In February Byron talked of getting up *Othello,* "and rehearsals of a few scenes took place. Perhaps Lord Byron would have made the finest actor in the world," Medwin wrote. "His

[44] Medwin, *Shelley,* pp. 360–362; Medwin, *Conversations,* pp. 258–260.
[45] Medwin, *Shelley,* pp. 340–341, 346.
[46] *Ibid.,* p. 253.
[47] Medwin, "A Cast of Casti," followed by "The Diavolessa, Translated; The Origin of Lord Byron's Don Juan," in the first number of *The New Anti-Jacobin,* April, 1833.

voice had a flexibility, a variety in its tones, a power and pathos beyond any I ever heard; and his countenance was capable of expressing the tenderest, as well as the strongest emotions. I shall never forget his reading Iago's part in the handkerchief scene."[48] Medwin was, also, "in his best days an admirable reader."[49]

After ten days the project was laid aside. Teresa, not speaking English, could not be included. "All at once," Medwin wrote, "a difficulty arose about a Desdemona [to be played by Mary Shelley], and the Guiccioli put her Veto on our theatricals." According to a marginal note made in 1825 or after by Trelawny, he was to play the title role, Byron the role of Iago. That left only two other male roles of any consequence, and Williams, Trelawny noted, was cast as Cassio, Medwin as Roderigo. Taaffe is not named. It was he, however, despite the role assigned to Medwin, who was the butt of Byron's remarks in Pisa and earned for himself finally the name of False-Taaffe. Medwin may have made awkward blunders, but he was incapable of the ridiculous gaucherie described by Claire in her journal for June 9, 1821: "Taaffe sent two guinea pigs to Mary, and said at the end of the letter, Ah! that I were one of those guinea pigs, that I might see you this morning!"[50]

Williams's continued affection and admiration for Medwin is made clear by his journal entries during February and March. He read to Medwin the tragedy he was writing, *Gonzaga, Duke of Mantua*, and Medwin criticized it for him.[51] There is nothing to suggest that Medwin maintained anything but the most cordial relations with all the members of the circle, including Trelawny, in whose company he dined repeatedly at both Shelley's and Williams's. Before he left Pisa, Byron presented to him an autographed copy of *Marino Faliero*, and Shelley allowed him to make extracts from his "notes on the wonders of art" in the gallery at Pisa.

[48] Medwin, *Conversations*, pp. 160–161.
[49] Medwin's obituary, *Albery's Horsham Journal*, Sept., 1869.
[50] Unpublished journal of Claire Clairmont, June 9, 1821.
[51] Williams, *Journal*, p. 132.

On March 8 Byron gave for Medwin a parting dinner, in the course of which Shelley "repeated some of the finest lines of Childe Harold," Williams recorded in his diary. "Lord B. after listening to a stanza—cried 'Heavens! Shelley, what infinite nonsense are you quoting?'" Medwin wrote to Mary Shelley from Geneva, "I look upon the time spent at Pisa among the happiest days of my life."[52] The night before he left for Rome and Naples, he dined at Shelley's house, on March 10, with the Williamses. Jane, as both the Shelleys knew, had always been one of his favorite people.

Trelawny provides a final glimpse of Medwin before his departure. Shelley, after a trip with Trelawny to Leghorn, to get money from his banker, emptied the bag of scudi onto the floor, divided the pile with a shovel, and then said, of one quarter of it, "I will give this to poor Tom Medwin, who wants to go to Naples and has no money."[53] This has the true Shelleyan ring. Money was dirt to him, to be handled with a shovel, and Medwin had little more sense about it, although a great deal more interest in it. Did Shelley lead Medwin to believe that the money was a gift and tell Mary it was a loan? On December 5, 1822, mistakenly thinking Medwin married, Mary wrote that she could not, even so, "prevail on myself to ask for the crowns. L. B[yron] offered to write to him as executor—I refused then but perhaps I shall request that he will."[54]

By leaving when he did, Medwin missed the famous affair of the Italian dragoon on March 24, which caused Byron so much trouble, after one of his servants had wounded the man. But Mary wrote him a long and friendly letter on April 12, 1822, describing it all, and sent, "at Lord Byron's desire . . . copies of some of the documents concerning the row . . ." Copies

[52] Medwin to Mary Shelley, July 10, 1824, a letter in the Abinger Collection.

[53] Trelawny, *Records*, I, 121. The date of the Leghorn trip may have been Feb. 20, 1822; see *Mary Shelley's Journal.*

[54] Mary Shelley to Claire Clairmont, Dec. 5, 1822, a letter in the Abinger Collection; Jones prints only a small fragment of it in *The Letters of Mary Shelley*, I, 208.

were also sent to Douglas Kinnaird, Sir Walter Scott, and Hobhouse.[55] Mary makes Taaffe appear properly ludicrous and cowardly: "what between insolence and dastard humility . . . [he] kept himself in hot water when in fact he had nothing to fear." She sends to Medwin news of Mrs. Beauclerc, "removed to Florence," summarizes the summer plans of Byron, the Shelleys, and the Williamses, informs him that Shelley has received *Hellas,* recently published in England, and that Byron has received David Lyndsay's *Dramas of the Ancient World* (1822), which deals with "three subjects treated by Lord Byron; Cain, the Deluge, and Sardanapalus." Mary explains how Lyndsay's treatment differs from Byron's and recommends the volume for its "considerable talent, and strength of poetry and expression." Mary was later to meet Lyndsay in England and gossip about Medwin to him.

She closes with news of Williams's and little Percy's health, suggests that Jane will probably write to him, and hopes that "we will be favoured with a visit on your return northward . . ."[56] He had promised, before leaving, to return in the summer.[57] The letter offers clear evidence of the intimate and respected place that Medwin had made for himself in the Pisan circle, and Byron's continued interest in him is apparent.

After leaving Pisa, Medwin went first to Rome. Here he called upon the great Canova, who at the time was completing his "Mars and Venus," commissioned by George IV. Upon discovering that Medwin was an Englishman, Canova ceased his labors, although still holding his chisel and mallet, and talked freely. Medwin asked "whether he thought the female form had degenerated since the golden days of Athens, or if he imagined that Greece possessed better models than we *barbarians* could boast of." Canova thought this was not the case, and they talked of the beauty of the Princess Borghese, a cast of whom Medwin had seen at Venice. In Rome he had heard

[55] Cline, *Byron, Shelley and Their Pisan Circle,* p. 239, note 40.
[56] *Letters of Mary Shelley,* I, 166–168.
[57] Medwin, *Shelley,* p. 379.

that the Princess's husband had prohibited her statue from being seen but that "a nephew of hers, to whom she was accustomed to accord the *entrée* in the Roman fashion, in bed," asked to look at it, nevertheless. "Putting her little foot out of the clothes, she said," as Medwin heard the story, "'you may judge of it by *that.*'"

Then Medwin and Canova talked of Napoleon and Napoleon's mother, both of whom had been executed in marble by Canova. The sculptor now returned to his work and asked Medwin what he thought of the group before him. Medwin was forced to reply that he liked the feminine figure "least of all his Venuses"; she was "too mature, too much *embonpoint.*" Medwin preferred the Aphrodite of Alcamenes, with both her hands lifting up her wet hair, although he did not admit this to Canova. After listening to Medwin's ecstatic praise of the Aegina marbles at Thorvaldsen's and the bashful "Paris" at the Justiniani, which he had recently seen, Canova asked which of his own works Medwin preferred. He selected the early "Magdalen"; when he saw it in Paris, it brought tears to his eyes, uniting as it did beauty and suffering. Canova was not particularly pleased with this choice, and other visitors arriving, Medwin took his leave, promising to call again. But he never did; instead, he went on to Naples, and Canova died in October. Medwin recognized his genius but thought much of his work studiously theatrical, his models taken from the stage or the ballet: he lacked a "deep sense of intellectual beauty." Medwin preferred the art of Flaxman.[58]

He wrote to Williams from Rome and from Naples, both letters arriving on May 16, 1822.[59] Julian says in the *Angler* that in 1822 he lived at the Chiatamone in Naples, from which he could see the Bay.

[58] Medwin describes his interview with Canova in "Canova: Leaves from the Autobiography of an Amateur," *Fraser's Magazine*, XX (Sept., 1839), 370–375. His dating of the interview in the spring of 1821 is an obvious error for the spring of 1822.

[59] Williams, *Journal*, p. 149.

I used nightly to watch the motion of a broadly reflected, rapidly moving torch [to attract the fish], opposite my windows; and on inquiring what it meant, learned that it proceeded from a boat, to which it was attached, and which boat contained "Ferdinando, il re dei Lazzaroni" [the most degraded class of the Neapolitan people], as he was properly called, for none of them could vie with him in imbecility of intellect, in vulgarity of manners, or in dexterity at their own particular occupation.[60]

Medwin does not exaggerate. Ferdinand IV, King of Naples, was one of the most contemptible monarchs ever to sit on a throne, ignorant, brutal, and treacherous, repeatedly violating his solemn oath, as he had recently done following the Congress of Laibach, when he had sworn to maintain the new constitution. But after the Austrian Army entered Naples, in the spring of 1821, Ferdinand dismissed the parliament and initiated a period of Gestapo-like tyranny, fed by a network of spies and informers. Julian says in *The Angler* that he was in Naples in the spring of 1821 and saw the "triumphal entry of the King of the Pulcinelle into that capital"—but Medwin was not there. He had missed another historic event, this one by a year. What Julian says about Ferdinand and his people, however, was soundly based on Medwin's own knowledge, confirmed on the spot: ". . . A monarch, after breaking the most solemn engagements to his own people, [had been] thrust down their throats by foreign bayonets. Ages of misgovernment . . . had reduced to destitution and misery half the population; and the late persecutions for liberty's sake, and exile, and confiscation . . . had so infested the roads with brigands, that daily accounts reached our ears of some horrible murders (or worse crimes) that . . . these savages committed."[61] Sick of these events, Julian returned to Rome, but Medwin on July 5, 1822, sailed from Naples for Genoa.[62]

[60] Medwin, *Angler*, I, 292.
[61] *Ibid.*, II, 37–38.
[62] Medwin, *Shelley*, p. 391.

Here he arrived, he says, on July 9, having had very light winds for the first two days, "lying becalmed one whole night off the Pontine Marshes," and being caught in a squall when "five or six miles from the bay of Spezzia"—the same squall in which Shelley was drowned. "The appearance of the sky was very threatening. Over the Apennines, which encircle Genoa as with an amphitheatre, hung masses on masses up-piled, like those I have seen after the explosion of a mine, of dark clouds . . . The squall at length came . . . in the afternoon; and neither in the bay of Biscay, or Bengal, nor between the Tropics, nor on the Line, did I ever witness a severer one . . ."[63] At the Hotel de l'Europe in Genoa, he says, he heard a rumor that an English schooner had been lost near Lerici and two Englishmen drowned, but suspecting nothing, he wrote to both Shelley and Williams at the Villa Magni, where he knew they had planned to spend the summer.

Before he left Genoa, he saw Pietro Gamba for the last time, who with his father had moved there in the latter part of July.[64] Medwin remembered this brother of Teresa Guiccioli as an "amiable man, . . . adored by his sister . . . He was a man of no talent, but pleasing and agreeable, and carried with him the passport of a very handsome person."[65]

And so Medwin went on to Geneva and did not learn of Shelley's death until after his arrival there, when he received a letter from Byron.[66] Shelley dead, Mary unburdened herself to Medwin as she had never done before, perhaps, sharing her grief with him in the unquestioned knowledge that he too had loved Shelley. She wrote, on July 29,

I ought to say something more about that which has left us in desolation—but why should I *atrister* you with my despair. I will only mention Jane, since you will be interested & anxious perhaps— She is not well—she does not sleep—but I hope with care she

---

[63] *Ibid.*, p. 392.
[64] Cline, *Byron, Shelley*, p. 184.
[65] Medwin, *Shelley*, pp. 370–371.
[66] Medwin, "Memoir of Shelley," *The Athenaeum*, Aug. 18, 1832, p. 535.

may get better—God knows!—she must have struggles & no one is more unfit for them—no woman had ever more need of a protector—but we shall be together & until she joins either her Mother or Edwards brother who is expected next year [from India] I shall be with her. Seven weeks ago—just three weeks before this blank moral death visited me I was very ill—near dying—but I have got through it all— I had not been out of the house from illness when Jane & I posted to Leghorn from Lerici to get intelligence of them & without intelligence—without rest we returned—to wait ten days for the confirmation of our sentence of a life of eternal pain— Yet not eternal—I think we are all short lived—but for my child I would take up my abode at Rome—Rome is a good nurse & soon rocks to a quiet grave those who seek death

I scrawl all this nonsense I know not why—I intended to have written two words only—but grief makes my mind active & my pen in my hand I run on by instinct I could do so for sheets.

Adieu—I hope you will be happy—

Yours very truly

Mary W Shelley

[P. S.] S. & I were united exactly 8 years ag[o] yesterday—on the 4th of August he wd have been 30— Except that his health was getting better & better I wd not selfishly desire that his angelic spirit shd again inhabit that frame which tormented it—he is alive & often with me now— Every one feels the same, all say that he was an elemental spirit imprisoned here but free & happy now— I am not now—one day I hope to be worthy to join him— My life is chalked out to me—it will be one of study only—except for my poor boy—[67]

Medwin "without delay recrossed the Alps,"[68] learned at Spezia where the bodies of his friends had been thrown up out of the sea, and arrived at Pisa again on the evening of August 16, it seems—just after Byron and Trelawny had finished cremating the body of Shelley.[69] In his *Conversations* he dates this event August 18 and, using Trelawny's account, implies

[67] *Letters of Mary Shelley*, I, 177–178.
[68] Medwin, *Shelley*, p. 393.
[69] Medwin, *Conversations*, pp. 306, 319; Medwin, *Shelley*, pp. 394, 395, 398.

without saying so that he was present; but he manfully corrected the erroneous impression in his *Memoir of Shelley* and again in his *Life of Shelley*: "I say, I arrived at Pisa too late." He was bitter about it even into his old age. The most dramatic event of his life—and he had arrived late for it by a few hours! His chagrin was so great that he trembled precariously on the brink of an outrageous lie. That he, who had loved Shelley best, should have been late, his place supplied by Hunt, whose weakness had forced him to retreat from the burning pyre into the protection of his carriage, some distance away! It was too much, the temptation too great.

But all his accounts agree that he arrived on the day of the cremation. Perhaps it is of little importance now whether he got there on August 16 or August 18. He found Byron suffering from a fever and badly sunburned after his long swim in the sea on the sixteenth, but Byron recovered rapidly, and they discussed the wreck of the *Don Juan*, the "strange occurrences" in Shelley's life, and his wish to die young. Byron compared the dispute between Mary Shelley and Leigh Hunt, for the possession of Shelley's heart, snatched from the fire by Trelawny, "to that between Ajax and Ulysses, for the arms of Achilles, and said, 'What does Hunt want with it? He'll only put it in a glass case and make sonnets on it.' Byron had heard also that Mrs. Williams meant to preserve her husband's ashes in an urn. His remark was, 'Why, she'll make tea in it one of these days.'"[70] Thus the two talked away in their old style. But the Pisan circle had ended.

Medwin also called on Hunt, then living under Byron's roof. Byron had talked very freely to Medwin of his difficulties with Hunt, and Medwin printed. It is not to be supposed, then, that Hunt's later references to Medwin would be remarkable for their charitableness.

Hunt wrote, in his *Lord Byron and Some of His Contemporaries* (1828), four years after he had read in the *Conversations* what Byron had said to Medwin,

---

[70] *His Very Self and Voice*, pp. 306–307.

Captain Medwin tells us that the noble poet's "voice had a flexibility, a variety in its tones, a power and a pathos beyond any I ever heard."—This is harmless, as an instance of the effect which his Lordship had upon the Captain; but, from all I ever heard of it, I should form a very different judgment . . . There may have been greater strength in his voice than it was my chance to witness; but the "flexibility," and the "variety of tones," to say nothing of the pathos, were assuredly in the Captain's imagination.

According to Captain Medwin, Lord Byron said of the writer of these pages, that till his voyage to Italy he "had never been ten miles from St. Paul's." The Captain ought to have known enough of his Lordship's random way of talking, not to take for granted every thing that he chose to report of another. I had never been out of England before; except, when a child, to the coast of France; but . . .

"I never met with any man who shines so much in conversation." That is to say, Captain Medwin never met before with a lord so much the rage. He says a little afterwards, that his Lordship "never showed the author," and that he "prided himself most on being a man of the world and of fashion";—that is, to Captain Medwin; whose admiration, he saw, ran to that side of things. The truth is, as I have before stated, that he had no conversation in the higher sense of the word . . . "His anecdotes," says Medwin, "of life and living characters were inexhaustible." This was true, if you chose to listen to them, and to take every thing he said for granted; but every body was not prepared, like the Captain, to be thankful for stories of the noble Lord and all his acquaintances, male and female . . .

I had the pleasure of a visit from Captain Medwin while "under the roof" that he speaks of, and should have said nothing to disturb the innocence of his *politesse,* had he abstained from repeating scandals respecting women, and not taken upon himself to criticise the views and "philosophy" of Mr. Shelley; a man of whom he was qualified to know still less than of Lord Byron. With the cautions here afforded to the reader, a better idea of his Lordship may certainly be drawn from his account than from any other. The warmth of his homage drew out the noble Bard on some points upon which he would have been cautious of committing himself with a less wholesale admirer; and not the least curious part of the picture, is the *mutual* excess of their position [italics mine].[71]

[71] *Ibid.,* pp. 307–309.

This is a remarkable tribute to Medwin's book, coming from an enemy, who was still smarting under his treatment at Byron's hands.

Medwin in his long and highly laudatory footnote on Shelley, occupying pages 306–317 of the *Conversations,* had called *The Necessity of Atheism* a "silly work" and stated Shelley's belief in the "perfectibility of human nature" to be "wild and visionary, and dangerous"; but he had closed by saying that Shelley's works were worthy of being placed on the same shelf with Plato's *Republic.* Hunt would worship (or criticize) alone, quarrelling even with the poet's widow, in the early weeks of her bereavement.

Medwin had seen the widowed Mary, of course, and also Jane Williams, from whom he heard with "melancholy satisfaction" the details of the last days and death of his two friends.[72] Jane described to him "the days and nights of horror" that she and Mary had lived through, waiting in suspense. This and more Medwin put into *Ahasuerus, The Wanderer* (1823), his poetic tribute, dedicated to Byron and laid at the feet of the dead Shelley.

In the fourth week of August, Medwin took leave of his friends, to retrace his journey through Genoa to Geneva and from there to go on to Paris and England, the need for change of scene strong within him.

He chose to travel to Genoa in a "*caratella,* with relays of one horse," and so was able to make a sentimental pilgrimage to the sites of his "friends' funeral pyres, . . . easily discoverable by their ashes."[73] He had another duty to the dead—to visit the Villa Magni at San Terenzo, where they had spent their last days alive. He must have written the following account on the spot, or very shortly afterwards, while the memory of the experience was still green.

From Sarzana to Lerici there is only a cross (and that a narrow) carriage road. After a somewhat difficult ascent of three miles, the

[72] Medwin, *Shelley,* pp. 398–399.
[73] *Ibid.,* p. 407.

calèche set me down at a bye footpath, which conducts to San Terenzo. The sky was perfectly cloudless, and not a breath of air relieved the intense heat of an Italian August sun. The day had been unusually oppressive, and there was a mistiness in the atmosphere, or rather a glow which softened down the distances into those mellow tints, in which Claude delighted to bathe his landscapes. I was little in a mood to enjoy the beauties which increased every moment during this walk. I followed mechanically a pathway overhung with trellised vines, and bordered with olive trees, contrasted here and there with the massy broad dark foliage of the fig-tree. For a mile or two, I continued to ascend, till on a sudden a picture burst on my view, that no pen can describe. Before me was the broad expanse of the Mediterranean, studded with islands, and a few fishing boats with their lattine sails, the sun's broad disc just dipping in the waves.

Thick groves of fruit trees, interspersed with cottages and villas, sloped down to the shores of the gulf of Spezzia; and safely landlocked, a little to the left, Lerici, with its white flat-roofed houses almost in the sea, stood in the centre, and followed the curve of this bay; the two promontories projecting from which, were surmounted with castles, for the protection of the coast, and the enforcement of the quarantine laws. The descent, now become rapid and broken, and deeply worn into the rock, only offered occasional glimpses of the sea, the two islets in front, and the varied coast of Porto Venere to the right. I now came in sight of San Terenzo, a village, or rather a miserable collection of windowless black huts, piled one above the other, inclosed within and imbedded, like swallow's nests, in the rocks that overhang and encircle it. The place is inhabited only by fishermen and their families, on the female part of whom devolves (as is common in Italy) the principal labours. However ungraceful in itself, the peasantry of most parts of Italy have some peculiarity of costume, but the women of San Terenzo are in a savage state of nature . . . They had neither shoes nor stockings, and the rags which scarcely hid their deformity, were strongly impregnated with the effluvia of the fish they were carrying on their bare heads to the neighbouring markets . . . The men I did not see . . .

Between this village and Lerici, but nearer the former, was pointed out to me the solitary villa, or *palazzo* as it is called, which was about to waken in me so many bitter recollections. It is built immediately upon the beach, and consists of one story; the ground-floor, when the Libeccio set strongly in, must have been washed by the waves. A deaf, unfeeling old wretch, a woman who had the care of the house, and had either witnessed or heard of all the desolation of which it had been the scene, with a savage unconcern, and much garrulity, gave a dry narrative of the story, as she led me through the apartment. Below was a large unpaved sort of entrance-hall, without doors or windows, where lay the small flat-bottomed boat, or skiff, much shattered, of which I have already spoken. It was the same my poor friends had on the Serchio. Against the wall, and scattered about the floor, were oars and fragments of spars,—they told too well the tale of woe. A dark and somewhat perpendicular staircase now led us to the only floor that remained. It reminded me somewhat in its arrangement, of an Indian bungalow; the walls were whitewashed. The rooms, now without furniture, consisted of a saloon and four chambers at the four corners; this, with the exception of a terrace in front, was the whole apartment. The verandah, which ran the entire length of the villa, was of considerable width, and the view from it of a magical and supernatural beauty.

Standing there, looking at the sea, Medwin relived the terrifying days when Mary and Jane had awaited news of Shelley and Williams, only to learn at last that their bodies had been found on the beach. "All this rushed upon my imagination," Medwin wrote, "and insensible to the heat, or fatigue of the ascent, I found myself, scarcely knowing how, where my *calèche* was waiting for me; and it was midnight, and after a twenty-two hours' journey, more harassing in mind and body than I had ever experienced, when I reached the inn at Spezzia." [74]

After the "pagan" rites of the cremation of Shelley, the burial of his ashes in Rome, presided over by two English clergymen, was an anticlimax, and no one of the Pisan circle was present. Two of Medwin's friends were there, however, the Rev. Richard Burgess and Sir Charles Slyte, and one of them sent to him an account of the burial, which he published in his *Life of Shel-*

[74] *Ibid.*, pp. 407–410.

ley.[75] It was surely no accident that Burgess later officiated at the christening of Medwin's first daughter, on Christmas Day, 1825.

In Geneva, the shock of Shelley's death still strong upon him, he sought out the house that Shelley had occupied in 1816, Montalègre, reliving what he knew of Shelley's and Byron's life together at that time. The scene burned itself into his memory, and his account of it is, "in spite of a few inaccuracies, the most graphic contemporary description of Shelley's house in Geneva."[76] Medwin wrote,

The Campagne Mont Allègre or Chapuis, as it was sometimes called, lay immediately at the foot of Diodati, being only separated from it by a vineyard, and having no other communication but a very tortuous, hedged in, and narrow lane, scarcely admitting of a *char-a-banc*. The spot was one of the most sequestered on the lake, and almost hidden by a grove of umbrageous forest trees, as is a bird's nest among leaves, and invisible from the main road. At the extremity of the terrace, is a secure little port, belonging to the larger villa, and here was moored the boat which formed so much the mutual delight and recreation of the two poets.[77]

[75] Medwin, pp. 412–415. This account first appeared in Medwin's story, "Pasquale; A Tale of Italy," *Bentley's Miscellany*, IV (Sept., 1838), 289–291, which may suggest perhaps that Medwin wrote the account himself. Burgess was still alive when Medwin published his *Shelley*. The other possible author, Sir Charles Slyte, did in fact send to Medwin an account of the burial, a portion of which Medwin copied in a letter to Jane Williams, Feb. 25, 1823, but this portion does not appear in the published account. I have followed Helen R. Angeli's spelling of the name (*Shelley and His Friends in Italy* [London, 1911], p. 318), which she herself is doubtful of, but in Medwin's letter both the taller letters are carelessly crossed with a single line, and thus the name may be "Styte" or "Style" or "Slyte." Burgess recalled that he found Slyte waiting at the grave when he arrived and Burgess described a procession through the streets, as does the account published by Medwin. There is one important inconsistency between Burgess's account and that published by Medwin. Medwin's friend said that he visited the grave of Shelley's son William; Burgess states that it could not be found.

[76] Häusermann, *Genevese Background*, p. 4.

[77] Medwin, *Shelley*, p. 145.

Perhaps the scene was too painful for him; perhaps he had
had his fill of melancholy recollections. In the fall [78] of the year
he returned to England for a brief visit, carrying a note from
Byron "to be read to Mr. Murray or his principal clerk." [79]
Medwin continues, in a marginal note to his *Conversations*,
"Not finding the Bibliopolist at home, who was as difficult of
access as a Prime Minister, I did so read [the note] in Albe-
marle Street to his said Clerk, couched in these words. 'Lord
Byron wonders he has not heard from Mr. Murray on the
receipt of his new Cantos of *Don Juan* and desires him to be
less negligent in future—!!'" Elsewhere, in a letter to the editor, written December 1, 1824, and intended for publication
in Galignani's *Weekly Register*, he dates this episode in September or October, says that he showed, not read, the note to
a clerk in Murray's office, but attributes the same words to
Byron in both places. On September 11, 1822, shortly after
Medwin had parted from Byron in Pisa, the latter wrote to
Murray, "by the two last posts [on September 7 and 11]—I sent
off to Mr. D. K[innaird] the four new Cantos of D. J.," Cantos
VI–IX; on October 24 he complained to Murray that he had
not yet heard of their safe arrival. [80] At some time between these
dates, presumably, he asked Medwin to inquire at Murray's,
giving him the note to be delivered there.

But London had ceased to interest Medwin. He wrote to Jane
Williams, shortly after his departure, "London seemed to me
a perfect Pandemonium—the people, climate, everything, in

[78] In a letter from Geneva, dated Sept., 1822, presumably near the end
of the month, Jane Williams wrote, "Medwin left three weeks ago"
(Williams, *Journal*, p. 164), and Medwin says he was at John Murray's
in September or October (an autograph letter to the editor of *Galignani's
Weekly Register*; in the Morgan Library).

[79] Medwin's unpublished marginalia in his *Conversations*, pp. 209–210.

[80] Byron's *Letters and Journals*, VI, 112, 130. Medwin says that Byron
gave the note to him when he left Pisa, but this seems improbable,
although Byron had finished the four cantos by August 27, when Medwin
may still have been with him.

short, quite detestable after the continent."[81] Julian says in
The Angler,

What a detestable, smoky, miry, brick and mortar Babylon this
"Swalool" is! I was never a week in it without wishing myself, to
my soul, in another place, which it well resembles, by Dante's lively
account. The question is (as was put to a Frenchman when about
to take a wife) where to pass one's evenings? Now, at Naples there
is St. Carlo; in most little towns in Italy good music; and *conversaziones* in all. And then at Paris, that darling little Opera Italienne,
where one does not miss a note.[82]

His friends were elsewhere, Paris glittered, and Sir John St.
Aubyn and his family would be there. By the end of October
or earlier he was in Paris, with an introduction to Thomas
Moore, given to him by Byron.[83] Shortly after arriving, he wrote
to Murray, a brief disappointed note.[84] Somewhere, it seems,
he had found time to finish *Ahasuerus, The Wanderer.*

> Hotel de L'Europe,
> Rue Richelieu
> 29th Oct. [18]22
>
> Sir/
> I wrote to you some weeks ago enclosing you two copies of a
> little work of mine and requesting your opinion on the subject of
> publishing it. May I beg you will send me as early as convenient
> your answer to the above address.
>
> I remain
> Your obed^t. Servt.
> T. Medwin

[81] Unpublished letter from Medwin to Jane Williams, (? Oct.) 22,
1822, in the Abinger Collection.

[82] Medwin, *Angler,* II, 283.

[83] *Letters of Trelawny,* p. 26; Medwin's unpublished marginalia in his
Conversations, p. 297; Thomas Colley Grattan, *Beaten Paths; and Those
Who Trod Them* (London, 1862, Second Edition), II, 76, note.

[84] Unpublished letter from Medwin to John Murray, Oct. 29, 1822, in
the possession of Sir John Murray.

Murray finally returned the manuscripts, without a word of comment, and the poem was published by G. and W. B. Whittaker in 1823. Meanwhile Medwin was delighted with Paris and wrote to Jane Williams, October 22, 1822,[85]

You will be surprized that you have not heard from me. I was in some little alarm about you owing to the gales in the channel and was not relieved from them [*sic*] entirely till I learned from Edward St. Aubyn that you only left Paris on the Saturday & could not therefore have arrived when I quitted London [two days before her arrival]. I wished and hoped much to have seen you and the Children—but it seemed we were not to meet, as we missed Each other on the road by some ill luck. Travelling however as I did night & day it was easy that it should be so. I need not say how anxious I am to hear about you. Your last letter to me was a dismal one indeed and made me very doleful too. I can imagine how much the sight of old scenes [at Geneva] must have affected you—& old friends. You do not say if you saw the Laines. They are to be in Paris in a few days to spend the winter.

Sir John St. Aubyn was much annoyed that he should not have seen you. The dear old man has had a severe attack of the gout which has confined him to his hotel ever since he came here. We have talked much about you. You know the goodness of his heart— & how much feeling he possesses. As soon as he is well, they all set out for Geneva. His little girls are quite charming, & her Ladyship [whom he had married on July 1, in England] just the same good creature as ever.

I must know how you find England, but London seemed to me a perfect Pandemonium—the people, climate, everything, in short, quite detestable after the continent. I expect you will not think much otherwise of it—& will be coming back here to settle. I know of no place that is to be compared with Paris for a Residence— I

---

[85] Unpublished letter from Medwin to Jane Williams, in the Abinger Collection. It is dated only the "22nd," but the month is rather clearly October, for on Nov. 13, 1822, Jane wrote to Mary Shelley from London, "I have not seen Medwin; he left England two days before I arrived [she was still in Paris on October 10, ill]; and I have heard from him only once; if you wish to write to him, his address is Hotel de l'Europe, Rue Richelieu, Paris" (from an unpublished letter in the Abinger Collection).

am delighted with it—having 3 or 4 families with whom I am domesticated. Mrs. Payne [to whom Medwin would shortly be engaged] would have called on you if she had known of your being here. I am sure you will like her.

Let me know that [*sic*] you have with all your law business & what your plans are & how I can be useful to you. It seems I am never to be made so. If you recross the channel let me know in good time before your arrival. You will excuse this short & [paper torn] Letter when I tell you I am summoned to attend some Ladies to the Louvre & have only time to pay my respects to your Mother & that you will kiss the Children for me. For the present then Adieu.

Yours affectionately,

T. Medwin

It is too bad that the Parisian excitement of Medwin's life blinded him for the moment to the depths of Jane's grief. He was usually more imaginative.

On November 15, 1822, at the home of Thomas Colley Grattan, Medwin met Thomas Moore, but not for the first time. Moore recorded in his journal, misleadingly, "Went at nine o'clock to Grattan, in order to sing to his wife (according to promise), and found some men assembled, which was contrary to compact. Among others, a Capt. Medwin, a friend of Lord Byron's, who passed a great part of last year at Pisa, and has written a volume of poems. Tells me Hunt's whole family is living in the same house with B., and he believes Mrs. Shelley also and her children [*sic*]."

But it was not Grattan who introduced Medwin to Moore; it was Moore who had introduced Medwin to Grattan—four days earlier, when Moore had "strongly recommended" Medwin to Grattan's "attentions in virtue of Lord Byron's warm letter of introduction." Grattan, after reading Moore's published diary, asked a pointed question: "Could it be that Moore composed this entry for his diary, or modified it, some years afterwards, when Medwin's *Conversations* had thrown him so much out of favour with Moore's particular world?" [86]

[86] Grattan, *Beaten Paths*, II, 76, note.

Medwin, who had very probably called with his letter of introduction on Moore, then living in a cottage owned by the wealthy and hospitable Spaniard M. Villamil, at La Butte, near Sèvres, had reasons of his own for developing a dislike of the Irish poet. These were encouraged, perhaps, by Byron's slighting remarks at Pisa. "Do but give Tom a good dinner and a lord," Byron had said to him, "and he is at the top of his happiness, for Tommy loves a lord." [87] From Villamil, Moore's landlord, Medwin heard that Murray had lithographed an embarrassing letter from Byron "and sent [it] about London to different literary men." [88] Medwin supposed that this story had come from Moore. Grattan, with whom Medwin was intimate, also observed of Moore at this time, "He was most positively no *friend* of the noble poet in the fine and generous sense of the term . . . I am pretty sure he had no strong attachment to Lord Byron." [89] Grattan was here remembering Moore's "refined obsequiousness" toward the great, the famous, or the noble; and it is very probable indeed that Moore, making his plans to leave Paris for England, paid no more than the scantest necessary attention at the time to Medwin, who very clearly was in no position to strengthen or advance Moore's position in life or letters.

Moore, however, did introduce Medwin to Grattan, then a young man who had published nothing except a poetical romance which he was trying hard to suppress. Perhaps Moore thought that these two obscure persons, both with a military past and a literary bent, were perfectly suited to each other. (He could not foresee that Grattan would serve as literary agent of Medwin's *Conversations of Byron*, offering the manuscript to Colburn and "giving him four-and-twenty hours in which to make up his mind as to the purchase and the price.") [90] The occasion of the introduction was the farewell subscription dinner given in Paris for Moore. It was limited to sixty "highly

---

[87] Medwin, *Shelley*, II, 198.
[88] Medwin's unpublished marginalia in his *Conversations*, p. 206.
[89] Grattan, *Beaten Paths*, II, 72–73.   [90] *Ibid.*, II, 62.

respectable" guests, who assembled at the Salon des Étrangers, in the Rue de la Grange Batelier. Lord Trimleston acted as presiding officer; Sir Godfrey Webster, one of the stewards, made a speech, and another was made by Patrick Lattin, "an Irishman of good fortune and great talent, who knocked down several glasses and decanters in the energy of his action." [91] Medwin would soon come to know Lattin very well. But what Medwin chiefly remembered was the conduct of Moore, who "refused to reply to Sir Godfrey's invitation to give his noble friend [Byron] as a toast, not wishing that any other should that day share in his divinity . . ." [92]

Sir Godfrey Webster, who had toasted Byron at the dinner, Medwin described in the following terms, when annotating his *Conversations*:

No man began the world with better auspices, a better fortune amassed during his minority, a very handsome home, talents (he was a Son of Lady Holland) that would have distinguished him in Parliament [where he served for Sussex, 1812–1820]. The fort[une] he ran out in a very few years. Among the small claims of his extravagance was £10,000 for [? some petty trifles] . . . He died [in 1836] of brandy in a miserable lodging at Hounslow . . . It is extraordinary to think that a man of his classical attainments and elegant taste should have inhabited such a place. [93]

In 1824, however, Webster still owned two of the finest seats in Sussex, Battle Abbey and Bodihan Castle.

Medwin at this time also met Lady Adelaide Forbes, to whom Byron considered proposing marriage in 1813, and "saw her set a little in Paris. This was in 1822 or 3," he wrote in the margin of his *Conversations*. We see emerging very clearly now, again, the weakness that was finally to destroy Medwin's happiness—the pressing need within him to move in society that he could not afford.

[91] *Ibid.*, II, 47–49.
[92] Medwin, *Shelley*, II, 199.
[93] Medwin's unpublished marginalia in his *Conversations*, p. 5.

But these acquaintances of Medwin also suggest something even more interesting: the fascinating possibility that Medwin read a copy of Byron's famed burned memoirs at this time and later incorporated portions of them, or recollections of them, into his *Conversations*. Lady Adelaide Forbes had the original in her possession "for a long time," and Lady Webster, wife of Sir Godfrey, had "industriously copied a good portion of it." Washington Irving, with whom Medwin was soon to become intimate in Paris, had read the memoirs. One of Moore's copyists was Dumoulin, "an Irish officer on half-pay" who was a "constant visitor" at Villamil's cottage, rented by Moore and later by Grattan.[94] Moore's original motive in having a copy made was his fear that "the original papers may become worn out by passing through so many hands." [95] Medwin was acquainted with all these people. Did one of them open to him the pages of Byron's memoirs? However this may be, it was already known in Medwin's circle that he had taken notes on Byron's conversations. Grattan writes, "It was to my own knowledge, as well as that of Washington Irving [whom Medwin did not meet until 1824] and others of Medwin's acquaintances in Paris in the year 1821 [*sic*], that he had then in his possession manuscript notes of his *noctes* with Byron and Shelley in Italy . . ." [96]

In late 1822, however, Medwin was thinking more about a Mrs. Payne than about Byron, for the false news that he had married her had reached Trelawny at Genoa by November 22 and was relayed by Mary Shelley to Jane Williams on December 5.[97] She was the sister of Sir Charles Gray, an old schoolmate of T. J. Hogg, and she was now a widow, with two daughters. Medwin had known her at Geneva in 1819 and 1820,

[94] Grattan, *Beaten Paths*, II, 60.

[95] Thomas Moore, *Memoirs, Journals, and Correspondence*, ed. Lord John Russell (London, 1853–1856), entry for May 7, 1820.

[96] Grattan, *Beaten Paths*, II, 67.

[97] *Letters of Trelawny*, p. 26; Mary Shelley's letter to Jane Williams, Dec. 5, 1822, in the Abinger Collection, unpublished except for a brief fragment.

before his reunion with Shelley, and there, it seems, Jane Williams and Trelawny had also known her.[98] She may be the Mrs. Payne, friend of Hunt, referred to in Mary Shelley's letters. In 1825, not yet remarried, she was travelling in Europe with her daughters and had been to Berne and to Baden. Hogg at this time thought that she was going to visit the newly married Medwin and his wife, but this seems unlikely.[99] On December 12, 1822, however, the prospect of his marriage to Mrs. Payne still seemed a real one, although noticeably dimming, and Paris was not quite the attractive city for him that it once had been. He wrote to Jane Williams,[100]

My dear Jane,

Do not attribute my silence to not thinking of you: there are few days—I may almost say hours—that you do not recur to my memory, and I wish you here, where I fancy you might be happier than in England. I was going to say *home*, tho' to you it is not a very applicable word.

I don't know what weather you have had, but here it has been most disagreeable—a fog thick, cold & penetrating has precluded week after week riding on horseback, almost walking, in that most enchanting of places to a French man or woman, The Tuileries. I cannot help contrasting this place and climate, both in themselves odious to me, with those of Tuscany, and were it not for the one person should have wished myself there a thousand times. I had a letter from Lord Byron about a week ago, in which he congratu-

[98] Unpublished letters from T. J. Hogg to Jane Williams, April 17, 1823, and Oct. 3, 1825; Mary Shelley's letter of Dec. 5, 1822, all in the Abinger Collection; Jane Williams's letter of Sept., 1822 (Williams, *Journal*, p. 164).

[99] *After Shelley: The Letters of Thomas Jefferson Hogg to Jane Williams*, ed. Sylva Norman (London, 1934), p. 44.

[100] Unpublished letter from Medwin to Jane Williams, Dec. 12, 1822, in the Abinger Collection. Medwin is correct in all essential details concerning Trelawny's mother and sisters. See Harriette Wilson, *Paris Lions and London Tigers* (London, 1825), who satirized them, and Lady Anne Hill, *Trelawny's Strange Relations* (Stanford Dingley, 1956). Harriette Wilson's book has a colored print which reveals clearly the masculine qualities of Trelawny's mother and sisters, shown surrounded by French officers.

lated me on *my marriage* as if it had actually taken place. When it will is not at all decided—perhaps not for many months.

I am very anxious to learn that you have settled all your law affairs—on which had I entertained any fears I should have written to you earlier. Mrs. W[illiams]'s offer was quite new to me—unexpected. I think you should endeavour for the sake of the dear Children to keep on terms with her—I heard she was in Paris—can you give me her address—perhaps I may call on her if she is.

The 8th Dragoons [Edward E. Williams's old regiment] are not yet returned—I find they are to be made Lancers. What are Captain Williams' plans [those of Edward's brother]—to remain with or leave them.

Sir John St. Aubyn & her Ladyship are the same kind people as ever—and both were much disappointed not to see you. They passed the winter here in consequence of the little girls having had the measles. I remain at the Nelson. Sir John is often talking *to me of you* and is acquainted with your story—was so—at Geneva this June. Nothing, he says, he has ever lamented so much as that you & Lady St. A. were not acquainted. The same reason that operated with you not to propose it at Geneva, also operated on her. You must be known to each other, she says, some of these days. You saw William John's marriage in the papers with [? no notice of Sir John's or Miss Lennan]. Edward is worth 50 of his brother—indeed I know no one to be compared with him.

Where is Mrs. Shelley & what is become of poor Clare. Do you hear from them. I wish to write, if I had their address. Trelawny you of course hear from. His Mother [Mrs. Maria Trelawny Brereton] and Sisters I have met here. They are the most masculine of their Sex. One of the Sisters is upwards of six feet high & the Mother a perfect Trelawny in petticoats . . . One of the Sisters is married to a Frenchman & the other most likely will be to Some of the Officers of the Garde . . . that ride with them every day & waltz with them every night.

Notwithstanding the dissipations of this vita plena, I never was in better health—tho' I turn night into day, seldom being in bed at 3 in the morning—a different life from the one I used to lead in Italy.

Pray let me hear from you in a few days & let me know with my best Respects how your Mother's health is. Kiss the dear Children for me & believe me

> My dear Jane
> Your affectionate friend
> T. Medwin

Four days earlier, on December 8, 1822, he had written to Byron about his postponed marriage, in a letter that rather fully reveals the nature of their relationship—its remarkable informality, their common interest in the more colorful forms of human life and in the literature and literary gossip of the day. The letter establishes solidly the honesty and accuracy of the account of their friendship as it emerges from Medwin's *Conversations*. He wrote,[101]

My dear Lord Byron,

Many thanks for your congratulations on my marriage—which has not taken place. When it will is not yet decided. You will have been expecting to hear from me on another subject—and I should have written earlier but have been awaiting an answer from England respecting the Yacht. The answer, I am sorry to say, is that *yours* is too small in tonnage for my friend, who however thinks the price so reasonable that you can have no difficulty in finding a purchaser. I will use my utmost exertions to do so at the Salon des Etrangers among all those coming into Italy—at [? that said] Salon our Compatriots have not been the only, tho' the greatest, Sufferers.

Mr. Ball, once called Golden Ball, by a means of alchymy has transmuted his precious metal into red and white counters—he left 40,000 at Brooke's before he came to Paris—so that Lady Jane Paget had rather a lucky escape—he is one of the most leaden-bullet-headed fellows in existence.

---

[101] Unpublished letter from Medwin to Byron, Dec. 8, 1822, in the possession of Sir John Murray. Medwin's translation did not appear in *The Liberal*, but Mary Shelley was "sure they would be glad to insert in The Liberal a good translation of the Mss. he [Medwin] read to us at Pisa" (from an unpublished letter in the Abinger Collection, Mary to Jane Williams, Jan. 12, 1823).

You saw an account in Galignani's of the dinner [on November 11] we gave to Moore at the Salon. We had the pleasure of drinking your health on that occasion. The toast was proposed by Sir Godfrey Webster, one of the Stewards, with a very appreciative and pretty speech. Sir G. is not the only one of your friends here. You may have heard of a Lady Oxford. She opens her house here to all the Liberals and there was considerable talk of her following Sir Robt. Wilson in his exile [in Spain; in 1821 his political opponents had succeeded in having him, a major-general, dismissed from the Army]. Her female acquaintances are not very select.

It is a question whether Lady Barrington reflects most credit on hers or she on Lady B's. Lord H— *looks* as if he had not given up all his old propensities.

Moore hastened home sooner than the others intended in order to forward the publication of his Loves of the Angels—and if possible to get it out before *yours* [*i. e., Heaven and Earth*]. I understand he says he *suggested* the subject. He told me that the passage in Genesis [VI, 1–2] was a mistranslation & that he meant to treat it simply as mythological. There is a third Loves of the Angels in the Press by a Mr. Wise, who married a Roman angel, a daughter of Lucien Buonaparte's.

I see Werner advertised [published November 23, 1822] but not Heaven and Earth [published in the second number of *The Liberal*, January 1, 1823]. Surely the Bibliopolist is not playing fool for his own sake & that of his pocket.

I overheard an anecdote of you the other day from a Mr. Darby who is paid £600 a year to furnish The King with a scandalous Chronicle. This Character is a kind of Grimm, and corresponds with royalty. He was telling a story of your travestying yourself as a Parish Clerk and instead of the Chapters of the day your fairly shouting some lines which were a Paraphrase. The Verses were certainly fine, and I should think yours—the rest of course a fabrication. I have met frequently a new married Lady from the North who is very intimate with Lady B[yron]. I thought your telling Lady B. that you had married a Blue stocking without wit and an Heiress without money not improbable. She said that your Daughter was a prodigy of talent but very excentric and difficult to manage. The story of the Portrait and the green cloth that is not to be removed till she comes of age you of course know. If we met I think I could amuse you with some of this Lady's conversations.

Lord Stair met with a curious adventure the other day. At a Soiree a Frenchman came up to him & said with an Oath that he was ugliest Dog he had ever seen. After some sharp words, it ended with the Aggressor giving Lord S. his Card. On Enquiry, it appeared that the Frenchman had so bad a Character that Lord S. would not meet him. He accordingly put the affair into the hands of his Courier, who at last discovered the gentleman sitting at an [? Illuminat, *i. e.*, a gathering of the illuminati] with some of his Cronies.

Shaking a stick over his back, he said that he came from Lord Stair to say he should use it the first time he met him, for that any other satisfaction was out of the question, but adding that he was not so particular as his master and that he was ready to have a Gallerie [*sic*] du Corps & Sabre whenever he liked.

The continued fogs of Paris often make me wish myself in Tuscany or rather passing the winter again with you at Pisa. In its society Paris is however rather an agreeable place. The Salon is a great recourse, and we have a Travellers Club, where a considerable quantity of Burgundy & Champaigne is consumed. That small character, and we call him [G. B.] Belzoni, belongs to it. Trelawny is a mere little gentleman to Belzoni. He is very full of a pretended discovery that has been made by one [Jean François] Champollion which serves as a Clue to the Hyeroglyphics. It is pretended that some of the Obelisks at Rome are inscribed with the names of the Emperors who sent them there, Trajan, Antoninus, &c. All the Parisian world are therefore mad for Egyptian antiquities. This is a very stupid Letter, but I have a dreadful headache this morning & you may help ease it. Remember me to Trelawny & believe me in all sincerity

> My dear Lord Byron
> Your attached and faithful
> T. Medwin

P. S. I enclose a Translation from Ariosto, if [? both] Hunts think it worth inserting in the next Liberal, against which there is a most violent outcry.

Perhaps it was Medwin's headache, perhaps his preoccupation with Ariosto which kept him from understanding that he was in the presence of a very great discovery, for Champollion had indeed read the hieroglyphic inscription on the Bankes obelisk and in 1824 published his *Précis du système hiéroglyphique*. The mystery had been finally solved, but Medwin was thinking of other things. Early in the new year, 1823, he wrote again to Jane Williams,[102]

My dear Jane,

Your kind and long letter has been a daily reproach to me. I am a sad correspondent at all times, but now every moment of my time is occupied by some bit of dissipation—and to you I ought to find time to write. This Paris is a detestable place—every day increases my dislike of it—it makes me more dissatisfied with myself and the way I spend my time or rather misspend it. Will you believe that I have not written a line or scarcely read a book since I came here now nearly three months.

I don't think Paris would suit you—it is abominably expensive—and the dirtiest town in the world. You may form some idea of the former when I tell you that I pay for a miserable lodging 200 francs a month, my Cabriolet & horse (which I bought) 100, my servant the same. This is a paltry part of one's expenses—in fact I spend three times as much as I did in Italy or Switzerland.

I shall leave Paris the first week in March, probably for Switzerland. I shall go in my Cabriolet—by Vetturino stages. I had some idea of passing the Spring in London but cannot afford it. One of my principal reasons for wishing it is to see you and the Children.

You do not tell me and I am anxious to know what can be the impediments to your obtaining the letters of administration. What and who can oppose it? If I recollect right the will [of Edward E. Williams] is so worded that your *foe* can have no claim in it. I am happy to find that you have so good a friend in Baird. I always thought him one of the best men in existence. You give an excellent

[102] Unpublished letter from Medwin to Jane Williams, in the Abinger Collection, dated only the "8th." The month is very probably January, for Jane wrote on Feb. 12, 1823, to Mary Shelley, "Medwin tells me his marriage is postponed for a year or two" (from an unpublished letter in the Abinger Collection).

account of the Children. Of Mrs. Williams' offers I know nothing but from one of your letters and am sure you have acted right in rejecting them. Indeed, I know not on any terms how you could have consented to part with either of the dear things to be educated by a woman such as I have always considered Mrs. W. Is she in Paris. If she were I think I should probably have met her—but there are so many different Societies here that I might not.

We often talk of you at Sir John's. They are both the best people I know—and I like their fireside better than all the gay parties in Paris. John (the *Parson*) is with them. I like him least of all the St. Aubyns. I always thought him a mere imitation of his father— the Copy for the original—a formal and ceremonious character. Edward is still unwell & the little boys are coming from Geneva. They go to Harrow at Easter. *My friends* leave Paris in March.

Your wishes for my happiness I know to be sincere, but they are not likely to be realized for some time; probably our marriage will be deferred for a year—perhaps even longer. Mrs. Payne talks of making an acquaintance with you in the Spring. You *will*, you *must* like her.

I was very sorry to hear of poor Clare's persecution. Her acquaintance with Lord Byron must have been the cause of her misfortune & probably that of her brother. What will become of Mrs. Shelley? Have you seen the Liberal? There is a reply to it published, called The London Liberal, that I am told speaks a good deal about Pisa—& the people who composed Lord B's Society. I am very curious to see it. There is a paper called The Stars of Pisa— another the Twin Sisters! I heard from Lord B a fortnight ago, but he gives me no news of Genoa. You tell me Trelawny has left it. Had B. & himself any quarrel which occasioned their parting. A very odd thing was told me of T—— the other day by an Officer in the Guards. Some years ago when on guard at the Opera T. did something that caused a public apology from him in the Morning Post. All his family are here—they are as odd as himself. One of the sisters is married to a French Officer who calls himself a Count, and the younger one is this day to be married to a Capt. Barlow, who was in the 8th Drgs. You may have heard his name. They have been acquainted about 3 weeks. The eldest is 6 foot 1, a fine Grenadier.

I suspect Capt. B. will have to fight his way thro' the whole Garde Du Corps, before he is permitted to carry off his prize. These said

Gents are the Locusts of Paris & infest every place. No private families admit them if possible, but they push their way every where. Their great Rendez vous is Mrs. Trelawny's.

People here talk of the War with Spain [liberated in 1814, with the help of the English, from the yoke of Napoleon] as a certainty—but I do not much concern myself with Politics. Let me know when you expect the 8th from India & if you hear from *Major* W[illiams]—probably he will quit the Regiment when they return. I was glad to hear that your Mother's health was reinstated. I thought her very ill when in London, pray give my best respects to her—Kiss the Children for me & believe me

My dearest friend
Ever affectionately yours
T. Medwin

P. S. Pray let me hear from you in a few posts. Do not follow my bad example. Adieu.

Jane thought the postponement of Medwin's marriage for a year or more was a "fearful chasm, and I know not what to think." [103] But Mrs. Payne had evidently thought better of marrying Medwin, and in his next letter to Jane, February 25, 1823, there is no mention of marriage. He wrote with news of particular interest to her—news of her husband and of the burial of Shelley's ashes in Rome, January 21, 1823. Medwin's great love is clear. [104]

My dearest friend,

I have indeed been anxious to hear from you—and am disturbed that your silence has been occasioned by the causes you mention. I am only surprized by one thing—that the event had not taken place before, from the knowledge I have of the parties. It must have proved a great affliction to your poor mother—and you my dear Jane have sorrows enough of your own.

A Circumstance has occurred here with which it is necessary you

[103] Unpublished letter from Jane Williams to Mary Shelley, Feb. 12, 1823, in the Abinger Collection.
[104] Unpublished letter from Medwin to Jane Williams, Feb. 25, 1823, in the Abinger Collection.

and Mrs. Cleveland [Jane's mother] should be acquainted. The wretch [Jane's legal husband] who has been the bane of your existence is about to pay the forfeit of his crimes with his Life or at least will be condemned to the Gallies for life. He has been in Paris for some months—during which he has sported a handsome equipage & servants. By means of his appearance he contrived to pass himself off as having been Consul at Java, and was received at several of the best French Houses, among the rest at the Duc D'Aumont's. There he happened to be seen by a friend of mine, Capt. Bergher of the 16th Drag[oons], who immediately recognized him as a person who had been turned out of a gambling house in London for issuing forged notes, and having been tried at the Old Bailey (after having been in Newgate *for stealing a Watch*). Bergher immediately communicated these facts to The Duke, who ordered him to be turned out. This occurred about three weeks since. Two days ago an Italian came to Bergher's Home and told him he had something of consequence to communicate. It was that he had been hired by that nameless Villain to assassinate him and mentioning the place and time fixed upon.

B. sent for a lawyer & having taken down his deposition, afterwards went to the Ambassador's—and I suppose he is before this in safe Custody. I suppose all this will shortly appear in the papers, but I will let you know more in a few days.

Every one here speaks of the War as a certainty—it is to me very doubtful what part the English ministry will take. I have no confidence in any of them. There is no doubt that their line of policy should be to protect the Spaniards. It would be the most popular war England ever entered upon. [Following the Spanish revolution of 1820, which restored the constitution and made a prisoner of Ferdinand VII, Spain existed in a state of Liberal anarchy. The French asked permission to intervene and restore order, Britain protested vigorously, but the majority of the powers granted the mandate, and French forces entered Spain on April 7, 1823. The Spanish people cooperated to restore to power the base Ferdinand VII.]

My hatred to the French increases every day, & my dislike to Paris, and I should be glad to see a war if it were only to drive home all the English that are colonizing in France. I was yesterday dining at Versailles—where there are not less than 2,000 English—

every Town is filled with them. Paris would not suit you after Italy. It is very expensive and a vile climate.

My plans are as unfixed or more so than they were. Sometimes I think of going home, at others I am inclined to join the Patriots in Spain, having had great offers of promotion. I am however determined to see you and the Children if possible—and shall not mind a journey to England, if solely for this purpose. In the present state of political affairs I could not recommend your coming on the Continent. Sir John has almost given up Geneva, and will most likely return to England in the Spring. I dine with them very often, and they always ask after you in the most affectionate way. They are dear good people. I find more real delight in their society than in all the fooleries of Paris dissipation. I am quite sick of Balls and Routs and wish heartily to be quiet.

I had little hope, from my knowledge of Sir Timothy's Character and my interviews with him, that he would do any thing for Mrs. Shelley. I was quite disgusted by the want of feeling displayed by the whole family and have a thorough contempt for them all. I had a letter some days back from my friend [Sir Charles] Slyte, mentioning the interment of his ashes at Rome. He ends by saying, "The high vale of the burial ground shaded the grave from the Sun that was beautifully bright. I could not forbear wishing that a last ray of its light might have fallen on all that remains of what was and ever will be dear in the recollection of you and me—Shelley, previous to its consignment to earth." This was written by a man who had never known him but in his writings! And his own family!—what wretches there are in the world, my dear Jane. If it were not for you and a few individuals, I think I should soon become misanthropical.

I rejoice to hear that Mrs. Williams has shown an intention of doing some justice to your dear Children. Is she in London? I long much to see the dear creatures. God bless you and them, my dearest friend, & believe me

Yours most affectionately,
T. Medwin

The details of Medwin's story about Jane's husband were confirmed in the newspapers, and Jane summarized the account in a letter to Mary on March 27, adding, "the papers say the agent is in custody but the principal is still at large in Paris. He will escape, be assured!" Jane had been trying to secure from Mrs. Williams a picture of the dead Edward, she wrote to Mary, and had chosen Edward's old friend F. Cox to carry on the negotiations. But Jane regretted her choice and decided that Cox was "a fool and cold hearted, and a luke warm friend . . . Medwin would have been a better person, for he is sincere at all events to me." [105]

Meanwhile, several other friends were thinking of Medwin, for the aid that he could offer. Lady Mount Cashell ("Mrs. Mason") wrote from Pisa in March to Mary Shelley, concerning Mary's efforts to persuade Sir Timothy Shelley to grant an allowance, "Why not employ Mr. Medwin to go to the old gentleman?" It is not clear that Mary ever gave this mission to Medwin, but on April 10, making her plans to return to England, she did write to Jane, "Pray tell me if Medwin is in Paris—& if he is, where? as I should wish to see him as I pass through—& should even write to him first to get an apartment for me for the few days I may stay there." [106]

But Mary did not get to Paris until August, and by that time Medwin had been five months or more in England. On April 22, 1823, he wrote to Byron again, from Stephens Hotel, Bond Street.[107]

My dear Lord Byron,

It is long since I have had the pleasure of hearing *of* you, *from* you I could have wished—but had scarcely any right to expect. When I write to you a second time, perhaps my letter comes with rather a bad grace, as it is accompanied with two requests. One is that you will permit me to dedicate to you a Dramatic Legend that

[105] Unpublished letter from Jane Williams to Mary Shelley, March 27, 1823, in the Abinger Collection.

[106] Unpublished letter from Mary Shelley to Jane Williams, April 10, 1823; letter from Lady Mount Cashell to Mary Shelley, March 4, 1823, both letters in the Abinger Collection.

[107] Unpublished letter from Medwin to Byron, April 22, 1823, in the possession of Sir John Murray. C. L. Cline (*Byron, Shelley*, p. 195), quotes two sentences from it.

I have written on the Subject of The Wandering Jew—entitled Ahasuerus, the Wanderer. It is to be published at Whittaker's. Mr. Murray I twice wrote to—proposing the work to him—but with an insolence common to that Autocrat (and which were he a gentleman would require chastisement) I received no reply.

Of the merits of the poem it does not become me to speak—but I have shown it to one of the Editors of the Edinburgh Quarterly, who promises to review it most favorably—& flatters me most highly in his commendation of it. In one of the characters under the name of Julian, I have attempted to give a sketch of our poor friend Shelley & this may perhaps prove some claim to your sanctioning my dedication. Now to my second request. You congratulated me somewhat prematurely in your Letter to Paris on my marriage.

Circumstances occur to defer that event for at least 12 months longer—and that interval I wish to occupy by some active employment.

At Paris I became intimate with the Duke San Lorazo & the Constitutional Spanish Party, & he kindly offered to take me on his staff, if I could obtain leave from the Horse Guards. This I failed to do, & the [?   ] has been thrown out [the sense may be that the Constitutional Party has been overthrown]. The same obstacle, though nominally existing, does not apply so strictly to the Greek Cause.

You, being in the Mediterranean & probably having sources of information not in my power to obtain, may rather assist me in this plan of joining that cause, which I know you have so much at heart, either with your advice or introductions. Mavro Cordato I passed a winter with at Pisa & am well acquainted with—so that I shall not be wholly a stranger.

I calculate that in the course of a month I can have an answer to these two requests. Remember me to Count Pietro & believe that there is no one more sincerely & faithfully yours than myself.

T. Medwin

Byron, in the midst of his own thoughts about Greece, Teresa, Lady Blessington, and other matters—on May 6 he completed the first draft of Canto XVI of *Don Juan*—took the trouble to write at once, on May 5, a letter to Hobhouse that would be "presented to you by my friend Capt. T. Medwin, who, at my request, will introduce himself to you as member of the Greek Committee, and explain some plan that he has formed with regard to offering his services to the Greeks,—a subject in which we are all interested. I need not say more than that any attention to him will be appreciated by me as an additional obligation due to you . . ."[108]

This letter of introduction must have been accompanied by a covering letter, in reply to Medwin's own, and he prints in his *Conversations* what he says is an excerpt from it, although it was either overlooked or rejected by Prothero, when editing Byron's *Letters and Journals*. It seems significant that the date of Medwin's excerpt is that of the note of introduction addressed to Hobhouse. The excerpt seems to ring true, even to Byron's slang use of the word *going*, his concession to Medwin or Medwin's style. And it is undoubtedly true that Medwin would not have dared to dedicate *Ahasuerus* to Byron without his consent. Byron replied to Medwin, then, it seems,[109] the etceteras being Medwin's,

"Werner" was the last book Murray published for me, and three months after came out the Quarterly's article on my plays, when "Marino Faliero" was noticed for the first time, &c.

I need not say that I shall be delighted by your inscribing your "Wanderer" to me; but I would recommend you to think twice before you inscribe a work to *me*, as you must be aware that at present I am the most unpopular writer going, and the odium on the dedicatee may recur on the dedicator. If you do not think this a valid objection, of course there can be none on my part, &c.

Perhaps one of the greatest assurances that Byron wrote these words is the note of reluctance in the last sentences. Medwin would not have invented it.

After a reviewer had implied that Byron had never granted permission for *Ahasuerus* to be dedicated to him, Medwin wrote an indignant note, years later, in the margins of page 211 of his *Conversations*, "Is it likely that I should venture to write

---

[108] Byron's *Letters and Journals*, VI, 201–203.
[109] Medwin, *Conversations*, pp. 210–211.

on the Title page, 'dedicated by permission to Lord Byron' without his sanction?" These words, in fact, do not appear on the title page. Instead, on the third leaf, the dedication page, we read, "To The Right Hon. Lord Byron, This Poem Is Inscribed By His Friend. Paris, March 1, 1823."

Medwin continues, in the marginal note just quoted, "The et caetera, which I did not give [in the *Conversations*] from fear of being taxed with vanity, was as follows: 'You showed me, I remember, a passage at Pisa, I suppose intended for the Poem, and which I thought well of. I pede faults, which rendered fully means—look to your feet—or you may be undone by the reviewers.' I was at no loss to understand the reference and his version from the circumstance of his having criticized one or two of the lines as lame *of a foot*, with a foot too short."

This, presumably, was the last letter Medwin ever received from Byron, if the poet did in fact write precisely the words attributed to him. Their friendship, as short as it was remarkable, had closed. In less than a year and a half, Medwin would proclaim it to all the world.

It would seem that he never presented Byron's note of introduction to Hobhouse, the man he came to regard as his greatest enemy, for when Byron's letter arrived in late May, Medwin was ill. Jane Williams wrote to Mary Shelley, June 15, 1823, "Medwin has never been well since he left my Mother's house [in London]; he has had a slow fever for 3 months and is only now out of the Doctor's hands. This has of course reduced him very much." [110] He convalesced at fashionable Cheltenham, famous for the effects of its waters upon complaints of the liver, and wrote to Jane from Stiles's Hotel. [111]

My dear Jane,
    I was sorry to leave town without seeing you. I thought it uncertain, your being at home at the hour we fixed—and there was a

[110] Unpublished letter from Jane Williams to Mary Shelley, June 15, 1823, in the Abinger Collection.
[111] Unpublished letter from Medwin to Jane Williams, dated only "Sunday," but written in the summer of 1823; in the Abinger Collection.

certain person that detained me beyond the time. I am one of those who think not there is a pleasing painfulness in parting with those we are fond of—tho' on the latter occasion the *substantive* predominated. I believe Presentiments are very fallacious and may be often placed to the state of the Stomach & too much or too little *Bile. This* makes me recollect that I am at its great enemy, Cheltenham, & you will expect that I shall give you some account of it.

Cheltenham differs little from other watering places. It has white houses with green sashes and sometimes Verandahs, and I have seen, tho' the pain that has been almost ever-present since my arrival quite precluded my going out, some spectral yellow faced people strolling about that might well give rise to Beppo's wife's exclamation & question,

'Well if ever
I saw any thing so yellow! How's your Liver?'

We travelled with such rapidity—near 10 miles an hour, that I had little time for reflection. In the road, I was so enveloped in my cloak to shelter from the rain (& that at last became a wet blanket about me) that I saw little of the country. This is however rich, & romantic. There is a hill in sight that is not unlike the [? Jalaun] & the Malvern range is visible when the atmosphere is clear—*once or twice a year.* To say the truth—with a pleasant companion one might pass a few weeks here not unagreeably. The verdure is most luxuriant. The Public walks when the acacias are in full bloom well gravelled and extensive. The country houses in the environs stand *single,* not in rows—& have an *Indian,* a[? Chouringee] look—and the air & water contribute to give an appetite—what a sensual conclusion to the sentence. Whether it be that all the world here talks of nothing but Bile, Biliary ducts, & Liver, & have *looks* a comment to the words, that by sympathy with *others,* the reflexes of their own, I have been suffering much, a kind which is equally bad from my head & side, to say nothing about my heart, since I came here.

I am living at a Pension—the oldest & largest in the place, which as far as the House, Table & accomodations go is excellent—& modest at 2 Guineas & a half a week. But Table D'Hotes in England are exotic things, and do not suit John Bullishness & [?]. Abroad you meet foreigners of all nations & well informed and travelled people. Here—let me look round: 3 or 4 old maids on a forlorn hope—mere old [? Madams] that ought not to have been *transplanted*—an apothecary who bores me to death—& Sirs and Madames coming in every instant, with an Oh coming in every minute like a Bass note—& several nondescripts male & female, in the whole 14. One Aesculapius told me for my comfort that my liver was seriously affected & wanted to put me on a preparatory course of a month before I began swallowing the Water—but I began immediately—& this morning swallowed to his astonishment half a dozen [Rolls *or* Bowls: *paper torn by seal*] for breakfast.

Miss Knight's address is 57 Berness Street, & beg her to make, when you call, a Copy of our dear for me, with your suggested alterations. Also of Byron, if you can not get me one of [? Wield *or* Wivel]. I enclose you the quadrilles & Waltz which I carried out of Town; they were employed till the last moment in copying them. I forgot to ask you, when I last saw you, to lend me this Summer, poor Edward's gun. I am too poor at present to buy one. You can send it me by the Cheltenham Coach, which goes every morning from the Bolt in Ten Fleet Street.

Pray write to me in a day or two. Tell me all about the dear little ones & kiss them for me. I think I shall kill a fortnight here but at least 10 Days more. You shall know my destination—but I hope to see you & them in the course of the autumn. Tell me when you hear from Mary—& believe me, my dear Jane

Most affectionately yours

T. Medwin

He was thirty-five years old; he had had adventures and had known two of the greatest men in the world, but he was sick and homeless. In his less cheerful moments he saw himself as a man whose

fine features had become marked and hard in their outline, his cheek shrunk and liny, and his figure, once distinguished for a rare beauty, and six upright feet of honest measure without his shoes, was bowed about the shoulders with no classic bend . . . He . . . had just arrived . . . with . . . half a liver, to pay his devotions to Hygeia, in that paradise of chemists [Cheltenham], where a decoction of Epsom salts and soda passes current for the genuine elixir vitae, an unadulterated spa.[112]

[112] Medwin, *Angler*, I, 3–4.

But in his fevered imagination he saw himself as the type of the cursed and homeless man, the Wandering Jew, outcast and incapable of loving, try as he may. For it is Medwin who is the title character of *Ahasuerus, The Wanderer,* completed in its final form in the spring of 1823. In his travels in the most distant and exotic lands, Ahasuerus has even seen the great cave temples of Ellora, but he remains the eternal spectator, never the participant, as men through the centuries turn from him, sensing in him some crime greater than they can commit, some guilt greater than they can incur. His handsome forehead is stamped with the "weight of weariless woe," and he carries "The memory of some joy forbidden,/ The forfeiture and loss of Eden." [113] His greatest wish is to die.

But Medwin, in all probability, went fishing in Wales for a month, "to make a new constitution amidst its mountains, its lakes, and rivers, and to seek a remedy for that *taedium vitae,* doing nothing and having nothing to do, in what had always been 'my passion and my enjoyment,' angling." [114]

He returned to London, his health restored, and it was probably during the latter months of 1823 that he "frequently met Mrs. Siddons at Lydia White's, where," he recalled, "I had the Entrée." [115] "She seldom missed the Literary Lady's 'Conversaziones.' I had been introduced to her at John Kemble's at Lausanne and reminded her of the circumstance. I had no idea of hurting her publicly, but she either was or affected to be so much affected by the reminiscence that she quitted her chair and crossed to the other side of the room." Perhaps Medwin did not know that Mrs. Siddons's brother, John Kemble, had died on February 26. Medwin continued,

[113] Medwin, *Ahasuerus, The Wanderer: A Dramatic Legend, in Six Parts* (London, 1823), Part I.

[114] Medwin, *Angler,* I, 5. The summer of 1823 is the most probable date for the Welsh tour that was the basis for the *Angler.* Julian is said to be thirty-five years old, as Medwin was in 1823; the tour begins at Cheltenham, where Julian had come for his health, as Medwin.

[115] Medwin's unpublished marginalia in his *Conversations,* p. 167.

She carried the actress with her into Society and was pompous as a Tragedy queen. The Circle at Lydia's was very small, on two occasions consisting of nearly the same individuals—Sir Humphry Davy, [William Stuart] Rose the Translator of Tasso [i. e., Ariosto], a pale, tall, serious looking man, Sotherby [sic; Byron had satirized Sotheby as "Botherby"], Cohen, whom Lord Byron mentions with thanks for his Translation of the Chronica di Sanuto [sic] relating to Marino Faliero, and two or three others.

After Shelley and Byron, who recently, on April 26, had included Lydia White and Sotheby in his satire of *The Blues,* this was very small literary beer indeed. Medwin turned with relief to Sir Humphry Davy and was delighted to hear him hold forth at length on his favorite sport, flyfishing.[116]

Medwin had been in London long enough. On December 28, 1823, he called on Mary Shelley and the great Godwin,[117] and by early January he was back again in Paris, where new adventures awaited him, as he tried to lose his unhappiness amid the glittering trivialities and the splendid treasures of the French capital.

[116] Medwin, *Angler,* I, 12–13.
[117] Unpublished diary of William Godwin, in the Abinger Collection.

5

Irving and
The Conversations of Byron

On January 8, 1824, in Paris, Medwin met an admirer of Byron quite as enthusiastic as he himself. It was Washington Irving, forty-one years old and famous as the author of *Knickerbocker* and *The Sketch Book* but his interest not yet seriously directed to Spain, which was to become a rich mine for him. For the moment a member of an idle society, trying unsuccessfully to write for the stage, he was polishing up *Tales of a Traveller* (1824) but otherwise leading a desultory and socially exhausting life. A literary lion on the loose, he was involved in a whirl of social engagements.

Medwin, however, was "always a stimulant to him," and their friendship "was one of the most interesting literary friendships of Irving's life."[1] According to Irving's biographer, Stanley T. Williams, "Medwin was one of the chief mediums of the influence" of Lord Byron upon Irving, "an influence that . . . is very noticeable in various essays of Irving's."[2] In addition, Medwin's tales of Italian banditti held him "deeply attentive," and their influence was also to appear in Irving's work, notably in *Tales of a Traveller,* in which three stories owed their existence to Medwin, who read to Irving a "journal of a painter while prisoner of the robbers near Rome," the subject of these

[1] Stanley T. Williams, *The Life of Washington Irving* (New York, 1935), I, 273, 454, note 30.

[2] *Journal of Washington Irving (1823–1824),* ed. Stanley T. Williams (Cambridge, Mass., 1931), p. 99, note 1. Hereafter referred to as Irving, *Journal.* If in the text the date of an entry from this journal appears, no footnote is attached.

stories.[3] Irving was so excited by what Medwin had read to him that he "awoke very early" the next morning, February 16, 1824, while it was still dark. "Full of uneasy thoughts," he lit his lamp to dispel them, talked at breakfast of an Italian story, and wrote all morning and afternoon on it, despite another visit from Medwin.

Later, on March 24, 1825, when Medwin was back again briefly in Paris, he gave to Irving his notes on the plot of a play or dramatic poem, supposedly drawn from a lost play of Calderón, which Byron had "projected" but never written. The main character was a Spanish nobleman plagued always by the presence of a mysterious stranger, who is finally revealed to be a second self, his conscience. Reduced to despair, all zest gone out of his life and existence itself become a Byronic burden, the nobleman challenges the other to a duel, which proves fatal to the latter. "The mask and mantle of the unknown drop off, and Alfonso [the nobleman] discovers his own image,—the spectre of himself: he dies with horror."[4] Medwin informed Irving that "the idea was taken from a Spanish play, called . . . the *Encapotado,* and was furnished to Byron by Shelley, as his Lordship did not understand Spanish." The play, Medwin wrote, "is so rare, that Washington Irving told me he had hunted for it, but without success, in several of the public libraries of Spain."[5] Medwin noted the similarity of the story to that of Cypriano and said that the play had been attributed to Calderón, whose works the two men may have discussed in 1824.

This plot fascinated Irving, and he gave to it at least three separate expressions. The day after talking with Medwin, he sketched out a play based on it. He never completed the play, but in the August, 1835, issue of the *Knickerbocker New York Monthly Magazine,* he published "An Unwritten Drama of Lord

---

[3] Williams, *Life of Irving,* II, 292–293; Irving, *Journal,* p. 128.

[4] Irving, "An Unwritten Drama of Lord Byron," *Knickerbocker New York Monthly Magazine,* VI (August, 1835), 142–143.

[5] Medwin, *Shelley,* p. 405.

Byron," which was a polished version of the notes given to him by Medwin, and the same article appeared also in *The Gift, A Christmas and New Year's Present for 1836.* (It has been pointed out that Edgar Allan Poe's "William Wilson" is also indebted to this plot, through Irving.) But in 1841 it received its most triumphant expression in Irving's "Don Juan: A Spectral Research," when Don Manuel "lost all self-command, rushed up to the bier, and beheld the counterpart of himself."[6]

The diligent searches of modern scholars have been no more successful than the inquiries of Irving in finding the play of Calderón which was, supposedly, the original source of the story. Did Medwin make up this narrative of man's dual nature, the seed of it Byron's relation to him of a waking nightmare or vision Shelley had at San Terenzo in 1822?[7]

But more important than this Spanish plot was Medwin's enthusiastic interest in Calderón and other Spanish poets, which helped to lead Irving to immerse himself for three years in the literature of Spain and to produce finally *The Conquest of Granada* and *Legends of the Alhambra.* The literary influence was also reciprocal, and Medwin's share of it will be pointed out later.

Medwin, who found the *Sketch Book* "delightful," thought the polished and amiable Irving "one of the best men I know, . . . reflected in all he has written."[8] They met at the home of Thomas Moore's landlord, the good-humored Spaniard Villamil, then confined with the gout. Present also were Lord John Russell, a son of Sir John St. Aubyn (perhaps Edward), and "the Last grand Inquisitor of Spain." Villamil delivered a dissertation on craniology, and Medwin told Irving that "Byron is very abstemious & has reduced himself quite thin— Is in excellent health." Irving identified his informant as "Capt Medwin a friend of Lord Byrons & author of the Wandring Jew." Irving

[6] See Williams, *Life of Irving,* I, 466–467, note 8.
[7] See Medwin, *Shelley,* pp. 404–405.
[8] Medwin, "Hazlitt in Switzerland: A Conversation," *Fraser's Magazine,* XIX (March, 1839), 283.

had been up since four o'clock in the morning, reading *Don Juan.*

This was on January 8, 1824. After Irving read Medwin's *Ahasuerus, The Wanderer* on January 26 and found in it, he recorded in his journal, "many beautiful passages," their friendship developed rapidly. On that day, after finishing the poem, he called on Medwin, promised to dine with him the next day and to go with him that night to Mrs. Popkins, a name which Irving used in "The Adventures of the Popkins Family," thus incurring the displeasure of the family. Medwin called that evening at nine for him, but they went first to the home of Lady Susan Douglas, an incurable party-giver who went "about haunting her own house in quest of the tea cup that any one of the company has set down. Misses silver &c. Looks like the ghost of a Housekeeper that had forgot to lock up the spoons before she died." At her house Medwin met a party of twelve or more, among them the Villamils, the Grattans, the American Miss Caldwell, Lord Miltown, Lady Milman, and several Spanish. Miss Caldwell, whose cousin had built a whole town on Lake George, was commonly called "Puss Caldwell," Irving noted. Having quarreled with her landlady and thus unable to give a party at her own house, she went "about asking people to other peoples balls &c. [and] so entertains her friend[s] miscellaneously at other peoples expense." She was capable of talking "slapdash" with Thomas Colley Grattan, who was, Irving observed, "one of those fellows that opens his mouth at a venture & trusts god will send him a meaning." Medwin at this time had a sharper satiric eye for this society than Irving had—in two months Medwin would write with a friend a satire on the English in Paris which Irving thought "cruelly severe"—and the two men must have had many a laugh at the follies of the travelling English and others. But Medwin was proud of his friendship with Grattan, who in 1823, the year before, had dedicated to Irving his *Highways and Byways*, had already written a poetic romance, and would go on to become British consul at Boston and help negotiate the Ashburton Treaty, between his country and the United States.

From Lady Douglas's party Medwin and Irving went on to Mrs. Popkins's hotel, where they found her rooms crowded but the music good and the women pretty, and they stayed until one o'clock, when "a little girl began recitations."

On the next day Medwin gave a stag dinner. He invited Irving, Edward St. Aubyn, son of Sir John, and Jenkinson, a painter with a "fine family of daughters & spaniels." The number of the latter was legion, and Jenkinson's house was overrun by them. Although Jenkinson had been painting landscapes only four years, Irving thought that he had achieved "great proficiency." [9] Medwin entertained this group with his conversation about "India Sports &c &c &c."

Pressing a little, Medwin made a call on January 29 and was not admitted by Irving, but Irving returned it on February 1 and stayed for an hour and a half. Medwin read to him "a poetical letter of Shelleys [the then unpublished *Julian and Maddalo*] giving a description of a ride near Venice with L. Byron & return to Dresden [*sic*] by water—with fine description of Lunatic, a mad house on an island &c &c." Irving left to make another call but returned to Medwin's and

drove with him in his cabriolet to Bois de Boulogne—all Paris in motion— Long talk ab[ou]t Ld Byron— He writes at fits—has intervals when he cannot write sometimes 2 & 3 weeks— Does not revise nor correct much—writes sometimes in Bed—rises at 12 sometimes 2—eats a crust in a cup of tea with Egg—rides out at 4. When in writing mood writes at any time—if persons are present he often writes & talks—does not seclude & deny himself. Never speaks ill of Lady B. When her father died [*sic*] he wrote a most affectionate & moving letter—wished a reconcilliation—recd no reply but a cold message thro his sister— When he dines by himself is very abstemious as to wine—when he has company he drinks freely—gives away large sums—reads miscellaneously all the mod-

[9] Irving, *Journal*, pp. 115, 128, 166.

ern works—reads much—does not study—never touches the classics
Is not a good Grecian—understands italian well—reads history &c
relative to the subject he is writing on—Has an excellent memory,
tho not for dates—a poetical memory. Does not like to meet
strangers who are desirous to see him—says they expect great
things, & he is but a common man in conversation—

An unpublished poem of Shelley's, one of his best, and a "long
talk" about Byron—Medwin had won Irving completely.

Medwin's next stag dinner, held on February 5, was larger
than the preceding one. He invited seven men: Lattin, Douglas,
Edward St. Aubyn, Grattan, James Kenney, Jenkinson, and
Irving, who knew all the guests present except Lattin and found
him from the first "very pleasant." Lattin told amusing mala-
propistic stories about the Irish, could relate the history of
famous duels and quote Lucian, shared his quarters with his
very beautiful daughter, Mrs. Mansfield, mother of five children, and entertained Rousseauistic notions about the ethical
advantages of breathing fresh country air, uncontaminated by
the flattery and other vices of the city. Irving became very
fond of Medwin's friend, who had excellent French connections,
among them the Count D'Armond and his sister, the Countess
D'Abeyne, "a very charming pretty woman & spirituelle." [10] But
Lattin suffered sadly from the gout, and Irving was forced to
conclude, after knowing him for about three months, that he
"Might be called a happy man if he did but know it." [11]

Another one of the guests at Medwin's dinner party was
James Kenney the dramatist, friend of Moore, Rogers, Mary
Shelley, and John Howard Payne. His *Sweethearts and Wives*
had been very popular the year before at the Haymarket theatre. A professional playwright, he was to produce more than
forty dramas and operas and at the time that Medwin knew
him was enjoying his highest success. He was full of anecdotes
of the theatre, many of them lamenting the dearth of good

[10] *Ibid.*, p. 126.
[11] *Ibid.*, p. 169.

actors and the mad jealousy of those available. It was an interesting company that Medwin had assembled.

Medwin saw Irving again on February 11, at a mixed dinner given by Lattin, "a very pleasant party," met Irving once more at the Louvre on the next day, and on the fourteenth, while out walking together, Medwin told Irving "how insolently he was treated by Murray who never answered his letters &c & finally when he requested an answer in London, having offered the Mss of his poem to be published at his own expense— recd the Mss back without a word in reply." Murray would soon suffer, in Medwin's *Conversations,* for this treatment. In the evening Irving read *Ahasuerus* aloud to his old friends the Storrows. One of the "many beautiful passages" that he found in the poem is perhaps the following one.[12] He would have explained to the Storrows that it describes Shelley's vision of love, the reality always escaping him in the poem, which quite ignores Mary Shelley.

> And momently, by day and night,
>> The vision of that heavenly maid
>> Stood ever by his side, array'd
> In hues and forms most fair and bright!
> The embodied soul of all that's best
> In nature, purest, loveliest—
> All sense of hearing, feeling, seeing,
> Lost in her universal being!
> No mixture dull of mortal clay,
>> A thing of lakes, and hills, and streams,
>> Of odorous plants, and rainbow beams—
> A radiant sister of the day!
> He saw her when the moonlight breaks
>> Upon the sea's marmoreal bosom;
> He saw her when the sunlight streaks
>> With lines of gold, leaf, bud, and blossom;
> He saw her in the clouds of even—
> He saw her smile in that of heaven!

[12] Medwin, *Ahasuerus, The Wanderer,* Part VI, pp. 88–90.

. . .
There seem'd from the remotest seat
Of the blue mountain's waste,
To the soft flower beneath his feet,
A magic circle traced!
A spirit interfused around,
A thrilling life of sight and sound,
One being his embraced!
And still he felt the centre of
The magic circle there
Was her fair form, that fill'd with love
The living atmosphere!

On the next day, February 15, Medwin read to Irving the painter's journal which was to interest him so greatly and influence him, with its account of the writer's imprisonment by robbers near Rome.[13] On the following morning, while Irving was writing "The Painter's Adventure," Medwin called and stayed "for some time." That evening, after leaving Lady Susan Douglas's, Irving met Medwin again, who went home with him and talked until after midnight. They could hardly have avoided discussing Italian banditti, about whom Medwin was to write stories in later years. Immediately after recording in his journal the time of Medwin's departure, Irving wrote a paragraph of rare isolated moralizing: "It is the convolutions & revolutions that have made all that is romantic and picturesque in morals & manners—what a dull world this would be for poets & painters had there been no deluges or earthquakes and no war—a milennium would be death to poetry . . ." This entry surely reflects some of Medwin's conversation that night, for Medwin was both poet and painter, Irving neither one.

Medwin called on February 19 and by February 24 he knew Frank Mills, Irving's old friend, well enough to invite the two men to dine, along with Jenkinson. Mills, also a friend of Moore, was an unsuccessful playwright whose wealthy brother Charles owned a lavishly furnished villa on Mount Palatine and there

---

[13] Irving, *Journal*, p. 128.

entertained the Blessingtons in 1828. In May, Frank Mills and
Irving would make a trip to England together, after Medwin's
departure for Geneva, but not before Medwin had come to be
on intimate terms with him and had seen much of him. The
results of a later conversation between Mills and Medwin were
to show up in Irving's *Tales of a Traveller*.[14] By March 22 they
had collaborated on a poem satirizing the English in Paris,
seemingly never published.[15] At this time Mills was also working on a manuscript dealing with the Knights Templars. Mills
and Medwin were on excellent terms until, it seems, Medwin
borrowed money from him, and in 1827 Mills, talking with
Medwin's enemy Hobhouse, was very bitter indeed.[16] After
Mills left Paris, he acquired some kind of connection or influence with Henry Colburn, publisher of Medwin's *Conversations,* for it was Mills, according to his own testimony, who
persuaded Colburn to suppress Medwin's pamphlet replying to
Hobhouse's review.[17]

But all this was still concealed in the future. Irving called
on Medwin on February 28, February 29, and March 2, 1824,
and on March 4 Medwin gave another dinner party, where
there was much "talk of Duels—of gallantry &c." It was again
a party of eight. Medwin had invited Mills, Irving, Jenkinson,
and Sir Frederick Henniker, among others. Sir Frederick told
a story of a Major "at the battle of Waterloo who had been
wounded eleven times & swore he would not quit his gun &
was killed on the cannon— A french officer who had three
times taken a cannon—swore he would not leave it—bestrode
it & was killed on it." In 1823 Henniker had published *Notes*

---

[14] *Ibid.,* p. 141, note; Williams, *Life of Irving,* II, 293.

[15] Irving, *Journal,* pp. 151, 155, 161.

[16] John Cam Hobhouse, *Recollections of a Long Life,* ed. Lady
Dorchester (London, 1910), III, 166–167.

[17] Unpublished portion of Hobhouse's diary, Feb. 5, 1827, in the
possession of Sir Charles Hobhouse. On Frank Mills see Irving, *Journal,*
p. 193; Lady Blessington, *The Idler in Italy,* II, 551; and Willard
Connely, *Count D'Orsay,* pp. 110, 123, who appears to have confused
the two brothers.

During a Visit to Egypt, Nubia, the Oasis, Mount Sinai, and Jerusalem.

Two days later Irving called on Jenkinson, who, accompanied by Medwin, "came in with the girls and a legion of dogs"—his daughters and the prolific spaniels. On March 18, Irving left his card at Medwin's lodgings and on the twentieth saw him at a dinner given by Frank Mills. One of the guests was Sir Henry Mildmay, whom Byron remembered as one of the four reigning dandies of his London years. He, with Brummell, had been one of the hosts of the famous ball held in 1813 at the Argyle Rooms, when the Prince Regent upon entering met him and Brummell with a blank, unrecognizing stare. In the silence that followed, it was Brummell who said, clearly enough for all to hear, "Alvanley," to whom the Prince had bowed, "who's your fat friend?" [18] This was heady company for Medwin, and he did not talk about Byron, it seems, in the presence of one who had once moved on intimate terms with the Prince Regent. Unable to compete on these terms, he discussed poetry with Irving and told him that "Moore had talents but not genius . . . He shines in smaller pieces but not in great attempts." So the two authors drew together, and Medwin's judgment of Moore was vindicated by the years.

The next day, March 21, Medwin called, and Irving read to him one of his Italian stories, just completed for *Tales of a Traveller*. That evening they met again at Jenkinson's home, and the following afternoon they walked together, when Medwin told him about the satire he had written with Mills, at whose quarters they met again on March 24 and March 26.

The next day Medwin and Irving dined with Mills and met there the celebrated Theodore Hook, whom Medwin had last seen in Mauritius. At this time the famous wit, who had known Byron at Harrow and been the friend of the Prince Regent, was editing the high Tory newspaper *John Bull*, which he had founded in 1820, following a criminal charge that his accounts as treasurer of the Mauritius were £12,000 short. In 1824 he

[18] Kathleen Campbell, *Beau Brummell* (London, 1948), pp. 116–117.

published *Sayings and Doings, A Series of Sketches from Life,* and in the same year was accused by John Hunt's *Examiner* of taking bribes from West India planters ("an unholy alliance with the Jamaica Slave-owners") in return for favorable treatment in *John Bull.*[19] Before his death, his name had appeared on over forty volumes. Medwin, we may be sure, listened appreciatively as he told an "excellent story" about the learned and formidable Dr. Samuel Parr, to whom Byron had listened "with admiring ignorance, and respectful silence."[20] At Mill's dinner there was "some discussion on Dr. Ps character who was pronounced a great Humbug," and the host, who could not have been much of a scholar, "doubted him as a grecian."[21]

Medwin attended a ball given by a Dr. De Coucy L'Assan on March 29, which Villamil, Grattan, and Irving also attended, there talked to the latter, and on the next day promised Irving "a sight of his Journal in India and also his Italian Journal." Irving lost no time in calling on Medwin and on March 31 "sat for some time with him reading his Journals."

He called again upon Medwin on April 1 and walked with him, and on April 2 dined with Medwin, along with Mills and Jenkinson. They talked of smugglers, and Jenkinson told stories about their chivalry and their ability to negotiate bogs impassable to all others, especially Excisemen.

Medwin met Irving the next day at a dinner given by a Miss Fitzgerald, at which Mr. Dinon "denied that Mad[a]m Tallyrand had mistaken him for Robinson Crusoe," and "a Poet from Caen went about complimenting every one." In the evening Baron Weber, foster brother to Marie Antoinette, came in. Grattan was also there. Medwin must have interested his hostess, for she invited him to dinner again on May 1.

The round of parties continued. On April 5, Medwin dined at the home of Mills in a company that included Sir Henry Mildmay and Charles Cavendish Fulke Greville, who found

[19] *The Examiner,* Oct. 3, 1824, p. 628.
[20] Byron's *Letters and Journals,* IV, 262.
[21] Irving, *Journal,* p. 156.

Irving "deficient in cultivation."[22] Mildmay told a story about an April Fool's joke involving a fictitious Hungarian Prince of Seidlitz who was forced to decline a dinner invitation in Paris. At nine o'clock a letter edged in black arrived, "regretting he could not attend as he had just heard of the death of his cousin the Bishop of Epsom Salts who died at Cheltenham—signed Poisson d'Avril," a catch for April fools. It seems that the expectant hostess was quite taken in by all this, helped along by a calling card which had been engraved with the name Prince of Seidlitz Powder, a laxative.

This life continued for Medwin, who saw Irving three more times before calling on April 17 to take his leave and say that he was going to Geneva.[23] But before he could depart, he was confined to his bed with a "touch of the Liver." This postponed his trip to Geneva but did not keep him in his bed longer than a day or two. When Irving called a second time to visit the sick, on April 20, he found Medwin out, but they saw each other three more times before Medwin left on the morning of May 2 for Geneva, a journey of eight days.

Medwin was to see very few of his Parisian friends and acquaintances again. He had fitted in well with this floating international colony, but when the hot weather approached, he moved on. He had not written to Jane Williams or Mary Shelley since Christmas.[24]

He was to see Irving only several more times in his life, between March 14 and March 24, 1825, when he was back in Paris again, mysteriously. He told Irving that he was thinking of "writing an answer to Hobhouse," who had reviewed his *Conversations* in the January, 1825, *Westminster Review*. For years Medwin thought that Hobhouse had also written the reviews that appeared in *Blackwood's* in November, 1824.

In the ten days that Medwin was in Paris, he and Irving met five times, the last of these meetings to leave an enduring in-

[22] *Ibid.*, pp. 162, 171, note 2.   [23] *Ibid.*, pp. 163, 166, 169.
[24] *Letters of Mary Shelley*, I, 291; Medwin's letter to Mary, July 10, 1824, in the Abinger Collection.

fluence on Irving.[25] They breakfasted together on March 16, "talked of Spanish literature—read passages in Cisma de la Ingleterre [*sic*]," Irving recorded. It was at this time that Medwin "spoke of a play by Calderon called sometimes 'El Embozado' and at other times 'El Capotado.' Lord B[yron] tho[ugh]t of writing something on it. Medwin promised to procure me a Ms. he had written on the subject"—which would haunt Irving for years. On March 24 Medwin delivered the promised manuscript, and Irving wrote in his album. They were never to see each other again, but Irving remembered Medwin, and on the very day of their parting he thought of a "plan for dramatic work on story of 'El Embozado.'" Before the end of the year he sketched out six scenes.[26]

He wrote to Medwin on December 12, 1824, and May 31, 1825, in reply to letters from Medwin.[27] It was presumably in one of these letters that Irving wrote, "Whilst reading your conversations I fancied myself page after page reading his auto- biography,"[28] that is, Byron's burned memoirs, which Irving had in fact read.

But all this was yet to come. When Medwin left Paris for Geneva, on the morning of May 2, 1824, Byron, as far as any- one in Paris knew, was still alive, and the *Conversations* was still a mass of notes and memories.

The news of Byron's death had been published in the London papers on Saturday, May 15; Medwin must have heard of it during the following week. By July 10, he had "compiled a volume," his *Conversations of Lord Byron,* although it was not

[25] *The Journals of Washington Irving,* ed. W. P. Trent and G. S. Hellman, II, 102–107.

[26] *Ibid.,* II, 171–174.

[27] *Ibid.,* II, 69, 70, 126, 128.

[28] Medwin's unpublished marginalia in his *Conversations,* p. 33. Irving read the *Conversations* on Nov. 13, 1824 (*Journals,* II, 47), wrote for a copy of *Ahasuerus* on Dec. 9 (*Journals,* II, 69). The last word, perhaps, that he had from Medwin was a letter enclosed in one from John Howard Payne, perhaps addressed to Payne, which Irving received on March 9, 1826 (*Journals,* III, 13).

until July 16 that Goethe finished writing his *Beitrag*. On July 10, Medwin wrote to Mary Shelley,[29]

My dear Mary,

The last six months of my life have passed I know not how. I have written to no one—not even to Jane—and was afraid to write to you. You must think me—I know not what.

You must have been as I was much affected with poor Lord Byron's death—all parties seem now uniting in his favour, and the papers are full of his praise. There was no one who knew him better than you—and it is a melancholy satisfaction to me to have passed some months with him. I look upon the time spent at Pisa among the happiest days of my life.

What changes have taken place since. I seem to have lost all my friends—and have hardly courage to make new ones. I have seen here scarcely any family but the St. Aubyns—& have a disinclination for all society. How do you think I have been employing myself. With writing, and the subject I have chosen has been Memoirs of Lord Byron.

Everyone here has been disappointed in the extreme by the destruction of his private biography, & has urged me to give the world the little I knew of him. I wish I was better qualified for the task. When I was at Pisa I made [*or* took] very copious notes of his conversation, for private reference only, and was surprised to find on reading them (which I had never done till his death, and hearing that His Life had been burnt) that they contained so many anecdotes of his life. During many nights that we sat up together, he was very confidential, and entered into his history and opinions on most subjects. And from them I have compiled a Volume which I am told is highly interesting. Shelley I have made a very prominent feature in the work, and I think you will be pleased with that part at least of the memoir, and all the favorable sentiments of Lord Byron regarding him. But I shall certainly not publish the work till you have seen it—and would give the world to consult you in person about the whole. You might be of the greatest possible use to me, and prevent many errors from creeping in. I am told it cannot fail of having the greatest success, and have

[29] Medwin to Mary Shelley, July 10, 1824, in the Abinger Collection; privately printed, with a number of errors, in *Shelley and Mary*, p. 1018.

been offered £500 for it—a large and tempting sum, in consequence of what has been said in its praise by Grattan. I have not attempted to write a panegyric. I have endeavored to draw him as he was. It is only a rough sketch. Some very valuable communications have been made me by Goethe—& I am daily expecting a second letter from him—with original letters of Lord B's to the German Poet—& some unpublished Sonnets of his on him.[30]

Before deciding finally on the publication, the[re] are many things to be thought of—I have had to speak of many living characters—and must expect to be assailed by a swarm of hornets. Lady B. will not be pleased with my account of the mar[riag]e & separation—in fact I shall be assailed on all sides. Now my dear friend what do you advise—let me have your full opinion—for I mean to be guided by it.

I hea[rd] t[o]day that Moore is manufacturing 5 or 6 Volumes out of the *burnt materials,* for which Longman advanced £2,000 & is to pay £2,000 more—*they* will be in a great rage.

If I publish, promptitude is everything, so that I know you will answer this soon.

Tell me how you are getting on, & Percy. I often think of the last evening we passed at your fathers. When shall we meet again. My plans are quite at sea for the winter—but Paris will probably be again my destination.

Are you coming abroad—Jane tells me she is. Her last letter was a most melancholy one—& I have not been able or had courage to answer it but shall in a day of two. I hear that *John Shelley* is to marry one of the Miss [? Beauclerks]—which is it—& that Mama has been making the tour. So says the scandalous Chronicle. Is Sir Timothy [Shelley] likely to weather another Winter. In fact give me all the news you have of the family. Will you not have a great loss in Lord Byron as Executor. Who was made joint Trustee with him. I have been scribbling for 6 hours & can hardly hold my pen—but will promise to be more legible & less unintelligible in my next. Adieu, believe me your affectionate friend,

T. Medwin

Mary indignantly (and fearfully) declined having anything to do with a book made up of "notes on conversations . . . with

[30] The second communication from Goethe, Medwin, it seems, never received.

L. B. (when tipsy)," [31] as she put it, and wrote to Hobhouse on November 10, shortly after the publication of the *Conversations,*

Medwin requested me to correct his MS. I declined even seeing it. He afterwards sent me his Memoir of Shelley—I found it one mass of mistakes— I returned it uncorrected—earnestly entreating him not to publish it—as it would be highly injurious to my interests to recall in this garbled manner past facts at a time that I was endeavoring to bring Sir T[imothy] S[helley] to reason. When I have the book I will point out a few of these misstatements— The book has been a source of great pain to me & will be of more— I argued against the propriety & morality of hurting the living by such gossip—& deprecated the mention of any of my connections— to what purpose you see. [32]

In short, it was highly inconvenient for Mary, with her "invincible objection to the seeing my name in print," [33] to have published at this time the facts in the life of a great poet. She objected not so much to Medwin's few errors, in his long footnote on Shelley, as to the truth that Medwin published. Of her, Medwin wrote only that Shelley had married her and that she was "an amiable wife" and a "disconsolate widow." Her position, however, was a highly vulnerable one, for a few years earlier she had held the most advanced views on free love, was prepared to put them into practice, and had in fact borne Shelley two children while his first wife was still living—not to mention her association with Claire Clairmont and Jane Williams, who had also defied sexual convention. But Victorianism was already to be sniffed in the air, and Hobhouse, who had been carrying on an illicit love affair, wrote in his diary, [34] as he was contemplating an attack on Medwin and his book, "If I publish this, it will be only from a sense of duty for I am not

[31] *Letters of Mary Shelley,* I, 308.

[32] Unpublished letter from Mary Shelley to Hobhouse, Nov. 10, 1824, in the possession of Sir John Murray.

[33] *Ibid.*

[34] Diary of Hobhouse, Nov. 13, 1824, quoted by Doris L. Moore, *The Late Lord Byron* (Philadelphia, 1961), p. 110.

injured—indeed I am on the whole better treated than any one—but then if no one dares to contradict these falsehoods what is to become of biography? *What is to become of private life?*" (Italics mine.) Hobhouse told Moore in the course of a long discussion about Moore's projected biography of Byron, "that there was a very general feeling against life writing as unfair and unprofitable. He agreed with me there ought to be" [35]—and went ahead and wrote his admirable life of Byron.

But this too was in the future. Let us pause, on the verge of publication of Medwin's book and look at him through a last pair of unbiased eyes, for after the appearance of the *Conversations* one of the greatest storms in English literary history broke, and the view of him is thereafter often clouded—by hatred, hurt, and fear of damaged reputations. For Medwin was to become midwife to a dead man, whose voice came back from the grave to laugh and sneer at the living. In addition to those whom Byron had attacked, Medwin had to deal also with friends of the damaged principals, as well as those (and their friends) who merely disliked the publicity attendant upon being mentioned by name in a book reporting Byron's conversations.

In the summer of 1824, in Geneva, Medwin met Sir Samuel Brydges, shy and retiring but testy, and one of the most prolific authors of any age, who operated for a time his own press, at Lee Priory, and wrote or edited one hundred and thirty-seven books. Irving was only five years older than Medwin; Brydges was twenty-six years older, at this time a man of sixty-two. He was completing his *Letters on the Character and Poetical Genius of Lord Byron,* the one-hundred and third book to appear with his name on it. He was much impressed by Medwin's talents and wrote of him in early July, 1824.[36]

[35] Unpublished entry, May 14, 1826, in the diary of Hobhouse, in the possession of Sir Charles Hobhouse.

[36] Sir Samuel Egerton Brydges, *Letters on the Character and Poetical Genius of Lord Byron* (London, 1824), pp. 276, 278, 280–281. The quotation referring to Medwin is dated July 3, 1824; the preface is dated July 14, 1824.

I have since [June 20, the date of the preceding "Letter"] conversed intimately with a gentleman who, at a late period of Lord Byron's life, spent many of his days with him: I have hitherto learned nothing to contradict my ideas, and much to confirm them; nay, my ideas of the great poet have been even raised; and some conjectural apologies I have made for him have been proved to be well-founded . . . I have had the advantage of trying my speculative opinions on Lord Byron by the test of the personal intimacy of one, whose qualifications to observe with soundness and comprehension have appeared to me quite indisputable.

Brydges, who had read Medwin's manuscript, trusted that "my friend's *Anecdotes and Records of the Conversation*" of Byron would soon be published.

But Medwin, his mind focused on Byron, also talked enthusiastically about Shelley and talked so well that Brydges included in his edition of Edward Phillips's *Theatrum Poetarum Anglicanorum* (Geneva, 1824) a memoir of Shelley written by Medwin as well as lyrics from the *Posthumous Poems,* just edited by Mary Shelley. Brydges, persuaded by Medwin, overcame his earlier distaste for Shelley and thus became one of the very first outside Shelley's circle to celebrate his genius.[37]

It was perhaps with the help of Brydges, who lived in Geneva in 1818–1819 and 1821–1824, that Medwin met several distinguished or well known Genevese at this time. Medwin remembered the venerable Bonstetten well, "as a little old man who went about in a little old Demi-faeton [*sic*] made expressly to hold his little person. What he ever wrote I could not find out, but to have been [Thomas] Gray's friend gave him a lasting vogue."[38] Perhaps Medwin never saw Bonstetten's *Etudes de l'homme, ou Recherches sur les facultés de sentir et de penser,* reviewed in the same volume of the *Bibliothèque universelle* that contained the last two installments of Medwin's article on the cave temples of Ellora.

[37] Mary K. Woodworth, *The Literary Career of Sir Samuel Egerton Brydges* (Oxford, 1935), pp. 143–144.
[38] Medwin's unpublished marginalia in his *Conversations,* p. 12.

Medwin was also on good terms of some kind with Charles Hentsch, Byron's Genevese banker, who wrote to Medwin[39] concerning Edward E. Williams's boat, left on the Lake when he went to Italy to rejoin Medwin and meet Shelley, "Je donnerai le tout en garde au Batelier Maurice, compagnon de notre célèbre ami," Byron. Medwin finally disposed of the boat for Jane Williams in 1825.

Brydges, who knew both Professor Pictet and Charles Victor de Bonstetten,[40] may also have introduced Medwin to Frédéric Soret, a Genevan scientist who was tutor to the Duke of Weimar's grandson. More important, he was a friend of the great Goethe, and it was through Soret that Medwin approached Goethe,[41] who on June 15 wrote the first draft of his strangely stilted *Beitrag* to Medwin's book, the German text marred by typographical errors and Goethe's words translated out of his own third-person point of view into the more informal first person.

Medwin, fearful of the character and quality of his manuscript, had allowed Brydges to read it with an eye to revision but then, changing his mind, it would seem, had taken it out of Brydges's hands before there was time to make any changes.[42] Perhaps in recompense he wrote for Brydges, at a single sitting, the memoir of Shelley which appeared as an appendix to Brydges's book and as a long footnote in Medwin's. With Brydges, Medwin discussed his publication plans and told him, at some time before July 17, that he had secured Henry Colburn as publisher of the *Conversations*. On that day Thomas Moore recorded in his journal,

Asked her [Mary Shelley] whom she thought this person could be, whom Sir Egerton Brydges had announced to the Longmans as about to bring out a sort of Boswell diary of Byron's Conversations,

[39] *Ibid.*
[40] Sir Samuel Egerton Brydges, *Autobiography* (London, 1834), II, 117–118.
[41] E. M. Butler, *Byron and Goethe* (London, 1956), pp. 104–105. See Goethe's *Briefe*, XXXVIII, 197, July 14, 1824.
[42] Irving, *Journals*, II, 94.

having lived much with him, and noted down all he said. Supposed it must be a Mr. Barry, a partner in the bank at Genoa, . . . did not think it could be Captain Medwin.[43]

But Medwin, at this date, very probably had already received his money from Colburn. Weeks ago he had written to Grattan, asking his advice on publishing, received Grattan's letter of encouragement offering to serve as his agent, and sent off to him his manuscript, for which he expected only "a couple of hundred pounds." (He had also been encouraged to publish by Sir John St. Aubyn, who had read a portion of the manuscript.) When, after considering it for twenty-four hours, Colburn offered £500, Grattan accepted at once, and immediately mailed the bills to Medwin.[44]

Mary as yet knew none of this, for she had not yet received Medwin's letter of July 10, informing her of his book, then complete, it seems.[45] Between that date and the preceding May 15, when the news of Byron's death had been published in London, less than two months had elapsed, the longest possible period for the composition of the *Conversations* and a very strong indication that the book was written up chiefly from notes made in Pisa. In the copy which he annotated and revised years later for a final edition he wrote at the bottom of page 336, descriptive of his last parting with Byron, "and here I closed my journal." In his new preface for this projected edition, never published, he wrote of his book, "It occupied scarcely 3 weeks and was taken literally from my Diary. Whilst

[43] Moore, *Memoirs*, IV, 220–221, July 17, 1824.
[44] Grattan's dealings with Colburn are related in *Beaten Paths*, II, 61–62.
[45] Medwin was responsible only for the first 17 pp. of the appendix, the remainder, pp. xviii–ciii, being inserted in London, he says in his marginalia to the *Conversations*, without his knowledge or consent. This statement is confirmed by that of the editor on p. xviii. In the copy which Medwin annotated and revised for a final edition, he deleted the last five words on p. 336 and all else that followed except the translation of Goethe's letter, pp. 343–351, the depositions of Byron and others concerning the Pisan affair of the dragoon, and the German original of Goethe's letter, pp. i–xvii. The translation of Goethe's three stanzas on pp. 348–349, he states, was done by Coleridge.

employed in it, I swear, I had no means of consulting a single English book by way of reference." In the last sentence, we have the explanation of Medwin's more obvious errors. He dated the preface August 1, and for the work of somewhat less than two months at most received £500, a sum which could have supported him, living decently but frugally in Italy, for five years.[46] Mary Shelley was offered in 1835 only £600 for "an edition of Shelley's works with life and notes."[47]

Thomas Jefferson Hogg, who remembered Medwin from his calls at Poland Street in 1811, following the expulsion of Shelley and Hogg from Oxford, and who had undoubtedly heard much of Medwin recently from Jane Williams, wrote to her on September 26, 1824, "I rejoice that M[edwin] is to have £500 [for the *Conversations*], because he is a good tempered fellow, & I dare say wants it: but I wish he co[d] get it in a more reputable manner."[48] This was the man who in later years, when preparing his own *Life of Shelley*, was to alter the poet's letters in order to protect himself from the results of his own youthful indiscretions and who had already made love to both of Shelley's wives, was now courting Jane Williams, also beloved of Shelley, and in 1827 would take her as his "wife."

A last glimpse of Medwin before the full force of the storm broke over him is provided by his letter to Mary Shelley, written from La Tour, near Vevey.[49] Mary does not seem to have

[46] Hogg wrote to Jane Williams in 1823 that Mary Shelley could support herself and Percy on £100 a year if she lived "in common with the N.s" (*sic*), perhaps the Novellos (*After Shelley*, p. 18). In 1824 Sir Timothy Shelley allowed Mary and Percy only £100 a year to live on in England; she hoped for £300, in 1825 was receiving £200 from him (*Letters of Mary Shelley*, I, 300, note 4).

[47] *Letters of Mary Shelley*, II, 91. In 1825 Colburn paid £2,200 for the copyright of the diary of Pepys, edited by Lord Braybrooke (*Encyclopædia Britannica*, 11th ed., article on Henry Colburn).

[48] *After Shelley*, p. 29.

[49] Medwin to Mary Shelley, dated only "13, 1824," in the Abinger Collection; privately printed, with errors, deliberate substitutions, and omissions in *Shelley and Mary*, pp. 1045–1048. The postmark may be August, although the letter might have been written in August, September, or October.

protested the publication of the *Conversations* nearly as strongly as she later maintained, although it is perhaps significant that he addresses her as Mrs. Shelley.

My Dear Mrs. Shelley,

I have received your kind and delightful letter at the divinest of places, where I have taken a cottage for two months, and am living in the midst of a few friends with *one* of whom I have been long intimate, and whose society might and ought to make any but the most discontented of mortals, comparatively happy. My quitting Geneva was no easy matter, as I had all the St. Aubyn family against it, but I have promised to visit them occasionally, and that promise (which, now I am here, will not be soon accomplished) in some measure made my peace. It is not, indeed, easy to tear oneself from this place, which, in point of scenery, has a manifest advantage over that of the rest of the lake; in fact, it is perfect from my rooms. Mountains, pine forests, vines, and an expanse of lake, a perfect Mediterranean, with its villages at the foot of its Savoy Alps, and all the Pays de Vaux to the right; but you know the place, and your imagination being much more beautiful than mine, can supply by memory what I should fail in painting. I have a friend here who is, perhaps, the best landscape painter of the day (a male one), and I mean to send you an oil painting of the view from my windows as a souvenir of one you and Jane may well have forgotten. I am the most idle, most unhappily distrait of mortals, never doing what I ought, and doing, &c., &c.; but for the last six months I hardly know what I have been doing, at least could give a very indifferent account of myself. My MS. is by this time in London, and would have been there long ago, but that I was waiting to close it by a communication from the celebrated Goethe, who has kindly sent me, at last, a detail of his acquaintance with Lord Byron, and has added to it an original poem—both great prizes—and, perhaps, the only valuable part of my work. I can easily enter into your objection. There are some topics I have cautiously avoided, and of course you are one. Your name does not occur in the Memoirs [*i. e.*, in the body of the text], nor have I made the slightest allusion to you. Our poor dear lost friend makes a very considerable portion of them, and I think you will be pleased with the little memoir of him which I have added by way of note. This I should much wish you to see, and there are some dates, &c. that I am doubtful about. Poor Shelley was so intimately acquainted with Lord Byron for so many years that it was impossible to avoid the mention of their intimacy. There is one thing that I cannot easily forgive, with all my admiration for Lord Byron, his not mentioning him in his note to the Two Foscari, which is a circumstance that, knowing, as I do, from such repeated expressions, of his friendship, regard, and admiration for Shelley, I have always been at a loss to account for. But he was full of inconsistencies. Nil fuit unquam sic impar sibi.

Your reminiscences of Lord Byron would indeed be invaluable, and if you were about to write them, I should most certainly consign mine to the flames, because you knew him perhaps better than any person living, and, considering that most of my knowledge of him was derived from you and Shelley, I have very little opinion of my six months' [*sic*] endeavour; but they tell me it is highly interesting, and there is at this moment a longing after and impatience to know something about the most extraordinary man of the age, that must give my book a considerable success. Moore's serious life my memorandum will not interfere with; but as he is a very costive writer, his five or six volumes will not appear for many months, perhaps years. You delight in his singing. I have often heard him in Paris, and *Grattan* sings his songs to my taste quite as well; with more voice and quite as much feeling. Between ourselves, I am no great admirer of Moore. I am no believer in his friendship for Lord B[yron], and saw a proof of it in Paris when, at a public dinner we gave him, he refused to give Lord B[yron] as a toast.

Moore has a great deal of littleness in his character and no small share of jealousy in his composition. W. Irving I delight in, he is one of the most unassuming, friendly, amiable characters I know. I wrote to him the other day through a Genevese going to London, a letter which I hope he got.

The enemies I shall make by this work are not easily counted. But I am very indifferent to the rage or resentment of the literary men of the day. All I have to say is that the opinions are Lord Byron's, not mine. Murray will cut a very bad figure in them, and Rogers not a very good one.

As to Lady Byron, I have given the detail of several very long and confidential conversations respecting her, in which he throws the entire blame of their separation on her; justly or not, the world will decide. I have, myself, no delicacy regarding her, or the authoress of 'Glenarvon' [by Lady Caroline Lamb], which hero, over the whole continent, is thought no caricature.

My work is very short and does not exceed 400 pages. I might have swelled it out into another volume, but hate book making for the sake of book making. There is one thing I wish to ask you. I have mentioned the Guiccioli at considerable length, but in a manner very flattering in itself. Her being associated in print with the greatest poet of the age, with whom she was notoriously so in the face of the world, cannot offend her. I was always a great admirer of the Guiccioli, and have spoken of her as very beautiful and amiable. She will go down to posterity as his Fornarina. How many women would envy her! What would I not give to be at Kentish Town with you and dear Jane and the children. I have you all in my mind's eye, and I wish there was magnetism enough between us that my mind might travel to and communicate with yours. Adieu! Give my love to Jane and believe me, my dear Mary,

                                Yours affectionately and truly,
                                              T. Medwin

P. S. Tell Jane this letter is half intended for her; that I hope to send her in a few weeks what I can get for the boat.

Meanwhile, in October, there were daily puffs of Medwin's *Conversations* in the *Courier*, proclaiming it to be the work of a "Captain in the 24th Dragoons" who was also "the Cousin of the late P. B. Shelley." [50] The book was published on October 23, but prepublication extracts had appeared in the first and only issue of the *Attic Miscellany* (established by Grattan, Henry Bulwer, and Charles Sheridan) and had been reprinted in *The London Literary Gazette and Journal of Belles Lettres* on October 16 and in *The Examiner* on October 17. [51] Before

---

[50] Unpublished letter of T. J. Hogg, Oct. 16, 1824, in the Abinger Collection.

[51] *London Literary Gazette*, Oct. 16, 1824, pp. 657–658; *Examiner*, Oct. 17, 1824, pp. 665–666. Grattan was responsible for the excerpts which appeared in the *Attic Miscellany*, where they formed part of an article which he wrote on Byron and the burned memoirs.

the *Conversations* finally went out of print, Medwin thought it had gone through ten or twelve editions;[52] actually there were even more.

By the end of the year, following publication of the original handsome quarto volume, Colburn had issued a "second edition" and also a "new edition," both octavos and the latter omitting the attack on Lady Caroline Lamb. In 1825 he published an edition in two volumes, and in 1832 the remaining sheets of these were reissued as "two volumes in one, complete."[53] The same year saw the appearance of the book as number XIV in "The National Library," edited by the Rev. G. R. Gleig, "assisted by eminent writers." This edition was late, but it was clearly respectable.

There were at least two American editions, one published in New York in 1824 and the other in Baltimore in 1825. In France, in 1824, both Galignani and Baudry published English editions, thus bringing the number of editions in English up to ten, and there were also two French translations, one by Amédée Pichot for Ladvocat, another by Davesiès de Pontès for Pellet.[54] Pichot's translation also appeared as an appendix to his translation of Byron's complete works in 1827. The two-volume edition read by Goethe with such interest was published at Stuttgart in 1824 as *Gespräche mit Lord Byron, Ein Tagebuch geführt während eines Aufenthaltes zu Pisa in den Jahren 1821 und 1822.*[55] Medwin states that there was an edition published in Belgium,[56] and in 1842 appeared in Padua

[52] Medwin's unpublished preface for a final edition of his *Conversations*.
[53] Medwin, *Shelley*, p. 496.
[54] The only copy of the rare Baltimore edition of 1825, published by Etting Mickle, that I am aware of is in the possession of Mr. Seymour Adelman of Philadelphia. Edmond Estève, *Byron et le Romantisme Français* (Paris, 1907), p. 21, lists the French editions. On Nov. 29, 1824, Lady Mount Cashell wrote to Mary Shelley that the *Conversations* was "selling fast in Paris" but had not yet reached Pisa (unpublished letter in the Abinger Collection). It would be reviewed in the Florence *Antologia*, XVII (Jan., 1825), 32–64.
[55] Solomon Liptzin, *Shelley in Germany* (New York, 1924), p. 5, note 11.
[56] Medwin's unpublished preface for a final edition of the *Conversations*.

the *Opere complete di Lord Byron voltate dall' originale Inglese in prosa Italiana da C. Rusconi, con note ed illustrazioni . . . dei signori Moore, W. Scott, . . . Hobhouse, . . . Medwin, . . . Lady Blessington, Mrs. Shelley, . . . Contessa Guiccioli, etc. a cui si aggiungono i dialoghi di Lord Byron compilati da M. Medwin*—all in two volumes. Altogether, at least fifteen separate editions and translations appeared.

The Captain was famous, and almost before he knew it, he married, at Lausanne, on November 2, 1824, ten days after publication of the *Conversations.* In the December issue of *The London Magazine,* at the end of a carefully selected list of twenty-one marriages of socially prominent persons in England, in Scotland, and abroad, among them the Earl of Glasgow and the daughter of Lord Erskine, we read of the marriage of "Thomas Medwin, Esq., late of the 24th Dragoons, to Anne Henrietta, Comtesse de Starnford" [57] by her first marriage. The angler had at last made his catch, and a very good one it was indeed, promising a lifetime of secure happiness; for Anne Henrietta, born the Baroness Hamilton of Sweden, brought with her a very sizeable fortune. Medwin, confident and happy, suspecting only that his *Conversations* might raise "a swarm of hornets," little knew of the tremendous storm that was already forming above him.

And when he was, as Grattan expressed it, "more terribly mauled by reviewers" than any other writer had ever been, when "his veracity was denied, his morality attacked," no man could have been more surprised or hurt. For "Medwin thought he was doing honour to Byron's memory in giving these fugitive conversations to the world," Grattan observed. "He held him in high estimation as well for good fellowship as for talent, and he was aware that any misrepresentation was liable to immediate contradiction." [58] Medwin thought that he had written an honest and accurate book.

[57] Medwin's marriage was also announced in *The Examiner* on Nov. 21, 1824, p. 750. There seems to be no authority for the spelling "Stainfort" in the *Dictionary of National Biography.*
[58] Grattan, *Beaten Paths,* II, 68.

6

Fame and Furor

No book was ever more timely than Medwin's *Conversations* or had a subject placed more repeatedly before the public eye. John Hunt's weekly *Examiner* describes the Byronic background against which Medwin and his book appeared, on October 23, 1824. On May 16 *The Examiner* announced the death of Byron, which had occurred on April 19. The most famous and notorious poet who had ever lived had now become the sacrificial victim to the cause of Greek liberty. On May 23 John Hunt made a vicious reply to a vicious attack by Dr. Stoddart in his *New Times* on May 17, the day that the court's decision was made in the libel suit brought against Hunt for publishing Byron's *Vision of Judgment*. Hunt accused Stoddart of trying to influence the court and called him "a Liar of the first magnitude" and a "bastard Englishman." Another article in the same issue regretted the destruction of Byron's memoirs but honored "the disinterestedness and zeal" of Moore. There was also an anonymous poetic "Lament on the Death of the Noble Poet, Lord Byron." The next issue, May 30, reprinted Moore's letter to *The Times*, describing his part in the burning of Byron's memoirs, and included an article on Byron's will. This article stated, "it is thought that Westminster Abbey will receive his remains."

The first page article of the June 6 issue refuted rumors recently published in newspapers about Byron's relations with the actress Mrs. Mardyn and reprinted Sir Walter Scott's tribute to Byron. On July 11 there was an account of a supposed consultation between Byron's sister Augusta Leigh, his lawyer Hanson, and his friend Hobhouse on the question of burying Byron in Westminster Abbey or in the family vault at Newstead

Abbey, that is, at Hucknall Church. This issue also described in detail Byron's coffin and the funeral procession to be:

Six cloakmen on horseback. Two Mutes attired in Black Silk Surplices and Bearing Batons. A Black Charger, stately caparisoned, bearing his Lordship's Coronet, on a Velvet Cushion. The HEARSE, containing the BODY, drawn by Six Horses, the Hammer-cloths richly ornamented with the Ensigns Armorial, and either side of the Carriage decorated in the same manner.

Four pages marched on each side of the carriage. The next week's issue described the funeral procession as it had taken place, giving the route followed, with an account of the autopsy and the Greek orphan boy of eight years who was befriended by Byron and came to London with his body, to sit in the first coach after the hearse and be adopted by the Duke and Duchess of Leinster. The issue of July 25 described the burial of Byron at Hucknall Church.

On August 15 appeared "The Last Moments of Lord Byron," collected "from the mouth of Mr. Fletcher," his valet, and reprinted from *The Westminster Review*. August 22 brought forth Dr. Bruno's "Answer to the *Westminster Review*, Respecting the Last Moments of Lord Byron," which had been presided over by the young doctor.

The October 17 issue contained "Lord Byron in Greece," extracted from a personal letter, "a pleasant and minute Narrative of an Interview with Lord Byron . . . , written a short time previous to the death of the patriot Poet." The same issue reprinted from the first number of the *Attic Miscellany* "Lord and Lady Byron." This was a prepublication extract from Medwin's *Conversations*. October 24 saw a preliminary review of Medwin's book: "It is a production which, as the phrase runs, 'all the world will read.'" On October 31 appeared a front page review-article signed "Q," who wrote, "The publication of Captain Medwin's *Journal of the Conversations of Lord Byron* has once more rendered that extraordinary genius the most prominent object of public attention." The reviewer noted that the passage dealing with Lord and Lady Byron's separation had "appeared in every periodical publication for the last week almost without exception" and dealt with Medwin's book as a serious and interesting contribution to knowledge. The *Conversations* "will tend to correct some prevalent impressions in regard to the character of Lord Byron very materially."

Long excerpts from Medwin's book appeared, without editorial comment, on November 7, but the next week's issue brought forth "Lord Byron and Mr. Murray," which refereed the bout between Medwin and Murray, the latter's statement having "appeared in the daily papers." Hunt gave the laurel to Murray but happily seized upon the attacks on Murray in the *Conversations* to further his own quarrel with Byron's old publisher, whom Hunt had succeeded. Madame Louise S. Belloc's biography of *Lord Byron* was reviewed on November 21, with quotations of Stendhal's account of Byron, contained in the book, and a poem by Lady Byron, "To Ada," dated December 10, 1816, the first birthday of Byron's daughter. The same issue announced Medwin's marriage on November 2. Dallas's *Recollections of Byron* received a review, twice mentioning Medwin, on November 28; and the same issue, in the opening paragraph of "Newspaper Chat," contained the following statement: "A letter has been received from Captain Medwin, in which he says, 'as to answering all the people who may take it into their heads to be angry with me, it would be endless; but I shall never shrink from responsibility, personal or otherwise.'"

December 5 saw a further reply of Hunt's to Murray, concerning Murray's conduct relative to the libelous manuscript of Byron's *Vision of Judgment* (Murray had turned over an uncorrected proof to Hunt, who had published it and then been sued). The same issue of *The Examiner* quoted again, without comment, from Medwin's *Conversations*, this time Byron's remarks on Lord Edward Fitzgerald. "Dr. Southey and Lord Byron" appeared on December 19. It was an article on Southey's letter to the *Courier*, replying to Medwin's book, and it con-

tained quotations from *The Times* and the *Globe and Traveller*
on the controversy, in the course of which Southey wrote, " . . .
that his lordship spoke to this effect [as reported by Medwin],
and in this temper, I have no doubt . . . I take these Conversations to be authentic . . ."[1]

As early as November 19, 1824, when Pietro Gamba's *Narrative of Lord Byron's Last Journey to Greece* was being translated by William Petre—Hobhouse looking over his friend's
shoulder, comparing translation with original—Edward Bla-
quiere (*Narrative of a Second Visit to Greece, Including Facts
Connected with the Last Days of Lord Byron*) and William
Parry (*The Last Days of Lord Byron*) were both busily writing,
and Hobhouse was fearful that their books would appear before
Gamba's. All three appeared in 1825, along with Leicester
Stanhope's *Greece in 1823 and 1824, to which are added,
Reminiscences of Lord Byron.*

Meanwhile, Medwin had been reviewed in *The New
Monthly Magazine* (October, 1824), *The London Literary
Gazette and Journal of Belles Lettres* (October 23, 30, Novem-
ber 6, 13), *Blackwood's, The Gentleman's Magazine,* and *The
London Magazine* (all in November), *The Monthly Magazine;
or British Register* (December), and *The Westminster Review*
(January, 1825), among other English journals. There were
also reviews in the United States and in Italy.[2] Three of these
reviewers were friends of Byron: John Galt and William Harness, both in *Blackwood's,* and John Cam Hobhouse, in *The
Westminster.* Even Fletcher had contributed an anecdote about
Medwin to Harness's review and had written out his list of
contradictions of the *Conversations.*[3]

---

[1] Robert Southey's letter to the *Courier,* Dec. 8, 1824, reprinted in
Byron's *Letters and Journals,* VI, 395.

[2] *Minerva,* Dec. 25, 1824; *Atlantic Magazine,* Jan., 1825; The Florence
Antologia, Jan., 1825; the *Giornale dei letterati di Pisa* (No. 29), 1826.
Medwin was also discussed in "Noctes Ambrosianae," *Blackwood's,* XVI
(Nov., 1824), 590–591.

[3] Galt and Harness are identified by Alan Lang Strout, "Some Miscellaneous Letters Concerning *Blackwood's Magazine,*" *Notes and Queries,*

Before it was all over, "The Editor of *The Conversations*," perhaps Colburn himself, had defended Medwin in *The Morning Chronicle* against Murray's pamphlet attack; the Editor of *The Times* had defended him against Hobhouse; "Vindex" had published a pamphlet, *Captain Medwin Vindicated from the Calumnies of the Reviewers,* defending him against Harness; and the great Croker had written an article for the *Quarterly Review,* run off in page proof but so favorable to Medwin that, at the request of Murray, it was never published.[4] It is the most effective defense of Medwin's book ever written, and a very impressive one it is, even though it damns Medwin for "a most unjustifiable breach of private confidence." Croker went on to edit Boswell's *Johnson,* containing more conversations than Medwin's book (although not such shocking ones), and Colburn earned a net profit of £3,000.[5]

CXIX (July, 1954), 311. Fletcher's largely unpublished manuscript is in the Pierpont Morgan Library.

[4] A copy of the article by "The Editor of *The Conversations*" is in the possession of Sir John Murray. Hobhouse saw the article by the Editor of *The Times* on Jan. 22, 1825, when he wrote, in his diary, ". . . I found a scurvy article saying it was more likely that Byron should have *lied* and *gabbled* [? garbled] than that Medwin, dull as he is, should have invented, and that Mr H— must be a very simple gentleman if he thought to persuade the public to the contrary. This is infamous! What does the editor of the Times know of the real character of Byron? I thought of going to the Times and remonstrating and I actually walked to Printing House Square—but 'Cynthius aurem vellet'—I would not go in—Gamba was with me . . ." Published in large part by Doris L. Moore, *The Late Lord Byron,* pp. 114–115.

The unpublished page proof of Croker's article is in the possession of Sir John Murray.

"Vindex," author of *Captain Medwin Vindicated from the Calumnies of the Reviewers* (London, 1825; Printed for William Marsh), is most certainly not Medwin, although the pamphlet is sometimes ascribed to him. The author is too critical of Byron, too objective in his estimation of the virtues and vices of Medwin's *Conversations,* his tone a much cooler one than Medwin was master of at this time on this subject. Further, "Vindex" mentions neither Murray nor Hobhouse; these omissions make it virtually certain that the author is not Medwin.

[5] Medwin, *Shelley,* II, 218.

The Captain was famous (or infamous), and his fame brought him into intimate, if usually unfriendly, association with a number of other well known persons, notably Lady Caroline Lamb, John Murray, and Hobhouse.

Lady Caroline probably suffered most. Byron had said to Medwin, in a conversation which was deleted from the "new edition" of 1824 and which Medwin never reinstated,[6]

About this period I became what the French call *un homme à bonnes fortunes,* and was engaged in a *liaison,*—and, I might add, a serious one.

The lady had scarcely any personal attractions to recommend her. Her figure, though genteel, was too thin to be good, and wanted that roundness which elegance and grace would vainly supply. She was, however, young, and of the first connexions. *Au reste,* she possessed an infinite vivacity, and an imagination heated by novel-reading, which made her fancy herself a heroine of romance, and led her into all sorts of eccentricities. She was married, but it was a match of *convenance,* and no couple could be more fashionably indifferent to, or independent of one another, than she and her husband. It was at this time that we happened to be thrown much together. She had never been in love—at least where the affections are concerned—and was perhaps made without a heart, as many of the sex are; but her head more than supplied the deficiency.

I was soon congratulated by my friends on the conquest I had made, and did my utmost to shew that I was not insensible to the partiality I could not help perceiving. I made every effort to be in love, expressed as much ardour as I could muster, and kept feeding the flame with a constant supply of *billets-doux* and amatory verses. In short, I was in decent time duly and regularly installed into what the Italians call *service,* and soon became, in every sense of the word, a *patito.*

It required no Œdipus to see where all this would end. I am easily governed by women, and she gained an ascendancy over

---

[6] Medwin, *Conversations,* First Edition, pp. 211–215. Medwin did not intend to replace these pages in his finally revised edition, never published. For other accounts of the scene at Lady Heathcote's ball, July 5, 1813, see *His Very Self and Voice,* ed. Lovell, pp. 69–70, 617, note 57.

me that I could not easily shake off. I submitted to this thraldom long, for I hate *scenes,* and am of an indolent disposition; but I was forced to snap the knot rather rudely at last. Like all lovers, we had several quarrels before we came to a final rupture. One was made up in a very odd way, and without any verbal explanation. She will remember it. Even during our intimacy I was not at all constant to this fair one, and she suspected as much. In order to detect my intrigues she watched me, and earthed a lady into my lodgings,—and came herself, terrier-like, in the disguise of a carman. My valet, who did not see through the masquerade, let her in; when, to the despair of Fletcher, she put off the man, and put on the woman. Imagine the scene: it was worthy of Faublas!

Her after-conduct was unaccountable madness—a combination of spite and jealousy. It was perfectly agreed and understood that we were to meet as strangers. We were at a ball. She came up and asked me if she might waltz. I thought it perfectly indifferent whether she waltzed or not, or with whom, and told her so, in different terms, but with much coolness. After she had finished, a scene occurred, which was in the mouth of every one. [Four lines of asterisks follow. The gossip was that Lady Caroline, when at Lady Heathcote's ball on July 5, 1813, had attempted suicide with some sharp instrument.]

Soon after this she promised young——   *   *   if he would call me out.   *   *   *   *   *   *   *   *   *   Yet can any one believe that she would be so infatuated, after all this, as to call at my apartments? (certainly with no view of shooting herself.) I was from home; but finding "Vathek" on the table, she wrote in the first page, "Remember me!"

Yes! I had cause to remember her; and, in the irritability of the moment, wrote under the two words these two stanzas:—

> Remember thee, remember thee!
>   Till Lethe quench life's burning stream,
> Remorse and shame shall cling to thee,
>   And haunt thee like a feverish dream!
>
> Remember thee! Ay, doubt it not;
>   Thy husband too shall think of thee;
> By neither shalt thou be forgot,
>   Thou **** to him, thou **** to me!

On November 1 Hobhouse called on Lady Caroline and wrote in his diary afterwards, "She is in the utmost rage at Medwin's Conversations representing her as not having been the object of Byron's attachment and she showed me a very tender letter of his which she wishes to publish. She told me that her brother William Ponsonby was not against the publication as he thought with her that no imputation was so dreadful as that of not having been loved by her paramour . . . She is certainly very mad."[7]

She had done all that she could to make reconciliation impossible between Byron and his wife, gossiping about his relations with Augusta Leigh; Byron had revenged himself, and Lady Caroline wept over the *Conversations*. She then wrote to Medwin a letter of well over two thousand words:[8]

Sir,—I hope you will excuse my intruding upon your time, with the most intense interest I have just finished your book which does you credit as to the manner in which it is executed and after the momentary pain in part which it excites in many a bosom, will live in despight of censure—and be gratefully accepted by the Public as long as Lord Byron's name is remembered—yet as you have left to one who adored him a bitter legacy, and as I feel secure the lines "remember thee—thou false to him thou fiend to me"—were his—and as I have been very ill & am not likely to trouble any one much longer—you will I am sure grant me one favour—let me to you at least confide the truth of the past—you owe it to me—you will not I know refuse me.

[7] Hobhouse's diary, Nov. 1, 1824, quoted by Doris L. Moore, *The Late Lord Byron*, p. 105. Lady Caroline Lamb, in an unpublished letter of Oct. 21, 1824, wrote to William Godwin, "What hot water it puts every one in to hear of His conversations being published—if I am named it must be unkindly—therefore it grieves me." After reading Medwin's book, she wrote again to Godwin, in an undated and unpublished letter, "Pray have you read Medwin's Book—the part respecting me gives me much pain . . . I feel flattered by your letter—a little flattery is now perhaps of use—for I have been *deservedly*—no doubt—deeply & painfully humiliated." Both letters are in the Abinger Collection.

[8] Reprinted in Byron's *Letters and Journals*, II, 451–454, from a copy seemingly made by Henry Colburn.

She *"had married for love,"* she told him, "and love the most romantic and ardent" (no matter what Byron said), although she confessed to Medwin that she was soon false to her husband. She described her first meeting with Byron, as well as his introduction to his future wife: "What you say of his falling upstairs and of Miss Milbanke is all true." But, she continued, "Byron never could say I had no heart. He never could say, either, that I had not loved my husband . . . Recall these words, and let me not go down with your book as heartless." She denied being "a woman of the world," and the proof of it, she said, was that Byron had written to her "perhaps ten times in a day," despite the "few personal attractions" that Medwin had referred to.

The main thesis of her letter is that "Byron did not affect—but he loved me as never woman was loved. I have had one of his letters copied in the stone press for you; one just before we parted. See if it looks like a mere lesson." At the last, she says, confirming Medwin again, they were invited everywhere together, "as if we had been married."

Although she had wept over Medwin's *Conversations*, which had given her much pain, "I had rather have experienced it," she wrote, "than not have read your book. Parts of it are beautiful; and I can vouch for the truth of much, as I read his own Memoirs before Murray burnt them."

She described for Medwin her parting from Byron and the cruel conduct of her rival Lady Oxford.

The scene at Lady Heathcote's is nearly true—he had made me swear I was never to Waltz. Lady Heathcote said, Come Lady Caroline, you must begin, & I bitterly answered—oh yes! I am in a merry humour. I did so—but whispered to Lord Byron "I conclude I may walze *now*" and he answered sarcastically, "with every body in turn—you always did it better than any one. I shall have pleasure in seeing you."—I did so you may judge with what feelings. After this, feeling ill, I went into a small inner room where supper was prepared; Lord Byron & Lady Rancliffe entered after; seeing me, he said, "I have been admiring your dexterity." I clasped a knife, not intending anything. "Do, my dear," he said. "But if you mean to act a Roman's part, mind which way you strike with your knife—be it at your own heart, not mine—you have struck there already." "Byron," I said, and ran away with the knife. I never stabbed myself. It is false. Lady Rancliffe & Tankerville screamed and said I would; people pulled to get it from me; I was terrified; my hand got cut, & the blood came over my gown. I know not what happened after—but this is the very truth.

If one may judge from Byron's account of this epsiode, written the day after, Medwin's book had stimulated Lady Caroline not only to "fancy herself a heroine of romance" but also to write a scene for it, herself the injured and helpless heroine. She continued,

It *is* true I went to see him as a Carman, after all that! But it is also true, that, the last time we parted for ever, as he pressed his lips on mine (it was in the Albany) he said "poor Caro, if every one hates me, you, I see, will never change—No, not with ill usage!" & I said, "yes, I *am* changed, & shall come near you no more."—For then he showed me letters, & told me things I cannot repeat, & all my attachment went. This was our last parting scene— well I remember it . . .

Shortly after he married, once, Lady Melbourne took me to see his Wife in Piccadilly. It was a cruel request, but Lord Byron himself made it. It is to this wedding visit he alludes [in Medwin's *Conversations*]. Mrs. Leigh, myself, Lady Melbourne, Lady Noel, & Lady Byron were in the room. I never looked up. Annabella was very cold to me. Lord Byron came in & seemed agitated—his hand was cold, but he seemed kind. This was the last time upon this earth I ever met him.

Although all her facts are not straight, her suffering is. Byron hated her (with good cause), but Medwin removed the offending pages before the end of the year. The damage, however, had been done. Her husband, William Lamb, who had lived through so much and, as Lord Melbourne, would live on to become Queen Victoria's prime minister, had no choice now. Caroline's scandalous relations with Byron, long known to all their intimates, had now been published for all the world to read, and William Lamb withdrew from her. Although she took increasingly to drink and to collecting men younger than she, she would not admit any hatred for Medwin or for Byron. (She had merely wanted Byron for herself, she thought, and if she could not have him, Lady Byron, she was convinced, certainly should not.) She wrote to her friend Lady Morgan in Dublin,[9] "I am done for would to God you had believed me and come to see me it is not Byron's last legacy which killed me in Medwin's book—it is unkindness . . . Lady Morgan be kind enough to tell Captain Medwin I liked and admired his book—that I wrote him a letter."

One of Lady Caroline's recently acquired young men, Edward Bulwer, wrote to Medwin, asking him to delete Byron's references to her incoherent novel *Glenarvon*. This Medwin declined to do, and in his reply he revealed a statement represented in the *Conversations* by asterisks: [10]

I am sorry I was not in England at the time your note was written, as I think I should have felt inclined to have complied with your appeal so feelingly urged. I am sure, however, that in justice to Lord Byron's memory I should not have felt authorized in omitting the mention of *Glenarvon*. On the continent at least Lord Byron's character has suffered more from that publication than from any other cause, as it is to the circumstance of his having been made the hero of that novel more than to any intrinsic merit in the work that it has owed so much of its popularity in France and Germany, where it has been looked upon as the real history of his life. Goethe, almost copying the words of the authoress, says in an essay on The Genius and Character of Lord Byron: "when a young, bold and

[9] Unpublished letter from Lady Caroline Lamb to Lady Morgan, no date, no postmark; in the Humanities Research Center of the University of Texas.

[10] Letter from Medwin to Edward Bulwer, Sept. 10, 1825, quoted by Michael Sadleir, *Bulwer: A Panorama*, pp. 53–54. Sadleir is mistaken, p. 53, in stating that Medwin deleted Byron's remarks on *Glenarvon*, which appear in the "New Edition" of 1824 on pp. 273–275. In connection with Goethe's remarks on Byron, quoted in Medwin's letter, Sadleir refers the reader to *Glenarvon*, first edition, II, 83–85; second edition, II, 81–82.

highly attractive personage, he gained the favour of a Florentine lady. The husband discovered this and murdered his wife. But the murderer was found dead in the street on the same night under circumstances that will not admit of attaching suspicion to anyone. Lord Byron fled from Florence and seems to drag spectres after him for ever."

It was one day after reading this passage that Lord Byron entered into the subject of *Glenarvon* and of the lady who shall be nameless. The particulars of the liaison with her were never a secret and what occurred at Lady Melbourne's [*i. e.*, Lady Heathcote's] was in the mouth of all the London world. I cannot think, therefore, considering the notoriety of this circumstance that her Ladyship has suffered much in the public estimation lately by what has appeared.

Whether some of the misery inflicted was unmerited I will leave it to your candour (and putting aside private friendship) to decide, when you have read the following two anecdotes which I pledge myself as having come from Lord Byron.

A lady whose name I am not allowed to mention told Lord Byron that when *Glenarvon* was in the press she received a letter threatening her with cutting a very prominent figure in the novel unless she sent £300 as hush-money. Since his death I have made enquiries of the lady mentioned, who not only confirmed the anecdote but added that the sum was paid.

The second anecdote is this and one which gave occasion to the dreadful lines written in a blank page of *Vathek*—"She offered" says Lord Byron "young Grattan her favours if he would call me out." With the truth of this I have nothing to do; but, if a fact, can we wonder that he who never forgave should have called up in judgment against her what he did.

John Murray was so incensed by the *Conversations*, tradition has it, that he considered sueing Medwin for libel.[11] Instead, he contented himself with addressing a letter to *The Times*, with writing twice to Colburn (demanding that a copy of a deleted, asterisked passage obviously referring to him be sent to him and that the passage be restored in any future edition, meanwhile guaranteeing not to sue), with suppressing Croker's

[11] T. J. Wise, *Catalogue of the Ashley Library* (London, 1922), XI, 136.

too favorable review,[12] intended for the *Quarterly*, and with privately printing, on November 2, a pamphlet entitled "Notes on Captain Medwin's *Conversations of Lord Byron.*" Although it is signed J. M., it omits the names of author, publisher, printer, and place; and Murray refers to himself throughout in the third person. Circulation was limited, and copies were sent around to Murray's friends, twenty-two of whom thanked him and congratulated him in letters which he carefully saved. However, the pamphlet was reprinted in its entirety in the November issue of *The Gentleman's Magazine*, with a post-script lacking in the original pamphlet.

Murray's rebuttal was a dignified one and attempted to refute Medwin by printing, alternately, an excerpt from Medwin followed by one from Byron's letters to him. But what Murray could not effectively deny was that Byron had quarreled with him and had changed publishers, not to mention their smaller, less serious disagreements over the years. On November 14, Hunt's *Examiner* had summarized Byron's relations with Murray since the autumn of 1822 and had published Byron's very severe letter to Murray of October 22, 1822, castigating Murray for failing to turn over to John Hunt the important preface to *The Vision of Judgment.*

Medwin, at Vevey, saw Murray's pamphlet before the end of November. It had been tipped into the appendix of Galignani's English edition. Without delay, by courier, Medwin says, he sent to England a "Reply to be inserted in one of the daily London Papers." Perhaps this was the letter from which *The Examiner* quoted on November 28. On December 1 he also wrote to Pichot,[13] his French translator, asking that his point-by-point reply, enclosed, be published in "Galignani's Weekly Register," and also that it be added to the appendix of the French translation of the *Conversations.*

---

[12] These proofs, with the letters from Murray and Colburn, are now in the possession of Sir John Murray.

[13] Autograph letter from Medwin to Amédée Pichot, Dec. 1, 1824, in the Pierpont Morgan Library. I have not discovered that it was ever published.

By way of introduction, he stated that he had been "very anxious" to see the translation

and hope you will send it me by return of Diligence, and with your permission [I] propose to pass a strict examination of it—as to fidelity &c.—in order that the second Edition may be perfect— besides that it will of course be a great advantage to its sale, that the author of the Original Work has revised and corrected it himself. I also mean to send you notes and remarks for the proper under- standing of many of the Allusions, which must otherwise be lost to the French reader.

This business done with, he moved on toward the serious matter of his reply to Murray, which, he says, he has already requested Colburn to tip into his next edition. Medwin's style shows how excited he was, and his defense is correspondingly weaker than it might have been. Frequently descending in the most deplorable fashion to personalities, he tried to prove what is now easy to prove, "that at that time Don Juan was still a sore subject [with Byron], and that Mr. Murray and his Lord- ship were then at least not altogether on the intimate footing which Mr. Murray would wish to lead the public to suppose had never been interrupted." Murray had made the mistake of claiming that "nothing had occurred to subvert [Byron's] friendly sentiments" toward him.

In replying to Murray on Galignani's offer to purchase the French copyright of Byron's works, Medwin resorted to the argument that in one way or another supported him in most of the questioned reports of Byron's conversation: Byron may have been mistaken. "Lord Byron certainly appears to have supposed that Galignani paid Mr. Murray handsomely for the privileges afterwards assumed, of an exclusive right to print his works in France." The delayed notice of *Marino Faliero* in the *Quarterly Review*, which Byron had complained of, Medwin explains in the same way: "Lord Byron certainly did attribute such delay to the interference of Mr. Murray," whether correctly or not. (Murray and Canning had founded the *Quarterly* in 1809.)

In reference to the £15,455 which Murray stated that he had paid for Byron's poems, although not all paid to Byron, Medwin can only write defensively,

As to whether £15,000 was an exorbitant price for the works of the most popular writer of the Age (Walter Scott has been said to have received £100,000), The Trade will be the best judge. I should however think with Lord Byron that The Corsair and Lara, its continuation, *were* given away, the one at £525, the other at £350 [Murray had stated he had paid £700 for *Lara*] . . . But it is a Subject Lord Byron would never have mentioned had not Mr. Murray as he said pretended to have lost money by being his publisher.

That Byron had attacked Murray in conversation with Medwin is certain, for otherwise Medwin would never have dared to write to Byron, as he did on April 22, 1823, of Murray's "insolence, common to that Autocrat (and which were he a gentleman would require chastisement)."[14] They had discussed the man of trade, and Murray certainly heard Byron's voice echoing out of Medwin's pages. Murray's case had not been helped, of course, when he refused to answer Medwin's letters offering him *Ahasuerus*.

That part of Murray's pamphlet which seemed to Medwin to come nearest his honor as an officer and a gentleman was at the end, indeed, in the form of a postscript. Colburn had finally replied to Murray's request for a copy of a deleted passage which was represented by asterisks but which referred in some way to the deed or contract for *Cain, The Two Foscari,* and *Sardanapalus*. This much had appeared in the first edition of the *Conversations*. The deleted words, which Murray had just seen, were these: "it contained a clause," Byron had supposedly said, "which had been introduced without my knowledge, a clause by which I bound myself to offer Mr. Murray all

[14] Unpublished letter from Medwin to Byron, April 22, 1823, in the possession of Sir John Murray.

my future compositions." Medwin had stated that he had witnessed this deed, in Pisa.

Murray's closing words about himself were, "He has only to observe upon the subject, that, on referring to the Deed in question, no such clause is to be found; that this instrument was signed in London by the Hon. Douglas Kinnaird, as Lord Byron's procurator, . . . and that the signature of Capt. Medwin is not affixed."

What could Medwin reply to this? What had Byron actually said to him? Medwin made two starts. "I certainly did witness on the 28th Novr a Deed . . ." This he deleted and began more convincingly:

I perceive by reference to my notes that on the 28th Novr 1821 about the time *Cain, The Two Foscari,* and *Sardanapalus* were in the press [all three published December 19, 1821] I witnessed a Deed which I understood to be the Copyright of these Dramas. Lord Byron observed that all the witnesses to it had written books. I remember replying that the wonder nowadays was to meet with a person who had not . . . I must therefore have confused some other copyright about which Lord Byron was speaking with this— but there is one fact about which I am not mistaken, and which perhaps is the only one of importance in this question: Lord Byron speaking of some Copyright certainly did make use of words to this import.

And then Medwin quoted the suppressed passage that Colburn had supplied to Murray.

"The Editor of *The Conversations*" had defended Medwin more effectively in a letter to the Editor of the *Morning Chronicle*: [15]

Sir— In the absence of Mr. Medwin, who is on the Continent, and who will doubtless eventually substantiate by original letters or other documents in his possession, the general authenticity of his work, I beg leave to observe, the extracts of letters published by Mr. Murray, in answer to certain statements affecting that gentle-

[15] A copy of this letter is in the possession of Sir John Murray.

man, contrary to the first impression produced by them, and on a mature consideration, to corroborate the truth and authenticity of the *Conversations*, except in the single instance of the deed; and even on this point the letters were not very conclusive . . .

Mr. Murray answers this by referring to the deed for the Two Foscari, Cain, &c., in which no such clause is to be found, and which is signed in London by Mr. Kinnaird, and witnessed by Mr. Williams. Now, it is to be observed, that it does not appear very conclusive that this is the identical deed referred to by Mr. Medwin; it might have been a deed relative to some former purchase which the party had taken this opportunity of sending for Lord Byron's signature, for it is well known, that although that respecting the *Two Foscari* was not [sic] signed in London, yet others were sent to Italy to be executed by Lord Byron himself. If Capt. Medwin had desired to practice any deception (which is quite improbable), is it likely he would have committed himself in so unguarded a manner? Certainly not. And I have no doubt, if Mr. Murray had chosen to refer to other deeds, he would have found one witnessed by Mr. Medwin, and containing a clause of the nature alluded to.

What neither Colburn nor Medwin knew was that the deed to Byron's three plays no longer existed. Shortly after publishing his pamphlet, Murray wrote to Croker, "I told you at the same time I could make oath that I never observed the man's name to the deed—which deed is no longer in existence." [16] Murray, then, in the heat of controversy, had relied on his memory; he had not, as he wrote, consulted the non-existent deed.

But Colburn, even so, may well have hit close to the truth when he referred to "other deeds," and there is one other interesting possibility in Medwin's favor. It was in November, 1821—the month in which Medwin stated that he signed the deed—that a "joint assignment" of Byron's memoirs was made to Murray by Moore and by Byron, complete "with all legal technicalities." [17] Was this then the deed that Medwin had

[16] Autograph letter from Murray to Croker, in the possession of Sir John Murray, dated only "Wednesday" but discussing Croker's review article on Medwin, then completed. Murray found this impartial examination "most distressing to my feelings," and thus it was never published.

[17] Doris L. Moore, *The Late Lord Byron*, p. 30.

witnessed? If so, it seems unlikely that he would have forgotten or confused the nature of the literary property involved—unless, as may well be, Byron had failed to make the matter clear or had deliberately misled him.

In his own defense, to return to it, Medwin turned back to Murray's pamphlet to deal with Byron's letter of February 25, 1824, which Murray had published as proof that "nothing had occurred to subvert [Byron's] friendly sentiments" toward him. The letter described in detail Byron's health, his recent "convulsive attack," and affairs in Greece, but it also contained an expression of friendship for Gifford. It was this portion of the letter, irrelevant to Murray's thesis, that Medwin chose to comment on. In so doing, however, he added another stroke to his portrait of Byron: "Affecting as he did thro' his whole poetical career to despise public opinion, no man was a greater slave to it, no writer of the day, however subaltern, held the Critics in more sovereign awe." Medwin had not seen, presumably, *The Examiner's* demolition of Murray's thesis on November 14.

In closing, he took two or three parting shots at Murray, recommending, rightly, that Kinnaird, "the most Confidential of all Lord Byron's friends and Correspondents," might be able to explain to him fully why Byron ceased publishing with Murray. A little less fairly, he wrote that Murray's "endeavour seems to prove that the Patronage and Benefits were bestowed on Lord Byron rather than received by himself." Then he asked Murray if he had or had not privately printed and circulated a letter "tending to throw ridicule on Lord Byron."

There is one question and only one I would put to Mr. Murray at Parting. Did or Did not Mr. Murray, shortly after or about the time of his difference with Lord Byron, have printed, and circulate among his (Mr. Murray's) friends the autograph of a private letter, or a very familiar paragraph, a private letter of Lord Byron's to him, tending to throw ridicule on Lord Byron. I hope Mr. Murray will be able to answer in the negative.

I now take my leave of Mr. Murray, and embrace this opportunity of declaring once for all that I do not consider myself responsible in any way for the materials or liable in the most distant degree to be called upon to advocate the authenticity of any one of the facts or anecdotes contained in my Publication. These must rest with Lord Byron, must stand or fall upon the authority of *Lord Byron,* for to me, who have consumed the greater part of my life in another hemisphere during the last 14 years, scarcely passing as many months in England, and been occupied in other than Literary pursuits, most of the topics of his Conversations were new, almost all the characters among his contemporaries, who were the subject of them, as well as their works, unknown, the name of Murray no otherwise known to me than through the medium of the Title pages of Lord Byron's Publications.

T. Medwin

Medwin then drew a line through his signature and added another paragraph. "As I am about to close my letter, one from Paris has just reached me saying that Mr. Murray has announced a forthcoming Pamphlet entitled 'A further Exposure of the Misstatements in Captn Medwin's *pretended* Conversations.' To this I shall probably deign no reply. The insolence of such a Title demands other chastisement than Words." Then he signed his name again. The pamphlet advertised was the work of Hobhouse (assisted by Kinnaird, Pietro Gamba, Augusta Leigh, Wilmot Horton, and Mary Shelley), but it had been suppressed since November 14 (after Hobhouse had consulted with Edward Ellice, Sir Francis Burdett, the Reverend George Croly—Byron's Reverend Rowley Powley—various other members of the Literary Fund Club, Lord Brougham, and Francis Place).[18]

[18] Hobhouse's diary, Nov. 4–14, largely unpublished, in the possession of Sir Charles Hobhouse; unpublished letters from Hobhouse to Murray, Nov. 14, 1824; from Wilmot Horton to Hobhouse, dated "Wednesday morning," before Hobhouse's pamphlet was printed; from Mary Shelley to Hobhouse, Nov. 10, 1824—all in the possession of Sir John Murray. On Nov. 19, 1824, Dr. Lushington wrote to Wilmot Horton, from Doctors Commons, "I am clearly of opinion that Hobhouse will do himself,

In a prefatory letter addressed to Murray, November 12, Hobhouse wrote, "After you have read it [the pamphlet], you will, I think, agree with me, that Mr. Medwin's authority is hardly sufficient to establish the authenticity of a single conversation in the whole volume. Pray give what currency you please to the enclosed statements, for which I hold myself now, and at all times, responsible."

Medwin never saw this pamphlet, printed and bound as *Exposure of the Mis-statements Contained in Captain Medwin's Pretended "Conversations of Lord Byron,"* but the insulting title was enough, and he composed a "very warlike" letter, as Hobhouse was to describe it. The contents of the pamphlet were reprinted almost exactly, however—minus the name of Hobhouse as author and the prefatory letter—in the January, 1825, issue of *The Westminster Review.* There Hobhouse changed his tune and wrote a new introduction: "As Mr. Medwin has been a dragoon, and as, moreover, he has recently sent a letter to England of a very warlike complexion, we suppose we must content ourselves with saying that he has mis-heard, not misrepresented lord Byron." Hobhouse then proceeded to publish twelve double-column pages that point out in parallel passages over fifty questionable statements or clear errors of fact, and

---

Lord Byron's memory, & all persons interested, infinite prejudice by suppressing the publication [of the pamphlet]. That such a publication was preparing, nay that it was printed, is matter of public notoriety; how it became so I know not, but such is undoubtedly the fact. The suppression will be attributed either to the impossibility of contradiction, or to fear on Hobhouse's part, & Captn Medwin's Memoirs will derive additional claim to credence . . .

"No publication in the Quarterly can supply its place. A Review is the very worst channel for a contradiction of facts." (Quoted by Doris L. Moore, *The Late Lord Byron,* p. 111.) On Nov. 19, Horton confessed that he had spoken to "several persons" about Hobhouse's pamphlet and had shown it. At this date Horton thought that Hobhouse's material was to appear in the *Quarterly.* It was Horton who pointed out to Hobhouse, contradicting Medwin, that the "£10,000" of Lady Byron was not spent, "as it was in trust." Horton later saw Hobhouse's proofs and made further suggestions. All these letters, presumably unpublished, are in the possession of Sir John Murray.

the implication is that Byron never made any of the remarks referred to. But Hobhouse protested too much, assuming without question, when Medwin's statements revealed any element of factual error, that Medwin must have invented the entire conversation and was in fact a monstrous liar without conscience. And that was the way the problem presented itself to all the interested parties attacked in the book: either Byron lied or Medwin lied, for the precise facts were obviously not those always reported. It never occurred to Hobhouse to ask how Medwin had become acquainted with all these most intimate details of Byron's life, which would allow him to weave together his rich and intricate tissue of accuracies and inaccuracies. For the true ghost of Byron still hovers over the book, and anyone who has ever read a page of Medwin's fictional dialogue will know that in the *Conversations* he is reporting Byron. Hobhouse was a violently partisan reporter who had worked hard over his review, at a time when he was in a state of nervous exhaustion; he had gone through the experience of suppressing his pamphlet; he had seen it declined by the *Quarterly;* he was helping with the translation of Gamba's book; he had seen too many scoundrelly publications about his friend Byron, the latest being Dallas's *Recollections of Byron,* which he finally reviewed along with Medwin. By January or before, his tone had changed considerably from what it had been on the preceding October 25, when he first became aware of Medwin's book and wrote in his diary,[19] "The papers this morning full of Captain Medwin's Conversations of Lord Byron— alas, my poor friend! into what society did he fall—but the attaching so much contemptible gossip to his name more than punishes him for that love of low company which I think distinguished him in his latter days. The honorable Captain has put into Byron's mouth three falsehoods respecting myself . . . Some other anecdotes mentioned by Medwin may I think have come from Byron's mouth—but such anecdotes! !"

[19] Hobhouse's diary, Oct. 25, 1824, quoted in part by Doris L. Moore, *The Late Lord Byron,* p. 102.

Medwin saw Hobhouse's anonymous review, and he replied to it at length in a pamphlet, "judiciously suppressed,"[20] which was dated from the Chateau de Blonai, August 20, 1825. John Galt had seen it and stated in reply to Hobhouse that Medwin had "refuted [him] in upwards of fifty statements."[21] Colburn, responsible for its suppression, it seems, still had a copy in 1828 and offered it to Leigh Hunt to use "the indisputable part of the materials" in his *Lord Byron and Some of His Contemporaries,* which he was then writing.[22] "It would make a piquant *dozen pages,*" Colburn wrote to Hunt; "—so that we give nothing that could embroil Medwin with Hobhouse, the former would no doubt be glad even thus late to see his refutation in print—and he would no longer be responsible for its appearance." It seems clear that Medwin's pamphlet had been judged libelous; for the libel laws were in a most confused state at the time.[23] Out of Medwin's suppressed pamphlet, which has disappeared, Hunt did not get a dozen pages, as Colburn had suggested; he got less than two, but he left the only description of the pamphlet in existence:

An article was written in "The Westminster Review" (Medwin says, by Mr. Hobhouse) to show that the Conversations were altogether unworthy of credit. There are doubtless many inaccuracies in the latter; but the spirit remains undoubted; and the author of the criticism was only vexed that such was the fact. He assumes, that Lord Byron could not have made this or that statement to Captain Medwin because the statement was erroneous or untrue; but an anonymous author has no right to be believed in preference to one who speaks in his own name: there is nothing to show that Mr. Hobhouse might not have been as much mistaken about a date or an epigram as Mr. Medwin; and when we find him giving us his version of a fact, and Mr. Medwin asserting that Lord Byron

[20] John Galt, *The Life of Lord Byron* (London, 1830), pp. v–vi.
[21] John Galt, "Pot *versus* Kettle," *Fraser's Magazine,* II (Dec., 1830), 536.
[22] *My Leigh Hunt Library: The Holograph Letters,* ed. Luther A. Brewer (Iowa City, 1938), p. 143.
[23] See *The Westminster Review,* III (April, 1825), 308–309, an article discussing two recently published books on libel, one of them by John Hunt.

gave him another, the only impression left upon the mind of any body who knew his Lordship is, that the fault most probably lay in the loose corners of the noble Poet's vivacity. Such is the impression made upon the author of an unpublished Letter to Mr. Hobhouse, which has been shown me in print; and he had a right to it. The reviewer, to my knowledge, is mistaken upon some points, as well as the person he reviews. The assumption, that nobody can know any thing about Lord Byron but two or three persons who were conversant with him for a certain space of time, and whom he spoke of with as little ceremony, and would hardly treat with more confidence than he did hundred others, is ludicrous; and can only end, as the criticism has done, in doing no good either to him or them.[24]

As reluctant as this support of Medwin was, and not always clear, Hunt, writing in 1828, nevertheless placed Medwin's book in the first of his five Byronic ranks. "The only publications that contained any thing at once new and true respecting Lord Byron" were those by Dallas, Parry, Gamba, and Medwin.

As early as February, Medwin had seen the review by Hobhouse (whom he took to be the author of *Blackwood's* insulting review also—simply because it was signed "Harroviensis," Byron had gone to Harrow, and Hobhouse was a friend of Byron's youth); but being on his honeymoon he delayed taking immediate action. It was Hazlitt, he says, who advised him at Vevey to write a pamphlet in reply to Hobhouse; Hazlitt, who indeed corrected it and added to it the following passage: "Hobhouse is known of old as a heavy hand; he comes down with a ponderous sledge-hammer contradiction, as though he were forging a thunderbolt, and, with all his din and smithery, fuss and fury, only displaces a comma, or corrects a date. The date and the comma are alike unimportant; not so the critic; whatever he does must be great, and while he thinks the circle around him are astonished at his hard hitting, they only wonder

[24] Leigh Hunt, *Lord Byron and Some of His Contemporaries* (London, 1828, Second Edition), I, 171–172; see also I, 160.

at his want of breath and temper."[25] Opposite this passage published in his *Life of Shelley*, Medwin wrote on an interleaf, bound into his copy, these words:

and Hazlitt adds, "the charges against you are in themselves nothing, all that one can make out is the wonderful air of business, dogmatism, & pedantry & self-importance with which they are brought forward; *au reste* he has the laugh against you in one or two places, for blunders or slips of the pen, a triumph well suited to his good nature & magnanimity." This tribute from so uncompromising and impartial & clear-sighted a critic as Hazlitt, took the sting out of the envenomed shafts of my remorseless enemy. It is the best answer to his malicious & vindictive attacks.[26]

As Medwin wrote, finding "more than thirty instances" of Hobhouse's lying,[27] his temper rose. His honor had been clearly challenged. Hobhouse had written, before subjecting Medwin to a treatment of parallel passages, the column on the right boldly labelled throughout THE FACT, "Certain, however, it is, that the Conversations, such as they now appear, never could have been uttered by his lordship; who, amongst his other noble qualities, was distinguished for a scrupulous regard, even in trifles, to truth." And "Harroviensis" (William Harness), whom Medwin took to be Hobhouse, had published a scandalous story in which Byron had instructed Fletcher, if Medwin ever again borrowed a book without permission, to "Kick his ———."

On September 2, 1825, Hobhouse received Medwin's challenge and on that day set the record straight in his diary:

[25] Medwin, *Shelley*, II, 212–213; compare Medwin in *The Literary Gazette*, Feb. 11, 1832, p. 88. On Feb. 19, 1825, Mary Shelley wrote to Hobhouse, "Yours was a most powerful article in the W[estminster] R[eview]— Dallas must feel rather uncomfortable & I know that Medwin does." From an unpublished letter in the possession of Sir John Murray.

[26] Medwin's unpublished marginalia in his *Shelley*, facing II, 213; in the Pierpont Morgan Library. Compare Medwin in *The Literary Gazette*, Feb. 11, 1832, p. 88. The Hazlitt quotation, if indeed Hazlitt wrote it, must be taken from a letter rather than from any passage that Hazlitt supposedly added to Medwin's pamphlet.

[27] Medwin, *Shelley*, II, 216.

I had also this morning a letter from the scoundrel Thomas Medwin dated 22 August, stating that the Westminster Review of his *work* had only *just* reached him, that he had heard from unquestionable authority I was the author—that it was a tissue of lies and calumnies—and that if I would give him the satisfaction which would enable him to *wipe the stain of* [sic] *his character* he would come to England.

[Sir Francis] Burdett advised me not to answer or notice this billet doux—the time which the fellow had taken to make up his mind to this step—for I am sure the review reached him long ago (Mrs. Shelley told me so by letter in April last)—the nature of the charge, and the character of the accuser would have fully justified my silence—but after some reflexion I thought it would be the shortest way to let the infamous defamer know that I was ready to be met with whenever he might choose to enquire after me, so I wrote to him thus.

Sept. 2, 1825

Sir,

You must know that your letter admits of no answer, but if you have any thing to say to me personally I shall remain in England for the next six months and am always to be heard of at No 6 Albany Court Yard in London.

I am

Your obdt hble sert

J. C. H.

It would not have been right to acknowledge that he had the right to fasten an anonymous publication on me, or even to ask me if I was the author, for the interests of society require that folly and impudence and villainy should be chastised by anonymous criticism. If, however, the rogue does come to me I will tell him in good set phrase what I think of him before I let him have a shot at me. It will be a sad thing if I should be forced to put myself on a level with such a miscreant. When one does fight one likes it to be with a man of character—but whatever happens I have the consolation of thinking that I interfered in this instance merely to do good to society by the exposure of a base fraud and to rescue my late friend's character from the hands of an imposter.[28]

[28] Hobhouse's diary, quoted by Doris L. Moore, *The Late Lord Byron*, p. 120.

At the time that Medwin sent his challenge to Hobhouse, he must also have informed Jane Williams or Mary Shelley of it, for Mary wrote to Hobhouse about it, and he replied on September 17:

Dear Madam,

Many thanks for your letter. I have now only to request that you will be so good as to consider the communication on the subject quite private; at least, for the next six months. I was obliged to answer the billet doux before I received your letter, but I trust the direction which the gentleman gave me to his chateau will be sufficient. I agree in everything you say, except that I do not understand how the conversations could have been more nefarious. Take your choice between the betrayal of confidence and the falsification of facts, and in either case you have a consummate scoundrel in the reporter, or misreporter, of the sayings of our departed friend. But I know more than half of the conversations to be downright forgeries. I cannot therefore comprehend how Mr. Thomas Medwin could have done much worse than he has.[29]

But there were others who took it all a good deal less seriously. Writing to William Blackwood, soon after mid-October, David Lyndsay related another version. His source is almost certainly Mary Shelley, whom he had recently met and whom he had praised warmly in the paragraph immediately before the following story:

Are you aware of the row which has occurr'd between "Hobby O" and that Blockhead Medwin? if not, I write in confidence since I have heard of the affair from Friends, but think it too good to be kept a secret, since I firmly believe the parties concern'd would be sorry it were so—Medwin indignant at Hobhouse's attack in the quarterly [sic] has nerv'd himself up to challenge him, notwithstanding he has only lately become a Husband to an Italian Beauty [sic] of some consequence. Mrs. Shelley, whose Relation Tom Medwin is, wrote to Hobhouse on business, and to him, ridicul'd the idea of fighting for any literary subject with any body. Hob-

[29] *Shelley and Mary*, p. 1240, corrected from the original letter in the Abinger Collection.

house return'd a somewhat angry reply, and treating Medwin very roughly, without declaring any intention either to fight or let it alone. In the mean time Medwin wrote his purpose home to another Lady [probably Jane Williams], and unless he arrives suddenly in England, and meets Hobhouse before any person has information of his landing, I shall believe the whole thing plann'd, in order to secure the interference of the Ladies, and the interposition of the Bow St. Officers. Do not think I judge harshly—the thing to me is apparent.[30]

Lyndsay's account seems to be much closer to the truth than such gossip usually is, perhaps because his source, almost certainly Mary Shelley, knowing both principals, understood the situation better than either one of those directly involved. Hobhouse in literal fact, in so many clear words, had not accepted Medwin's challenge. As Lyndsay observed, he had not declared "any intention either to fight or let it alone." He had merely left the gate open (he could do no less) for Medwin to make the next move—"if you have any thing to say to me personally."

And Medwin, so he said later, "at that moment . . . fell in with Hazlitt. This happened at Vevay. He told me that, in his opinion, my proposed way of settling literary disputes was a bad one, and requested to see the reviews, and my MS. journal. Having convinced him from the perusal of the latter, that every word in the Conversations had been copied from my daily notes, I next . . . , at his advice, wrote a pamphlet" replying to Hobhouse.[31] Colburn printed but never published, and Medwin presumably never saw it.

Thus closely had Hobhouse missed being shot at by Thomas Medwin. (Hobhouse would go on to become William the Fourth's Secretary of War and Victoria's President of the Board of Control.) To this narrow—or not so narrow—miss, Mary

[30] A. L. Strout, "Knights of the Burning Epistle (The *Blackwood* Papers in the National Library of Scotland)," *Studia Neophilologica,* XXVI (1953/54), 96–97. The approximate date of the letter is established by the statement, "Leigh Hunt is returned, and Trelawny is coming."

[31] Medwin, *Shelley,* II, 214–215.

Shelley had contributed a substantial share. She had, in fact, been involved from the first in the relations between the two men. Hobhouse approached her through Gamba, sent her what he had written on Medwin's book, and she replied on November 10, 1824.

My dear Sir,

I have read over your sheets—& have made the following remarks only. If I had Mr. Medwin's book by me I might have enlarged them.

P. 1.—While the dayly [*sic*] occurences of my life were at all interesting to me I kept a kind of journal—more for the sake of dates than for any thing else. In this I find on Tuesday, August 27, 1816, "Shelley dines at Diodati with Mr. H[obhouse] and S. Davis—& remains there all the evening—they go out for a short time in the boat."—The circumstance is immaterial—but this is a war of facts & Medwin may appeal to me. There was certainly no storm—but if my memory do not fail me, a boat was wrecked during the expedition. By the bye Medwin is Captain by courtesy only—is it courtesy to *print* a Lieutenant a Captain? I am not aware of the etiquette on this point.

P. 2.—Is not the Cardinal's name Consalvi?

P. 4. Methinks I have heard Lord Byron complain of the presence of the lady's maid in the [honeymoon] carriage—but if you were there you must know best.

P. 7. L.B[yron] was incapable of praising his own verses—& was certainly satisfied with the opinion all present had of his talents—Shelley was a warm admirer of his poetry.

P. 10. Mazi was a Sergeant not a Major [he was a Sergeant-Major; hence Medwin's mistake].

Not being able to refer to the book, I can only mention a mistake or two that I remember to have struck me. The conversation said to have been held at Diodati is fictitious, since I never saw [Monk] Lewis in my life—and the stories alluded to (with the exception of that of Lewis) were never *related*. As I have an invincible objection to the seeing my name in print, this were as well passed over—unless you chose to observe that the Preface to Frankenstein proves that that story was conceived *before* Lord Byron's and Shelley's tour around the lake [June 22–July 1, 1816], and that Lewis did not arrive at Geneva until some time *after* [in mid-August].

Medwin could also have mentioned that as soon as Dr. Nott heard that he was accused of the impropriety of preaching against Shelley, he paid us a visit to exculpate himself from the charge.

How completely he spoils your story of the Definite Article; I have it as recorded by one of abler memory where it cuts a much better figure.

You justly remark that Lord Byron could not have made an inaccurate quotation—his memory was admirable—Medwin requested me to correct his MS . . . The book has been a source of great pain to me & will be of more—I argued against the propriety & Morality of hurting the living by such gossip . . .

Hence has arisen a "Narrative of a Voyage" &c—When in fact Shelley was never at sea with Lord Byron— In times past when a man died the worms eat him, now in addition viler insects feed on his more precious memory—wounding the survivers by their remorseless calumnies.

Count Gamba has promised that I shall have the book tomorrow when I will again write. He tells me also that he has mentioned to you my wish to have certain letters—but as he gives me hopes that I shall have the pleasure of seeing you, I will defer speaking of these until we meet. Perhaps you will do me the favour to accompany him some morning to Kentish Town.[32]

It was only right, of course, that Mary should trade her comments on Medwin's book for "certain letters" written to Byron, which were now in the possession of his executor, Hobhouse, and the contents of which it was inconvenient to have known. Thus she did not hesitate to associate Medwin's book with the purely fictitious *Narrative of Lord Byron's Voyage to Corsica and Sardinia during the Year 1821.* Hobhouse thanked her on November 12 and made use of her suggestions: "I flatter myself that the Captain will never show his book again; as for his

[32] Unpublished letter from Mary Shelley to Hobhouse, Nov. 10, 1824, in the possession of Sir John Murray. In her comment on p. 1, Mary has combined two entries from her journal and changed her original phrasing.

face, it would be rather satisfactory if he would come here and give some of the relations of the ladies whom he has belied an opportunity of resenting his unmanly conduct."[33]

What should Medwin's defense have been? Croker provided it, although it never saw the public light of day. After noticing that all the inaccuracies and misstatements in the *Conversations* had been regularly laid, by Hobhouse and Murray, among others, to the charge of Medwin, Croker wrote,

But after an anxious examination of the subject, conducted certainly without any partiality towards Mr. Medwin, we cannot be of this opinion. We, on the contrary, believe that Mr. Medwin's notes were made with perfect sincerity, and a desire of fairly reporting what he had, perhaps not so fairly, undertaken to report. It is we think impossible to read his notes without seeing in them all the marks of general authenticity. No doubt he has been guilty of some inaccuracies of detail; . . . but after all, we see no good reason to suppose that his inaccuracies are more frequent than the transmission of recollected conversation to paper is necessarily subject to, and the instances in which errors of any considerable importance have been detected are not many, nor such as to affect in any serious degree the credit of the reporter . . .[34]

Croker reached this conclusion only after a detailed examination of numerous passages which mixed "truth and falsehood"; these he scrutinized at length in his review and was forced to decide that they could derive *only* from Byron: ". . . after great hesitation and with great reluctance, we find ourselves forced to the conclusion that Mr. Medwin's reports are substantially correct, and we must leave to abler pens and more discriminating understandings the task of clearing Lord Byron's memory from the stain which they at present seem to affix to it."[35] Here it was again—the white-hot center of the fire: the "stain" must be attached to someone, and there were

[33] *Shelley and Mary*, pp. 1189–1190.
[34] Unpublished page proof of Croker's review of Medwin, p. 5, in the possession of Sir John Murray.
[35] *Ibid.*, p. 12.

only two to choose between, Byron and Medwin. More chose Medwin than Byron. Croker, however, who had selected most of Medwin's controversial passages from Murray's pamphlet and effectively refuted it, wrote similarly of Hobhouse's: ". . . Mr. Hobhouse's Notes tend mainly to support Mr. Medwin's general veracity." He was right.

Somewhere along the way Medwin informed Grattan that he had also sent a "cartel" to the younger Dallas, who had seen through the press his father's *Recollections of Byron* and written a concluding chapter for it, mentioning Medwin. Perhaps Medwin did not know that A. R. C. Dallas was a clergyman.

Grattan thought that public opinion would have shifted to Medwin's support, "had he, instead of writing transalpine summonses as little likely to bring forth their objects as were Owen Glendower's calls to the 'vasty deep,' put a pair of post horses to his carriage and come to London, with a brace of pistols in his portmanteau . . ." But then Grattan concluded, thoughtfully, "Perhaps he was right; for the loss of a life one side or another goes but a small way towards deciding an argument." [36]

[36] Grattan, *Beaten Paths,* II, 71.

7

High Life and Downfall

The storms following the *Conversations* did not at first touch Medwin, who had been married on November 2, 1824, the very day that Murray's pamphlet appeared. The marriage ceremony took place in the picturesque little town of Lausanne, with its memories of Gibbon (and *Childe Harold*). Perhaps the newly married couple rode on the Lake of Geneva in the new steamship which had begun regular operations the year before, although Medwin later came to feel that it was "hideous . . . , with its blackening column of smoke [and destroyed] the connexion of the present with the past."[1] He and his bride moved almost at once, presumably, to Vevey, only twelve miles from Lausanne. Years later, he thus described the honeymoon of the two main characters in *Lady Singleton*, his novel:

They took a campaign on the Swiss side of Lac Leman, and immediately on it, the pleasure grounds running down to the water's edge.

It was the *petit Eté*, as it is called, and which nature seems to have invested with a peculiar charm, as if willing to put back the evil hour—the approach of winter.

The air was peculiarly soft and windless. The Mont Blanc, a circumstance rare at any other period of the year, was, day after

[1] Medwin, "The Innkeeper of Andermatt," *Bentley's Miscellany*, III (Feb., 1838), 143. This steamer was operated by Edward Church (1779–1845), U. S. consul, who offered Byron one of his steamships in which to travel to Greece in 1823 and later tried to persuade the poet to establish a steamship line in Greece. Byron replied that the Greeks were "too ignorant to become interested in such an undertaking" (*The National Cyclopædia of American Biography* [New York, 1929], XX, 52).

day, distinctly visible in its soft and majestic outline, and assumed at sunset those rose-hues that blend so singularly with the twilight, already begun, as they reflected themselves in the glassy mirror of the lake. Its banks covered with sloping vines had exchanged their monotonous green for crimson and gold . . .[2]

Medwin was happier than he had ever been in his life. On February 22, 1825, Mary Shelley wrote, innocently, to Trelawny,

Medwin's book made a great sensation. He is lately married to a Swedish lady of rank—a baroness by right of birth—a countess by the rank of her late husband—with a good fortune, he says, pretty, & some thirty years of age. However the two latter circumstances may be apocryphal—it is certain that she has some money & consequently that he has made a good thing of it. Moreover I received a letter from him the other day whose seal bears arms . . . supported by griffins with the motto . . . *Nous ne changeons jamais*— happy Medwin! he says that he & his bride think of settling at Florence (they are now at Vevai) & that the last two months have been the happiest of his life. His letter is principally taken up with excuses for having (against my earnest desire) published a very blundering & disagreeable memoir of our Shelley in his Conversations . . .[3]

Medwin's wife was in fact not thirty but thirty-six years old, being three weeks older than her husband. She was born in London and very probably spoke English, for she brought up her two daughters to "know English well and [to be] mindful of their English origin."[4] Her first husband, Count of Starnford,

---

[2] Medwin, *Lady Singleton; or, The World as It Is*, II, 7–8.

[3] *Letters of Mary Shelley*, I, 315.

[4] F. Chance, "Captain Medwin," *Notes and Queries*, Fifth Series, V (Feb. 26, 1872), 161–162. See also *Notes and Queries*, Sixth Series, VI, 168, 293. F. Chance quotes from Medwin's wife's memorial card, printed at Siena, where she died on June 28, 1868: "Nata Baronessa Hamilton, nacque in Londra 26 Febbrajo, 1788." The last reference, above, quotes from Cartwright's *History of Western Sussex*, which describes her as "by her first marriage Countess of Stainforts." There seems to be no basis for this form of the name, and the error was perpetuated in the *Dictionary of National Biography*. I adopt the spelling that appeared in *The Examiner* and *The London Magazine*, when the marriage was announced,

was on such intimate terms with Edmund Burke that the great Englishman had given to him an unpublished manuscript in his own handwriting, a reply to a review of his *Reflections on the Revolution in France.* She may well have been related to the great and greatly prolific noble family of Swedish Hamiltons. However this may be, she brought with her a sizeable fortune, estimated to be as large as £10,000.[5]

The couple continued their long honeymoon at Vevey, and when the summer came, Medwin was delighted to rent the very Chateau de la Tour which William Beckford had lived in while writing *Vathek,* one of Medwin's favorite books. Here, Medwin was told, Beckford buried his wife—in the garden. "There was a tradition," Medwin recalled, "that he used to cross over to an old ruin at Yvoire and that there he composed that marvelous scene in the Cave of Eblis. It was the work of his Daemon . . . If ever a Man was [? serving with] the Devil, it was Beckford."[6] It was a bad omen, sleeping in a house that had been occupied by such a man, but Medwin thought only of Beckford's fame and the beauty of the country.

Very probably he went picnicking to St. Gingolph, which he thought "the most picturesque spot, perhaps, in Europe,"[7] and was bothered there in the beautiful woods by nothing worse than gnats. He saw, probably at this time, the famous *fête des vignerons* at Vevey, put on by the ancient guild of vinedressers.[8]

---

although her name may be spelled "Stamford" in the register of the Certificates of Marriage which was kept in the archives of the British Legation in Berne. The name is also spelled "Starnfold" in Medwin's obituary in *Albery's Horsham Journal,* Sept., 1869. On her memorial card her first name appears as "Anna."

[5] The Burke manuscript and the size of Mrs. Medwin's fortune are mentioned in an unpublished letter from Charles Armitage Brown to Leigh Hunt, June 1, 1830, in the British Museum.

[6] Medwin's unpublished marginalia in his *Conversations,* p. 328. Beckford took up residence at La Tour shortly after his honeymoon, and there his daughter in 1784 was born and died. He was living again in the Chateau de la Tour in 1786, when he was revising *Vathek.* His wife died there in the same year.

[7] Medwin, *Angler,* I, 156–157.

[8] *Ibid.,* I, 210.

He later made a "tour in the small cantons, to compare the glaciers of Grindelwald with those of Chamouny . . ."[9] and decided that those of the former were "finer than the boasted Mer de Glace at Chamouny, that forms the Aviron."[10] Although a complete picturesque tourist, comparing view with view, he was also a devotee of Isaac Walton and surely fished in some of the Alpine streams at this time. It was a pursuit not allowed by any of the standard treatises on the picturesque. Julian, in *The Angler*, says that he "knew every inch" of Switzerland, and indeed there are innumerable quite specific references to Swiss scenes in that book—the Simplon Pass, the Saint Gotthard Alps, a trip from Interlaken to Lauterbrunnen or the Vale of Water-falls, the remarkable bridge of St. Maurice, a single span of more than two-hundred feet, said to have been built by the Romans.[11] There is a description of a Swiss tour from Chamouny to Martigny to Bagne, where an avalanche had held up the waters of the Dranz, which normally empties into the Rhone, with resulting great destruction when the natural barrier broke. There is a set piece describing the "enchanting panorama from the castle" at Thun:

To the east, the sides of hills, covered with vines and country houses; above tower Alp above Alp, the imposing summits of Misen, and Stockhorn, their glacier'd heights contrasting with the sombre verdure of the midway forests of pines; whilst to the west, the eye reposes on the Jura, and between looks over a vast and fertile plain, abounding with cattle and interspersed with fruit-trees."[12]

Medwin may have remembered that Byron had spent a night at Thun, where he had been inspired to write some of his most splendid prose, in the journal kept for Augusta Leigh. One thing is certain: Medwin saw at one time or another the best part of the splendid sights of Switzerland, whose magnificent scenery he remembered vividly years later.

[9] Medwin, "Hazlitt in Switzerland," *Fraser's Magazine*, XIX (March, 1839), 283.
[10] Medwin, *Angler*, I, 243.
[11] *Ibid.*, I, 201, 231, 242.   [12] *Ibid.*, II, 25; I, 245.

Before leaving Vevey for his tour of the Alps, it seems, he met Hazlitt, who was there from mid-June to September 20. Medwin called two or more times at Hazlitt's cottage, which he found in a "lovely and secluded" spot about half a mile from Vevey.[13] They talked about the relative merits of France, Switzerland, and Italy as places to live, and they agreed that at Florence, because of its art treasures, "one is never at a loss how to pass time." Medwin thought " 'la belle France' one of the ugliest countries in the world." Hazlitt objected; he never tired, he said, of "corn plains." These comfortable subjects disposed of, Medwin was forced to listen to an attack on Byron's "avarice." Medwin countered with the details of a story he had outlined in his *Conversations*: [14] Byron had sent £50 to a needy ex-officer in the East India Company's army. Medwin said to Hazlitt, "I told Byron that he had been very shamefully treated in India. On very incompetent evidence, he had been drummed through the country down to Bombay before his trial, and afterwards dismissed the service." Hazlitt replied with other details of Byron's avarice, saying that he insultingly "doled out to Leigh Hunt a weekly allowance," and concluded, "It is the manner of a gift, not the making of it, . . . that stamps its value." Medwin, who had noticed that Hazlitt had not shaved for several days and looked tired or bitter, eagerly seized on this generalization to agree and tried to shift the conversation to the Marquess of Wellesley, who, instead of ordering that a man be given fifty rupees, Medwin stated, used to say, "Give that man a handful of rupees." But Hazlitt persisted and only later did the conversation turn into other channels.

They discussed Manzoni's *I Promessi Sposi*, the first volume of which, much admired by Medwin, appeared in 1825. They discussed the problem of Shakespeare's learning, Medwin find-

[13] Medwin, "Hazlitt in Switzerland," *Fraser's Magazine*, XIX (March, 1839), 278. In this article Medwin states that he made his "tour in the small cantons" after meeting Hazlitt. However, it is possible the tour preceded this meeting, for Medwin's first child was born on Nov. 3, 1825, in Florence.

[14] Medwin, *Conversations*, pp. 225–226.

ing echoes of *Agamemnon* in *Hamlet* and *Macbeth*, as well as other debts of Shakespeare to Aeschylus.

The conversation seemed for the moment to be going better, and Medwin confessed that he, too, was "a disciple of the true romantic, not the pseudo-classical school." But this betrayed him into a reference to Byron's controversy with Bowles over the merits of Pope, and Hazlitt was off again, attacking Byron's tragedies, among other matters, and the conversation ended with "a long discussion on the present state of dramatic literature."

When Medwin called a few days later, Hazlitt's temper was showing even more, and he attacked Scott, Washington Irving, and Byron again, although allowing Shelley to pass unscathed. Medwin tried to placate him by saying,

Byron could write well if he chose, but he preferred being *en dishabille* in prose; besides, he disliked to reason on paper as much as he hated to argue in conversation. He looked upon both as a recreation, not an exercise of mind; he even studied, if I may say so, to be slatterly, and was even ungrammatical at times—a strange affectation: I have some letters of his which would have disgraced a school miss.

But Hazlitt was a bitter man, not now to be pleased. Three years before he had divorced his wife because of his passion for his landlady's daughter, a very ordinary girl who thereupon declined his further attentions. He had relived all his anguished pain while writing *Liber Amoris*, published in 1823, and then in the spring of 1824, cured of both wife and mistress, he astonished his friends once more by marrying a widow, from whom he speedily parted. When Mary Shelley saw him, less than a year before his acquaintance with Medwin, she "never was so shocked in [her] life—gaunt and thin, his hair scattered, his cheek bones protruding . . . the most melancholy of ruins . . ." Only his smile, which brought tears to her eyes, assured her, she wrote, "in a dark night of the identity of a friend's ruined and deserted abode."[15]

[15] *Letters of Mary Shelley*, I, 307.

This is essentially the man described by Medwin. At the end of their conversation Hazlitt "entered into a long history of his own literary wrongs, his neglect by the public, his bitter persecution by the reviewers," and verged on hysteria. ". . . He spoke for half an hour with much rapidity, and with an attempt, at times, to suppress his feelings, that was no less distressing to me than himself. He dwelt upon the personality of these attacks of the reviewers, and their calling him, I think he said, a barber's son, which he denied." Hazlitt's father was not a barber; he was a Unitarian preacher. There was no more virtue extant, Hazlitt maintained, his voice becoming increasingly shrill. "No one, said he, nowadays, can get his bread by his talents, however great they may be, who does not prostitute them—who is not a hypocrite and a bigot. It is because I am neither, that they hate and decry me . . ."

Medwin was uncomfortable in his own new prosperity. "The conversation," he wrote, "had become painful and distressing to me; I knew not what to say to calm him, and shortly took my leave." He went home, he says, and wrote it all down in his commonplace book.

But this was the embarrassing end of a brief acquaintance. Before it had reached its conclusion, Medwin had been able to say that he too had been attacked infamously in the reviews, by Hobhouse, writing, he thought, both in *Blackwood's* and *Westminster*. Hazlitt helped and comforted him, as seen above. They were two injured men, trying to console each other, and Medwin had recorded the conversation of another famous writer. Of Medwin's presence at Vevey, only one voice spoke, other than his own—that of an anonymous "Swiss Gentleman, who spoke of him with regard," to Hogg, who arrived about ten days after Medwin had left in late September or early October, 1825.[16]

[16] *After Shelley*, pp. 41–42. The earliest possible date for Medwin's departure would seem to be about Sept. 17, 1825. T. J. Hogg left Berne on Sept. 20, hoped to be in Geneva on September 27, found Medwin "about ten days" gone when he inquired for him at Vevey.

The time had come to bring an end to this long honeymoon and choose a permanent abode, for Medwin's Swedish baroness (who had dropped her title in favor of plain Mrs. Medwin) "was so near her confinement" that Medwin's friend, the anonymous Swiss gentleman, "almost doubted whether they would reach Florence." [17] Meanwhile Medwin had decided to be remarried, and the second ceremony took place on August 10, 1825, in Berne,[18] at the British Residence. Here, it would seem almost certain, Medwin chose to be remarried in order to have the marriage recorded in the London Registry Office, in the book kept by the Bishop of London.[19] The first marriage at Lausanne would not have been a matter of official English record. Thus he safeguarded the legitimacy of his child, shortly to be born. The honeymoon was now over. Ten days later he dated his reply to Hobhouse, from the Chateau de Blonai.

He had reason to remember this second ceremony, which bound him to the British divorce law, and years later he wrote a grim little story of seduction and suicide (or murder) entitled "The Three Sisters. A Romance of Real Life." It opened, bitterly,

I was at Berne on a very particular occasion—a very particular one indeed, so that I cannot help remembering it. What object other than most travellers in Switzerland have, do you suppose led me there? To see the view from the terrace? No! To save you the trouble of any more guesses, I will at once come to the point, and say, that I went to the capital of the Canton to—be married. As the

[17] Unpublished letter from T. J. Hogg to Jane Williams, Oct. 17, 1825, in the Abinger Collection.

[18] A military form, called a "return of service," which Medwin filled out in March, 1829, indicates that he was remarried in Berne on August 15, 1825 (letter to the author from Mr. D. W. King, Librarian of the British War Office Library). However, in the register of the Certificates of Marriage deposited in the Archives of the British Legation, the date is given as August 10, 1825. I assume Medwin's memory to be in error.

[19] "By an order of Castlereagh's (7 May, 1816) all records of weddings celebrated at British Residences abroad were to be sent to the Bishop of London for entry in the book kept at his London Registry Office" (Ivan Roe, *Shelley: The Last Phase* [London, 1953], p. 172).

car drew up to the door of the minister—I do not mean the divine,—
I found before it a vast crowd of the citizens, who, with shouts and
hisses, were dragging along two persons, both young, and one very
handsome, a boy and girl, I might almost call them; I tell you no
fiction,—to be yoked together, whether they would or not . . . We
were shown into a room, till the ceremony—the wedding—was
concluded; and then came our turn.[20]

If true, it was a bad second beginning.

From among all the cities of Europe, Medwin and his bride
of a year chose Florence in which to settle, "Florence the magnificent, with its fortressed palaces—its Piazza Vechia, crowded
with statues, its Santo Croce, and Cascine and Gardens, and
splendid galleries . . ."[21] These words appear in his biography
of Shelley; writing his novel, *Lady Singleton,* he expressed his
love for Florence with even greater enthusiasm.

Florence! How shall I apostrophize thee? Shall I call thee the
gem of gems, the treasury of the arts?—speak of thy gates of
paradise—thy Venus, that enchants the world, the mighty conception of a colossal spirit—thy night and morning—the inestimable
riches of thy galleries—thy Andreas—thy Baroccios—thy Frates—
thy Bronginos? Shall I hail thee as the birthplace of the greatest
poets, save one, and the most enchanting of prose writers? Or shall
I address thee as magnificent Florence—call thee a city of palaces—
zoned with palaces?—Ask the reader to pace with me the Lung
Arno, or ascend the heights of Fiesole, and look around, below, on
thy world of beauty?—to thread with me the classic gardens of the
Pitti, or drive through the shady avenues of the Cascine? Or shall I
ask him to carry back his thoughts to the past?[22]

Medwin would never forget it. The dust of Cawnpore was
half-way round the world, six months' voyage away. He had
finally found his home, although he did not live there long.

Here Thomas Jefferson Hogg, who in 1827 would form a
union with Medwin's favorite, Jane Williams, found him and

---

[20] Medwin, "The Three Sisters. A Romance of Real Life," *Bentley's
Miscellany,* III (Jan., 1838), 66.

[21] Medwin, *Shelley,* p. 231.

[22] Medwin, *Lady Singleton,* II, 46–47.

the expectant baroness on November 2, 1825. ". . . The poor countess was in bed in the next room," Hogg wrote, "waiting . . . to get worse before she gets better." [23] Her sister had come, and a doctor was in attendance. They were living in the "quiet Square" of Santa Maria Novella, "dull," Hogg observed, "but favorable to parturition." The child was born the next day, November 3, and on December 25, "according to the rites and ceremonies of the Church of England," was baptized Catherine Mary Anne Pilfold Hamilton Medwin,[24] thus perpetuating the name of the child's mother as well as that of Medwin's mother, to whom he remained deeply attached over the years. He chose as the officiating clergyman, the Reverend Richard Burgess, one of the two clergymen present at the burial of Shelley's ashes in Rome. Pilfold, it may be recalled, was also the maiden name of Shelley's mother.

When Hogg called again, Medwin showed to him a letter from the wealthy Sir John St. Aubyn offering to be the child's godfather. Thus much he left her, with her English name and blood. Medwin had been "very good" to Hogg, the latter wrote on January 6, 1826; "the Countess is quite well, & the little girl is a fine child." [25] Medwin promised Hogg that he would write to Jane Williams.

And so the little family settled down to the life it would live for the next three years or less, and Medwin delighted in it all. The spirit of Shelley still hovered over the city for him, and he still kept Shelley's beautiful description of Florence, as seen from the Boboli gardens—"a smokeless city" of "domes and spires," framed by the Apennines, their green valleys gently unfolding upon the plains, and bisected by the Arno.[26] Like

---

[23] *After Shelley*, pp. 47–48.

[24] A copy of the baptismal certificate in the Public Record Office. The original was signed "R. Burgess of St Johns College Cambridge and Domestic Chaplain of the Rt Hon Lieut Genl Lord Aylmer." The document was witnessed by Medwin and Harriet Hamilton, who was very probably the sister of Medwin's wife.

[25] *After Shelley*, p. 61.

[26] Medwin, *Shelley*, pp. 198–199.

Shelley, he too was a "constant visitor to the Uffizi Gallery," and he lovingly recalled the *Niobe,* the *Apollo,* the *Dancing Faun,* the Medician *Venus,* the *Laocoön,* the *Bacchus and Ampelus,* all in that gallery. In later years he was also to make perceptive comments on the collections he had already seen at the Louvre and at Rome.[27] He was a dedicated dilettante. Nor was he less passionately interested in music than in sculpture. We read in *The Angler,*

It was a grand piano of Broadwood's, and on the desk lay the opera of "Semiramide." I was familiar with the music of that chef-d'oeuvre of Rossini, for I had been at Florence in 1826, and during six weeks drank deep of the inspiration of the divine and soul-piercing Pesaroni.

The book was open at a cavatina which had stilled, night after night, the noisy "palchi" of the Pergola . . . She began to sing: the enchantment increased; her voice was a magnificent "contr'alto"— her accompaniment faultless, for she indulged in no variations of her own, and contented herself with the notes as they were written, which I perceived, by the sharpness of the character, were French . . .

Her deep notes now penetrated the bottom of my heart, and now she played with her voice like a humming bird fluttering over the tops of flowers; and when she ceased, I was so charmed to silence that I had no breath to utter a single "bravo." To conceal my emotion, I involuntarily turned over the leaves of another book lying on the rack, and happened to light on a 'duo' in Odoardo and Oloiska, which I had heard— But no matter.[28]

Beethoven, however, with his "unutterable tenderness and beauty, [was] the Shakespeare of German composers," and Shelley's "Stanzas Written in Dejection" affected him "like the slow movement in some of the Sonatas of . . . that incomparable composer."[29] There was no higher praise he had to give. He felt the kinship of these sister arts and knew that the highest pleasure comes only when the poem is read repeatedly, the music heard time after time.

[27] *Ibid.,* pp. 222–224, 197, 216–217.
[28] Medwin, *Angler,* I, 272–275.
[29] Medwin, *Shelley,* pp. 209, 310.

Only rarely was he able to hear more music than he wished, but when he was living in the Piazza Santa Maria Novella, "so called from the splendid church of that name," he heard so much that he was forced to change his residence. The occasion was a Roman Catholic jubilee, given once every fifty years, and it continued for several months, while "daily, almost hourly, priests, 'black, white, and grey,' passed [by his house] in long procession, chanting in their monotonous, melancholy, deep-toned drawl, suitable passages from the breviary; the bells—how I wished, with Voltaire, the ropes round the necks of the tormentors—jangling, in horrid discord, an accompaniment to the dismal psalmody. It was too much for mortal endurance."[30]

By March, 1827, or before (secure in his knowledge that another jubilee would not be held for fifty years) he had moved into the splendid Casa Filicaja, on the Piazza d'Ognissanti, across from the old church of the same name, with its grand figure of St. Augustine by Botticelli. Once again Medwin had expressed his veneration of the poets, for the name of his house perpetuated that of the seventeenth-century Florentine poet whose famous sonnet "Italia, Italia" Byron had translated in *Childe Harold*, IV. From this address, on March 27, 1827, he wrote to Mary Shelley, who had perhaps inquired about the effeminate soprano Giovanni-Battista Velluti, whom she defended in two articles written in 1826.

My dear Mary,

What shall I say to you to excuse my long silence—I believe I had best say nothing—& yet I ought to have long ago thanked you for your kind letter & remembrance of me & my wishes in sending me my dear lost friend's Posthumous Volume—which I have read and re-read but always with additional delight— No that is not the word—In there were many of the beautiful poems it contained that reminded me of him, & of the past.

I don't know how it happened, but we saw little of Velluti during his stay here. My wife was ill, & did not go out— & his time was so much occupied at Lady Burghersh's & by Lord Burghersh

---

[30] Medwin, "Doctor Crispinus," *Ainsworth's Magazine*, II (1842), 317.

that he could not spare any portion of it for others—What exquisite taste he has—what wonderful intonations of voice—what powers peculiar to himself— When he left us he was quite recovered from an attack that had nearly proved fatal (at Venice), a mal di Petto— Would you believe that Boy, as he lives, he is 54 [he was born in 1781]—I had this from good authority—

Pasta [the soprano] has left or is about to leave Naples, where she has given better satisfaction. Il Carlo was too enormous for her weak organ—When she first saw it she burst into tears & soon relinquished the attempt to be heard in it, singing afterwards at one of the minor Theatres— She did not honor us in her way thro' Florence—indeed she passed thro' it in the night— Her reason for doing so was a poor one— She said she did not mind singing at Ld Burghersh's but could not bring herself to sing Lord Burghersh's Music.

Every Thursday during Lent we have had this purgatory—& last week it was more like High Mass than any other thing human or divine. Her Ladyship is finer than ever— But her airs & graces are quite lost on everybody this year. The Saturday Concerts at Court are quite delightful.

Who do you think is to be here in a few days—the Guiccioli—on her way to Rome from Ravenna. Old [? Juliani] whom you may remember at Pisa tells me that she is again separated from the Count, whom he describes as an old Profligate. When she arrived at Venice [in July, 1826] she found her place occupied it seems [by a Venetian prostitute]. It is said that the old Russian has beat her more than once—the *last* of which seems a favorable reason for Separation. Sgricci has given up Improvising—at least before the English, of whom he has taken a thorough hatred— He came back from England foaming at the Mouth like a Mad Dog & his Rabies has not yet left him.

At Paris they have struck a Gold Medal in his Honor & he has published a Drama on the subject of Missolonghi—taken down in Short Hand from an Improvisation at Paris—rather calm stuff.

Pacchiani has again made his disappearance from the world— It is said that he has been in bed for some months with an attack of *Spleen*—but the cause of his concealment has been otherwise accounted for—& in a probable way— There has been published here a most atrocious & Sanglante letter—which passes in review all the nobili of this highly Moral City— Their names appear at full length—& you may conceive what a Sensation it has occasioned— The Grand Duke has exiled an Abbé, a great friend of the Ex Professor's [Pacchiani], for having borrowed and kept one of the letters in the pesky affair, & probably the Professor keeps out of the way till the Storm has blown over— So much for our general acquaintances here.

Do you and Jane still adhere to your intention of revisiting Florence— We are fixed here in all probability for several years— having far the best House in Florence—one of those old Palaces built in the Republic & modernised 50 or 60 years ago. I hope you will one day see us in it— We opened the other day 10 Rooms & had upwards of 400 people. So large is the Society of Florence— This letter is intended for Jane as well as yourself—give my kind love to her & tell her to think of me as I think of her— I shall hope to hear soon that Percy & her dear Children are well—& believe me

Yours affectionately

Medwin

P. S. We have had Mr. [William Alexander] Madocks here all the Winter—who speaks always with the greatest affection of our poor Shelley— Give me some literary news when you write. Gal[ignani] has printed your Last Man [Paris, 1826]— My friend Dr. Lamartine is a great admirer of it. What are you doing now? I hope not idle. You promise more of Shelley's prose writings— Do you mean to perform it. I hope so. Lady Byron is at Genoa & coming to Leghorn, where we shall pass part of the Hot months & part at the Lucca Baths, where we lodged last year with Chiappa [Shelley's old land-lord], who showed me some letters of Shelley's to him— he has a very nice cottage near the Villa Bridge— I want to see the rooms where you lodged [in 1818]. Adieu.[31]

[31] Unpublished letter from Medwin to Mary Shelley, March 27 [1827]. Medwin does not name the year, and the postmark is almost illegible, but the events referred to in the letter suggest 1827. *The Last Man* was published by Colburn in Feb., 1826, by Galignani later in the same year. Teresa Guiccioli separated a second time from her husband about Dec. 1, 1826 (Iris Origo, *The Last Attachment*, pp. 389–390). E. C. Mayne, *Life of Lady Byron*, pp. 309, 311, says Lady Byron "spent a year on the Continent" and returned in Dec., 1828. If, however, Mayne's "year" is anything less than two years, Lady Byron might have been on the Continent as early as Jan. 1827.

Even at the height of his prosperity the details of Shelley's life remained dear to him. And high estate it was indeed, with ten rooms opened up for his nearly four hundred guests, a very fashionable neighborhood. There, on the Piazza d'Ognissanti, which opens upon the Lungarno, Caroline Murat, sister of Napoleon and queen of Naples, owned a residence, where she died in 1839. Was Medwin thinking of his own house, when in his novel he described the Florentine palace taken by Lord and Lady Singleton?

They had fixed their domicile in one of those palaces so common in Italy, that seem made for giants, and serve to remind us the more of pigmies to whom they belong. This pile is said to have been built after a design by Michael Angelo, whose architectural genius was generally shown in what the painters call breadth—in the grandeur of the proportions rather than details—unity of parts and a certain stern simplicity, being his general characteristics. But in this building, as in the celebrated *Ritter Saal* at Heidelburg— perhaps the finest known specimen of the Ornate, enriched as it is with its caryatides, its niched statues, and relievos, and medallions— he has not disdained to employ a style almost as elaborate. These two edifices bear a marked resemblance to each other; and whether constructed or not after a design of Buonaroti's, there can be little doubt but that they sprang from the same hand—the projecting blocks composing the basement story, for the purpose of resisting cannon, in the turbulent times of the Republic, being imitated in the celebrated ruined castle hall of the Palatines.

The interior of this noble edifice corresponds with its facade. The hall was only second in size to that of the Lanfranchi, at Pisa; and a vast suite of rooms, hung with silken arras, and gorgeous with gilding—their ceilings painted by some good artist in the palmy days of the Florentine school—when illuminated by thousands of tapers, and filled with the *elite* of that luminous capitol, furnished a scene of enchantment.[32]

Byron paid only 200 zecchini or about £90 per year for the Lanfranchi in Pisa, which Shelley described as "the finest palace

[32] Medwin, *Lady Singleton*, II, 48–49.

on the Lung' Arno."[33] At this rate, Medwin may well have thought he could afford his palace, with its hall smaller than that of the Lanfranchi. His military pay, about £85, would probably have paid the rent—after the place had been furnished.

Florence, city of beauty, was also a city of gaiety, especially at Carnival time, and in this Medwin delighted, writing of it,

It was the Carnival at Florence; and the Florence Carnival, since Venice fell under the domination of Austria, is the most brilliant in Italy. This year it was in its very zenith; and the great influx of foreigners of distinction, of all nations, made it for some months every day a *jour de fête*. The *Corsos* had been more than unusually splendid, the fours-in-hand would not have disgraced any race-course in England, and, indeed, the horses, carriages, and servants were mostly English. A Neapolitan prince drove his team, *à l'antique*, the horses nearly naked, and the court added to the splendour of the endless procession, by appearing in the liveries, and with the running footmen of the time of the Medicis.

Among the equipages, that of a Russian nobleman [Nikolay Demidov] did not attract the least notice; he had brought with him from his own country, the mixture of grandeur and meanness, the magnificence and bad taste that are found in the establishments of these polished barbarians . . . And to crown all, . . . a company of French comedians were among his singularities. Twice a week Vaudevilles were acted at his theatre, afterwards transformed into a ball-room . . .

The Palace of a native prince [? Prince Borghese] was also open weekly, the Austrian ambassadress, herself one of the finest con-tr'altos in Europe, figured in the 'Barbière di Seviglia'; at the palace of another Ambassador [Lord Burghersh] were represented his own operas; and another English nobleman, who had himself a great talent for the histrionic art, got up private theatricals [in a theatre in his own palazzo: this was Lord Normanby, counselor of the legation and author of *The English in Italy* (1825), a collection of romances in three volumes].

These were some of the weekly festivities of the season.[34]

---

[33] Shelley, *Works*, X, 318 and note 1.
[34] Medwin, *Lady Singleton*, II, 69–71.

Medwin was moving in the most exclusive circles. He thus describes a masked ball at Florence given by the Prince Borghese:

Not only the rotunda, whose perfect proportions and elegant design have been the admiration of all Europe, but the great gallery that runs through one wing of this gorgeous Siennese palace, supported by its columns of marble, almost equal to the *giallo antico*, were open; also the vast suit of rooms branching on all sides from them, and brilliantly illumed by thousands of tapers, that made an artificial day.

It was a *bal costumé*, and nine hundred persons from every country, habited in the costumes of all nations and almost all times, formed an assembly, such as Florence, in these degenerate days, can vainly boast.[35]

Nine hundred guests—more than twice as many as Medwin had invited, but no matter; he was "doing the great man at Florence, giving parties etc.," Mary Shelley wrote. She thought that the English there, some two hundred families altogether, "were very shy of him" because of the *Conversations*, "but if he regales them that of course will wear off," she prophesied to Trelawny.[36] Medwin, for his part, discussed her with the Grand Duchess of Tuscany,[37] and his wife became "a great favourite at court."[38] In June, 1824, the mild and enlightened rule of Ferdinand III, patron of the arts and sciences, had been succeeded by that of his son, Leopold II, "mildest and least reactionary of all the Italian despotisms of the day."[39] Both Medwin's daughters were to marry into the Tuscan court circle.[40]

[35] *Ibid.*, II, 79.

[36] A copy of an unpublished letter from Mary Shelley to Trelawny, Easter Sunday, 1827, in the Abinger Collection. Hunt, *Byron*, II, 385 (2nd ed.) refers to the number of English in Florence.

[37] Medwin, *Shelley*, p. 375.

[38] F. Chance, "Captain Medwin," *Notes and Queries*, Fifth Series, V (Feb. 26, 1876), 161–162.

[39] *Encyclopædia Britannica*, 11th ed., articles on Ferdinand III and Leopold II.

[40] Chance, "Captain Medwin," pp. 161–162.

Lamartine, "dressed so perfectly like a gentleman, that one never would suspect him to be a poet" and recently married to a young and beautiful English heiress, had been transferred in 1824 to Florence, as a member of the French diplomatic service. His *Le Dernier Chant du Pèlerinage d'Harold* appeared in 1825, the year that Medwin settled in Florence, and it is virtually certain that the two men discussed Byron at length. In later years, when Lamartine came to write his *Vie de Lord Byron*, published serially in *Le Constitutionnel*, he acknowledged in his preface the assistance of Medwin, whom he knew, he said, and who had given him documents relating to Byron.[41] Medwin recalled hearing the Grand Duke tell Lamartine "that he had had his Meditations in his pocket for two years"—presumably trying to understand the poems.

At the home of Lamartine, Medwin often encountered, among other literati, "the celebrated poetess" Delphine de Gay (Madame de Girardin) and her mother, Madame Sophie Nichault de la Valette Gay. It has been said of the latter's salon that it "was the resort of all that was most brilliant in French society under the Empire."[42] The daughter was such a social success among the literati of Rome that in 1827 she was crowned in the capitol. Medwin must have been very happy.

Among the English at Florence that he knew during these years was Lord Dillon, friend of Moore and Mary Shelley, a zealous disciple of Kant, and author of *Eccolino, the Tyrant of Padua*, which he insisted was an epic, reading it aloud to all who could be cornered to listen. Leigh Hunt, when he lived in Florence, was honored to name the bizarre viscount among his acquaintances, although he confessed that Dillon "ought to have been eternally at the head of his brigade, charging on

[41] *Le Constitutionnel*, Sept. 26, 1865. Lady Blessington, *Idler in Italy*, II, 476, describes Lamartine's appearance; Medwin's recollections of him appear in *The Athenaeum*, "Foreign Correspondence," June 13, 1840, p. 476.

[42] Medwin's unpublished marginalia in his *Conversations*; Byron's *Letters and Journals*, V, 104, note.

his war-horse, and meditating romantic stories," instead of living in the present prosaic age.[43]

Medwin also knew William Alexander Madocks, to whose Tremadoc Embankment in Wales Shelley had subscribed £100 and helped to raise more. The wealthy and philanthropic Madocks had built a model village on land that had once been under three feet of sea water, but in the 1820's his financial condition had become so reduced that he had retired to the Continent. With both Madocks and Dillon Medwin discussed his idol Shelley, and Dillon in his way was almost as enthusiastic as Medwin, who upon this foundation came to know him well.[44] He met Lady Burghersh, wife of the British minister plenipotentiary at Florence, and found that her "beauty, grace, elegance, and talents" made her palazzo "the charm of Florence."[45] He was particularly impressed by the fact that she had taken up painting after she had passed the age of thirty (she was born in 1793) and was approaching a level of distinguished excellence. She was also an accomplished linguist. She and her husband, known as Lord Burghersh until 1841, when he succeeded his father as Earl of Westmorland, set the tone of the English and international society in Florence. Only four years older than Medwin, he had seen military action in Egypt, Portugal, and France and had been minister at Florence since 1814. Further, "as a musician he was not less distinguished than he had been as a soldier and diplomatist."[46] In 1823 he had founded the Royal Academy of Music. Some of his seven operas were performed at Florence. He also wrote masses, cathedral services, anthems, hymns, and canons. It is to this religious music that Medwin refers in his letter of March 27, 1827, to Mary Shelley: "Every Thursday during Lent we have had this purgatory—& last week it was more like High Mass than any

[43] On Dillon, see Moore, *Memoirs*, IV, 180; *Shelley and Mary*, pp. 1111–1112, 1121–1122, 1165; Hunt, *Byron*, II, 377.

[44] Medwin, *Shelley*, pp. 116, 225.

[45] Medwin's unpublished marginalia in his *Conversations*, p. 33.

[46] *Dictionary of National Biography*, "John Fane," 11th Earl of Westmorland.

other thing human or divine." Medwin suffered, but Burghersh never knew it and set to music a seranade written by Medwin. It began,

> When I crost the Ocean wave, Love,
> Far—far from love and thee,
> The plighted faith you gave, Love,
> Was something still to me.

Among other English, Medwin knew Sir William Drummond, then an old man. His *Oedipus Judaicus* (1810) had explained the Old Testament in terms of astronomical allegories. Medwin had heard Byron "speak more than once of his *Academical Questions,*" which Medwin thought "a good analysis of the different schools of philosophy."[47] But he decided that Drummond was "a better Metaphysician than Connoisseur in Pictures, for he told me that his Collection, which cost him £12,000, sold in London at auction for £1,200. He said that he travelled into Germany on purpose to purchase a small Raphael, for which he gave £500. He added that he . . . now felt suffocated in the air of a gallery." Medwin commented, "Well he might!" Medwin would soon understand perfectly this sense of suffocation in an art gallery, but the evil day had not arrived yet.

He met Shelley's and Mary's friends the Gisbornes at the Baths of Lucca, in the summer of 1826 or 1827, and introduced them to the Prince of Lucca and to Demidov, one of the famous Russian family. He found Mrs. Gisborne "an amiable & interesting person" and her husband "not ill read," but "a great Bore."[48]

Here also he met Teresa again, after seeing her in Florence, on a visit at her aunt's. She told him that "she was often closeted" with her husband, the old and wicked Count Guiccioli, from whom she had secured a Papal decree of separation, "and that he was a *very bad man.*" Medwin met her also at

[47] Medwin's unpublished marginalia in his *Conversations,* p. 157, also the source of Medwin's other remarks on Drummond in this paragraph.
[48] Medwin's unpublished marginalia in his *Shelley,* I, 313; in the Morgan Library.

a ball given by Prince Borghese, where he introduced her, he says, to William King, later Lord Lovelace, "and little thought then that he would have married Byron's Ada," as he did in 1835. He noticed that Teresa's beauty had faded badly and wrote to Mary Shelley that she was "the ugliest woman he ever saw in his life." Mary observed that Medwin had become "a great man at Florence."[49]

Pacchiani, "the devil of Pisa," was now operating in Florence again and haunted Medwin "like an unquiet spirit," not allowing him to forget their old acquaintance at Shelley's. One day, Medwin wrote,[50]

when at my house, he said mysteriously,—"I will introduce you to an old friend—come with me." The coachman was ordered to drive to a part of the city with which I was a stranger, and drew up at a country house in the suburbs. The villa, which had once boasted considerable pretensions, was in great disrepair. The court leading to it, overgrown with weeds, proved that it had been for some years untenanted. An old woman led us through a number of long passages and rooms, many of the windows in which were broken, and let in the cold blasts from "the wind-swept Apennine;" and opening at length a door, ushered us into a chamber, where a small bed and a couple of chairs formed the whole furniture. The couch was covered with white gauze curtains, to exclude the gnats; behind them was lying a female form. She immediately recognized me— was probably prepared for my visit—and extended her thin hand to me in greeting. So changed that recumbent figure, that I could scarcely recognize a trace of the once beautiful Emilia [Viviani]. Shelley's evil augury had been fulfilled, she had found in her marriage all that he had predicted; for six years she led a life of purgatory, and had at length broken the chain, with the consent of her father; who had lent her this long disused and dilapadated *Campagne.*

She wept over the departed Shelley, whose *Epipsychidion* she had inspired. And she must have wept for herself, for the cruel

---

[49] Medwin's unpublished marginalia in his *Conversations,* pp. 19, 26; Medwin, *Shelley,* pp. 327, 381; *Letters of Mary Shelley,* II, 4, 14.
[50] Medwin, *Shelley,* p. 289.

marriage, now broken, which Shelley had tried to protect her from, wept for her four dead children.[51]

If Medwin wept also, it too may have been in part for himself. His time was running out, and he would soon be ruined. "Pisa and economy are at an end," Mary Shelley had written,[52] without fully knowing the implications of her words. For by the middle of 1828 Medwin had suffered the most serious financial losses.

His amateur's love of painting, coupled with his extravagances, his imperfect understanding of the use or management of money, had betrayed him. Trying to recoup his losses, incurred when living beyond his income in Florence, he had speculated in Italian oil paintings, returned to England to sell them, and there found them to be of little value. He had been cheated. Mary Shelley wrote to Jane Williams, in a letter postmarked July 17, 1828, "Trelawny [who had just returned to England] tells me that Tom is in difficulties & that he has returned to Italy—a picture speculation (witness Shorediche) is the last resort of men— With his palace—his horses—his routs & his passion to *fai figura*, I can easily believe that Tom, had he a million a year, would get encumbered. What does the Countess say?"[53] In his adversity, she found it easy to pity him: "Poor Medwin!—from first to last—poor Medwin!"[54]

The details of his downfall must have been very similar to those he described in an anonymous article called "Autobiography of a Picture-Fancier," contributed to the first number of *The New Anti-Jacobin*, April, 1833, and identified in the table of contents of his copy as his own.[55] The anguish of the story

[51] R. Glynn Grylls, *Mary Shelley* (London, 1938), p. 138 note.
[52] *Letters of Mary Shelley*, II, 14.
[53] Unpublished letter from Mary Shelley to Jane Williams, postmarked July 17, 1828, in the Abinger Collection. Shorediche was the name of Jane Williams's sister Sarah, it is stated in a note in an unknown hand preceding a group of Jane Williams's letters in the Abinger Collection.
[54] *Letters of Mary Shelley*, II, 4 (June 28, 1828).
[55] Medwin's annotated copy of *The New Anti-Jacobin*, identifying his own contributions, is in the University of Pennsylvania Library. Medwin's article occupies pp. 74–79.

is genuine, the circumstantial details overwhelming. I quote the account in full.

I am acquainted with a person who till he reached the "mezzo cammin" of life had never shaken a dice-box or entered a gambling-house. Being at Paris, curiosity took him to Frascati, whose pestilential atmosphere he has breathed ever since. There is some similarity between my friend and myself. Cards have been "the devil's books" to him; paintings his hooks for me. The rage for play is said to be innate: Gall and Spurzheim have discovered the boss. I forget whether the love of pictures is laid down in their chart; but I look upon it as a facetious one,—at least this passion never developed itself in me till after my crossing the Alps, and I was then turned thirty. I had, it is true, as a lounge, gone more than once to Lord Grosvenor's and the Marquess of Stafford's, and walked twice through the half mile of rooms at the Louvre; but if in these places I ever stopped to look at a group, or head,* or landscape, which pleased me, I never inquired who was the master, nor should I have thought less of them had the artists been obscure, or their names absolutely unknown.

I have since blushed for myself, and wondered how nature and beauty in the abstract could have charms for any man who has the slightest pretensions to *vertù*. This was after I fixed my residence at Florence, where I thought it indispensable (would I never had!) to become a connoisseur.

Some demon whispered, "Visto, have a taste!" But I anticipate.

If my observation had been confined to the human face and forms divine of our fair countrywomen, as exhibited in the "Tribune," instead of its being directed to the walls, it had been better, even if I had endangered the loss of my heart at every successive visit; but, alas, I gazed on the Fornarina till I fancied myself bound to fall in love with her, though I never before could endure brunettes or masculine women. As ill luck would have it, I happened to meet in this Temple, sacred to Venus, one of those gentry who live by their good spirits, yclepted a *cicerone*, who had picked up sufficient English to dilate, with all the jargon of his tribe, on the distinguish-

---

* The price given in England for single heads astonishes the Italians, who properly estimate the value of pictures of fine masters by the number of figures they contain.

ing merits of different schools, of course giving the preference to his own. Every word he uttered seemed to me an oracle. I became his echo; he followed me like a shadow; but of all masters, he most encouraged my predilection for Carlo Dolce—and I soon got desperately smitten with the Sant' Agnese of that *pretto naturalista* in the Baroccio-room. One day when I had arrived at the point my new acquaintance wished, he told me, in a "sotto voce," that a certain Marchesa, a descendant of the Medicis, had a Carlo Dolce infinitely finer, and that he would take me to see her. I gratefully accepted his offer, and accompanied him to the palazzo. We were shewn into a deserted, sun-unvisited, fireless, enormous saloon, with a plentiful lack of furniture, and what there was, apparently coeval with the structure. It was of a kind such as aristocratic bad taste and folly have lately brought into fashion in England—marble-slabbed tables, supported by tarnished cherubim, and chairs which it required a dowager's hoop to fill, and a porter to lift. Our Marchesa presently made her appearance, and with her an attendant, carrying an antique carved case, which, as I supposed, contained the *chef-d'oeuvre*.

No relic was ever more carefully enshrined. Had it been painted by St. Luke himself, like the celebrated miracle-working Virgin and Child at Bologna, it could not have been better secured against all possible mishaps. The casket was at length unlocked, a favourable light chosen for the exhibition, a green curtain drawn aside, and this wonder of wonders displayed. Suffice it to say, that I was dazzled, entranced—nay, more, that, overcome by my entreaties, and the eloquence of my *disinterested* friend, the noble dame was persuaded to accept a draft for 100 sequins, and make me master of the treasure.† The scene was pathetic—she wept bitterly at

† On coming out of the Royal Gallery of T——, where I had greatly admired a small Flemish painting, the *custode* whispered me, that if I wished I might become the possessor of the landscape; and added, seeing I was surprised at the offer, "You know we do not esteem the Dutch school, and I have the privilege of selling, to buy with the money." At the Duke ——, at Genoa, are on sale some curious landscapes, that formed the sides of Charles the Fifth's bed, painted by Titian. Cardinal Fesch's collection is waiting for a new owner, and Madame Mère's is already gone; in fact, there would be hardly a good picture left at Rome, if the government wisely (though by a great stretch of arbitrary power) had not made them heir-looms in families.

parting with the last of her "Lares," and I had tears of rapture in my eyes. I took home my prize. What a bargain!—50*l.* for a real Carlo! Many times a day did I open my chest, and pore, like a miser over his gold, on the charms of my Madonna, till I almost adored her, doted on her as a lover does on a lock of his mistress's hair, the first token of an acknowledgment of a mutual passion. I no longer wondered at Pope Innocent's idolatry of St. Agnes, or at the magnificent temple in the Piazza Navona he erected in honour of that Venus of the calendar; but Bernini's Donna Olympia, for she sat to him for the saint, seemed to me a cold and lifeless shape in the mere form of woman, in comparison with *my* Virgin. How soft and velvetine was her complexion, how animated with love her eyes, in which something of earth mingled with heaven, how voluptuous the full and flowing contour of her form! In short, it would have required little, I am convinced, at that time, to have made me a devout convert to the Romish faith; but I soon had other idols to divide my worship.

The fame of this exploit soon got wind. From the *"Terreni"* to the *"Quinti Piani,"* it was immediately noised about, that a new *"Compratore di quadri"* was arrived, in the person of a *"Signor Inglese,"* rich as a *"Milordo."*

All the picture-sellers, picture-dealers, picture-restorers, and picture-frame makers, were in a bustle and uproar of delight. My *"anticamera"* was filled, from an early hour in the morning till dark, with *"Mezzani,"* the messengers of mysterious Counts and Marcheses, inviting me to their galleries, and handing me their catalogues. Sometimes these hawkers would bring with them, on commission, paintings they had no scruple of baptising with the highest and most *sacred* names. In short, the fascinating rogues understood their craft so well, that not a day passed without my adding to my stock some *"studio studiato"* of Allori, or *"bozzo"* of Andrea del Sarto, badly drawn indeed, and worse coloured, but full of thought and sentiment,—and an indubitable original. But these issuers of base coin were petty rascals compared with the licensed pickpockets in the *"Lung' Arno"* and *"Piazza Santa Croce."* There is a proverb which says, that it takes three Jews to make one Tuscan. O the insinuating, uncircumcised dogs! How many falsely-certificated and wrongly-cited pictures did they not palm off upon me! How many execrable daubs was I not wheedled into buying against my better reason, solely through their importunity, and the lies with which these *dealers* in iniquity varnished over their impostures! I now began to make a *"catalogue raisonné"* of my pictures, with engraved outlines, and asked *my friends* to bring *their friends* to look at them. I was surprised that they were not in ecstasies; but attributed their silence to ignorance or envy, or pitied their want of taste when they could not see the beauties even after I had so eloquently pointed them out. My collection at length swelled into a gallery, for I bought by wholesale, and spoiled my crimson, green, and yellow-damasked walls, by nailing on them worm-eaten and dingy frames, which enclosed more dismal-looking inmates. I knew, indeed, that they were not all *capi d'opere*, but consoled myself with their being *originals*, all, of some master or other. But what originals, and of what masters? Oh—such Holy Families, with the usual sheepish-looking Saint Joseph at his book or carpentry, and saucer-faced and goggle-eyed cherubim, with green and golden wings, as bright as Rubi's in the *Loves of the Angels*—such St. Sebastians, those catholic Marsyases—such *Stregonerie* of Salvator—such St. Francises in the black stage of the cholera—such Salvatores Mundi, *"alle stimmate"*—such frightful-looking Lanfranchis of St. Peter, from the recollection of which Lord Byron probably formed the wish that he had been *"sweeter"*—such martyrdoms, such grilling, and roasting, and shearing, and spiking, and flaying alive, better suited to Juggernaut or Moloch than the living God—such lively representations of purgatory and hell, that instead of drawing-rooms one might fancy one's-self in the chambers of the Inquisition, and be afraid of shewing a lady in, lest the sight of such horrors might produce the same effect on her that the Furies are said to have done in the play of Æschylus.

I have often wondered since at the complacency with which I used to look at these devildoms, and been surprised at my blindness and credulity. As an instance thereof—a notorious picture-smuggler ‡ came to me one evening with a most mysterious face, telling me he had got a real portrait of a great master. I followed him outside the walls, where, sure enough, on a panel was written, "This is the *Ritratto* of ―― Buonarotti, father of, and painted by, Michael Angelo Buonarotti." The date, the ugliness of the wretch, who had a broken nose, which gave him a strong family resemblance to

‡ Pictures pay a duty on entering Florence, according to their value.

Michael Angelo, made me conclude I had got a capital prize in the lottery; but—horrible discovery!—I soon found, after I had made the purchase, that the subscription was a forgery, that beneath it was another, purporting that the hero was a doctor, and the artist some painter not to be found even in Baldinucci or Vasari, those chroniclers of many a dauber whose works are only known in their pages, and whose names might as well have perished too, without much loss to the world of art.

This trick and some similar ones, which I kept to myself, at length gave me a dire suspicion of the unauthenticity of my Raphael—that my Baroccio was not sufficiently "impasted," and looked too fresh to have been painted in the fifteenth century,—that my "Woman taken in Adultery" was a Bonifaccio instead of a Titian; and, to crown all, I had it hinted that my dear obliging Marchesa's "Madonna" was no other than the entire production of a certain Florentine called Fineschi. Will you believe, that when I taxed him with the fraud, the funny rogue confessed it, and laughed in my face? He was, indeed, the Raphael of restorers. He had purchased, for five pauls, in the street, a half-length panelled picture, discarded by the gallery. It had really once been an angel of Michael Angelo, of which nothing remained but one arm. Now there happened to be an engraving of this very picture; and our fortunate artist, by dint of two or three years' indefatigable labour, contrived to work it up—ay, in such a manner, that, if one eye had not been rather out of drawing, no Peacock, Woodburn, or Emerson, could have detected the renovation. He modestly asked 2000*l.* for this curiosity, and was once fool enough to refuse 1000*l.* He outstood his market—outwitted himself, and still has, and is likely to retain, his Angelo-Fineschi, or rather Fineschi-Angelo. How many Honorio Marinaris, Alessandro Lomis, Mancinis, or Agnese Dolces, has not this incomparable imitator passed off upon poor John Bull for Carlo Dolces! § How many Elisabetta Siranis for Guidos, how many Pandolfos and Ghisoltis for Salvator Rosas, have come out of his manufactory! Nay, how often has he not even persuaded the directors of the gallery, with Benvenuto at their head, to certify

§ Not fewer than 500 *Carlo Dolces* have been sold at Florence since the peace. Carlo Dolce died young, and worked with infinite care and labour. All the pictures he painted are cited by a contemporary historian, and do not amount to fifty; very many of which are in the Pitti, Uffizi, the Marchese Ferronis, or other galleries in Tuscany.

their originality! O *fine* Fineschi! O miracle-working *Fineschi!* It was through you that I became initiated in all the mysteries of your high calling, and was let into the system of depredation called *dealing*, that supports half the population of Florence, Rome, Venice, and Bologna. Your English dealer makes a freemasonry of his virtuous art, but you made no secret of yours. I was persuaded, good easy man! that because Florentine pictures were black with the sun, or rotten by damp, from their having been exposed in processions, or hidden in cellars during the French revolution, that *all* old ones were in a similar predicament—that they lost nothing of their value by being retouched all over—that a general coat of varnish and water-colours would last as long as the original oil-paint.

But the film at last fell from my eyes. I asked an Englishman, who had for forty years been enriching his country with some of the finest specimens of ancient art it possesses, his opinion of mine. He had the sincerity to undeceive me. I restored my walls to their primitive cheerfulness, had my paintings packed and sent to Leghorn, where I almost freighted a vessel with a cargo for the London market. They unhappily reached the place of their destination too safely. Would they had gone to the bottom of the Mediterranean! I should, in that case, have got my insurance! No such luck for me. I think I see them at Christie's now. His great room was completely crammed from top to bottom with them. The day of sale came—there were hardly twenty people present.

Do not suppose, reader, that I had nothing but copies or daubs. Among the first in the catalogue were two landscapes. They had been hung high in a bad light, and in a corner of the exhibition-gallery, as being of no consequence. They happened to be Canalettis—were views of the Tiber, with some old brick buildings. The colours seemed put on with a trowel, and were rich and varied, and as true to nature as in a camera obscura. I remember there was a squall coming on in one, that blackened the river as the wind passed over it in the distance, and that the sun gleaming partially through a cloud on the mass of masonry, was magical in its effect. The first offer was 5*l*. Going! going! My poor Canalettis, they would have been knocked down!—I said 10*l*., and they were finally sold for 250 guineas, to the solitary bidder against me, the only one of the famed connoisseurs in London who had discovered that they were not Guardis. I had several other pictures of a high class; but it is the interest of dealers to decry all those that are not known and pedigreed in the market. I was forced to buy in the best part of the collection. To end the melancholy story: from Christie they went to Phillips, from Phillips to Foster; till, after warehousage, commission, and duty, were deducted, they barely repaid the cost of their frames.

Sir William Drummond's collection cost him 12,000*l*., and only brought 1200*l*.; he turned pale at the name of a painting, and felt suffocated in the air of a gallery. So it is with me; I had rather be in a charnel—where I heartily wish all venders of patched canvas, for my sake.

Should England ever form a gallery, let it be a national one; let her not again buy Schedonis for Corregios, but encourage her own artists, who will then no longer confine themselves to portraits, but, in their treatment of historical and other subjects, vie with, if not surpass, the old masters. And if this doleful tale should be the means of weaning one compatriot abroad or at home from a similar dupery and folly, I shall not have been writing or suffering altogether in vain.

If the account is at times colored—which is far from certain— if he altered prices of purchase and sale and sometimes misspelled the names of his painters, the main outlines are surely set down with honesty and accuracy, along with many of the details. For Medwin was not given to making up stories which placed himself in a bad light—and here he looks very foolish, indeed. How like him to buy first and then give his greatest admiration to an imitation of a Carlo Dolci Madonna, to be thus led into the whole heartbreaking business of folly. For Carlo Dolci, it has been said (by William Michael Rossetti), "holds somewhat the same rank in the Florentine that Sassoferrato does in the Roman school. Without the possession of much genius, invention or elevation of type, both these artists produced highly wrought pictures, extremely attractive to some tastes. The works of Dolci are easily distinguishable . . . ," but not by Medwin, alas, who must have been attracted by the "pathetic or at least strongly sentimental emotion" which marks the sacred heads of Dolci. Rossetti concludes, "There is a want of character in his pictures . . ."[56]

One fact is clear: Medwin had lost a vast sum of money. In little more than a year his great household in Florence was broken up, and he had separated from his wife, leaving behind him two small daughters, the second named after her mother, Henriette.[57] Sadly he left the auctioneers in London and returned to Florence.

A brief and unpleasant glimpse of Medwin's crumbling financial position (and his consequent irascibility) is afforded by his treatment of one of his servants, a German named Frederick Novak, who charged that Medwin had dismissed him from his service while still owing him money on several counts ("per vari titoli"). This suggests that something more than wages may have been involved. On September 17, 1828, Medwin was called before the Commissario of Santa Maria Novella, the ward in which he lived. The Commissario and his assistant tried to persuade Medwin of the advantages of a friendly settlement out of court, but Medwin replied that he would pay nothing and that the tribunal was not a competent one. Then he turned to leave. Perhaps all he meant to say was that the court did not have jurisdiction over his case.

Before he had left the building, he was called back, and the Commissario tried, he said, with the greatest courtesy, to persuade Medwin to an agreement with Novak. But the fiery Captain interrupted, would not let the Commissario finish speaking, said that he did not intend to pay Novak a penny, that the Commissario did not understand the matter, that this was not a competent tribunal—and left, in a very unbecoming fashion.

Novak was instructed concerning his right to apply to the Magistrato Supremo, and Medwin, charged with insubordinate conduct, was ordered to appear before His Worship the Auditor

[56] W. M. Rossetti, "Carlo Dolci," *Encyclopædia Britannica*, 11th ed.
[57] Medwin's obituary, *Albery's Horsham Journal*, Sept., 1869.

and President of the Buon Governo (Foreigner's Division).
Here he was severely admonished, threatened with the withdrawal of his visitor's permit and expulsion from the Grand
Duchy, if he should ever again fail to show the proper respect
and subordination to the public authorities. Presumably he
never again made this mistake in Florence, and it seems that
Novak never sued.[58]

Early in the next year, toward the end of February, 1829,
Trelawny arrived in Florence, and it was at this period, it seems
most probable, that Medwin "gave" to him the four and a half
Shelley letters published in Trelawny's *Records*. Trelawny,
writing about fifty years afterwards, stated, "The first time I
met Thomas Medwin, shortly after Shelley's death, was at
Florence." It is quite unlikely, however, that the two men were
in Florence "shortly after Shelley's death." Medwin, Trelawny
continued, "called to thank me for some service I had done
him." Is this a reference to Medwin's unauthorized and misleading use in his *Conversations* of Trelawny's account of the
cremation of Shelley's body? Did Trelawny, in effect, blackmail
him, in return for the letters? It does not seem impossible.
"Some service I had done him"—the words have an ominous
ring. And the dialogue that follows is too neat: in it Medwin
not only suggests that Trelawny write Shelley's biography but
also disposes of Mary, Godwin, Peacock, Hogg, and Hunt as
potential biographers. That any conversation resembling the
following one ever took place is uncertain, although of course
it may have occurred exactly as Trelawny described it. Medwin
is reported as saying,

"You ought to write Shelley's life. You and Williams were his
inseparable companions the last and important year of his life. He
loved Williams, but Williams died with him. I was at Naples; you
alone did all that could be done to the very last. He liked you
exceedingly from the first of his seeing you; your enthusiasm and

[58] Unpublished court records of 1828, in the state archives of Florence,
case no. 1769, involving Medwin and Frederick Novak (Buon Governo
Comune).

unselfishness charmed him; the same qualities made him like Williams. I have two or three letters of his, and might have had more; but I have been careless of letters, and when moving about I burn them. I will write down things I remember, and give them to you. The public are quite ignorant of him, and, now he is gone, they will perhaps listen to the truth."

I asked, "Why cannot his wife write? She has been with him for some years."

Medwin said, "No, women cannot write men's lives and characters—they don't know them: much less his—he was so different from ordinary men. She told me she could never get him to speak of the past. He disliked being questioned, was impatient, left the room whenever she attempted it; and never spoke of himself. She knows very little of his early life, except what I and others have told her."

TRE.: There are his early friends, Godwin, Peacock, Hogg, and Hunt.

MEDWIN: They were his book-friends, fellow-students. They admired his great abilities, his generosity of character; but they had no sympathy with his writings, they laughed at his transcendentalism and enthusiasm. Shelley said that men herding in great cities might differ widely in theory, but all of them did the same things in their daily life, and though they denounced abuses and clamoured for reform, any changes that interrupted their habits they would have abhorred; they exhausted their strength in words. They will grieve at Shelley's death, some of them, because of his many amiable qualities.[59]

And then Trelawny proceeded to attack in his own voice the potential biographers that Medwin had named, reserving for the climactic position Mary Shelley, who in April, 1829, the year of Medwin's catastrophe, had refused to authorize Trelawny as Shelley's biographer. So he has Medwin authorize him. Or did he? At this time, in Florence, Trelawny was writing his "autobiography"—a mixture of some nine parts fiction to one part fact. An unpublished letter from him to Mary, June 24, 1829, reveals some of his motives and the climate in which

[59] Trelawny, *Records*, II, 20–22.

the book was composed: "But she [Jane Williams] thinks me
a scoundrel to—& that I have outlived my honesty,—had I died
in Greece—I should have been still blessed—at least in your
memorys—and yet if I had told you a plain Tale—your hearts
would have been softened towards me—however I am writing
an honest confession of my life—and then you will see—what
conjuration & mighty magic—for such proceedings I am
charged withall I have used—and for which I am called
worldling." [60] He never got over the fact that Byron had cast
him as Othello. Mary decided that he had been "destroyed by
envy and internal dissatisfaction." [61]

It was this man who on October 20, 1829, devoted an entire
letter to the subject of Medwin (and his own good services).
Trelawny wrote to Mary, from Florence, [62]

After what I told you in England about Medwin's goings on—
you will not be surprised at any folly—or vilainy he may have
committed you used to like and laud him to and thought me rash
& violent in asserting him to be a coward—a liar, and a scoundrel—
nevertheless he has proved himself all three be the judge—yourself—

A Month back Mrs Medwin sent a message desiring to speak to
me—I had just returned from Ancona—Medwin was in England—
Mrs M—— said on my entering the room I must remark it was only
the 3 time I had seen her—"that she wished to consult me";—after
the usual apologies—says—"that she had not herd of or from her
husband for nearly two months—that a Banker *Orsi* had been to
her—& told her that Bills he had cashed to the amount of £800 of

[60] Unpublished letter from Trelawny to Mary Shelley, June 24, 1829,
in the Abinger Collection.

[61] *Mary Shelley's Journal*, p. 202.

[62] Unpublished letter from Trelawny to Mary Shelley, October 20,
1829, in the Abinger Collection. In an unpublished letter from Claire
Clairmont to Jane Williams, postmarked Feb. 26, 1830 (in the Abinger
Collection), Claire wrote of Trelawny, ". . . when his brain is once
heated, out of every thing that is cast in, it forges something new [*i.e.*,
false]; not out of willfulness, but from the laws of its nature and kind."
Claire was commenting on Trelawny's assertion that Mary Shelley had
supplied materials to Moore for his *Life* of Byron; Mary had falsely
assured Claire that no such aid had been given.

Medwins had been dishonored & returned him" "I said well is that all,—" "No she said other people had applied to her for money due;—" " well I said have you the means of paying them! "no she said;"— he went away suddenly and left me no money—and I am ignorant of his affairs:" I said if you are Mrs. Medwin so am I,—I was told you brought Medwin a considerable fortune—and thought he was living on that—for I never heard that he had any of his own— Oh yes she said—I had when I married nearly ten thousand pounds—originally it was eight but by economy in Switzerland I increased it— And Medwin told me his Father allowed him £800 a year—and that he was very old & infirm and on his death he would come into 3,000 pr annum.— "Well I said had you any other authority for believing it to be true— No she said only his declaratin.—" And you fully relied on his apurances.— "certainly, and have & do still;— I then got up and said very well then of course when you write to Medwin and tell him of these trifeling debts—he will remit the money—for a man with the income you say he has can have no difficulty in procuring a £1000— What do you mean she said has he not told me truth— I have no friend here and no relations living—oh pray tell me has he not £800 a year— £800 a year I said I dont believe—he has £80 of his own a year or once had— She nearly fainted— I said can you have been married to him five years & not know this— I then told her a plain tale—but I said— Still Mrs. Medwin as you said your money was intailed on you—you have still enough to live here well on— Oh no she said— I have been his victim—he under different pleas got me to [? recipt] my money to his custody—

I suppose it is unnessesary for me to say more—since that time— (such is my destiny)—I have been taken up with Mrs. Medwin affairs—and selfish as you & Jane think *me* unlike a worldling I have exerted myself to serve Mrs. M. now that she is in poverty— ruined & abandoned— I alone—that neither feasted or visited her during the prodigal days of her Husband—am now set to work counting arranging seling & economising—and doing all those things I would never do for myself—and at the same time I do this—I know to a fraction what will be my reward—that her & her husband will shun me & denounce me [? some day]

Yours & Truly
E. J. T.

This is Trelawny's letter exactly as he wrote it. The violence of his tone is to be explained in part perhaps by the fact that one of Medwin's creditors had seized some carriages which Trelawny claimed as his own. Meeting the banker Orsi at the palazzo of the British Minister, Lord Burghersh, Trelawny in a loud voice had called the Italian a "blackguard." Orsi promptly petitioned the court for redress, and Trelawny, for the first time in his life, it may be, was forced to apologize.[63]

How much of Trelawny's letter is to be believed? That Medwin's wife was left to live on a greatly reduced income is certain. About a year later, on October 6, 1830, John Gisborne wrote in his journal, " 'Muso' [Tonelli, whom Gisborne had met that very evening] gave me the news of the breaking up of Medwin's splendid establishment in Florence under very deplorable and, it is insinuated, under very dishonorable circumstances— His wife, the poor 'Baroness born,' and his two children, in a state next to destitution, have found an [? asylum] at 'Sienn.' "[64] Medwin's family was not quite in the destitute circumstances described by Gisborne, for Mrs. Medwin "was a great favourite at the Court of the then Grand Duke of Tuscany (the Court of Lorraine, as it was called), and the Grand Duchess took charge of the two little girls, and had them carefully educated in a convent at Florence."[65] This part of the story ended happily enough, for Medwin's elder daughter grew up to marry the Grand Chamberlain to the Court of Tuscany, M. Arreglio; and his younger daughter made a brilliant match. She married the wealthy Marchese Nerli, who inherited a rich estate from his friend Count Pieri (on condition that he take the latter's name and title), and in 1876 Count Pieri Nerli, still

[63] R. Glynn Grylls, *Trelawny* (London, 1950), pp. 167–168.
[64] Unpublished journal of John Gisborne, in the Abinger Collection, Oct. 6, 1830.
[65] F. Chance, "Captain Medwin," pp. 161–162; Medwin's obituary, *Albery's Horsham Journal*, Sept., 1869. Medwin's second daughter was born at some time in 1829, after March 19, when as a half-pay officer he filled out a "return of service" form, which stated that he had only one child.

married to Medwin's Henriette, had two palaces, five or six large estates, one daughter, and five sons.

But what was Medwin doing back in England when Trelawny called at the Casa Filicaja in Florence about September 20, 1829, and was told, supposedly, that Mrs. Medwin had not heard from her husband for nearly two months, or since the latter part of July? Had he in fact run out on his family without a word, simply disappeared, as Trelawny implied? There is a much more likely explanation. On September 4, 1829, at the age of seventy-six, Medwin's father had died, after a lingering illness.[66] After his return to Italy, following his catastrophic losses in London, Medwin, informed of his father's last, long illness, must have very shortly returned again to England. No wish would be more natural for him, the elder surviving son, named after his father, than the wish to be at his father's deathbed. Now, more than ever, he needed his inheritance, for with it he could mark off his losses and live again (for some years, at least) as he had become accustomed at Florence. When the will was read to him, the shock was probably the greatest one he had ever suffered. His father had left him ten guineas for a memorial ring. He had indeed had great expectations, and at this most critical point in his life he was left almost penniless, a gentleman of expensive tastes without a gentleman's income. He was trained for nothing except a lieutenancy—and writing for a living. On March 19, 1829, he had declined returning to active military service.[67] Quite incapable of supporting his family on his own earnings, it seemed, he decided to leave them, reduce their number by one (the most expensive one), and allow the Baroness to try to live on the remnants of her fortune and her influence at Court. She did, and she lived to be eighty. He turned increasingly to his pen, which, it seemed

---

[66] From the tablet in Horsham Church. Sir Timothy Shelley wrote on Dec. 15, 1829, "Medwin is dead at last. Voltaire could not suffer more in agony for three days" (Shelley's *Works*, VIII, xliii). This I take to imply a lingering illness.

[67] Medwin's "return of service" is preserved in the Public Record Office.

just barely possible, might support him, author of the famous *Conversations of Lord Byron.*

In his absence, in early January, 1830, Donato Orsi and Company, bankers, sued him before the Royal Supreme Court of Florence and won a judgment against him. Medwin was notified of the first hearing, held on January 2, but chose to be neither present himself nor represented by anyone. Orsi, one of the most innocent bankers in all history, stated that he had made loans to Medwin which were secured by certain property to be assigned to him in the event of nonpayment. This property was said to be located outside or beyond ("sopra") London. Becoming suspicious of this security, Orsi had then requested, as further collateral, jewelry, silver, and a hunting rifle—all of which were deposited in three locked chests, Medwin retaining the key. Upon investigation, it proved impossible to secure the legal title to the English property. At this point, Orsi sued. The amount that Medwin owed, secured in fact by nothing more than his own signature, is startling, almost beyond belief. Including interest, miscellaneous banking charges, and court costs, the sum amounted to 30,000 lire, defined by the court as the equivalent of 18,000 Tuscan florins. He was notified of the judgment against him through his servant, Gabbriello Martelli, who presumably informed the Baroness.[68]

Trelawny was not alone in helping her through this difficult period. Charles Armitage Brown wrote to Joseph Severn, in early 1830, probably in February,

I have been very much occupied in Mrs. Medwin's affairs, battling with bankers, and lawyers, with my hands day after day full of documents in Courts of Law; let this be my apology, especially when I tell you I have been of service to that ill-treated lady, with whom every one in Florence sympathises. I have had much con-

[68] Unpublished court records, in the state archives of Florence, of the suit brought against Medwin in 1830 by Donato Orsi and Co., case no. 8, Magistrato Supremo.

scientious responsibility on my head, little able to think of any thing else." [69]

Brown continued to interest himself in Mrs. Medwin's affairs and on June 1, 1830, wrote to Leigh Hunt that she was "anxious to turn every thing of value into money . . ." He was trying to sell for £25 the Burke manuscript which she still owned, and he thought that Hazlitt or Colburn might be interested.[70] Medwin was far away, already in Genoa. He could do no good in Florence, and the advantages of returning were uncertain.

Exactly how had he perpetrated this astonishing swindle? This is probably impossible now to ascertain, from existing records. At worst, he had signed a legal document, accepted without investigation by Orsi, stating that he owned the English property in question. It is difficult to believe that any banker would unquestioningly accept as collateral such a document. At best, it would seem, Medwin had stated that he would inherit, as elder son, from his father, who was aged seventy-five years in 1828. There is no evidence that Medwin ever felt he had dealt dishonorably with either Orsi or the Baroness. Undoubtedly, he thought that his intentions were of the best, from first to last.

[69] William Sharp, *The Life and Letters of Joseph Severn* (London, 1892), p. 161.
[70] Unpublished letter of Charles Armitage Brown to Leigh Hunt, in The British Museum.

8

Literary Labors

Following the death of his father, Medwin, left now with £10 and the half-pay of a lieutenant, returned again to Italy, the land he knew best and loved most in all Europe. Characteristically, he chose Genoa the Superb, a city he had repeatedly passed through but never lived in. He who had looked upon beauty so often and possessed it so seldom would now try once more to sustain himself upon it. Perhaps he made the journey this time by sea: he vividly remembered in later years the passage through the Strait of Gibraltar, the great rock towering above him:

There is not on the face of the whole world a spot that in sublimity can match with this, uniting, as it does, in one point of view, outlines so varied and picturesque; exciting emotions so profound, and reviving recollections so heroic. For we behold, on either hand, two continents, where civilization and barbarism meet; two quarters of the globe the most dissimilar, and hostile to, each other.

After a brief further voyage through the smooth waters of the Mediterranean, the ship glided between the two gigantic moles stretching out into the Genoa harbor, and Medwin, familiar with the bloody history and the beauty of the city, anticipated the splendors that he would soon live in the midst of.

Here stood the Doria Villa, with its terraces, quarries of marble; its frescos, painted by Perin del Vaga, one of Raphael's most distinguished pupils. To the left I saw the San Pier D'Arena, through which old Andrea [Doria, in 1547, the year of the Fiesco conspiracy] fled after the death of his nephew Jiannettino. On the hill to the right was pointed out to me the site of La Inviolata, the palace of his rival, the princely Fieschi.

I visited in thought, the D'Arena, where he sank in all his armour, on crossing a plank to a mutinous galley; and the gate against which was nailed the head of the Brutus of the conspiracy, Verrina.

I walked in idea through these streets of marble palaces, the Balbi, Nuova, Novissima, and Carlo Felice, entered the splendid churches of San Lorenzo and San Siro.[1]

The churches of Genoa, their color and their music—these are what he chiefly recalled:

The churches of Genoa are perhaps the most splendid in Italy. It is the only state that has preserved almost entire its monastic institutions and the immense revenues of its clergy, and the *Fêtes d'Eglise* are celebrated there with a pomp that I have observed nowhere else. Brilliant illuminations, the walls, the pillars completely covered with crimson damask, give San Siro the semblance of a theatre, and we might almost fancy ourselves, so exquisite is the music, at the representation of *Mose en Egitto*. Indeed, it is not uncommon to adapt the operas of Rossini, or any favourite maestro of the day.[2]

And he goes on to refer to the "gorgeous dresses of the officiating priests" and the "elevation of the host through clouds of incense." But here too, in this church, he was a mere observer, not a participant. This religion was not his. Nor were the Genoese struggles toward Italian independence his—although because of them he was investigated by the police as a former associate of Byron and a suspected Carbonari, and was ultimately given twenty-four hours to leave this city of informers and revolutionaries.[3] Genoa, by a secret clause in the treaty of Paris, had been incorporated into the realm of the King

---

[1] Medwin, "The Quarantine," *Bentley's Miscellany*, V (May, 1839), 502, 504.

[2] Medwin, "Pasquale; A Tale of Italy," *Bentley's Miscellany*, IV (Sept., 1838), 292.

[3] Medwin, "Memoir of Shelley," *Athenaeum*, Aug. 11, 1832, p. 523, note.

of Sardinia, and in 1830 Mazzini, whom Medwin met,[4] was arrested and imprisoned. In 1833 an uprising planned by Mazzini was put down with cruel severity by Charles Albert.

Unable or unwilling as an Englishman to participate openly in Italian intrigue, Medwin turned to his pen and to the most ambitious subject he ever attempted: an attack upon tyranny in the form of a poetic drama dealing with the first part of the Prometheus story. He called his play *Prometheus the Firebearer* and dedicated it, on a beautifully hand-lettered title page "to the memory of Shelley."[5] It was never published in English, but it was translated into Italian and so published in Genoa in 1830. The translator was the distinguished Lorenzo Antonio Damaso Pareto, translator of Shelley's *Adonais* and the collaborator of Mazzini. In Italy Pareto is regarded as "il primo Shelleyano."[6] Undoubtedly the two devoted Shelleyans discussed their idol together.

The translation of Medwin's play, *Prometeo portatore del fuoco,* was enthusiastically reviewed in the Florence *Antologia* for July, 1830, where an advertisement of Pareto's translation of *Adonais* had appeared earlier in the year. The reviewer, "K. X. Y.," noticing Medwin's disclaimer in his preface of making any "profane attempt to revive a lost play of the Trilogy" of Aeschylus, found the work to have a new and beautiful boldness ("bello e nuovo ardimento"), to be original in its imitativeness of Aeschylus ("originale nella imitazione"), and quite splendid in its many genuinely ancient beauties ("splendido di molte e veramente antiche bellezze"). The passages chosen by the reviewer to illustrate such beauties are these:

> De'suoi capelli le diffuse anella
> Dalla benda di perle ivan disciolte
> Ondeggiando dintorno alle leggiadre
> Membra, e qua e là, come di vite errante

[4] Maria Luisa Giartosio de Courten, *Percy Bysshe Shelley e l'Italia* (Milano, 1923), p. 137.

[5] Medwin's autograph manuscript is in the Humanities Research Center of the University of Texas Library.

[6] Giartosio de Courten, *Shelley e l'Italia,* p. 139.

Teneri tralci van cercando appoggio,
S'intrecciavano ai miei . . .

. . . Così giaceva:
E com'io con delizie più profonde
Ad ogni sorso nuovo amor bevea
Con sete insaziabile, che sempre,
(Dissimile da quella ond'arde l'uomo),
Maggior si fea . . .

Parmi null'altro amar, poi ch'io l'amai.
Più bella ancor del corpo è la sua mente,
Sede ai pensier più cari, a le sue belle
Fantasie, che s'affollan numerose,
Quai conchiglie che al mar fan pavimento,
O quali gemme che del ciel la volta,
Quasi occhi della notte, ornan fiammanti.
S'ei parla . . . immagini e pensieri
Sorgono in me, che il labbro non accenna,
Quasi memorie di più lieta vita
Pria di questa vissuta . . .
Quella sua voce, ond'è ogni cor rapito,
S'io potessi morire, a nuova vita
Mi torneria . . .

. . . Muto ei non è mai;
Che sovra il volto allora io leggo i moti
Dell'anima, che tutta in quel trasfonde
Il suo raggio, e traluce in quella guisa
Che da questa lucerna alabastrina
Traspare innocuo lume; e qual dal sole
Si distende una luce, onde il creato
Si veste e si ravviva. Oh s'io nol veggo,
Pur mel sento vicino. Allor che i suoi
Occhi incontrano i miei, nel più profondo
Del mio core mi vibra ogni suo sguardo
Ineffabile armor, dolce desìo,
Care lusinghe, e nuova gioia.—Un solo
Fossimo almeno! un essere in due spoglie!
E gli spiriti e l'alme e gl'intelletti
Sempre annodati e concentrati in uno!

What had Medwin attempted, and what had he achieved? His purposes he describes in his preface: to piece out in dramatic form the Prometheus story, the middle part of which had been dramatized by Aeschylus in *Prometheus Bound* and the final third by Shelley in *Prometheus Unbound*. Medwin's play would thus take its place in the timeless but ever shifting order of the literary past. He wrote, more particularly, ". . . my principal object was, in Saturn and Jupiter, to typify the present tyrannical oppressors of a country where the press is so fettered that allegory alone can be resorted to. This Drama was written at Genoa . . ."[7] Although the "allegory" is of a very general kind indeed and there is nothing like the many-faceted symbolic depth of Shelley's play (Medwin "aimed at the style and manner of Aeschylus," not of Shelley), *Prometheus the Fire-bearer* is a very respectable performance, if not of the same quality of his translations of Aeschylus. Finally, its theme is the salvation of man in a world of tyranny.

Medwin, who states in his preface that he had "been sacrificing for the last twelve months" at the "shrine" of Aeschylus, "the God of my poetical idolatry," deliberately constructed his plot from all the known classical sources, among them Hesiod, Orpheus, Empedocles, Callimachus, and Ovid. He was proud of his learning, and the *Antologia* reviewer complimented him on it. The plot, therefore, is consciously and carefully given a conventional, familiar form. Despite this fact, however, the theme is handled upon occasion not without a certain subtlety, and the verse usually bears the weight of its meaning. For example, the first act, which establishes Prometheus's humanitarian concern for mankind and his role as saviour, also conveys to him, in the form of a vision, his knowledge of Saturn's approaching overthrow. This knowledge comes to him on his nuptial night, after hours of love, while he still lies beside his bride and sister, Hesione. It is brought to him in a vision of his mother, the majestic and venerable Themis, who is also the mother of Justice and most resembles this her eldest daughter.

[7] Medwin's unpublished preface.

The clear implication thus is that love (Hesione) calls forth, or is somehow the essential condition of, a vision of the mother of justice (Themis), who is also the mother of man's salvation (Prometheus). Love, justice, and the agent or principle of revolt against tyranny are thus seen to be all members of the same family. Much of this symbolism derives from Medwin's sources, to be sure, but it should also be said that he had wits enough to see it and use it.

The play closes with the lamentation of Hesione, as she watches Prometheus departing to begin his punishment: "The Earth/ Shows itself what it is: one sepulchre/ . . . The Air is still,/ The Night drops deadly dew upon the World." The present day is an evil day: the first to be rewarded by Jove are brute "Strength and Force, who now stand night and day/ Beside his throne and run before his chariot." Despite such pessimistic elements as these, however, the play as a whole, reflecting Medwin's own tough resiliency, expresses an almost Victorian confidence in the future of man, who is, even before the beauty and orderly wonder of the stars, "the great miracle" of the last act. All the fruits of settled civilization shall grow out of Prometheus's civilizing gift of fire, until, one day, men shall

> defy the elements,
> And breast the wind without a sail,
> And then shall visit distant countries, join
> Continent with continent, making them one,
> As is this stream that girds as with a zone
> The pendant world, and every heart unite
> In brotherhood of peace and joy . . .

Prometheus's greatest gift to man, however, is not fire but the promised knowledge that those who love purely in mortal life shall live and love forever. Thus the last act is characterized by a paradoxical note of victory in defeat, of miracle to be born out of suffering. The structure of the play was intended to achieve a kind of exhilarating catharsis. But Medwin had attempted more than he was able to achieve. He must have known it: Pareto's translation, he wrote in his preface, with a show of mock modesty, "so far surpassed the original" that when the *Antologia* gave to him its praises, "so little merited, . . . I was half inclined to consign my feeble sketch, a mere improvisation and prologue, to the fire . . ." Then he made a weak joke about the punishment suiting the crime and the fiery element that he had had "the temerity to handle." He was at his best when he had a collaborator of genius, like Byron or Aeschylus.

Prometheus the Fire-bearer was his last original poetic work of major proportions, and he turned increasingly to prose and to translating. Before he left Genoa, however, he had completed another tragedy, presumably in prose. It was "written solely for Representation, & without any intention of publication," he informed Henry Colburn.[8] Although it remained unpublished and probably was never produced on any stage, it hastened his departure from Genoa. For the title of his five-act play was *The Conspiracy of Fieschi,* and a government informer used one of its speeches to implicate the budding playwright, who obligingly translated a radical or republican passage into Italian verse for him. That very night, at eleven, the police searched his room for revolutionary papers or letters, and the next day his passport was returned to him, with a written order to leave Genoa within twenty-four hours. He wrote later,

Not being remarkable for command of temper, I tore it into pieces, and threw it in the face of the bearer, telling him to inform his employers that I intended to remain where I was as long as suited my convenience . . . In defiance of the police, I remained for fourteen days in Genoa,—made public, in no measured terms, the unwarrentable conduct exercised towards me, a British officer,—

[8] Unpublished letter from Medwin to Henry Colburn, Jan. 1, 1831, quoted by permission of The Carl H. Pforzheimer Library. There seems to be no evidence that Medwin knew that Byron had also considered a tragedy on this conspiracy. See Lady Blessington, *Idler in Italy,* II, 74.

called the carabinieri, who pursued my steps whenever I went out, my lackeys,—and when I had *bearded* the authorities to the utmost, took my place by the courier for Turin.[9]

Although some of these details may be colored or invented, it is clear that Medwin was ordered out of Genoa and that the subject of his play would be highly distasteful to the authorities at this time, shortly after the Revolution of July, 1830, in France, when, Medwin noted, the Genoese were "not a little suspicious of strangers, . . . especially the English and French," and "every hotel was beset with spies."[10] For Medwin had written a play about the conspiracy which had taken place at Genoa in 1547, that of Giovanni Fiesco (de' Fieschi) against Andrea Doria. No subject could have been more carefully chosen to inflame the Genoese authorities. Fiesco belonged to the French or popular party and received French aid; the Dorias led the aristocratic and Imperialist party. Upon the failure of the armed conspiracy, Andrea Doria confiscated the Fiesco estates, despite a promised amnesty, and tortured and executed some of the conspirators, including Verrina, for whom Medwin was writing a speech when the police spy entered his room to request a passage from the play as a friendly memento. Medwin says he was only "killing time" by writing the play, "having been inspired so to do by reading Bonfadir's eloquent account" of the conspiracy, a source which Schiller also used, he says. But it was enough, despite the protestation of political innocence. Genoa turned out to be only an interlude.

Besides, if he intended to support himself by his pen or supplement his pay of four shillings and eight pence a day, London was the only place. He was already thinking of a memoir of Shelley and a biography of Byron. Furthermore, he had been too long an exile, living among foreigners and Roman Catholics. He would try England again. His manuscript trunk was full; he had not been idle. On January 1, 1831, still on the

[9] Medwin, "My Moustache," *Ainsworth's Magazine,* I (1842), 54.
[10] *Ibid.,* p. 53.

Continent but planning his return to England, he offered to his old publisher Colburn four manuscripts; "a Translation of Aeschylus in 2 Volumes—a Play called The Conspiracy of Fieschi in 5 Acts—A Drama—Prometheus The Fire Bearer accompanied by an Eclogue or Elegy on Shelley, & two Indian Scenes,"[11] the latter refurbished versions, probably, of "The Lion Hunt" and "The Pindarees." The elegy on Shelley was perhaps a revision of portions of *The Wanderer*. Offering these manuscripts as security, no one of which Colburn published, he asked for a loan of £50. His precarious financial state is suggested further by the fact that he entrusted the manuscripts not to the mails but to a man who was "almost a stranger" to him. A year and a day after being sued in Florence for 30,000 lire, he was very nearly without funds.

He was back in England early in 1831, and on February 1 he exchanged his commission on the half-pay list with Lord Kinnaird (nephew of Byron's friend Douglas Kinnaird) for a Lieutenancy in the very exclusive 1st Life Guards. Two weeks later he sold out and resigned from the service[12] Mary Shelley (and H. Buxton Forman, the editor of Medwin's revised *Shelley*) thought that the brevity of his service with the Life Guards reflected discredit upon him. Mary wrote, maliciously, "I suppose the officers cut him at mess . . ."[13] But Medwin's move was almost certainly a financial one, for there was a flourishing trade in commissions,[14] and his maneuver was no more disgraceful than moving in and out of the stock market today, within a period of two weeks. Kinnaird, who had very recently succeeded to the title upon the death of his father in 1830, wished to be relieved of active duty; Medwin needed money. The ex-

---

[11] Unpublished letter from Medwin to Henry Colburn, Jan. 1, 1831, quoted by permission of The Carl H. Pforzheimer Library.

[12] *The London Gazette*, Feb. 1 and Feb. 15, 1831, quoted in Forman's edition of Medwin's *Shelley*, p. xxvii.

[13] *Letters of Mary Shelley*, II, 41.

[14] See "Promotion by Purchase in the Army," *New Monthly Magazine*, XC (Nov., 1850), 279–282.

change was easily made. Medwin probably made his arrangements with Cornet Edward Hammond, who purchased from him, before closing with Kinnaird.

The exclusiveness of the 1st Life Guards is suggested by the regulation price for a Lieutenant's commission—£1,785, or £788 more than a Lieutenant's commission in the 24th Light Dragoons. By selling out, Medwin thus secured again, at the very least, the price of his commission in the 24th, £997, worth approximately twenty-five thousand 1962 American dollars, which, if invested at 5 per cent, would give him an annual return of about £50, or the equivalent of approximately twelve hundred such dollars. But Medwin probably received a sum "very much in excess" of the regulation price.[15] If he could protect his principal, he could exist, and he could live reasonably well if he could supplement this income by means of his pen. He set to publishing.

But before anything of his appeared that had been written for money, he sent on January 28, 1832, a long letter to *The Literary Gazette,* which was printed as "Original Correspondence" in the issues of February 4 and 11. He had just seen Moore's *Life* of Byron and took the opportunity to defend himself, as well as to add new and sometimes sombre colors to his own portrait of the poet, now only great, it seems, "in his moments of inspiration; he was else an ordinary mortal." More interestingly, we learn that Byron made Teresa miserable in Pisa "by his low intrigues and infidelities . . . and went to Greece principally to shake off a connexion that was become irksome to him." Byron, he tells us, knew that the infamous Brougham was the author of the review of *Hours of Idleness* which then gave rise to *English Bards and Scotch Reviewers* and knew further that Brougham had made "unwarrantable allusions" to him in the course of the separation proceedings. "I have seen Byron, more than once, in a *whiteness* of fury

[15] Letter to the author from Mr. D. W. King, Librarian of the British War Office Library.

when on this topic, and heard him vow, that if ever he came to England, he would call to account that personage . . ." We hear for the first time of Byron's debt in *Don Juan* to Casti, a subject that Medwin would shortly write at length upon. And Medwin provides further evidence of Byron's shifting pronunciation of his name. "I was present when a person asked him how his name ought really be pronounced: his answer, with one of his *smiles*, was, What does *b y* spell? Now, as he always called Lady B. Bur-on himself, he was only dealing, of course, in one of his usual mystifications." And this is the first, although not the last, of Medwin's self-protective references to Byron's tendency to "mystify" those with whom he conversed.

The reviewers of his *Conversations* had dealt harshly indeed with him, and he could not forget it. He set about again trying to clear his name, making the first of his several confessions that Trelawny was the author of the cremation scene introduced so misleadingly into his book. But this was only the beginning. He explained that the original title was merely *The Conversations of Lord Byron* and that "Mr. Colburn changed it, as more attractive, without my consent," adding the damaging words (for which Medwin had suffered), *Noted during a Residence with his Lordship at Pisa* . . . This, however, was only a detail, however important. The most effective defense of himself that Medwin ever made, perhaps, was his offer to show his original journal, "which has been seen by several of my friends, at any time, to any person whom Mr. Murray may appoint." This challenge, it appears, was never taken up. Medwin moved on.

His "Memoir of Shelley" appeared originally in six weekly installments in *The Athenaeum*, between July 21 and August 25, 1832, the "Shelley Papers" following at once at weekly intervals until the issue of October 6, which was given over almost wholly to the death of Sir Walter Scott. Publication was resumed on October 20, and following this date installments appeared on October 27, November 10, 17, 24, and December

8, 1832,[16] and April 20, 1833. These installments, eighteen in all, were collected in 1833 as *The Shelley Papers; Memoir of Percy Bysshe Shelley.* It was the first memoir of Shelley of such comprehensiveness to appear, and in it appeared for the first time a substantial quantity of Shelley's poetry and prose.

For the next twenty-five important years (until 1858), when the reputation of Shelley was being formed, Medwin remained the chief and almost the only major authority on the whole life of the poet. What kind of book had he written? At the time when Shelley's fame stood most in need of a biographer in perfect sympathy with his subject, Medwin filled that need, although his "Memoir" stops sensibly short of adulation. For example, he did not recall, he wrote in his first installment, that Shelley showed any "precocity of genius"; he points up his "girlishness" and his shock upon encountering the rough language and manners of the boys at Syon house; he notices his relative friendlessness at Oxford. But he also discusses his personal bravery and his extreme generosity or selflessness.

Medwin has so often been charged with an utterly callous disregard for the feelings and privacy of the living that his biographical treatment of Claire Clairmont and Mary Shelley in the summer of 1816 deserves comment here. At that time both women were living out of wedlock with their poets, Byron and Shelley being still married. Medwin refers to Claire only as "C——," describes her generously, and does not mention Mary at all. And Mary is not mentioned by name in his account until she became the wife of Shelley. But at this point, Medwin, tactful and considerate as he had been, dropped a remark which we would not lose but which Mary would gladly wish away: "Byron told me, that . . . it was by his persuasion that Shelley married again."[17]

[16] Sylva Norman, *Flight of the Skylark* (Norman, Oklahoma, 1954), p. 93, note 19, states that the Dec. 8, 1832, contribution, Shelley's "Lines Written During the Castlereagh Administration," was made not by Medwin but by T. F. Kelsall.

[17] *Athenaeum*, Aug. 4, 1832, p. 502.

The portrait of the mature Shelley which emerges is, in fact, the one familiar today, and the main outlines of the poet's life are correctly given. Considering the fact that the "Memoir" was written with the benefit of only the merest handful of letters, it is a quite remarkable achievement. But Medwin's qualifications were impressive: he knew his man personally, he knew the scenes of Shelley's life, he also was a poet and classics scholar, and he was no mean critic. At a time when many were still ridiculing Shelley's genius, Medwin recognized it and proclaimed it. He recognized Byron's poetic debt to Shelley in 1816 and the change that Byron's poetry consequently underwent at that time. Although he did not at the moment admire the work of Keats (he refers only to *Endymion,* an example of "sickly affectation"), he pronounced Shelley to be "the second master spirit of the age," Byron being the first.[18] The latter judgment is one that most would agree with today.

But Medwin's confidence in Byron had been tested under a very heavy fire, by the reviewers of his *Conversations,* and in 1832 his attitude was already shifting a little this side of idolatry. We hear to Byron's supposed discredit of his £1,000 bet with Shelley and of his fondness for "mystifying," a trait never mentioned in the *Conversations.*

This is interesting, for the February 25, 1832, issue of *The Athenaeum* announced, without comment, "Mr. Medwin is preparing for publication a Life of Lord Byron," and in the same month *The Gentleman's Magazine* included in its list of "New Works announced for Publication" the same title, "A Life of Lord Byron by Medwin."[19] At some time before July 21, when the first installment of Medwin's "Memoir of Shelley" appeared, he had made a pilgrimage to Harrow, where he saw the poet's name carved "in three places, in very large characters—a presentiment of his future fame, or a pledge of his

---

[18] *Ibid.,* Aug. 25, 1832, p. 555. Medwin had praised Keats's *Hyperion* in his *Conversations,* p. 295.

[19] *Ibid.,* Feb. 25, 1832, p. 133; *Gentleman's Magazine,* CLI (Feb., 1832), 155.

ambition to acquire it." [20] This journey was undoubtedly made
in preparation for writing a biography, and Byron bulks very
large indeed in *The Angler in Wales,* published in 1834. But
Medwin had suffered from the furious attacks of the reviewers
of his *Conversations;* these he refers to querulously in his
"Memoir of Shelley," and his sense of pain would grow, not
decrease with the years, as he remembered with less and less
certainty what Byron had actually said to him and began to
wonder if Byron had not indeed been pulling his leg, as the
reviewers had said. Thus his enthusiasm waned, and the new
Byron material he collected appeared chiefly in *The Angler*
and his *Life of Shelley.* The biography of Byron remained
unwritten.

"I am at no loss to account for the inveterancy with which
I was assailed by the press," he wrote, "through the influence
of the all-mighty of bibliopolists [Murray], and the persevering
attempts that were for a time but too successfully exerted, to
cast doubts on the authenticity of Byron's Conversations . . .
The fact is, that Messrs. Moore, Murray, and Hobhouse [now
Secretary at War and a Privy Councillor] looked upon Lord
Byron as an heir-loom, as their private property; and were
highly indignant that any one should presume to know any
thing about their noble friend." [21] He was understandably bitter,
and all the more so because, as he points out, Moore in *The
Letters and Journals of Lord Byron, with Notices of his Life*
had treated him "as so far dead in the world of letters" as to
quote generously from the *Conversations* without acknowledgment, silently appropriating several of Byron's poems and
Goethe's *Beitrag.* Medwin closes with an appeal to the copyright law.

One final word about the "Memoir of Shelley." It is more
consistently well written than the *Life of Shelley* and is indeed
the work of a diligently cultivated mind. Any press would be
delighted today to publish a similar work dealing with an im-

[20] *Athenaeum,* July 1, 1832, p. 472, note.
[21] *Ibid.,* August 18, 1832, p. 536, note.

portant twentieth-century poet. *The Metropolitan Magazine,* edited by Thomas Campbell the poet and Frederick Marryat the novelist, found it "written with perspicuity and elegance."[22]

By the time that the last installment of the "Shelley Papers" had appeared, Shelley's "System of Government by Juries," Medwin had become the editor of the ephemeral *New Anti-Jacobin: A Monthly Magazine of Politics, Commerce, Science, Literature, Art, Music, and the Drama.*[23] It advocated anything but such Shelleyan and revolutionary doctrines as government by juries. Published by Smith, Elder & Co., it lasted for two issues only, those of April and May, 1833, and included among its contributors Horace Smith and John Poole the playwright, author of the popular *Paul Pry.* Medwin may have met them both as early as 1822, when Poole lived outside Paris and Horace Smith lived at Versailles.

It is difficult to understand why the magazine failed so early—unless it had insufficient financial backing. There was no advertising. Perhaps it ran too obviously counter to the rising tide of political reform. Each issue of 110 pages dealt with an admirably balanced variety of subjects, as the title promised. Most of the articles show a professional level of competence, and many of the humorous pages are still alive with laughter today, although there are sometimes regrettable outbursts of violent language in the political articles.

Together, the two extremely rare issues provide such important insights into the mind of Medwin at this period (as well as interesting and sometimes startling glimpses into the life and thought of the day) that they deserve to be considered in some detail.

[22] Quoted by S. Austin Allibone, *Critical Dictionary of English Literature* (Philadelphia, 1870), II, 1259.

[23] Medwin's editorship is established by his unpublished letter of Sept. 26, 1835, to "A. V., Care of Mr. W. Edwards, 12 Ave Maria Lane," in the Morgan Library. Medwin's contributions and those of Horace Smith and John Poole are established by Medwin's annotated copy of the *New Anti-Jacobin,* in the University of Pennsylvania Library.

Medwin opened his first issue with an article attacking "the besotted idolaters of the Typhon of Radicalism," specifically, "the 'Princes and Potentates' of Reform's pandemonium," chief of which are Cobbett and O'Connell. This is followed by "Renewal of the Bank Charter," a spirited defense of the Bank of England. "Man versus Machine" argues that the use or abuse of machinery is "grinding day by day our artisans into paupers" and encouraging child labor and a sixteen-hour work day. Revolution is predicted if governmental regulation of the cotton manufacturing industry is not imposed. A page and a half "On the East India Question" follows, indignantly resentful of any diminution of the Company's powers.

After the unrelieved toryism and violent tone of these articles, it is pleasant to come upon Medwin's first contribution, "A Cast of Casti" (pages 30–35), which establishes for the first time Byron's debt to the Italian poet, with whom he became acquainted in 1816, as Medwin observes.[24] Medwin's essay is followed by his translation of Casti's *The Diavolessa; or, The Spanish Dons Juan and Ignazio* (pages 35–54) in ninety-three ottava rima stanzas. This is the story of the love adventures of Don Ignazio, culminating in the abduction of Ermenigilda, who is placed aboard a vessel bound for Sicily. There are a storm and shipwreck, however, and all are drowned except the Don, thrown up on the coast of Africa, where he is converted to virtue. Here he resists all the Devil's efforts to seduce him until Satan assumes the form of the drowned Ermenigilda. The poem ends with Ignazio's descent into Hell, where he meets Juan, and there the two old friends duel with firebrands.

Several stanzas will illustrate Medwin's understanding of his two poets, Casti and Byron. *The Diavolessa* opens with a stanza quite *Juanesque*:

[24] The respectability of Medwin's scholarship is suggested by the fact that Willis Pratt in the *Notes on the Variorum Edition* of Byron's *Don Juan* (Austin, 1957) twice cites Medwin's article, without however recognizing the author.

All goes to prove, fair ladies! that the Devil
  Of late has become liberal beyond measure;
Indeed, I must own he's grown wondrous civil—
  Quite a philosopher, and finds no leisure
To prowl about the world in doing evil:
  All think, and act, and talk, as is their pleasure.
He about others' conduct makes no fuss—
We about his—'tis best for both of us.

The next stanza (28) describes Ermenigilda's abduction and
ends with a typically Byronic sting in its tail:

And lo, the cortège comes, nor longer hide
  Those wretches in the covert;—with a shout,
They draw their swords, and pounce, on every side,
  On the defenceless boors, who, put to rout,
Leave to her fate, an easy prey, the bride.
  Ignazio seizes, throws his arms about
Ermenigilda, laying her across—
In spite of all her sobs, shrieks, prayers—his horse.

Following the storm and shipwreck, described quite as realistically as those in Byron's *Don Juan*, Ignazio tries virtue (stanza
59), after setting up his defences:

The outer hut, that needs no more description,
  Supplied the place of ante-room: this he fences
With trunks of trees and stakes; his habitation
  On all sides to protect by such defences
He seeks—which gave him no small occupation—
  And as a penitence for his offences
With a rope's end he wished his back to cuff—
But as he found it hurt him, he left off.

Medwin's translation is followed by Poole's "Pomponius Ego,
A Character," which is an amusing but predictable dialogue
between Ego and Friend. Next comes an informed and boldly
reasoned attack on Wilkins, the architect of the proposed National Gallery in London. The writer objects to the site chosen,

which would shut out the front view of St. Martin's Church, and also to Wilkins's "general architectural creed." The argument is convincing, but Medwin's issue went to press too late: a footnote informs the reader that the plan in question had already been abandoned. "Autobiography of a Picture-Fancier" (pages 74–79) follows, Medwin's account of his financial downfall, already quoted.

The serious tone of this article is relieved by two humorous articles: "Punch's Patent Rights. The Legitimate Street Drama" and " 'The Wondrous Tale of' Ikey Solomons! !" The first laments the fallen state of Punch, due chiefly to streets too large, the late dinner hour of the leading poor, lack of encouragement from the nobility, "the anti-dramatic taste of the New Police," and competition from performing white mice and organ grinders with monkeys in red jackets. The body of the article is composed of "Extracts from the Minutes of Evidence taken before a Select Committee of the Magistrates appointed to inquire into the Laws affecting the Regular Street-Drama." Among those examined are Herr Nasaltsinger, Mr. Sixteenstring Jack (Street Inspector of Nuisances), and Signor Tambouri, whose job is "to play on the people, *not* on the tambourine." The other humorous article pretends to be a précis of a novel written by one Asher Levi and shown to a friend who plagiarized it. It is a tale of Jewish low life, complete with thieves' cant. The Jewish humor is not malicious.

Three poems follow. "Anacreontic. The Invitation" is a conventional love poem. "Incantation to Canidia. For an Album" pleads, sometimes satirically, with a beauty to give up writing and devote herself to her proper business. "Lines Written in Hampton-Court Gardens, in 1831, By James Smith" is identified in the table of contents as by Horace Smith, laments the changed scene since the time of Pope.

"The Theatre-Patents" is a scholarly and historical account of the subject from 1574, when a patent was granted to Burbage, down to 1792, when the Killigrew patent was purchased by the proprietors of Drury Lane Theatre.

"Bigarrures" (pages 102–103), as the title suggests, is a miscellany of short paragraphs, on theatre gossip, Italian opera,
politics, and literary figures. It was probably written by Medwin, who wrote the second installment of this department. He
did identify himself as the author of "The Drama" (pages 104–
106), which opens, "The revival of the stage—the regeneration
of the drama—such are the objects to which this department
of the *New Anti-Jacobin* will be directed." Public taste, we are
told, is now vitiated but not dead. "It shall be our earnest
endeavour to put down that system of clap-trap for point,
punning for wit, and bustle for interest, that has taken possession of the stage." Medwin recognized the dearth of good
plays and lamented the fact that "no play has been produced
for years that has so much real merit, and pretension to originality" as James Sheridan Knowles's comedy, *The Hunchback,*
produced April 5, 1832, at Covent Garden.

Among actors, Kean, Farren, Macready, Vestris, Liston, and
Meadows are to be praised; but we learn that the high salaries
demanded by actors inflate admission prices: twenty, twenty-
five, or thirty guineas a week give to them "an income such as
the most indefatigable author could not in twice the time
obtain . . ." And finally Medwin appeals to managers to admit
the work of gentlemen playwrights; at present, "no person, who
has not been bred to the art, as if it were a trade, can get a
play presented, or even read . . ." The clearly evident personal
note here suggests that Medwin's own play may well have been
rejected.

The last article of the first issue is given to the department
of "Music," written by an enthusiastic and competent critic,
who finds the state of music in London, by and large, a flourishing one. But Medwin as editor had the last word, on page 110,
in a footnote. He suggested to the parodists of *Rejected Addresses,* about to appear in another new edition, a subject: "The
Bond-age of Greece," a country whose war for independence
had been financed largely by English and European loans.

Medwin's second issue, May, 1833, need not be described in its entirety. It continued to preach and sometimes scream high tory principles and to prophesy quick disaster if the tide of reform were not turned. Catholic emancipation and equal civil rights for Jews, we are told in a "Letter to the King," are "but the prelude to the annihilation of the church." In another article, revolution is predicted if paper money, secured upon a gold and silver standard, is not reintroduced, thus driving up prices. A concern for the poor, however, is more clearly evident in "Man versus Machine," continued from the first issue. The basic argument is that machines (particularly power looms) tended by women and children throw men out of work and lower the wages of those left on the job; depress the wages of handicraft workers, forced as they are to compete with the machines; and kill off the handicraft trades and arts, thus reducing purchasing power and driving up the poor rates to nine million pounds annually in England and Wales. Examples of the distress of workmen refer to weekly wages for men of five shillings net, "clear of expenses of winding." "A Diplomatic Note. Russia and the Porte" is pitched in a startlingly modern key. The postwar settlements following 1815 are damned on every score but especially for admitting Russian influence into Poland and thus giving Russia a European base. The results are, ". . . Russian agents are actively at work in every part of the continent; they are to be found in the highest walks of English society, and amid the frenzied peasantry of Ireland, sowing the seeds of disunion and discord. But it is the East that presents the widest and most favourable field for her Machiavellian policy." The solution suggested is for England and her allies to strengthen the Turks and so halt the Russian advances.

Medwin's own contributions bulk large in his second issue, beginning with a savagely personal attack in verse on Cobbett, with a full page picture facing it. "Horace in Parliament. Ode to William C[obbet]t," he called it. Very different from this is

Medwin's "A Scene in the Life of an Artist. Imitated from the
German" (pages 166–178). The first-person narrator and main
character is a young man of vaguely Germanic but clearly
provincial background, who runs away with two touring Italian
vocalists, pretty young sisters. He is a pianist and composer.
They perform at court, and after a period an Italian tenor joins
the party of three. In his presence, the sisters ridicule the
pianist, who overhears them and disappears without a word of
farewell. Fourteen years later, now a successful composer in
Rome, he meets the sisters again.

The two sisters were very urgent in their request that I would,
as early as possible, arrange some pieces for them; but I quitted
Rome without paying them a visit. And yet it was they who had
awakened in me the passion for music, and a crowd of musical
ideas and impressions: this very reason it was that prevented my
going to see them again. Every composer doubtlessly retains, like
myself, the influence of a first impression that time cannot weaken
or efface—he remembers when the genius of harmony first inspired
him—when the striking of a magic chord asserted its power over
his soul. As soon as a singer has made the artist comprehend the
melodies that dive into the depths of his being, the future immediately opens on his view and commences for him. But it is our lot,
poor weak mortals that we are, and chained down to clay! to wish
to limit and confine to the narrow circle of our wretched realities
that which is celestial and infinite. Let the singer become your wife,
the charm is broken; and that melodious voice which had opened
to you the gates of paradise, serves to express some vulgar plaints,
or to scold about a broken glass or a spot in a new dress.

And in the final paragraph of this, Medwin's first published
tale, he goes on to generalize upon the clash of the actual and
the ideal, and the necessity of the artist to preserve and protect
the latter in the purest memory, free of the taint of the actual.
Perhaps so, for the purely Romantic artist, but Medwin's bent
lay elsewhere, with the Byron of the *Conversations at Pisa*,
although he did not always know it.

Medwin's "Goethe and his Faust" (pages 198–204) is the introduction to his translation following, "Specimen of a Translation of Faust" (pages 204–210), the Forest and Cavern scene. He argues against "all literal servile translation" in favor of "the full and perfect transfusion of an author's ideas in our own true idiomatic form." He then attacks Abraham Hayward's translation of *Faust* (1833), meanwhile defending Shelley from Hayward. Shelley "alone, perhaps, of all men that the present age has seen, was fitted to take up Goethe's mantle." We are told further that Shelley made his own translations of *Faust* "*for* Byron," although this seems doubtful. Medwin's own very respectable translation opens with the following lines:

> Spirit of Spirits! All I possess is thine—
> All, all I ask thou grantest—nor in vain
> On me thy countenance in fire has beamed;
> To me this glorious universe of things
> Thou gavest as a kingdom, nor with it
> A lifeless admiration, but the power
> And faculty to feel and to enjoy
> Nature, and dwell upon her mysteries,
> And look through her deep bosom, as we read
> The bosom of a friend—before my eyes
> Thou makest all created things to pass,
> And teachest me to know my fellow-creatures,
> And love as brothers all the forms that breathe
> The breath of life, in the still woods disporting,
> Peopling the air, or gliding in the waters.

The next article (pages 211–213), "The Connoisseur," is also Medwin's. It is comprised of discussions of the Laocoön, indebted to Shelley's note on the same sculpture, and of the Dying Gladiator, each discussion prefaced by the appropriate quotation from *Childe Harold*. Of the Laocoön he wrote, "nothing that remains to us of antiquity can surpass it." He briefly discusses Byron's lines on these two statues, both representing the moment before death, and then compares the two, chiefly

in terms of the manner in which the figures represented appear
to face death. He does not hesitate to describe the thoughts
suggested by the facial expressions and attitudes of the figures.
It is controlled impressionistic criticism by a sensitive observer
with no special knowledge.

"Bigarrures" in this issue has resolved itself into "The Bard
at Bay" (pages 217–218), Medwin's account of Byron, Samuel
Rogers, and the bull dog that cornered the elderly visiting poet,
to Byron's vast amusement. Medwin does not pretend to have
been present. "We think we see Byron in his jacket, stumping
round the billiard-room, with the heavy sound that once heard
could not be mistaken, and, after making some successful hit,
bursting out into one of his usual jibes or flashes of merriment
which success always inspired, or dividing his caresses between
Jocko [the monkey] and Tiger [the dog]." This is Medwin at
his *New Anti-Jacobin* best, the retailer of amusing and convincing anecdotes about the famous, with dialogue.

Medwin's contributions close with a single paragraph on the
drama (page 218), ridiculing the anachronistic and space-
defying marvels of Ducrow's *Siege of Troy*, and a brief review
(page 220) of Frederic Mansel Reynolds's novel, *Miserrimus*,
dedicated to Godwin. Medwin damns this "charnel-tale," whose
main character, he says, has been a villain "from the cradle."

On the last page of the issue is a two-line notice of the forthcoming *Woman, the Angel of Life*, a poem in three cantos by
Robert Montgomery, which went through five editions. Opposite the title, Medwin wrote in his own hand, "hear! hear!
hear!" followed by his initials at the bottom of the page. And
so the last issue closed, along with Medwin's life as a magazine
editor. Perhaps he was not sentimental enough for his readers.

His uncomplimentary note on the title of Montgomery's
poem, however, with its assertion about women and angels,
would not appear to refer to the poet. For Montgomery thought
highly of Medwin and recommended to Charles Dilke, editor
of *The Athenaeum*, an essay by Medwin on the *Agamemnon*
of Aeschylus. Montgomery commented, "Do not judge Medwin

by the *Conversations*—they were a *three-weeks' child*—he is a fine enthusiast, an accomplished scholar."[25]

Although it is not certain that the essay "On the Agamemnon of Aeschylus" which appeared in *The Athenaeum* for May 19, 1832, is Medwin's, his translation of that play was published, along with translations of all the other plays of Aeschylus except *The Suppliants,* a play which was "much neglected in those days, on account of its corruptions."[26] The six plays which Medwin did translate into verse represent his highest achievement as a poet, and that achievement is of no mean order. As he himself observed, he "possessed the advantage of studying these Tragedies with two of the most elegant, not to say the best scholars I have ever known"—Shelley and Prince Mavrocordato of Greece.[27] *Prometheus Bound* and *Agamemnon,* published in companion octavo volumes by William Pickering in May, 1832, were rapidly followed by the four other plays, which appeared in *Fraser's Magazine.* In November, 1832, appeared *The Choëphori;* in January, 1833, *The Persians;* in April, 1833, *The Seven Against Thebes;* and in May, 1834, *The Eumenides.* The translation of *Prometheus Bound* had appeared in 1827 at Siena; it appeared again in *Fraser's* for August, 1837; and in November, 1838, *Fraser's* reprinted the *Agamemnon.*

Why did Medwin, recently disinherited, separated from wife and children, turn to the austere genius of Aeschylus? One can only speculate. Shelley, he knew, would have approved. But there were also themes or other elements to be found in Aeschylus, the soldier-poet, that would speak clearly to Medwin. He may have sensed that the severity of Aeschylus's art would be an effective antidote to his own native diffuseness, his tendency to formlessness, that Aeschylus's assured and lofty style would help sustain his own uncertainty of tone. The Greek plays, voicing repeatedly the sadly precarious nature of human

[25] Quoted by John Drinkwater, *The Pilgrim of Eternity* (New York, 1925), p. 320.
[26] Forman's edition of Medwin's *Shelley,* p. 243, note.
[27] Medwin's preface to his translation of *Prometheus Bound,* p. iv.

happiness (which Medwin now knew well), also expressed
other themes that would be congenial to him. *Prometheus
Bound,* which Medwin thought "the sublimest of all the compositions that have come down to us from the Greeks," [28] had
at its lyric center an injured hero suffering all the torments of
unjust punishment. The *Oresteia* stated the theme of justice
finally delivered. And he would have felt comfortable in the
presence of the martial spirit of *The Persians* and *The Seven
against Thebes.*

In addition, translating Aeschylus was most eminently the
occupation of a gentleman and a scholar. As the reviewer in
The New Monthly Magazine pointed out,

> Time was, when, if an author sought fame and fortune, he could
> scarcely have taken a surer road than through a vigorous and
> spirited translation of some classical author. That time is gone by;
> and if now a writer exercises his pen on such a topic, our apprehen-
> sion is, that he is not attracted to it by an ambitious or selfish
> motive, but by the pure love of the subject, and by a strong admira-
> tion of the mighty Greek or Roman whom he desires to clothe in
> English dress. Such is our judgment of Mr. Medwin.[29]

Further, the time was ripe for a new translation of Aeschylus,
who had been neglected in both France and England during
the eighteenth century and whose reputation had begun to rise
only in recent years.[30]

After the virulent animosity of the reviewers of the *Conversations,* the chorus of critical praise for Medwin's translations
must have been sweet music indeed. *The Literary Gazette* led
off, on April 28, 1832, with a review of *Prometheus Bound:*

Most sincerely can we say, that in no translation which we have yet
perused have the text and meaning of Aeschylus been so correctly
exhibited, and eloquently rendered, as they are by Capt. Medwin.
He has brought to his task the prime qualifications of a poetical

---

[28] Medwin's final footnote to his unpublished *Prometheus the Fire-bearer.*
[29] "Critical Notices," *New Monthly Magazine,* XXXVI (Nov., 1832),
479–480.
[30] "On the Agamemnon of Aeschylus," *Athenaeum,* May 19, 1832, p. 320.

translator, viz. an admirable acquaintance with the language, style, and sentiments of his author, a noble mastery over his own tongue, a thrilling sense of the beautiful and sublime, together with a thorough sympathy with the freshness and glory of the classical drama.

The Athenaeum followed, on May 12, with a review of the same play,[31] which "has no parallel in the literature of the world," the reviewer stated in his first sentence. "It stands alone in its naked majesty unapproached and unapproachable—a gigantic conception filling the mind with wonder and awe . . ." After committing himself to two columns of such unqualified praise, the reviewer could hardly admit that Medwin had done full justice to the original. But he did his best: "Of Mr. Medwin's translation, we can speak in terms of great but not unqualified praise. It is by far the best version of the Prometheus in our language . . ." And then he lamented the death of Shelley. This was followed a week later by an article "On the Agamemnon of Aeschylus," in which the great playwright was again given his due, and the numerous quotations from the play were identified as those of Medwin. A review was promised, and it appeared on June 9. Meanwhile, J. S. Harford's translation of *Agamemnon* had been reviewed and damned on May 26: "the dialogue merits only feeble praise." *The Literary Gazette* agreed, on the same day: "After a comparison of the two versions of this play, we must, according to our judgment, award the palm of superiority to Medwin . . . We again bestow our unaffected eulogy on the fire, spirit, and general correctness of Mr. Medwin's version . . ." Medwin found the *Athenaeum* review worth waiting for: the reviewer congratulated him "on having produced a version of the Agamemnon, almost worthy of being compared with the sublime original."[32] He then proceeded to damn the translations of Potter, Symons, Harford, and Kennedy, the first two for hiding "the naked majesty of the [Aeschylean] marble beneath a rich dress of brocade . . ." This sad fault Medwin in fact avoided, although the reviewer does not say so explicitly.

[31] Pp. 301–302.   [32] P. 363.

The reviewer in *The Gentleman's Magazine* for June, 1832, was equally enthusiastic about Medwin's *Prometheus Bound* [33] and began by including the translator among those men who, "like Aeschylus, Xenophon, and Caesar, . . . have sacrificed 'tam Marti quam Minervae.'" Medwin was coming into his own, clearly. This reviewer contrasted his version with "those by Potter and Morell, neither of whom can compete for a moment with Mr. Medwin," noted that Medwin had "infused into his translation the spirit of the original," and observed that "not the least of the merits of the translation is the facility with which he adapts himself to the changing moods of his author." *The Gentleman's Magazine* reviewer writing in August, 1832,[34] liked the *Agamemnon* even better: "In our June number, . . . we spoke in praise, and yet not more than it deserved, of Mr. Medwin's translation of the Prometheus; and it is now our gratifying pleasure to express in even higher terms our opinion of his successful attempt." The review in *The New Monthly*, which appeared in November and dealt with both plays, was less enthusiastic but still favorable.

All but the last of Medwin's reviewers criticized him adversely for departing on occasion too far from the literal meaning of the original. No one of them seems to have understood, however, that the very qualities they admired derived from Medwin's conviction that such departures were essential. He wrote in the preface to his *Prometheus Bound,*

. . . the aim of a translator should be the full and entire sense, and not a servile adherence to forms or expressions . . . If in our language could be found words that are exact synonyms to his, and a correspondent idiomatic phraseology, then indeed, not to be literal, would be little less than sacrilege . . . But what would have been the effect of such an endeavour; to produce a clumsy mosaic instead of a painting, to involve my meaning in twofold darkness, to render my verses hard, dry, and inharmonious . . .

Although Medwin's translation would seem to suggest well enough the famous "helmeted phrases" of Aeschylus, sonorous

[33] Pp. 532–534.   [34] Pp. 142–144.

and polysyllabic, Medwin also knew that a certain naturalness of diction is also essential to the flowing, time-pursued drama. One of the great virtues of his translation is that he wrote idiomatic English. However, the element of Aeschylean formality is further suggested by the skillfully varied verse structure, sometimes stanzaic in organization, sometimes not.

The important, moving eloquence of the dance as an adjunct to Greek drama and a visible comment on it may be overlooked by the casual reader. The close association of dance and choral ode, however, the moving feet of the one in varying harmony with those of the other, makes a prose translation quite false. The same principle makes a loose or freely flowing verse translation of uncertain accentual pattern, unpunctuated by rhyme, only somewhat better. A useful and meaningful convention in suggesting an approximation of the Greek original, therefore, is to employ blank verse for the dialogue and rhymed couplets of differing lengths along with a variety of stanzaic forms for the choral odes. This is Medwin's method, and he is remarkably successful with it, achieving by this means and others an effective illusion of the varying metrical pattern and the shifting tones of the several dramatic voices in the original, as the drama develops from point to point.

All of this may be illustrated from Medwin's *Agamemnon*. The opening speech of the Watchman is rendered in good, solidly idiomatic English blank verse, in lines that may be spoken aloud: [35]

> Once more I ask the gods, once and for all,
> To end this heavy duty. 'Tis a year
> Since I've been crouching on this palace-roof,
> Most like a watch-dog; and, for company,
> Have had the stars, been present at their courts,
> Attended every congress of the chiefs
> Of the bright corps spangling the air, whose counsels
> Bring heat and cold; and have beheld them rise,

[35] Quotations of Medwin's *Agamemnon* are from *Fraser's Magazine*, XVIII (Nov., 1838), 505–539.

And marked their setting. But I long to see
A different light, the coming of a star,
To bring from Troy a message, that, I trust,
Will prove, with hers, the symbol of the fall
Of one, a man in everything but form.
Meantime, my restless pallet's wet with dew,
Unvisited by dreams; or if I chance
To doze, Fear comes, and stands by my bed-side,
Instead of Sleep, and will not let him set
Upon my eyelids a fast seal, and then
I try to drive my drowsiness away,
By whistling or by singing, if such ditties
Can be called songs, accompanied, as they are,
By groans, for the changed fortunes of this house,
No more well managed, as it used to be.

Much more formal and elaborate is the first choral ode, using
lines of six, eight, or ten syllables, rhyming alternately or in
couplets or otherwise. Short-line couplets are used with telling
effect in the choral account of Calchas's prophecy:

"Time, the hunter, shall destroy
Priam, and the state of Troy;
Destiny, with eagle-hand,
Sack the town, and tear the land.
Towers be by a tower subdued,
Pregnant with a mightier brood,
Should no fate-sent storm arise,
To o'ercloud our enterprise,
Tarnish the bright bits of steel,
Break the curb our foe should feel.
Dian hates the hounds of Jove,
Mother-hares are Dian's love;
Dian, with resentful breast,
Loathes the eagle's cruel feast;
Dian chaste, with pitying eyes,
Views that embryo sacrifice."
Chant the hymn, the presage hail!
Chant it, may the good prevail!

More complex in structure is the Epode describing the flight
of Helen and the consequent grief of Menelaus:

Leaving her citizens the din of spears,
  And shields, and arming ships, and as a dower
To end in Troy's destruction, carrying tears,
    Through the tall portal at night's shrouding hour,
      Daring intolerable things, in haste,
      With steps that left no sound, so soft their tread,
      That woman went; whilst, sobbing on the blast,
      Prophetic voices echoed, as she passed,
        These words: "O palace! palace towers!
        Deserted, silent, nuptial bowers!
        Abandoned and adulterous bed,
        Where still the print of her who fled!
        Prince! O for thee! now lorn and lone,
        Thou body of a soul that's gone!
        Bitter, alas, the memory
        Of former joys—but most to thee,
        Whose loss is harder to be borne,
        Imbittered as it is by scorn,
        That hides, yet cannot stifle grief,
        Nor finds in words or tears relief.
        I see him tortured by the fire
        Of shame, and inextinct desire
        Of her now far beyond the seas.
        He comes, how squalid, pale, and wan,
        More like a spectre than a man,
          Pacing his marble galleries;
          And when her statue there he sees,
          Feigns that its beauty all is fled,
        And turns as if he loathed the spot,
        Saying, 'Where woman's eyes shine not,
         There every spark of love lies dead.'
To him shall airy shapes appear by night,
  To cheat his dreaming fancy, and to trace
Those features gazed on with a fond delight,
    That worshipped form of more than mortal grace:
      And when to clasp her to his breast he tries,

And stretches forth his arms, from his embrace
   Along the paths of sleep the winged vision flies."

The Herald's speech on the hardships of war was translated
by one who knew them at first hand:

Need I repeat the hardships, fastings, toils,
Endured at sea—the brief and broken rest
On the hard deck? What day, what hour of the day,
Did we not mourn our destiny? On shore
'Twas even worse: beneath the enemy's walls,
Our sleep was still more insecure; and there
The dews of heaven, and fogs from the damp ground,
That was our only bed, rotted our garments,
And tangled, like the mane of some wild beast,
Our shagged and matted locks. And who can tell
The savage cold that Ida's snow sent down,
When died the birds? or the fierce summer-heat,
When on his noontide couch, in heavy sleep
Outstretched, the interminable ocean lay,
Waveless and windless?

Medwin's blank verse is also skillfully varied to accommodate
character and situation. Agamemnon's blind step into hybris,
as he treads on the purple to please Clytemnestra and in the
same speech orders her to welcome Cassandra into the household, is executed without false heroics:

Then be it so, since 'tis your pleasure. Come!
Loose from my legs the sandals, that no god
May see me walk upon the figured purple,
And cast his envious glances at my feet.
It shames me much to soil with idle state
Such household wealth, and silver-woven tissues.
Something too much of this. Queen! may it please you
With gracious courtesy to welcome in
This stranger; he who reigns above looks down
With friendly eye on those who rule with mildness.
None bear with a good will the servile yoke.

And so this maid—she follows in my train
Of all my spoil the choicest flower, and gift
From the whole army: let us on, and since
You have persuaded me to grant your prayer,
Behold, I pass the vestibule of the palace,
Treading upon the purple as I go.

The tone of this blank verse is quite different from that spoken by the Chorus in dialogue with Cassandra, after her prophecy of Agamemnon's death:

You are seized
With some oracular spell, and in your ravings
Sing your own funeral dirge; as the dark bird
Of night, who never ceases to complain,
And all her life weeps bitterly, and calls
From her deep bower of woes on "Itys, Itys."

As a final example, consider Medwin's translation of Clytemnestra's first speech after the murder. Here was a great temptation to melodrama, but Medwin avoided it, and the coldly murderous hatred, nourished for years, emerges clearly:

How is an enemy to cheat an enemy,
But by returning hate for hate, and taking
A garb of friendship, thus to compass him
In a high net that is beyond his leap?
I have been wrestling with myself in thought
For years upon this conflict, my old wrongs
Rankling within me—and, at last, the morrow,
Too long delayed, has come for vengeance: what
He did, that did I—I deny it not—I slew him;
Just price for his offences—with such art
Contrived the stratagem, that to escape,
Or ward the blow, was vain. A circling cast-net,
Without a flaw in 't, as they spread for fishes,
A precious robe involved him in its folds:
I struck him twice, and twice he groaned aloud;
And as he groaned a second time, his limbs
Were loosened, and he fell—one more, a third

And last libation poured I forth, to please
That subterranean Jove, who saves the dead,
As he above the living—then escaped
His spirit with a sigh . . . and on its breath
Came rushing forth a mighty shower of blood,
That sprinkled me all o'er with its black dew,
Making me glad as a field newly sown,
When falls the divine rain, and wakes to life
The flowers.

Under Medwin's hand the characters of Aeschylus do live again, for he had an ear for dialogue as well as a practical and practiced acquaintance with a number of traditional metres and measures. These qualities, along with his usual avoidance of pompous, ornate, and archaic diction, help to explain why his translations may be read today with greater ease and pleasure than many a Victorian translation or even certain limp and prosaic-poetic renderings of the twentieth century. Even H. Buxton Forman, who disliked the man whose *Life of Shelley* he edited, was forced to pay grudging tribute to his enduring qualities as a translator. Writing in 1913 he stated, ". . . fifty years ago classical scholars referred to him as one of themselves." [36] This is good to hear of Medwin, at that time, in 1863, an old man come home to England to die, and Forman goes on to contemplate the republication of "his six by no means contemptible translations," which undoubtedly had their first origins in Shelley's *vivâ voce* renderings of *Prometheus Bound* during Medwin's first winter in Pisa. This, it will be recalled, was the first of Aeschylus's plays which Medwin published, in 1827.

Medwin had loved the drama since boyhood, when he took Shelley to see his first play; he and Byron had talked at length of plays and actors; he had himself written a tragedy for the stage; he had assigned to himself the drama section of *The New Anti-Jacobin*, and at the present period of his life he was acquainted with one of the greatest actors of the day, Charles

[36] Forman's edition of Medwin's *Shelley*, p. x.

Macready, who in the sunlit and happy complacency of his fame and fortune, surrounded by his loving family, did not like Medwin. "I do not like thee, Dr. Fell," he commented in his diary on October 25, 1833. Medwin, in his poverty and out of his love for the drama, asked Macready on at least four separate occasions for free tickets to the theatre.[37] The last time was on May 10, 1834, when Macready answered a note from "Captain Medwin, who dates South Molton Street, and is described by his messenger 'as the gentleman living at Mr. Tibbs's, Dean Street.' He seems a complete shuffler; his request was for an order to Sardanapalus"—*Sardanapalus,* the deed to which Medwin thought he had witnessed, a play that took him back to the days of his glory with Byron and Shelley in Pisa. Being poor was not easy for him; his pride ran too high. One did not grow rich by translating Aeschylus, nor acquire the respect of actors, who preferred less Grecian and more romantic plays. As for South Moulton Street, Medwin at this time repeatedly gave this address on his letters to Bentley the publisher. The number was 42. It is possible, at least, that Medwin's messenger misled Macready.

Medwin must have found more pleasant the company of old Joe Manton, the famous gunsmith who had taught Byron in the days of his youth to control his shaking hand when firing a pistol and who still remembered him. "When I was in London in 1833 or 4," Medwin wrote in the margin of his *Conversations,*[38] "I had a visit from old Joe Manton about a gun. He talked to me much about Lord Byron. He said that if his hand had not trembled so much he would have made an excellent shot." Medwin noted that the old man, after suffering reverses, had "opened a new shop in Holles Street."

Medwin too made another new start at this time, with a book unlike any he had ever written and one that proved to be his last book published in England. It was *The Angler in Wales,*

[37] *The Diaries of William Charles Macready,* ed. William Toynbee (New York, 1912), I, 72, 73, 132.
[38] Medwin's unpublished marginalia in his *Conversations,* p. 14.

or Days and Nights of Sportsmen (1834), handsomely printed, with seventeen illustrations in the two volumes, by Richard Bentley, Publisher in Ordinary to His Majesty. The frontispiece of each volume was engraved by the well-known Thomas Landseer, who was also in charge, it seems, of the fifteen woodcut vignettes that decorate the book, although these are signed variously.[39] Most of these illustrations were taken from sketches made on the spot by Robert Allen, to whom the book is dedicated. Medwin was so fond of his angling friend Allen, who also contributed "about 20 pages of the Text,"[40] that he wanted his publisher to send the book forth as "Edited and Illustrated by Two Brothers of the Rod."

He undoubtedly intended that his book should take its place within the tradition of Izaak Walton's *The Compleat Angler, or the Contemplative Man's Recreation*, to which he more than once refers, although his immediate model seems to have been William H. Maxwell's *Wild Sports of the West* (of Ireland), 1832.[41] Like *The Compleat Angler*, however, *The Angler in Wales* takes the form chiefly of dialogue; it too makes a show of defending the sport of angling, but in fact deals with innumerable other subjects at great length; it too evokes the author's love of the countryside as well as of the poets dear to him. Both men even believed or pretended to believe that fish could hear. From both books emerge clearly the minds and personalities of their authors. But Medwin was not Walton; he could not say, with Walton, "I write not for money, but for pleasure." The writing of Medwin's *Angler* was hard labor, done in illness, and this shows at times in the book, which is by no means characterized by the cheerfulness of tone or the spirit of innocence that pervades Walton's book. For Medwin

[39] Unpublished letter from Medwin to Richard Bentley, postmarked May 20, 1834, quoted by permission of The Carl H. Pforzheimer Library.
[40] Unpublished letter from Medwin to J. Ollier, March 5, 1834, quoted by permission of The Carl H. Pforzheimer Library.
[41] Unpublished letter from Medwin to Richard Bentley, Feb. 19, 1834, quoted by permission of The Carl H. Pforzheimer Library.

lacked Walton's simplicity of heart, and nothing could be more different than the origins of the two books.

The painful course of *The Angler* can be traced in some detail in Medwin's letters.[42] By February 19, 1834, Medwin thought that he had completed the manuscript and offered it to Richard Bentley, writing that he would deliver it to any representative of Bentley's who might call at 42 South Moulton Street: he himself was too ill to make the journey to Bentley's offices on New Burlington Street. The manuscript was accepted almost at once, before the end of the month, and Medwin's relations with his publisher during the course of the book's printing would never again be so pleasant. It was perhaps during these few days that Medwin recommended to Bentley a friend of his, George Burges, as "a worthy successor of Porson, & well known in the Classical World." Medwin's faith in Burges, who had a manuscript to dispose of, was fully justified during later years, and the two classical scholars remained lifelong friends.

But almost at once the relations between Medwin and his publisher became worse. Bentley had decided that the manuscript was not long enough to make two volumes. Medwin replied in a letter marked "Private" and delivered by some unknown hand. "Dear Sir," he wrote,

Your letter found me in a high fever & the contents of yours did not contribute to abate it. How you can have the assurance, the barbarity—I may say (knowing as you do that I have depended on & anticipated part of this money) to make such a proposition astonishes me. You say that the Matter will not make 480 pages. My bargain with you says nothing about quantity . . . However to end all further Discussion, I shall supply you with Matter enough to make 700 pages—in the course of 8 or 10 Days.

Medwin closed by saying that the additional pages would come at the end of the book, and thus the printing need not be held

---

[42] Unpublished letters from Medwin to Bentley or Ollier concerning the *Angler* are quoted by permission of The Carl H. Pforzheimer Library, unless otherwise stated.

up. A part of this new material took the form of an appendix to volume one, made up of quotations from such works as "Swammerdam's rare Treatise on the Ephemerus" and Penn's *Maxims and Hints for an Angler*. The second volume was swelled out by a revised version of "The Pindarees," now called "Julian and Gizele," with the names of the chief characters changed and the original notes greatly (and interestingly) expanded. Significantly, for this amorphous book, Medwin's original title was "The Rambling Angler."

The printing of the book stretched out over the months, and Medwin complained in letter after letter: "we are getting on very slowly—I mean to go out of Town on the 23ᵈ, so that if the book is not printed by that time I must leave the proofs to you, which I should think . . . were best avoided— Pray stir up the Printers." Another undated letter voiced his anguished cries again: "We are getting on horridly slow," he wrote to James Ollier, now working for Bentley. "Pray try & expedite— for I am very ill & my Doctor recommends me change of air." On May 20, he informed Bentley that he was going to Ireland: "I perceive that there is no chance whatever of my work being printed for 3 months, for during the last 3 weeks I have only had two Sheets to correct . . . I have already lost the best part of the Season . . . my health has been much injured mentally as well as physically." He complained because the illustrations were placed on the same page with the text, and so reduced, instead of appearing on separate sheets; he complained about the late publication date for a book on angling. "It is doing it little justice to bring it out in July or August—indeed it ought to have appeared & might by the 1st of June . . ." He was suffering more than his share of the pains of authorship. On June 12 his cries reached their highest pitch, as he wrote to James Ollier,[43]

My dear Sir—It is quite dreadful this delay in the printing—I have only had one sheet this Week.—Is it ever intended that this

[43] Forman's edition of Medwin's *Shelley*, p. 499.

Book is to get thro the press—?—When the present matter is printed, I mean to write day by day just as much as they can print—but shall not put pen to paper till then. O God how sick I am of the Angler in Wales.—

Yours truly
T. Medwin

He escaped from London, a city he had never liked, with a great sigh. Ironically, he went not to Ireland but to Cheltenham, where the fishing trip described in *The Angler* begins and ends. After staying there for nearly two months, he wrote to Charles Ollier at Bentley's on August 31. He had run out of money again; he was leaving in a few days and had to pay his bills: "I tell you that I am really distressed for money—implore your good offices in endeavouring to get Mr Bentley to send me a small sum, even £20 on Account." Then he apologized for his words to Bentley when they had quarreled over the length of his manuscript. "My nerves were in that state of irritably [*sic*] from long illness . . ." He believed that he had been "very intemperate"—and in the last sentence announced that he had "half finished a Work—which will far outdo any thing I expected to do." Why Bentley ever again published anything by Medwin is difficult to understand, but he did, again and again.

The portrait of Medwin that emerges from *The Angler* is more attractive than that revealed by these letters, written during its printing, even though the book also deals in terms of sickness, frustration, and worse. The two chief characters are clearly autobiographical, and the man that Medwin was is to be found in them. The narrator, Stanley, whose journal and papers are supposedly transcribed in the book, represents the Continental Medwin. He has been "much on the Continent," at Rome, Naples, Geneva, Paris, and Florence, and now, "sick of London (as I always am in a week)," he was on his way to fish in Wales,[44] to recover his health. Of the pages of his own diary, Stanley writes, they are "a memorial of time misspent;

[44] Medwin, *Angler*, I, 4–5.

health destroyed—prospects foundered—fortune impaired—
and, to crown all, of a killing and deadly blight in love, and
an inseparable perpetual blister in marriage . . . I have, as you
know, lost all my early friends by neglect . . ."[45] But the other
main character, Julian, is even worse off: he dies, and it is he
who represents the Medwin of India, the brevet Captain who
tells all the Indian stories in the book and suffers from "half
a liver." On the last page we read of him, " . . . Julian fell into
a state of mute melancholy, and having refused to take any
nourishment for many days, passed, for the most part, in
wandering about Cader Idris, expired of inanition." Perhaps
this reflects no more than Medwin's belated farewell to his
youth—he was now forty-six—but it would seem singular and
significant that both characters suffer from a melancholy dissatisfaction with life, both are in search of health, and one dies.

Despite these qualities, however, the dominant tone of the
book is by no means melancholy. There is too much else in it,
including fresh air and an expert knowledge of angling. In
many ways these pages offer the most attractive image of the
man Medwin we have. For here is the outdoor Medwin, who
loved to tramp through the countryside, fish or hunt all day,
and take his ease that night at an inn, with a choice friend or
two, enjoying his cigar and his claret. Another attractive quality
of the book is Medwin's ability to ridicule the tall Indian tales
of Julian, "who never fails to find a climax for every marvel
of the creation, however marvelous."[46] Indeed, before his final
illness, Julian is "the same amiable, gentle, and gay creature
he ever was."[47] It is a man's book, full of weather and water
and Wales, the racked land of wild and rocky mountainous
terrain, one-family farms, small inns, and worse—tiny huts in
which people live like animals. None of this is blinked or
romanticized.

The book is formless, supported structurally only by the
strictly accurate geographical progression, as the characters fish
in one stream or lake after another, but it is not unskillfully

[45] *Ibid.*, II, 290.   [46] *Ibid.*, I, 157.   [47] *Ibid.*, I, 6.

formless, for it pretends to be chiefly a record of conversation on an extended trip. And into *The Angler* Medwin poured his varied reminiscences more richly than into anything else he ever wrote. In addition, he included poems of his own written as long ago as his Indian or early Italian years; portions, it seems, of his Indian journal; pages once intended for his biography of Byron; a Welch dialect sermon; a melodramatic Welch tale of treachery, and translations of Welch verse, along with pages and pages of angling. Of the value of these, opinion seems divided. The *Blackwood's* reviewer wrote, "Captain Medwin is an accomplished gentleman, but no angler, and his 'Fly-Fishing in Wales' [sic] though it contains much valuable reading—unless he sends a presentation copy—will never find its way into the library of the Walton Club." [48] Robert Blakey's *Historical Sketches of the Angling Literature of All Nations,* on the other hand, found in Medwin's book "much useful information," [49] and *The Literary Gazette* for July 19 and 26, 1834, referred admiringly to the author's knowledge of his sport.

One of the values of the book lies in the fact that it first published Shelley's translation from the *Purgatorio*, "Matilda Gathering Flowers," and his Italian song, "Buona Notte." But Byron figures more prominently than Shelley and is the subject of two valuable letters written by James Forrester, [50] surgeon of the *Alacrity*, who met Byron at Missolonghi. These show every sign of being authentic, but they derive from or are related in some other fashion to a letter published in *The Examiner* on October 17, 1824, "Lord Byron in Greece." It is possible that Forrester wrote two versions, although how Medwin secured the longer version he published is not clear. Forrester was drowned, we learn from *The Angler,* when serving as surgeon on a convict ship lost off Boulogne. His account of Byron contains some of the best pages in Medwin's book.

[48] *Blackwood's*, XXXVIII (July, 1835), 121.
[49] P. 265.
[50] I am indebted to Mrs. Doris L. Moore of London, who has consulted the Naval Lists, for the correct first name of Forrester, hitherto understood to be Daniel.

Byron also figures large in the supposed conversation of a character easily recognizable as Captain Daniel Roberts, still very much alive at the time. It would therefore seem probable that Medwin was in fact, as the book implies, on friendly and intimate terms with the naval officer who had built the *Don Juan* for Shelley and the *Bolivar* for Byron. Medwin would not otherwise have dared to place into Roberts's mouth so many of his own opinions of Byron, nor described Roberts's life in such detail. For Roberts is clearly the mouthpiece of Medwin: statements are attributed to him which had appeared in Medwin's *Memoir of Shelley* and would appear in his *Life of Shelley*. Further, the account of Byron at Pisa, attributed to Roberts, actually describes Medwin's association with Byron in that city.

Roberts, who had outrageously overcharged Byron for the *Bolivar,* did not like the poet,[51] and it is significant of Medwin's own changing views of Byron that he should have chosen a character representing Roberts to voice many of the remarks on Byron. Byron the man is still a subject that kindles Medwin's imagination, and his style takes on increased color and firmness when he writes of him. But he now passes judgment on the character of Byron, and this he never did in the *Conversations.* Byron the poet, however, is still for Medwin unchallenged: "Poetry died with Byron, and is not likely to have a second resuscitation." Thus the Byronic flame burned on in him, despite his persisting hatred of Hobhouse and the other reviewers who had dealt with the *Conversations* so harshly or shamefully.[52]

If he had enshrined the poetry of Byron, it was to Shelley, both man and poet, that he had given his heart. In 1835, the year after publishing *The Angler,* he was already collecting additional materials about the life of Shelley in Marlow, talk-

[51] See Roberts's letter in Trelawny's *Recollections,* chapter xiv: "God defend me from ever having anything more to do with him [Byron]." Byron lost nearly £600 when he sold the Bolivar, which in 1827 was owned by Roberts, who had himself purchased it for £100 (Roberts's unpublished diary, in the Keats-Shelley Memorial Library in Rome.)
[52] Medwin, *Angler,* II, 184, 189.

ing to people who had known the poet there in 1817, planning already, it would seem, a full-length biography. For nearly a month, with Shelley's *Revolt of Islam* in his hand, he observed the Thames and its banks in and around Marlow, between Oxford and London, comparing the scenery with Shelley's "strikingly faithful" description of it.[53] Shelley, he knew, had composed a good part of the poem in his boat, drifting down the river. Medwin, who thought that *The Revolt* was "perhaps the finest descriptive poem in the English or any other language," no longer wondered, after studying the beauty of the Thames, at Shelley's inspiration. Neither the Ganges nor the Rhine, he wrote,

made an impression equal to the Thames—with its clear and pellucid stream, now precipitate, now tranquilly flowing through meadows—vying with those of Asphodel, its lovely islands, whence the swans lead forth their cygnets—its venerable and sacred oaks, and beeches, and plantations, through which peeps some noble mansion, or runs down to the water's edge—fishing punts and pleasure boats moored in the foreground—some cottage *ornée* or Italian villa.[54]

As sensitive as Medwin was to natural beauty, he was drawn with equal force to the life of the town, and it was almost inevitable, sooner or later, that the author of the *Conversations of Byron* would make the acquaintance of Lady Blessington, whose *Conversations with Byron* had appeared in book form in 1834. Medwin had met her, in fact, in Florence, where she had lived in 1826 and again in 1827. He remembered Lord Blessington's daughter there, before her strange marriage to Count D'Orsay. Now, in London, he dared to renew his acquaintance and called at Gore House, where he met the impressive D'Orsay. Lady Blessington, he recalled,[55] "used to ring a bell that communicated with the Cottage in the Court where

[53] Medwin, *Shelley*, p. 193.
[54] Medwin, *Lady Singleton*, I, 229–230.
[55] Medwin's unpublished marginalia in his *Shelley*, I, 293.

that accomplished Gentleman and Artist (for he was both Sculptor & Painter) lived." Medwin was so impressed by the varied "talent of that remarkable Frenchman"[56] that he decided Byron in the last canto had turned Don Juan "into the Beau D'Orsay." But it was Lady Blessington who became his "old friend and correspondent," and at Gore House they traded talk of Mary Shelley. In later years, in 1845 or after, he was told by her that Mary had paid £40 to George Byron (who passed himself off as the poet's son) for letters supposedly written by Shelley and Mary shortly after they first met. The subject of the correspondence was the advantage of free love over the matrimonial state.[57] Lady Blessington, "a lady whose talents and accomplishments are thrown into shade by the qualities of her heart," also told Medwin that she had tried to help Claire Clairmont by securing for her "a situation as humble companion." But "Miss C. was too noble to conceal her story from the ear of her intended benefactress" or employer and so failed to get the job.[58] The end of this tale, however, seems highly doubtful: Claire actually made the most frightened efforts to conceal the fact that she was the mother of Byron's daughter.

The glitter of Lady Blessington's circle was probably too great, however, for Medwin, whose clothes must have seemed at times a little shabby or threadbare. This friendship was best cultivated by mail. In the autumn of 1835, a few months before Lady Blessington moved into Gore House, he had been reduced to answering an advertisement seeking an editor for some unknown paper. In his letter of application, September 26, he proposed himself as one whose "name is sufficiently known in the Literary World," listed his chief publications, and pointed to his editorship of *The New Anti-Jacobin* as "proof of my conservative principles." He closed, "I have also at times contributed to conservative papers— My terms will be very moder-

[56] Medwin's unpublished marginalia in his *Conversations*, p. 202.
[57] Medwin's unpublished marginalia in his *Shelley*, I, 212.
[58] Medwin, *Shelley*, p. 175.

ate . . ."[59] It does not appear that "A. V., Care of Mr. W. Edwards, 12 Ava Maria Lane," gave him the job.

He dated this letter from the Westminster Chop Club, but he may have moved already from London to Devon, where he was living in 1837.[60] If he lived in the little Devonshire village so lovingly described in his novel and again in his sketch called "The Two Sisters," it was very beautiful indeed.[61]

On the southern coast of Devonshire, within two miles of that fashionable watering place, Torquay, at the foot of a steep hill, almost inaccessible to carriages, is seen the village of Babbicomb. I have called it a village, though the name is hardly applicable; for the only houses it contains are seven, or eight in number, and these occupied, with the exception of the one inn, by the families of gentlemen.

It is then a hamlet of villas, or rather *cottages ornées,* not placed together, but separated by pleasure grounds, and gardens, and so nested in wood and hidden by the inequalities of the ground, that they are scarcely visible, one by the other. They are all covered with thatch, and the walls are so overgrown with ivy, and other creeping plants, that only the tops appear, even from the heights, that shut in this lovely dingle. The spots chosen for these abodes, are the most romantic and picturesque that can be imagined. Some stand immediately on the beach, shadowed by thick plantations of forest trees, that grow most luxuriantly down to the water's edge; others are raised on little platforms, that seem designed by nature for their erection.

If Medwin lived in one of these seven or eight houses, it is virtually certain that he spent many hours at that "fashionable watering place," Torquay, only two miles away. Torquay is, he writes,

[59] Unpublished letter from Medwin to "A. V., Care of Mr. W. Edwards," Sept. 26, 1835, in the Morgan Library.

[60] Giartosio de Courten, *Shelley e l'Italia,* p. 138.

[61] Medwin, *Lady Singleton,* I, 2–3; "The Two Sisters," *Bentley's Miscellany,* III (March, 1838), 279–280. In the second quotation, from "The Two Sisters," I have silently corrected "Torbay," presumably a typographical error, to "Torquay." Medwin's "Babbicomb" is properly spelled "Babbacombe" and is on the bay of that name.

the Nice or Pisa of England, and the great refuge of consumptive patients from all parts of the three kingdoms. This famed spot is protected from the northeasterly winds by range behind range of hills: here, carpeted with turf of eternal verdure; and there, surmounted by tors covered with plantations to their tops . . . So that Torquay is not only the most picturesque, but the most desirable residence on the coast of Devonshire. But if the environs are beautiful, what shall I say of the place itself, with its basin, like a small sea-port scooped out the rock, artificially formed by means of two piers or moles, the miniature of those of Genoa; terrace above terrace, its buildings and villas of the most elegant construction, with their verandas and balconies commanding a view of Torbay, seen from between two rival wooded cones, where many a thatched cottage peeps like a bird's nest out of the thick foliage of evergreens that embower them. I have called Torquay a winter residence; no! winter there is none: so mild is the climate, that the ilex, the arbutus, and the philarea, here grow to a size that they never elsewhere attain. The myrtle is seen clambering over the windows; the China rose has, throughout the year, a constant succession of buds and flowers.

But by June, 1837, his sojourn in Devon had come to an end, and he was back in London, where he learned that the Italian patriot Mazzini was living. After days of searching, Medwin found Mazzini's house. The Italian, who was busy writing and planning for Italian unity, had not attempted to find Medwin in London because, as he wrote on June 16,[62] "I like to stay alone as much as possible and because in this ocean-like city it was difficult for me to discover where he might live." But Medwin called too often on the serious young Italian, "almost every day," he wrote to his mother; "he begins now to come rather too often." Medwin told him that he earned enough ("abbastanza") from his writing—perhaps so, but not enough, certainly, to support himself, which is what Mazzini wanted to do. This was a very difficult thing in the days when Dickens received only £20 a month for editing the popular *Bentley's Miscellany* and only £2 more for his monthly contribution of

[62] Giartosio de Courten, *Shelley e l'Italia*, pp. 137–138.

original material, some of which included the chapters of *Oliver Twist*.[63] Mazzini was too busy to entertain Medwin and seemed glad, when he announced to his mother on August 9, 1837, that Medwin was going to Germany for several years.

For Medwin, it was the end of an era. He must have known that he would be gone from England many more years than several. Before he left he secured, as a "present" from the publisher, he said,[64] the first ten volumes (up through 1834) of *Fraser's Magazine,* in which his Aeschylus had appeared; and he requested Bentley to be "equally generous" with his *Miscellany.* To assist such generosity, he stated that for Fraser he had "written but little in comparison" with what he had published in *Bentley's.* If this is true, he may have delayed his departure until some time around April, 1838, for by that date seven of his contributions had appeared in *Bentley's,* but by the end of 1837 only three. Whatever the precise date of his departure, he was collecting his scattered works, in preparation for another, rather late beginning. It seems virtually certain that from now on he would be a remittance man, supported in large part by his brother or mother. For his tales contributed to *Bentley's* he had come to expect virtually nothing in payment: in the event that Bentley could not make a gift of the back issues requested, Medwin, without money to pay for them, offered to send to the publisher "a Tale to liquidate the amount."

[63] Una Pope-Hennessy, *Charles Dickens* (New York, 1946), p. 65.
[64] Unpublished letter from Medwin to Richard Bentley, undated and delivered "by favour of Mr. Hannen," quoted by permission of The Carl H. Pforzheimer Library.

9

The Last Long Years

Between 1837 and 1847 Medwin published, exclusive of the foreign correspondence contributed to *The Athenaeum*, twenty-six tales and sketches, enough to fill a volume of very respectable size. Eleven of these appeared in *Bentley's Miscellany*, twelve in *Ainsworth's Magazine* (which was illustrated by George Cruikshank), and the others in *Fraser's* and *The New Monthly*. Eight of the twenty-six, appearing in *Bentley's* in 1837 and 1838, received the editorial approval of Charles Dickens, when he edited the magazine in which his own *Oliver Twist* was appearing. Other contributors included Fenimore Cooper, Theodore Hook, Dr. Maginn, and J. J. Morier. All of this suggests that Medwin's contributions must have had a substantial popular appeal at the time. A sampling of them, along with his one novel, *Lady Singleton* (1842), will throw interesting light on the mind of Medwin as well as on the popular taste of the time.

The world of prose fiction that he created is essentially the world of the traveller, and in his tales he admiringly referred three times to Irving's *Tales of a Traveller*. The scene is variously international, as we move from tale to tale—a little village in Devonshire, a great house in Grosvenor Square, a cold back room on the fourth floor of a cheap hotel in Paris (where the heroine of "The Sacrifice" dies), a *palchétto* in the Scala theatre in Milan (where she is seduced, in French), at Poitiers an inn frequented by students and a café frequented by officers of the local garrison, where a duel is fought to the death on a billiard table. The great cities, along with the small towns and villages that Medwin knew, pass in review: Rome, Paris, Cheltenham,

Venice, Coire and Andermatt (in Switzerland), Cività Vecchia, Berne, Florence, Lausanne, Ghent, Genoa, each described accurately and at length. Not until 1842 does he publish a tale with a German setting, in Leipsic. Thereafter he places his narrative in Mainz, Strasburg, Jena, or Mannheim.

The descriptions of these backgrounds are solidly buttressed in factual, realistic detail, although the plots may be marvelous enough. Rather regularly, the marvelous or less easily believable rises out of the ordinary or the commonplace or the actual. By such use of circumstantial realism did he lead his reader on into belief. And here he is at his best—in description, not in plot structure, not insight into character or the nature of life. His art is primarily pictorial or visual. But in evoking the scene before him, he is perhaps the equal of Irving, to whom he is indebted, although he lacked Irving's warmth and genial humor. Nor is his skill necessarily limited to those scenes that had passed before his eye. It is by no means certain that he was ever in Spain, between Castile and Andalusia, but of that place he conjures up a vision convincing both in its color and solidity. We get the look and feel of the dry terrain, we sense the quality of the air—"an atmosphere of dust and flame." There are then heard the voices of the *arrieros,* as they stop their long train of mules before the *venta* or "refuge." Inside this vast, isolated, barnlike inn, a great single room, its raftered roof resting on square stone pillars, the only light comes through narrow openings cut into two walls only. Along the two dark walls are fastened the mules and horses of the caravan, hardly visible, and about the stone pillars the baggage is piled. Then a group of three young persons is singled out, their faces lighted up by the cooking fire—and the narrative begins.[1]

This scene may be an unfamiliar or uncommon one, but it is not falsely romanticized. When Medwin is not deliberately and openly attempting to suggest the picturesque or the sublime, his "principal aim" in description is that which he attri-

[1] Medwin, "The Contrabandista," *Bentley's Miscellany,* VIII (July, 1840), 17–22.

butes to the painter Jean Stein, whose "Cuisine Maigre" he says he saw in Ghent: it is "truth to nature; plain, unadulterated, disgusting, degraded nature, without caricature or exaggeration . . ." [2]

The characters in these tales and sketches live by and large in a world of violence and treachery. The heroine of "The Sacrifice" is sacrificed to a cold and heartless noble husband by the senseless social ambition of her worldly-minded aunt, whose name, interestingly, is Henrietta, the name of Medwin's wife. This innocent heroine, once on the Continent, is seduced by her husband's friend, a gambler, to be passed on to other gamblers, to end as their accomplice, and to die young, deserted and remorseful.

"The Duel" is a story of chance, senseless superstition, and desperation, arising from the accidental gathering of thirteen students at dinner and the suggestion of one of them that there is a "way of annulling the proverb that threatens death in the course of the year to one of a party of thirteen." [3] This is to risk death at once—in a duel. And so the thirteen coolly play billiards to select the duelist from their number, who then strikes in the face an officer of the local garrison. It is the officer who is killed.

"Mascalbruni," a formless tale which takes its name from the wholly villainous title character, relates the "biography," as Medwin calls it, of an international criminal—gambler, fortune hunter, and murderer—who preys upon the innocent in Rome, Paris, London, and the estate of an Irish bishop, among other places.

"The Last of the Bandits" is not a tale or story at all, but a sketch of the formidable and awesome Barbone which takes the form of an interview in the prison at Cività Vecchia. The significant movement is found not in the rambling recollections of Barbone, but in the reactions of the first-person narrator who

[2] Medwin, "The Cuisine Maigre," *Bentley's Miscellany*, III (April, 1838), 367.
[3] Medwin, "The Duel," *Bentley's Miscellany*, II (July, 1837), 76.

reports his words. At their end, he realizes that "the poetry of banditism had perished in the citadel of Città Vecchia." [4] Medwin's sketch is in effect the final chapter of Irving's "The Painter's Adventure," where Barbone first appeared. Medwin refers twice to it, for it was he who read to Irving the "journal of a painter while prisoner of the robbers near Rome," as Irving noted in his diary on February 15, 1824. It would seem, then, that Barbone (so called because of his great beard) was an actual bandit. Medwin states that his name was Gasparoni, that the painter of Irving's story was Charles de Chatillon, kidnapped at Lucien Bonaparte's villa at Frascati, where he was mistaken for the prince. I take the sketch to be what it pretends to be, an account of an actual interview; if not, the sketch is a remarkable tribute to Medwin's powers.

"The Three Sisters" is a tale of seduction, suicide, and retirement into one of the strictest convents of Rome—the several fates of the three sisters of the title. The narrator is represented as hearing this story on his marriage day, at the British Consulate at Berne, where Medwin in fact had been married. The narrator observes at the conclusion, "I cannot help considering it a bad omen of my own future happiness." [5]

The Innkeeper of Andermatt, in the story of that name, turns out to be a murderer for money who knowingly allows an innocent man to die for his crime.

"The Two Sisters" has for its subject that recommended by Poe as the most poetic of all, the death of a beautiful woman, but Medwin, perhaps to compensate for the tale's utter formlessness, gives us two beautiful women, both dying of consumption. The last days of the last to die are made miserable by a dissenting minister who persuades her to accept the "desolating doctrines of election and grace." [6]

---

[4] Medwin, "The Last of the Bandits," *Bentley's Miscellany*, II (Dec., 1837), 590.

[5] Medwin, "The Three Sisters," *Bentley's Miscellany*, III (Jan., 1838), 70.

[6] Medwin, "The Two Sisters," *Bentley's Miscellany*, III (March, 1838), 282.

"The Cuisine Maigre" is not a tale at all, but a description of a painting which depicts a numerous family ground down very nearly to the condition of hungry animals by years of undernourished poverty.[7]

"Pasquale: A Tale of Italy" relates the slow poisoning of the father of an unattractive middle-aged woman by his servant, who has already secured the love of the woman but not yet her inheritance. The startling pages in this story are those describing the funeral of the father, for we meet them again in Medwin's *Shelley*—as an account of the burial of the poet's ashes in Rome.

"The Quarantine" is the only one of these tales and sketches thus far that does not turn on violence or death. It relates the manner in which an entire ship's company is placed in quarantine in Genoa, at a time when cholera is raging. An ancient virgin who travelled alone had, out of vanity or thoughtlessness, falsified her passport, which stated that she was accompanied by a servant. The only conclusion for the port authorities was that the servant had died. The lazaretto is then realistically and sometimes brutally described.

"The Contrabandista" is another dueling story, this time set in Spain, and the contestants disagree over politics. The title character is a Constitutionalist sympathetic to the army of Christina, the Spanish Regent during the minority of her daughter Isabella II; the other duelist, who is killed, is an officer in the forces of Don Carlos, brother of Ferdinand VII and leader of the extreme monarchists. These details establish the time of the action as 1833 or shortly after, seven years or less before the date of publication.

"Sydney. From the Memoranda of a Physician" gives us Shelley as Sydney, Medwin as the attending physician, Emilia Viviani as Bianca, and Pacchiani the devil of Pisa as Torriagni, who is, interestingly, not only a dealer in old paintings but also

---

[7] Medwin states that he saw this painting in the "beautiful cabinet of Monsieur Schamps at Ghent," a collection also referred to in "The Two Sisters."

Bianca's confessor, and introduces the two lovers of *Epipsychidion* fame. The plot is startling in its implications for the biography of Shelley. The physician finds the melancholy Shelley wasting away in a psychosomatic decline and recalls a painting at the Louvre which suggests to him a cure: Love in the form of a young woman. (No character representing Mary Shelley appears in the story.) The devil of Pisa, whose description reappears in Medwin's *Shelley*, suggests Bianca, at the time in a convent. She is then described as a true "Cressid," and Medwin quotes several lines from Shakespeare's play: [8]

> Her very foot spake,
> Her wanton spirits looked out
> At every creek and corner of her body.

We read further, "So loose was the discipline of the convent, that I have reason to know that Sydney was frequently closeted with the fair pensionnaire." This character of Emilia Viviani quite agrees with that given her by Claire Clairmont, who noted that Emilia changed the saint she prayed to each time she changed her lover. It is not impossible, then, that Medwin took the name of Bianca from *Othello* (where another Bianca is the mistress of Cassio) and that in Medwin's story is to be found the true explanation of Shelley's sudden revulsion from Emilia, whom Shelley finally described as a "centaur," not Juno but a cloud.[9] In Medwin's story, however, Sydney never comes to understand the true character of Bianca; he dies, shortly after she marries and moves to the Maremma.

The year 1842, which saw the publication of Medwin's novel, *Lady Singleton*, also produced two short stories, the last two that need be glanced at here. "The Two Skeletons: A Tale of Florence" tells the tale of two cloistered lovers, a nun and a monk, who dig a tunnel linking their two cells. In it they perish,

---

[8] I have quoted the lines from *Troilus and Cressida*, IV, v, 56–57, as they appear in Medwin's "Sydney; from the Memoranda of a Physician," *Bentley's Miscellany*, IX (Feb., 1841), 179. Medwin quoted from memory.

[9] Shelley, *Works*, X, 401.

somewhat unconvincingly, because of the flawed nature of Medwin's plot, which he feels the need to explain in a footnote. "Desaga: A Fantastic Tale, after the Manner of Hoffmann" is better constructed. His first story with a German setting (Leipsic), it gives us an old man's mysterious double, who suddenly appears in the house of Desaga at the very moment that a character named Baron Vilde (of uncertain nationality) disappears from the hotel across the street. Desaga is found murdered, but Vilde is never found, and at the end of the tale it is revealed that Vilde is an anagram, in English, for Devil.

The tales and sketches contributed to *Ainsworth's Magazine*, between 1842 and 1847, do not differ sufficiently from Medwin's earlier work to deserve summary. All of his tales and sketches, however, may be said to be typically romantic in their fondness for the marvelous, the picturesque in natural landscape, and the foreign or remote in locale, but their view of human nature, significantly, is by no means idealized. Most of his main characters emerge from underground and live in a world of violence, from which they prey on the innocent.

The male characters are almost never sentimentalized, however melodramatic they may be at times, and the settings are faithfully or convincingly rendered. But Medwin's art was static and pictorial, his plots constructed in a loose or even, in several tales, a slovenly manner. A clear sense of structural form is not one of his virtues, nor does he usually see any significant meaning in his tales of violence, which never attempt to rise to the heights of tragedy. (This, however, is also true of Irving's banditti tales, which move primarily on the surface of life.) Medwin's tales are innocent also of Hawthorne's moral symbolism, but they show more common vitality than Hawthorne at his palest. The mind of Medwin was coarser, but it was also more robust, and he knew more about the varied surfaces of the world. In these stories, finally, there is nothing at all which is femininely decorous. Medwin was selected, significantly, to initiate the department in *Ainsworth's Magazine* called "The

Gentleman's Tiger," addressed specifically to male readers. This page, the editor wrote, "will overflow with milk and honey—to say nothing of whiskey-punch, humble port, and imperial Tokay. All things proper for gentlemen to discuss, the gentleman's tiger will monthly bring to them . . ." Medwin led off with "A Short Chapter on Beards." [10]

Whatever one may think of Medwin's tales and sketches, the respectability of his insight as a critic is revealed again by the choice that he made of masters to follow—Irving in his shorter fiction, Manzoni's *I Promessi Sposi* in his novel. The latter he described as "one of the best novels in any language; and in saying so, I do not forget Fielding's, or Walter Scott's, or the names of Le Sage, or Cervantes . . ." Of his own *Lady Singleton* he stated, "I mean to follow the example" of *I Promessi Sposi*. In so choosing, he demonstrated an understanding not only of the Italian novel but also of his own talents, for he recognized that the melodramatic bare bones of the Italian plot were unimportant. Manzoni, he wrote, referring to the travels of the Italian's hero and heroine,

not only describes the country through which they pass, but enters into the history of the times where the scene is laid, presenting to our eyes a gallery of landscapes, historical pictures, and more than all, of portraits, some sketchedly drawn, others highly finished; and yet, as occurs in every day life, we hear of them no more, though they cannot be dismissed from our memory.[11]

This was the example that he set before himself, and it is significant that again he falls into the language of painting. For violent and melodramatic as his plots may be, his art at its best is essentially static, his method primarily and solidly pictorial.

The latter quality may stand a reporter in very good stead indeed, and by early 1840 Medwin had sufficiently mastered the German language to serve as German correspondent for

[10] Medwin, "A Short Chapter on Beards," *Ainsworth's Magazine*, I (1842), 113–114.
[11] Medwin, *Lady Singleton*, III, 2–4.

The Athenaeum. It is very possible, however, that he did not go directly to Heidelberg immediately after leaving England. He must have lingered at least briefly at Ghent, if one may accept as genuine his realistic description of the painting, "The Cuisine Maigre," he states that he saw there. He may well have gone to Siena, where the narrator of "The Two Skeletons," it is stated, met Vincenzo Papi, Byron's coachman, who stabbed Sergeant-Major Masi in the Pisan brawl involving Byron, Shelley, and others.[12] This meeting is also described in Medwin's *Life of Shelley.* But if Medwin was at Siena, he could have been there for only one purpose: to see his wife and two daughters, the first born having become a naturalized Tuscan in 1836.[13] At some time during this period he was also at Prague and Vienna.[14]

By February 1, 1840, however, he was at Heidelberg, sending back to *The Athenaeum* his impressions of all manner of things German.[15] He informed English readers that a German optician had produced three daguerreotypes in accurate color. The "tone" of the Academy in Berlin had been wondrously reproduced "in all its truth, with the blue sky above, and the [Lime-tree] walk covered with snow . . ." He called the attention of English readers to Ernst Willkomm's nine-volume biographical novel, *Lord Byron, ein Dichter Leben* (1839), which, he noted wryly, was "in the main, borrowed from his different biographers," Medwin's own *Conversations of Byron* being among the sources of the novel. Of particular interest to English readers, he thought, would also be *Ideen und Betrachtungen über die Eigenschaften der Musik,* by the Crown Prince of Hanover, and a new edition of the poetical works of Immer-

[12] Medwin, "The Two Skeletons: A Tale of Florence," *The New Monthly Magazine,* LXV (Aug., 1842), 486.

[13] Enrica Viviani Della Robbia, *Vita Di Una Donna (L'Emily Di Shelley)* (Firenze, 1936), pp. 199–200.

[14] Medwin, "Foreign Correspondence," *Athenaeum,* March 14, 1840, p. 213.

[15] For Medwin's contributions to the *Athenaeum* in 1840, upon which almost all the following discussion is based, see the list of his publications.

mann, which, however, were marred, he observed, by extrava-
gantly artificial conceits. He looked forward to the appearance
of Schindler's biography of Beethoven, announced for Easter.

It was with the purest delight, however, that he discovered
and was elected to membership in the Heidelberg *Museum*—
which contained library, dining rooms, concert and ball rooms,
and a garden. The building was "large enough to contain a
regiment of dragoons, horses and all," he observed, and, indeed,
its exterior looked like a barrack. But inside, all was ordered,
at moderate cost, for man's comfort and intellectual sustenance.
The latest books were ordered from England, current periodicals from England, France, Switzerland, Italy, and Poland, in
addition to German publications. Here, in the foreign news
room, Medwin could read the London *Times, Galignani's Messenger,* the *Moniteur,* the *Quarterly Review,* the *Edinburgh,*
the *Athenaeum,* the *Revue des Deux Mondes,* the *Bibliothèque
de Genève,* and the *Biblioteca Italiana,* among others. This
internationalism presumably reflected the professorial element of the *Museum's* membership. In addition, there were
concerts and balls to be attended, where no formal introduction
to the ladies was required. Medwin was so impressed that he
recommended the institution to the English as a substitute for
the coffee house and the barroom. Indeed, a man might spend
most of his waking hours in the *Museum,* eating, drinking,
reading, writing, talking, or otherwise engaged, and Medwin
must have spent many. He was also pleased with the very un-
English mingling of ranks at the *Museum,* where, he noted,
"the citizen thinks himself on a perfect equality with the noble:
the host taking a hand at cards with the professor, or making
a beer or wein spiel,—*i. e.,* rattling dice for the reckoning with
his guests." It was a very perfect club.

But Medwin was less pleased with the rather complete do-
mestication of German women, in all but the great cities, and
their old-fashioned exclusion from most male society. He was
even more displeased by the wild and arrogant university students, with their scarred cheeks and seamed noses. Of their

dueling he highly disapproved. Few of them, he was glad to
report, came to the *Museum;* they had their own clubs, their
Verbindungs and their private *Kneipen.* These he had somehow
penetrated, only to be greatly disappointed, and he recalled, in
contrast, English undergraduate conversation at Oxford or
Cambridge:[16]

Instead of animated discussions on the politics of the day, on the
history of times present or past, and the great men of these times—
of disquisitions on classical subjects, poetry, or the drama, or the
fine arts—beer-laws and beer-fines furnish the staple of conversation
after the single combats of the day have been discussed, or the
coming ones of the morrow settled. Instead of the conviviality
produced by generous wine, which is an excuse for occasional
excess, all is gloomy and morose silence, or noise and uproar, with
them . . . Now as to their *Allgemeines*—when all the clubs meet,
one would suppose for good-fellowship, they assemble there to
insult and abuse each other—for the very purpose of so doing—in
order that they may give and receive challenges, until they are
carried insensible to the dead-room, where they lie wallowing, side
by side, on the straw, laid there on purpose to receive them!

Their pugnacity, it is explained, is the result of "sheer idleness . . . and having no pursuit."

They neither row, nor sail, nor angle, nor ride, nor drive, nor play
at crickets, tennis, fives, or any manly game, except that horrible
vulgar one of nine-pins. Their sole employment, out of lecture
hours, and we may suppose how much they learn there, how fitted
for study they are, after such orgies, is fighting or seeing fights, of
which upwards of eight hundred take place every year in Heidelberg. You may guess how much the spectacle of a man, covered with
blood, from wound after wound, serves to refine the feelings . . .

The only good word Medwin had to say for them was the
result of his attending an initiation or inauguration at one of
the student clubs. Here he witnessed an exhibition of "enthusi-

[16] *Lady Singleton,* III, 23–25.

asm—almost of poetry,"[17] as the students swore their solemn oaths upon the long dueling rapiers and chanted a solemnly chauvinistic German anthem. With all this he was much impressed.

The Germans generally he found to be a highly materialistic people, much more concerned for the actual than the ideal. "They eat more, drink more, and sleep more than any other people," he reported.

The author of a celebrated novel knows little of the Germans when he talks of "sentimental German Ladies," or of "metaphysical German Students." There is not a less ideal people on the face of the earth . . .

What sentiment can be expected from girls, who (those of the first families in Berlin even) take lessons in cookery; and of students, who pass their time, as I have here described. The positive, the actual, is all in all to them; as to metaphysics, they know not what the term means . . . I know that there is only one man in Germany, except the poet Körner, at the present day, who believes in the existence of any one thing that is not present to his senses.[18]

But Körner was dead, and this was an exaggeration. For he also knew, "The world of Germany is, at the present day, divided between the Pietists and Rationalists," Strauss being the leader of the latter group.[19] It did not occur to him, perhaps, that the Germans frequently expressed their intellectual energies in terms of religious controversy because politics was forbidden to them. "The censorship of the press weighs like the leaden mantle in Dante's *Inferno*, on German literature," he noted, with the result that few superior plays or books of consequence were produced, their place taken by translations from other languages. "Scarcely a novel known at home, but is immediately put into a German dress; and 'Boz' has as much fame here as in England."

[17] Medwin, "Foreign Correspondence," *Athenaeum*, March 28, 1840, p. 252.

[18] *Lady Singleton*, III, 31–32.

[19] Medwin, "Foreign Correspondence," *Athenaeum*, Feb. 22, 1840, p. 155.

All in all, however, Heidelberg was a very good town in which to live. Along with its other attractions, it had an excellent amateur orchestra, so good, Medwin thought, that the largest English city could not produce one to equal it. Heidelberg, he discovered, was one of the most delightfully musical cities he had ever lived in, and a summer music festival was celebrated at the Castle. He became acquainted with the aged Professor Thiebaut, "the possessor of the greatest private collection of MS. church music that perhaps exists in Europe." Medwin's own "particular predilection for sacred music [grew] almost to a passion" as a result of his acquaintance with Thiebaut, who held weekly *Academias* at which "no instrument is used but the organ, and no woman admitted." Medwin attended regularly and with the old *fanatico* discussed the generally admitted decline of church music. Thiebaut would banish "every instrument from the church but the organ." "All this blowing, scraping, and fingering," Medwin reported him as saying, "is to my mind heathenish, and unchristian." "The organ is the sole instrument fit for the worship of God," he thought. Medwin disagreed. He attributed the decline of church music to the "undevotional spirt of the age, and the consequent want of encouragement to write for the church, whilst the opera offers certain fame, however short-lived it may prove, and immediate remuneration." Nor could Medwin agree with the professor's sweeping denunciation of the moderns. Mendelssohn's *Paulus*, Medwin thought "an oratorio of great merit; I shall never forget the effect which that pathetic appeal, 'O Jerusalem, Jerusalem,' produced on me—Tomaschek, in his Requiem, deserves the highest praise . . . and Soboleski is of great promise . . ." Medwin was mistaken, it seems, in his last two judgments. It is clear, however, that he was a most enthusiastic and devoted amateur of music, by no means uninformed. He speaks with the very highest respect of Schumann's *Die neue Zeitschrift für Musik,* which effected a revolution in the musical taste of the time and in which most of Schumann's critical writings appeared.

He was repeatedly impressed by the Anglomania of the Germans, "not likely to decrease from Prince Albert's marriage," he wrote on the very day of the ceremony, February 10, 1840.

The English language is becoming as universal as French was . . . Half the shopkeepers now speak our vernacular tongue, and it is considered an essential in the education of the upper classes, who are become not only familiar with our classics, but well acquainted with all the ephemerides of our literature. Such are some of the fruits of the long peace—and the steam navigation of the Rhine.

But Medwin also realized that this admiration of things English had two other roots: a Germanic sense of national inferiority and an influx of English tourists, convinced that the German baths provided "remedy for all diseases . . . Baden-Baden, Carlsbad-Spa, Kissengen Ems . . . threaten to supersede Cheltenham, Bath . . ." Thus the shopkeepers learned English.

In late February, 1840, he went to Berlin, where he remarked the shockingly exotic character of the pre-Lenten Carnival, quite "alien to the spirit of the serious people of the north." Medwin thought of the Carnival at Florence, "when that city was a continued fête for *weeks*—and at Rome, where this Saturnalia is compressed into *one*, . . . the whole populace . . . giddy and drunken . . ." But at Berlin the Pietists were gaining so many converts that their puritanical fanaticism became the object of Blum's satiric comedy, *Schwärmerei nach der Mode*. Medwin found the comedy clever but no more: it lacked sufficient particularity to give him a clear idea of the tenets of the Pietists, who had, he thought, moved from self-delusion to intolerance of other opinions. He tried a sentimental tragedy by Gutzkow, *Werner, or Heart and the World*, and found it no better. A historical play by Raupach, *Elizabeth Farnese*, turned out to be "the very essence of dullness, . . . if it had forty acts instead of four, it could not have been more tedious."

In his articles from Berlin he ranged over a variety of literary productions and most of the arts. Tieck's new novel, he informed readers of the *Athenaeum*, "proved that the vigour of his intellect remains unimpaired." He noticed a learned new work on Dante which further developed the allegorical interpretations of Gabriele Rossetti, a critic whose views, he observed, were "diametrically opposed" to those of Ugo Foscolo. He described, for English readers, the two models of the proposed statue of Frederick the Great, to be erected in Berlin. One of these gave him a laurel crown and a Roman mantle but "left him with his Prussian long boots and holsters." Both showed him mounted. Medwin the old dragoon knew, however, that "Frederick was too good a general to trust himself to such chargers": they were too heavy and lifeless.

He was more impressed with the painting fostered by the *Kunstvereins* or Art Confederations, the purpose of which was "the extension of the fine arts, the improvement of taste, the adornment of the churches and public buildings, and the encouragement and remuneration of artists." Theodor Hildebrandt's "Lear and Cordelia" and Julius Hübner's "Fisherman and Water Nymph" he singled out for particular notice. He sent news to England of the summer music festivals held throughout Germany, of the second volume of "Rüppel's travels in Abyssinia," of a disappointing biography of Hoffmann, of a promised posthumous novel by Arnim (which never appeared), of Dieffenbach's difficult and metaphysical *Gedichte*, of a homeopathic magazine which argued, in the fourteenth number, that animals make better patients than men because they "follow their prescriptions more punctually." Thus variously did Medwin further the cause of Anglo-German understanding and cultural relations.

Although he chose Heidelberg finally as his place of residence, he continued to be a traveller, journeying throughout Germany, and it is virtually certain that he settled for a period in Baden-Baden. It is the scene of the action for more than one hundred pages in his novel, *Lady Singleton,* completed in the autumn of 1841. The city is described in the kind of realistic and lengthy detail that clearly demonstrates the knowledge of an eyewitness, probably acquired in 1840 or 1841. Although

Medwin recognized Baden-Baden as "the Queen of Baths," he did not like it: the government-licensed gambling houses had made it "the common sewer of Paris and London," and the high prices had driven most of the Germans from the town, now "almost exclusively colonized" by French and English. But he found the weather unusually good, and the "environs of Baden-Baden are indeed beautiful—the Black Forest and the Rhine . . . kissing each other." Lady Singleton and her young admirer, however, "did not confine their visit to the old Castle, or follow only that Tyrolian road which winds through the pine forest of Eberstein; they explored, in gipsy parties, other castles, and discovered points of view equally interesting." [20]

The chief biographical interest of Medwin's novel, perhaps, is the clear evidence it provides that he had already met Caroline Champion de Crespigny, whose verse appears at the head of a great many of his chapters, beginning with the first. He was to become her devoted slave. Poetess, translator, and daughter of the Lord Bishop of Norwich, she is almost certainly the "high-born and highly-gifted lady" whom Medwin thanks in his preface "for much of the matter and manner of these volumes"—which were "founded," nevertheless, he explains, on his story "The Sacrifice." The theme of the novel, the disastrous consequences of a loveless marriage made to achieve social position, Medwin did not derive from her. For Caroline's father had allowed her to marry very imprudently: her husband, the Rev. Heaton de Crespigny, a young man whom her father had admitted into holy orders without a degree, wound up in debtor's prison, where he still was in 1832, following the original "violent" and "disagreeable publicity." [21]

Caroline came from a colorful if unlucky family. Her father Henry Bathurst, nephew of the first Lord Bathurst and one of the stormiest and most liberal bishops in the House of Lords,

[20] *Lady Singleton,* III, 136–137.
[21] The Rev. Henry Bathurst, *Memoirs of the Late Dr. Henry Bathurst, Lord Bishop of Norwich* (London, 1837), I, 294; II, 6.

made himself very unpopular by his early and vigorous es-
pousal of Catholic emancipation, thereby losing much patronage, to his great regret, for he had regularly found places in
the church for his ministerial sons and other relations. The
Bishop's first son was Archdeacon of Norwich; his second son
a general, formerly military secretary to the Duke of Wellington. But another son, Benjamin, who had been appointed "En-
voy Extraordinary on an important secret mission to the Court
of Vienna," mysteriously disappeared without a trace in 1809.[22]
(Benjamin's daughter Rosa was drowned in 1824 when her
horse slipped down a steep bank into the Tiber at Rome. Caroline wrote a poem on this disaster.) In 1813 the Bishop's youngest son went insane, and another son, Coote, was "confined,"
presumably for insanity.[23] In 1828, on Christmas night, another
son, the Rev. Robert Bathurst, with eight children and £500
a year, cut his throat with a razor. Two years earlier, Benjamin's widow had played a "disagreeable and notorious part
[in] the celebrated abduction" of the fifteen-year old heiress,
Ellen Turner, by Edward Gibbon Wakefield, the Machiavellian colonial statesman, who persuaded the girl to marry him,
a complete stranger, at Gretna Green. The marriage was an-
nulled by special Act of Parliament, and the adventure was
terminated by Wakefield's sojourn in Newgate.[24]

Born in 1798, Caroline de Crespigny emerged, then, from a
background which was unstable, if sometimes distinguished.
Her brother the archdeacon described her as "a young woman
of great personal and intellectual endowments," "talented and
beautiful."[25] However, she had had to endure much before
Medwin met her. She had borne four sons by 1830 and was
trying to support them and herself on £200 a year, when the
Bishop observed that she was, "in her present nervous state, . . .
little qualified to attend to the education of her children."[26]
There was talk of the possibility that Caroline would have to

[22] *Ibid.,* I, 88.   [25] *Ibid.,* I, 294; II, 129.
[23] *Ibid.,* II, 101.   [26] *Ibid.,* I, 325.
[24] *Ibid.,* I, 293.

part with them, for the de Crespigny family was unable to assist her financially, and her father in his will left her a sum "wholly inadequate to supply her reasonable wants"—somewhat more than £4,000.[27] But she published three volumes of verse—*My Souvenir or Poems . . . with Translations &c.* (London and Heidelberg, 1844), a verse translation of Ernst C. F. Schulze's *The Enchanted Rose* (London, 1844), and *A Vision of Great Men, with other Poems and Translations from the Poetesses of Germany* (London and Heidelberg, 1848)—and she earned the name of bluestocking for herself in her adopted country. She was also an accomplished guitarist, harpist, and pianist. In 1849 she appeared to be about fifty years old but still dangerous, in the opinion of a reluctantly sympathetic feminine observer, Julie Gmelin, who wrote of Caroline,

She is considered a former mistress of Byron . . . has several grown sons, by whom I do not know, and in spite of her very florid cheeks, she is certainly pretty. Last evening we were once again asked to the Kerners for supper, where she played the harp; as we came in, she was sitting, in a bright colored dress, with bare arms, bare neck, necklace, headband, veils, flowers, and bows, behind the harp, which she played quite wonderfully with her beautiful arm and graceful hand movements. She has the beauty of an aristocratic Englishwoman, with alabaster skin, dark hair, and blue eyes. Her friend the Captain . . . is the model of a true worshipper.[28]

He became known as her "alten truesten Diener und Sklaven."

Their relationship was also sentimental and intellectual. He presented to her a copy of his *Shelley Papers; Memoir of Percy Bysshe Shelley,* with sixty additional pages bound into it. Here Medwin copied poems and verse translations of his own, of Caroline's, and of Shelley's. Much can be deduced from the

---

[27] *Ibid.,* II, 167.
[28] Letters of Julie Gmelin, June 19, 1849, published in the *Badische Post,* March 21 and 26, 1924, a typewritten copy of which was kindly sent to me by Dr. Herbert Derwein, Director of the Historische Bibliothek Des Kurpsalzischen Museums in Heidelberg.

little volume.[29] They had both suffered from life, and poetical
effusions of sentimental melancholy abound, which need not be
quoted here. Both had been unsuccessfully married; both knew
genteel poverty. They also shared an enthusiasm for Shelley.
On the back of the title page appear two poems, one an epigram on Shelley by Medwin, the other a sonnet "To Shelley"
written in another hand, perhaps Caroline's, and signed "C. de
Crespigny." Medwin's couplet may allude to her:

> Living—thou wert a morning star to us,
> Shelley—and dead art now our Hesperus.

Caroline's sonnet follows:

> From thy untimely grave where pitying Heaven
> [S]ent thee an early rest—if it is given
> [To] the imprisoned spirits here to roam—
> [Sc]orn not thy former uncongenial home,
> [O]h Shelley! first of Poets in whose mind
> The Virtues, Graces, Talents lived enshrined.
> Spirit of air, Oh deign to take the Wing,
> The ray of bright etherial glory fling,
> [? In] thy blest radiance mortal now no more,
> And light her path who dares thy name adore.
> Her feeble lay, her humble Muse inspire
> With but one spark of thy celestial fire,
> [S]o shall the world this meed of praise bestow:
> [H]er sweetest song was tuned by Shelley's woe.

Medwin's translations reflect a great breadth of intellectual
interests, and it is to be assumed that Caroline was impressed
by the variety of languages and centuries represented. There
are translations identified merely as from the French or Italian
or Latin, from Plato, Martial, and Casti, translations from
Goethe's *Faust* and a French version of the *Lusiad* of Camoëns,

---

[29] This interleaved copy of Medwin's *Shelley Papers* is in the Humanities Research Center of the University of Texas. Punctuation has been
added to Caroline de Crespigny's sonnet "To Shelley," the left edges of
which have been trimmed.

a translation of Alfieri's sonnet "To Genoa," of a poem on Byron by John Carlo di Negro, of Petrarch's sonnet 212, and translations into Greek and Latin of Byron's lines on Lord Elgin.

In addition to this varied intellectual fare offered up to Caroline, sentimental love poems abound, although no one of them addresses her by name. Perhaps she would understand that Medwin addressed the following "Epigram" to her:

> All own that thou art lovely—and it were
> In me most strange to say thou art not fair:
> An eye of liquid blue—a brow of snow,
> And cheek where all thy feelings pictured glow.
> In every motion of thy form we see
> The Graces have a Sister made of thee,
> But 'tis thy mind from that divinest frame
> Looks forth and tells us 'twas from Heaven it came.

Their relationship, however, as reflected in these manuscript pages, was substantially more robust than this "Epigram" would imply. Presumably they agreed on Robert Montgomery's long poem, *Woman, the Angel of Life,* of which Medwin wrote,

> He says that Women Angels are of Life;
> 'Tis clear the Poet never had a Wife.

Caroline also read an epigram "On a Coquette":

> You swear you never loved a man *more dearly;*
> Once in your life at least you spoke sincerely.

A couplet "On a Bon Mot of Sir J. Hamilton" is rather shockingly grotesque in its antisentimentality:

> " 'Tis spring and all things live, and breathe, and grow."
> "I hope you're wrong, for I've three wives below."

He even wrote a mock epitaph for his wife the Baroness, still very much alive:

> Here lies my wife; should I repine
> At her repose—as well as mine?

There are satiric attacks on John Murray, Samuel Rogers, Lord Burghersh, and a "Canting Preacher," the latter imitated from Martial:

> Snout nose—long shanks—a Camel mouth—pig's eyes:
> They say he has a heart—then Nature lies.

Of Burghersh's musical compositions he wrote,

> Who asks why neck cloths reach men's ears
>   Must surely be a *flat*;
> Whoever Burghersh's music hears,
>   Requires a high Cravat.

He would probably have married Caroline if he could, and in both his novel and his *Life of Shelley* he penned bitter and violent outbursts against the state of the divorce laws. "Barbarous and unnatural," he called them, "a disgrace to our civilization, the source of more miseries than all 'that flesh is heir to.'"[30] That there was more to his own separation than a heavy financial loss is suggested (although it cannot be proved) by his novel. There we read that there is "no compensation for the loss of domestic happiness." There also is to be found the knowledge that "love is an annihilation of self." But more startling is the interpolated story of the heroine's mother, over fifty pages which relate how an "unnatural" husband deserts the young mother, who then has to sell her jewels in order to live and who, thus reduced, initiates the central tragedy of the daughter, persuaded finally to marry a dastardly husband for wealth and position. In the midst of the mother's story occurs the dissertation on marriage and divorce law. Medwin seems to recognize no parallel between his treatment of the Baroness and the situation in the novel.[31]

The [English] law ranges itself on the side of the church. She [the wife] is as much his property as the horse he rides; her fortune he may dissipate, like the Count de Clairmont [the heroine's father];

[30] Medwin, *Shelley*, I, 188.
[31] *Lady Singleton*, III, 242; I, 92, 48–106, 100–101.

or squander it in the race course or at the gambling table . . . And all this a good wife must endure [under English law], not only uncomplainingly, but cheerfully. It may be answered that a court of justice holds forth a remedy, but what woman of delicacy would present herself before it—would so far forget the dignity of her sex, as to appear before a public tribunal to bear witness against her husband, the father of her children . . . Things are better managed on the Continent, a wife's fortune is sacred; it can by no chicanery of law be wrested from her; and irreconcilable diversities of character, incompatibility of temper, not to mention other causes, lead quietly, and without *fracas*, to the bursting of chains that are heavily dragged by both.

No useful purpose would be served here by a detailed discussion of *Lady Singleton; or, The World As It Is*, the preface to which is dated November 16, 1842, at Heidelberg. Except for a generally unfavorable review in *The Athenaeum*, December 17, 1842, the novel seems to have dropped very nearly stillborn from the press, although the reviewer notices its "force and reality." Its main outlines remain those of "The Sacrifice," published in late 1837, and its purpose is still nakedly didactic as expressed in the preface of the novel: "to furnish a salutary lesson to infatuated Mothers and intriguing Chaperons."

Perhaps Medwin at last had overcome his need to cut a grand figure by moving in circles he could not afford. It is significant that the first chapter is prefaced with twenty lines by Caroline de Crespigny, beginning, "Turn from the world—turn, and be free!" And early in the first volume, we read,

It is by no means necessary to be rich, in order to enjoy life . . . Such a sufficiency as may not render it necessary to calculate every penny spent, a competence without the harass of providing the ways and means, is as much affluence as a large rent-roll, or an immense nominal income, with an expenditure commensurate with or above it.[32]

And so Medwin settled down into a rather comfortable life in Heidelberg. The English colony was small. However, the

[32] *Ibid.*, I, 38.

prolific Howitts lived there, both William and Mary, between 1840 and 1843. They found Medwin to be a man of "culture and refinement, aristocratic in his tastes," and he regularly and politely lent to them his copy of the *Court Journal.*[33]

In the early 1840's Fanny Brawne Lindon, once Keats's fiancée, moved to Heidelberg, and through her, for the last time, Medwin's life touched that of a poetic genius—John Keats, who became for him the third member of the poetical trinity that rose out of his generation, along with Byron and Shelley. It all started when Medwin "by chance stumbled on" Keats's marked and annotated copy of Shakespeare, an 1808 reprint of the 1623 folio, in Fanny's possession.[34] Medwin, curious to know the history of the volume, "occasionally" asked her questions about Keats, but it was not until a copy of Shelley's *Essays, Letters from Abroad, Translations and Fragments* (1840) fell into her hands that she and Medwin "at all entered into the subject." Mary Shelley, the editor, had quoted a lurid account of Keats's last days, in which it was stated that "he might be judged insane." Thus Mary unwittingly opened the door to Medwin, who eagerly entered. To contradict this false account, Fanny first showed to him letters to her mother from Keats and from Joseph Severn, who was with Keats at his death. Veteran literary detective that Medwin was, however, he had not yet ferreted out the relationship that had existed between Keats and Fanny Brawne. It took Caroline de Crespigny to do this. She cunningly and fearlessly asked Fanny's husband "whether Mr. Keats had been an admirer of Mrs. Lindon's—and he, taken by surprise, knew just enough to answer yes."

Medwin made the most of his knowledge. In his *Life of Shelley* he published extracts from the Keats and Severn letters, as well as Keats's note to Shakespeare's *Troilus and Cressida* (I, iii,

[33] *Mary Howitt: An Autobiography*, ed. Margaret Howitt (London, 1891), p. 154.
[34] Hyder E. Rollins, "A Fanny Brawne Letter of 1848," *Harvard Library Bulletin*, V (Autumn, 1951), 372–375, on which the discussion of Medwin and Fanny Brawne Lindon is largely based.

13–17). Here, written on the blank leaves of Keats's Shakespeare, Medwin also read Keats's sonnet "On Sitting Down To Read *King Lear* Again" and his "Lines On Seeing A Lock of Milton's Hair." Fanny showed to Medwin the manuscript of Keats's *Otho the Great*, allowed him to have a copy made of Keats's miniature, and contributed to Medwin's *Shelley* her own comments on Keats. But Medwin had not completely charmed her. "If Medwin had known," she wrote, "that I possessed the Cenci by Shelley marked with many of Keats notes he would have been miserable till he got it, but I kept that and others out of his way." Thus did the world lose Keats's notes on Shelley's *Cenci*, for Medwin would most certainly have published them, and the book has since disappeared. Besides scattered references, Medwin wrote for his *Shelley* a single discussion of sixteen pages on Keats, and for his trouble Severn wrote him a very strong letter on the illegality of publishing another's correspondence.

It was in 1845 that he began actively preparing his biography of Shelley. From Heidelberg he wrote to Charles Ollier, requesting letters of Shelley or other material relating to him and offering to pay a portion of his profits from the book: "I shall consider it a matter of course to make you any proportionate remuneration I may receive for the work." [35] But Ollier declined to accept such indefinite terms. Medwin also told Ollier that Trelawny had refused to return the letters that Shelley had written to him from Italy and that he did not now know where Trelawny was. In addition, he confessed his failure to preserve Shelley's earlier letters to him, but these may have been few in number. He did, however, secure ten letters that Shelley had written, nine of them to Medwin's father. The other, addressed to Medwin's aunt, Catherine Pilfold, is the earliest extant letter of the poet. Medwin tried, unsuccessfully, to obtain correspondence that had passed between Byron and Mrs. Beauclerc in Pisa. He wrote to Lady Blessington and learned little, chiefly that Mary Shelley had purchased letters from George

[35] Medwin, *Shelley*, p. xvii.

Byron.[36] He wrote to Percy Florence Shelley, the poet's son, asking assistance,[37] but he did not approach Mary, it seems, until the book was substantially complete. (There is no evidence, significantly, that she attempted to see him when she was in Heidelberg and elsewhere in Germany in 1840.)

In the autumn of 1845 he returned to England and visited Field Place, which he found deserted and in need of repair. The visit turned out to be "a melancholy one."[38] As he later wrote to Mary Shelley, in mid-May, 1846, he found "the place dismantled—the family scattered—& who about to inhabit it— a London Alderman!" The published image of himself developed out of this elegiac note, as he recalled his distant past with Shelley:

I walked in moody sadness over the neglected shrubberies, paced the paths, weed over-grown and leaf-strewn, of the once neatly kept flower-gardens, where we had so often walked together, and talked in the confidentiality of early and unsophisticated friendship; there, too, he had in many a solitary hour brooded over his first disappointment in love, and had his sensitive spirit torn by the coldness and alienation of those dearest to him. All this passed through my mind.[39]

Medwin also visited the graves of his ancestors in the chancel of Horsham church, saw the monuments to his own and to Shelley's father, and was shocked to find none to Shelley himself. Medwin's aged mother was still alive, and his affection for her was great. "Were it not that I come to see my dear old Mother," he wrote, "I would never set foot in [England] again."[40] Following her death, he wrote in his own hand, on the last page of his *Odds and Ends*, "In Matris Cenotaphium," in imitation of Catullus:

[36] Medwin's unpublished marginalia in his *Shelley*, facing I, 212, in the Morgan Library.

[37] Percy Florence Shelley's reply to Medwin is in the Morgan Library.

[38] Unpublished postscript to Medwin's letter to Mary Shelley, May 17, 1846, in the Abinger Collection.

[39] Medwin, *Shelley*, p. 417.

[40] *Letters of Mary Shelley*, II, 288, note.

Per maria et terras multis erroribus actis
Fessos hoc templum visere tendo pedes
Ut caram hanc animam postremo munere donem
Atque iterum mutos alloquar heu cineres.
Persequor hoc votis longae post taedia vitae
Aeternâ tecum posse salute frui.

He loved her dearly without doubt; without doubt she had helped to support him over the years, out of her inheritance from his father.

In early May, 1846, he aproached Mary Shelley for assistance with his biography, asking particularly for information of the Chancery suit that deprived Shelley of his children. Presumably she did not remember, when she replied to Medwin, that on November 12, 1829, John Murray had paid to her £100 for her help to Moore while writing his biography of Byron. This aid included her written recollections of Byron's burned memoirs.[41] Despite all, it was her conviction, she wrote to Medwin, that "in modern society there is no injury so great as dragging private names and private life before the world. It is one from which every honourable and upright mind shrinks . . . In these publishing, inquisitive, scandal-mongering days, one feels called upon for a double exercise of delicacy, forbearance—and reserve."[42] Sir Timothy Shelley was now dead; there was no further need to fear him; she had inherited from him. As the comfortably situated widow of a great poet, as a professed lover of literature, she did her best to kill the publication of a biography of Shelley written by a man who had known her husband in boyhood and in maturity. No other living person had Medwin's qualifications.

He replied to Mary's letter on May 17, 1846, from Horsham:[43]

---

[41] The receipt and a copy of Murray's letter to Mary Shelley are now in the possession of Sir John Murray.

[42] *Letters of Mary Shelley*, II, 288–289.

[43] Medwin's letter to Mary Shelley, May 17, 1846, in the Abinger Collection; printed with errors and important omissions in *Shelley and Mary*, pp. 1241–1242. The postscript is wholly unpublished.

Dear Mrs. Shelley,

You tell me that my letter has surprised and pained you. Why it should pain you I am at a loss to grasp, & had thought that it was pretty generally known that I had long been engaged in this work.

When you say that you have vindicated the memory of Shelley & spoken of him as he was—you seem *to imply that I shall take a different course.* I have latterly met with Gilfillin's Gallery of Literary Portraits—& De Quincey's review of the same. I am disgusted with your English writers with their accursed Cant—their cold, false conventionalities—their abominable Claptrap. They should take a lesson from the Germans. I should like to show you a book just published, entitled "Burger Ein Deutscher Dichterleben." Poets are not to be squared by the rule and measure of ordinary mortals. But how bright does Shelley's Character come out. What a glorious creature he was, how infinitely above all those methodical hypocrites—that bow-wow at him.

I remember seeing, when we were at Pisa, a work of considerable length, that Shelley wrote, a book of "History of Xst" [*Essay on Christianity*], why do you not publish it? How did he differ in his opinions from [Heinrich] Paulus and [David] Strauss and the Rationalists, who felt the theological chains in Germany, and drag from them the Divinity of Xst. What does [Johannes] Ronge, the new Luther, teach? Why you are 100 years behind the Germans. I speak not of my own Profession of Faith. Every one has his own, and should have—but of the narrow-minded intolerance that reigns here. Every visit I make to England disgusts me more and more with it, and were it not that I come to see my dear old Mother, I would never set foot in it again. Germany is my foster mother, and there I have passed the happiest part of my existence; there I mean to lay my bones. It is cheap also to be *buried* there!!!

But to return to your letter. You cannot suppose that I shall undo the arrangement I have made for the publication, which will take place in about a month, or 6 weeks at latest, & you shall have a copy among the first. It will be translated in German by a friend of mine, a most accomplished person, a lady, who has done more justice in her translations, to our Lady Poets, than any I know of—Madm de Ploennies—who has admirably rendered some of Shelley's minor poems.

My hands are so cold, that I can scarcely write, and this is the middle of May.

Yours truly,
T. Medwin

P. S. I am much grieved to hear that you are still suffering from ill health, & think you do right to try the air of Italy, which I hope & trust will restore you—I think when I was here last Autumn you had such an Intention.

I saw Howitt when I was in town last week—& have promised to drive with him—I think you know Mary Howitt.—They were neighbours of ours in Baden—for a winter. He tells me a work entitled Homes and Haunts of [the Most Eminent British] Poets [? is to be published]. Of Course Shelley will find a place there . . .

Shortly afterwards, it seems, he wrote to her what has been called a "blackmailing letter." [44] But blackmail implies premeditation, and it is monstrous to suppose that he composed his loving portrait of Shelley, in two volumes, for the purpose of extracting money from Mary Shelley, who was not disgraced but honored by her appearance in his book. What she asked him in his poverty to do was to give up the £250 paid to him by his publisher and lose the time and money he had spent in writing the book and in travelling to England. What he in fact offered to do was to sacrifice his own fame and deny to posterity recollections of Shelley that no other man had, asking of her in her prosperity only that she repay his losses. He also promised to write no more about Shelley, sealing his lips forever. She treated him with silent contempt, refusing to reply to his letters but writing to Jane Williams Hogg and Leigh Hunt about what she called his "attempt to extort money" from her, "this threat." He was understandably angered and wrote a letter to Jane "that is very bitter against Mary Shelley & in which the writer plainly hints that he has materials for incriminating Shelley not only in the Viviani affair but also something that transpired at Naples." This is S.

[44] *Letters of Mary Shelley*, II, 289, note.

Leigh Hunt writing to Lady Shelley in 1898.[45] In Medwin's *Life of Shelley,* however, as it was published in 1847, Emilia Viviani remains a romantic and ethereal figure;[46] there is no mention of the birth of Elena Adelaide Shelley at Naples (although we do read of a beautiful young Englishwoman who followed Shelley there and there romantically died);[47] and the Chancery papers did not appear in full until the 1913 edition, delivered by H. Buxton Forman.[48] The book is by no means the libelous publication that Mary Shelley imagined it would be, and even she, "on reflection," began to be vaguely or uneasily aware that it might "not be so utterly abominable." [49] He offered to allow her to read the proofs before publication, but her irrational fear was so great that she persisted in seeing it as "a triumph of evil" and the author as a "fellow [who] goes about dealing wounds with a poisoned dagger." [50] Thus ashamed of the facts of her husband's life (and her own), she did not, it seems, ever read Medwin's book, although she remained firmly convinced that it "was never so injuriously written but for the sake of extorting money . . . I am sure the book will be a disgrace to dear Shelley's name . . ."

So little did she understand him, so much did she fear him who wrote of her husband,

All the poems indeed of Shelley, numerous as they are, resolve themselves into one . . . They present to the mind in their different episodes, their accidental details, or sites or costumes, but one type, always equally sublime, that of a man who devotes himself, suffers and dies for his fellow beings, a Christ deprived of his divine attributes, a philosophic Martyr, a Confessor of Liberty.[51]

Perhaps a part of her fear of Medwin stemmed from the recent memory of her dealings with the notorious forger George

---

[45] Unpublished letter from S. Leigh Hunt to Lady Shelley, Feb. 19, 1898, in the Abinger Collection.

[46] Medwin, *Shelley,* pp. 277–281.

[47] *Ibid.,* pp. 204–207.   [48] *Ibid.,* pp. 463–486.

[49] *Letters of Mary Shelley,* II, 307.   [50] *Ibid.,* II, 308–309.

[51] Medwin, *Shelley,* pp. 419–420, not in first edition.

Byron, to whom she had paid £30 on November 12, 1845. On July 8, 1846, George Byron also wrote to Medwin, identifying himself as the son of the poet Byron and inviting Medwin to call at 2 King Street, Greenwich. But Medwin had neither the money nor the inclination to be taken in: "I did not go to Greenwich as requested by Mr. Byron," he stated firmly.[52] Instead, he continued to polish his biography of Shelley, which appeared in late August or early September, 1847.[53]

What kind of book did Medwin write this time? It was the first full-length biography of Shelley, and being largely written abroad, it showed inevitably many faults. It is not a coolly dispassionate account in the modern scholarly style (nor was it authorized and censored by the family). There are overly warm attacks on Shelley's critics, as if they had written yesterday instead of a quarter-century or more earlier. There are hotheaded attacks on Medwin's personal enemies—chiefly Hobhouse and Moore, whom Medwin disliked for permitting the destruction of Byron's memoirs, bowdlerizing Byron's letters, and damning Shelley with faint praise, even after receiving material aid from Mary Shelley. There are numerous errors of date, fact, and quotation; for Medwin was careless. (But Medwin's illegible hand was an invitation to outraged frustration, and there is clear evidence that many of the errors were those of the printer, unable to read Medwin's scrawl.) All these mistakes were throroughly annotated by H. Buxton Forman in 1913.

Despite these objections, Medwin's book remains a most important major source of Shelley biography. Newman I. White's definitive *Shelley* (1940) lists Medwin's *Life of Shelley* as a "general" or major source for fourteen of its twenty-nine biographical chapters—almost one-half. Medwin is today the chief source of knowledge concerning Shelley's boyhood, the second

[52] Medwin's unpublished marginalia in his *Shelley*, I, 384.
[53] On August 21, 1847, *The Examiner* advertised that it was to be "immediately" published; it was first reviewed on Sept. 18, in *The Athenaeum*.

major source perhaps concerning Shelley in 1821–1822 (after Mary Shelley and before the unreliable and semiliterate Trelawny), and a significant source for scattered episodes throughout Shelley's life, as these were related to him by the poet. Written from the few sources available at the time—chiefly Hunt's *Byron*, Moore's *Byron*, De Quincey's four articles in *Tait's Magazine* (1845–1846), Hogg's articles in *The New Monthly* (1832–1833) on "Shelley at Oxford," and Mary Shelley's notes to Shelley's *Poetical Works*—his book is inevitably a rich mine of personal recollections. It no more can be ignored than his *Conversations of Byron*. Even Lady Jane Shelley, reluctantly publishing the *Shelley Memorials* in 1859, recognized the central position of Medwin, who became the excuse or the cause for the publication of her own book: too "many papers on Shelley, all taking for their text Captain Medwin's Life of the Poet," had appeared both in English and French magazines, she wrote in her preface. He had been, in fact, for years an international force, in Germany the chief source of knowledge concerning Shelley's life and character since 1824, when his long footnote-memoir of Shelley appeared in the *Conversations of Byron*. Goethe and Wilhelm Müller at first, later Gutzkow, Laube and Kühne (representatives of Young Germany), Adolph Friedrich, Graf von Schack, Seybt, Louise von Ploennies, Alfred Meissner, Moritz Hartmann, and others were indebted to Medwin.[54] To the extent that Shelley's personality and idealism helped to bring about the Revolution of 1848— and their influence was considerable—Medwin also was involved. For "it is Shelley's personality and not his work that impresses Young Germany,"[55] and Shelley's personality, clashing with a world of tyranny, was seen largely through the eyes of Medwin. Thus did he come to influence the course of great events.

English reviewers, however, were not all sympathetic to his

[54] See Liptzin, *Shelley in Germany*.
[55] *Ibid.*, p. 13.

Life of Shelley, by any means. *The Athenaeum* reviewer, John Abraham Heraud, began bluntly: "We are not in any way satisfied with this book," but among the very few concessions he made to Medwin, we read, "Nevertheless, he constantly manifests a deep and sincere sympathy with Shelley's condition of mind, body, and estate." [56] Heraud, interestingly, deals with the Chancery suit, which had so concerned Mary Shelley, as a thing well known already. *The North British Review* for November, 1847, which chose to deal in a single article of forty pages with Medwin, Mary Shelley's edition of *The Poetical Works* (1847), Hogg's *New Monthly* articles on "Shelley at Oxford" (1832–1833), George Gilfillan's *Gallery of Literary Portraits* (1845), and Shelley's *Address to the Irish People* (1812), discussed Medwin at length but concluded that his book was "unreadable and presumptuous." The *Spectator* was equally unenthusiastic: "Medwin's labours . . . are chiefly remarkable for the art of stuffing . . . nor does the author forget a scandal when he can pick any up." [57]

Medwin was received sympathetically, however, into journals edited by his friends, W. Harrison Ainsworth and William and Mary Howitt. The reviewer in *Howitt's Journal of Literature and Popular Progress* wrote, "Captain Medwin disarms criticism by the humility which he brings to his work . . . This admiration and love for his subject render Captain Medwin a biographer more to our taste than one who would be inclined, perhaps, to sit in judgment." [58] Ainsworth himself, presumably, wrote the footnote that preceded by a month the review of Medwin's *Shelley*: "It could not possibly have fallen into more competent hands. His name alone gives assurance that the work will be executed in a kindly and enlightened spirit." The review itself was equally laudatory: Medwin's "own high attainments in every way qualify him for the task . . . a valuable

[56] *Athenaeum*, Sept. 18, 1847, p. 971, and Sept. 25, 1847, p. 1004.
[57] Quoted by Sylva Norman, *Flight of the Skylark*, p. 174.
[58] *Howitt's Journal*, II (1847), 348.

addition to the literature of the country."[59] Thus *The New Monthly*.

His sojourn in England ended pleasantly with a visit in October at Mannington Hall, in Aylsham, Norfolk.[60] This had been preceded by a trip during the summer to Holland, made possible no doubt by the £250 received for his *Shelley*. When at the Hague, from which he planned to travel to Amsterdam and Utrecht, he was invited by a friend "attached to the court" to observe the ancient and noble sport of hawking at Loo, the summer palace of the Prince of Orange, Crown Prince of Holland.[61] And so Medwin made the journey, over the brick highways, from Amsterdam to Arnheim, the palace being some three leagues distant. Upon arrival he struck up a conversation with one of the falconers and learned that all of them had been trained in England. Nevertheless, waiting for the distinguished members of the very exclusive Société de la Fauconnerie to appear at four o'clock would have been very boring if it had not been for the lovely, melancholy sound of a musical voice emerging from a two-wheeled gipsy wagon. Listening, Medwin waited long for the owner to reveal herself, but the door remained closed. Suddenly, the colorful falconers appeared, wearing "top boots, highly polished, with spurs attached, light drab tights, bright-coloured waistcoats, and a dark green coat . . . Each had on a green hunting hat, with a tuft of heron's plume stuck jauntily in the band, while long buckskin gauntlets, coming far over the wrists, completed the gallant costume." The red-hooded falcons appeared in cages, and the company prepared to gallop to the scene of the hawking.

But the sport had lost for Medwin some of its attraction. He "had heard a voice more thrilling than the halloo." All at

[59] *New Monthly Magazine*, LXXXI (Oct., 1847), 232, note, and LXXXI (Nov., 1847), 296.

[60] Unpublished letter from Medwin to his publisher, Oct. 15, requesting copies of his *Shelley*; in the Carl H. Pforzheimer Library.

[61] Medwin, "Hawking at Loo, a Palace of the King of Holland," *New Monthly Magazine*, XCI (Feb., 1851), 157–167.

once, drawn perhaps by the noise of the assembly, the girl appeared at the door of her wagon, almost at Medwin's shoulder. The gallant Captain had not lost his eye for beauty, and her eyes, as she played her guitar and sang in her unknown language, scarcely moved from him. It seemed to Medwin at that moment that "Nature had but one form of loveliness, and gave it to the gipsy's daughter." She was seventeen. He offered to her a piece from his purse, and for the first time she spoke, in Italian: "E che il Dio vi renda felice." He went home and wrote, "I shall never forget her face nor her smile."

The "spectacle of another age," the not so gentle sport of hawking, offered an experience of a very different kind. Medwin was received by the members of the club, many of them wearing lorgnettes, with "great civility." He appreciated the skill and strength and beauty of the trained hawks, but he pitied the herons from the bottom of his heart, and he was left with "an unpleasant impression" of hawking.

Once back in Heidelberg, a much greater unpleasantness awaited him. He discovered a highly unfavorable review of his *Shelley*. He was now sixty years old, writing the biography had been hard labor, and his old irascibility showed up again, as he wrote to Charles Ollier. "After your *show* of friendship to me I *am* rather surprised to read your article in the Newspaper which you now Edit—an article, rather an attack on a rival Publisher than the work itself . . ." The review was "a word catching piece of Cockneydom," he stated, as he warmed up to his subject. "There is a goddess Nemesis who has her retribution, and it has so happened that I have never yet had an Enemy on whom I have not taken my *revanche*." [62]

Perhaps his warlike tone was provoked in part by the highly unsettled conditions which he found upon his return to Heidelberg. On March 5, 1848, the Heidelberg assembly had met, and this led directly to the Revolution of 1848, by way of the Frankfort parliament. There was armed revolt in the Grand

[62] Unpublished letter from Medwin to Ollier, concerning a review of his *Shelley*; in the Pierpont Morgan Library.

Duchy of Baden in 1848 and again in 1849, when the grand duke was forced to take flight and Baden was controlled by a revolutionary mob.

Taking Caroline de Crespigny with him, Medwin fled to the little town of Weinsberg in the kingdom of Württemberg, which remained free of revolutionary violence. Here was the home of Justinus Kerner the poet, whose house, already a literary shrine, became the natural center for all the displaced intelligentsia in the area. Here, in Kerner's home, on June 8, 1849, Caroline de Crespigny, attended by Medwin, entertained the company with her harp after dinner.[63] They formed a small but genuine literary circle. Kerner, two years older than Medwin, wrote a poem "An Frau v. Crespigny," and Medwin wrote one to Kerner, which was translated into German by Luise von Ploennies, who had promised to translate Medwin's *Shelley* into German but apparently never did.[64] He translated a sonnet sequence of hers and in 1851 published it under the title "Oscar and Giannetta."[65] This was the year when Medwin also published a translation of Kerner's poem "To the King of Wurtemberg," prefaced by a note from the translator.[66] Medwin explains that the German poet's son, Dr. Theobald Kerner, had been sentenced to ten months' solitary confinement for making a revolutionary speech in Heilbronn. After four of the ten months had passed, the father addressed a poem to the king, William I, and Theobald was immediately released. Medwin's admiration for William I is evident: he was "no tyrant, but the father of his people." Medwin's hatred of tyranny is by no means synonymous with a preference for an elected chief executive. Constitutional monarchy, with a legitimate king on the throne, remained his ideal. William I was legitimate, but he was also a great actor. Medwin was clearly impressed by the performance which he described in his prefatory note: "Finding that his army had been tampered with, the king

---

[63] *Badische Post*, as cited above.
[64] These poems appeared in Medwin's *Nugæ*.
[65] In the *New Monthly Magazine*, XCI (March, 1851), 360–361.
[66] *Ibid.*, XCII (June, 1851), 218.

ordered a review of his troops, and appealed to their loyalty by riding without his staff in front of the line, and baring his breast as a target for their balls." At this moment the band, perhaps by previous arrangement, struck up the national anthem, and the king had no more trouble with his army during the revolutionary period.

It should be emphasized that the distinction between a "good" king and a tyrant on the throne was very clear in Medwin's mind. Shortly after his return to Germany from England, he wrote a sonnet "On the New Heidelberg Bastille Now Constructing":

> Put not your trust in princes. Now when man,
>   Like a young eagle panting to be free,
> Would burst some links of the Oppressor's chain,
>   And walk erect in sovereign majesty;
> Is this the consummation? Hark! I hear
>   The clink of hammers, and the iron sound
> Of riveted bolts and bars, denoting fear
>   Of tyrants. Lo! up towers the grim huge mound,
> And circling walls that cover half a rood,
>   And speak of sunless dungeons damp and cold,
>   Such as are hid beneath yon ruins old,
> Strewn with the bones of captives soaked with blood.
>   How long must these to the deaf Heavens appeal
>   In vain? What did the French with their Bastille? [67]

But Germany was not France, and before the end of 1849 the revolution was dead in Baden, which was for a time occupied by Prussian troops. Medwin may have returned to Heidelberg at once, although the date is uncertain. If a poem addressed "To Justinus Kerner" and published in October, 1854, has any foundation in fact, Medwin plucked a branch from a bay tree in Kerner's garden, before his departure from Weinsberg, and wove of its leaves a wreath, which he then presented to the German poet.[68]

[67] *Ibid.*, LXXXIV (Nov., 1848), 310.
[68] *Ibid.*, CII (Oct., 1854), 196.

In the next month, the Crimean War now raging but Austria as yet not actively engaged in it, he addressed a poem "To the Emperor of Austria, on His Marriage." Francis Joseph, in 1853 nearly assassinated by the Hungarian patriot Lebenyi, had married in 1854 the very beautiful Elizabeth, daughter of a Bavarian duke. Russian forces had crossed the Danube and advanced ultimately as far as Silistria. Under these conditions, Medwin invoked the Austrian emperor:

> Whilst the new Goths, in many a Cossack horde,
> Slaves to the ambition of the ruthless Czar,
> Lay waste his neighbour's realms with fire and sword,
> Glad nuptial shouts outswell the din of war.
> Sovereign! tho' young in years, in wisdom old,
> Drive back the invader from *thy* Danube's floods,
> Back to their steppes and icy solitudes,
> And thy sons' sons shall bless thee. Rise! Awake!
> Or fall for ever! Join the Western band
> Of brothers harnessed to uphold the weak:
> Thy country's altars, hearths, thy native land,
> All Europe's independence is the stake—
> Prove not in vain struck down the Assassin's hand! [69]

Medwin disliked the Russians, but as an old dragoon he had no sympathy with the military stupidity that resulted in the frontal charge of the light brigade against the Russian artillery at Balaclava, nor with Tennyson's glorification of the disaster. In later years he published a parody, "The Charge of St. Leger or the Five Hundred." [70] The St. Leger is an annual horse race for three-year-old colts and fillies held at Doncaster, and the five hundred of Medwin's title is a bet of £500. He decided that "the Decadence of Poetry at the present day is proved in nothing more than the great analogy that exists between the Tennysonian School and the Catullan . . ." [71]

[69] "To the Emperor of Austria, On His Marriage," *New Monthly Magazine,* CII (Nov., 1854), 340.
[70] Medwin, *Odds and Ends* (Heidelberg, 1862), p. 69.
[71] *Ibid.,* p. 8, note.

Indeed, his years out of England and his manner of life abroad had left him unsympathetic with much that was Victorian. When he was seventy-four, he published a doggerel poem called "The Cabman" that rather accurately measures the distance which separated him from any typically Victorian propriety:

> Who would be
> A Cabman free,
> Sitting alone,
> Smoking alone,
> Like a king all gold
> Upon his throne?
> Said the Sweeper
> To the Dog-keeper

I would be a Cabman gay!
And when I'd no fare, would sing all day,
"If I had a Donkey wot wouldn't go,
Wouldn't I wallop him, Oh no no."
But at night I would drive thro' the lanes and streets,
And cut in and out every Bus that I meets,
Dressing the hide of my high-bred hack,
And when he's obstreperous, holding him back,
I would give him the thong just under his jaw,
And if that wouldn't do, touch him up in the raw,
                    Whackingly, Whackingly,
And then would drive without making a bend
To the City—the Station house or the West-End,
                    Crackingly! Crackingly!
> Oh this is the life that for me best suits,
> And when I'd no job, without delay
> I would rub down my Hoss
> And o'er his head toss
> A bag full of woats,
> And off to the Gin-shop over the way.
> And take a good swill at a Pewter pot,
> Or if it is cold, call for something hot,
>   Cheerily! Cheerily!

Would sing aloud in the Gaslit Hall,
Would call aloud, and whoop and cry
                    Beerily! Beerily!
And the young Ladies in pink and green
Laughing and clapping their hands between
                    Would foot it merrily!
And I would in spite of any Beak
Play with them at Hide and Seek,
                    Rompingly! Rompingly!
Then leaping out upon them unseen
I would kiss them often behind the screen,
And kiss them again till they kissed me,
                    Smackingly! Smackingly!
Oh what a happy life it would be!
With much to gain, and nothing to lose,
And no paddling in mud to wear out my shoes;
At the sound of "Cab", I would make a sign,
And take up a Gent to a Rout or to dine:
Oh such a Life as this would be fine!
                    Yes I would be
                    A Cabman gay
                    To smoke all day,
                    My mild cigar,
With nothing to do but pocket my fare.[72]

At some time around 1850 or after, he undertook to prepare his *Conversations of Byron* for a new edition. In the opening paragraph of his new preface, he wrote,

A friend of mine many years ago told me that I had thrown them on the world like a bastard child; the period is arrived for proclaiming the offspring, and that parental duty I now perform. To have done so before the appearance of Mr. Moore's Notices [of Byron's life] would have been lost labour, for then the tide of detraction and calumny would have been too strong to them; but as these Documents are now in all hands my task is easy, and on them I rest my defence.

[72] Medwin, *Odds and Ends,* pp. 71–73.

Much of his energy he spent on finding and copying passages in Byron's letters and Moore's *Life* that supported his accuracy. He was still bitter when he remembered: "Though the wounds I have received no longer bleed, the scars remain." This sentence he deleted. Then he compared himself to Boswell, reporting the conversations of Dr. Johnson, and asserted that he too had been "only a reporter or Editor." The new edition has not yet appeared.[73]

And so the years slipped by. The German custom of decorating an evergreen tree at Christmas no longer seemed strange to him; he became used to the students at Heidelberg; he collected a small circle of bluestockinged admirers about him—Caroline de Crespigny still faithful, Luise von Ploennies, Helmina von Chezy, and Elise von Hohenhauser, all of whom appeared in his *Nugæ*, which he edited in 1856. Here also Justinus Kerner appeared, along with German translations of Medwin's contributions to a mysterious volume called *Rhymes and Chimes*.

The little book of *Nugæ* is an international miscellany, with poems in Greek, Latin, English, and German. *Odds and Ends* (1862) is almost equally as varied in character. There are translations from Catullus (with learned notes), Virgil, Horace, Martial, Janus Vitalis, Scaliger, and (by Caroline de Crespigny) Antipater, translations from French and German and into Latin. He was in fact a very learned man, however inexactly learned or careless. *Odds and Ends* was his farewell to Heidelberg; his last contribution to *The New Monthly* had appeared in July, 1858, "Renderings in Latin" from Kerner, Sir William Jones, Doddridge, Shakespeare, Goethe, Heine, and, last of all, Caroline de Crespigny.

Back in England in 1862, he set to work at once revising his *Shelley*—with a plan very different from that later followed

[73] The present writer is now preparing for publication Medwin's corrected copy of his *Conversations of Byron*, to be edited also from other copies annotated by Lady Byron, Hobhouse, Trelawny, and Sir Charles James Napier, who knew Byron in Cephalonia.

by his editor H. Buxton Forman, who may well have worked from the copy first revised by Medwin. For there exists another, quite different copy, with additional pages bound in, revised in Medwin's hand, and it contains a new preface, lacking in Forman's copy. In it Medwin wrote, "As to the Errors of my work, I mean to make no alterations in the Text . . . The Additional matter will be found in brackets." Such an editorial procedure, if followed by Forman, would have resulted in a much more useful edition than the one he produced.

In his old age, annotating and revising his *Shelley*, Medwin reminded himself of his services to lovers of Shelley's poetry: "The world is indebted to me for having rescued from Oblivion the following Poems, of which all if not the greater part of them were unknown to Mrs. Shelley, who added them to his works after their publication in the Athenaeum & Fraser's Magazine. This is the list of them . . ." [74] But his memory failed him, and his list included poems published by Shelley himself and by Mary Shelley as early as 1824. To his credit, however, he did first publish and remains the present textual source of nine of Shelley's poems (including the beautiful "With a Guitar: To Jane"), plus three verse translations, three juvenile poems, and a substantial quantity of prose, not to mention the controversial *Wandering Jew*, upon which he and Shelley collaborated.

Nor was he unaware of Shelleyan textual problems, which unfortunately still exist: "A Mr. Garnet or Garble it should be," he wrote after the appearance of Richard Garnett's *Relics of Shelley* in 1862, "has taken the liberty either himself or for Lady or Mrs. Shelley to interpolate, correct or alter a vast number of Shelley's Lines—Shame on the Publication." [75]

He remained clear-headed and intellectually vigorous almost up to the very end. At some time following his last return to England, it seems, he produced a translation of Aristophanes's *Frogs* and a poetic version of the Book of Job. He remained

[74] Medwin's unpublished marginalia in his *Shelley*, I, 331–332.
[75] *Ibid.*, I, 332–333.

interested in political developments and had a clear insight into them. Percy Florence Shelley was sufficiently interested in him to invite him to Boscombe Manor. Medwin replied to the invitation on January 31, 1867.[76]

My dear Cousin,

As you wished to see my Frogs, I send the play to you & accompany it with a Version of that grand Poem Job. I flatter myself that I have thrown much light upon the Subject—and taken new views on many questions regarding it. Speaking of Aeschylus—the last of the Greeks my friend George Burges, who died [in 1864] since I came to England, when he lectured at Cambridge on the *Epta* [*Seven against Thebes*] took with him my version of that play & explained it from my Pages. It was a great Compliment. He thought it the best of my Translations.

I myself prefer the Coeforoe [*Choephoroe*] to the other Plays. It is full of Pathos & Dramatic Effects. The old Nurse reminds one of Romeo & Juliet— By the way Dionysus [in the *Frogs*]—what is he but Falstaff one can hardly think that Shakespeare was ignorant of this Comedy of Aristophanes— The Choruses in the Frogs are more didactic than poetical—& I am sorry I did not take the Birds—but I am too old now to undertake any more of these admirable Farces.

We are all on the *qui vive* about the opening of Parliament & the reform Bill—which will I fear be the Death-blow to the Administration— Whether D'Israeli tries to shelve the Bill or to bring it forward it will come to the same result— The Bill if brought on will aim at too much or too little— If it goes too far it will dissatisfy the Tories, and if too little discontent the Whigs, but whether knocked down or tripped up the Overthrow of the Conservatives is equally certain. Lord Russell knew what he was about in 1832 and his party saving for two short years have been in power ever since. They are ravenous for Office—and think Derby's Administration Usurpation— Perhaps you do not know any thing or take any interest in our Politics [? in Sus]. Fitzgerald is gone to his Bombay Governorship and it is said that Padwick is to stand ag[ains]t Hurest on a dissolution. This great Turf man is appointed by the

[76] Unpublished letter fom Medwin to Percy Florence Shelley, Jan. 31, 1867, in the British Museum.

Duke of Hamilton, who has £13,000 a year, his Commissioner: Agent, Receiver, &c.

Do you mean to go for a tour abroad. I fear my health which daily gets worse will not admit of my return to H[eidelburg]. My apartment has been [?] for fifteen months—& I shall have to decide in April whether to continue it or not. At present I am quite unable to travel even to go to town or to walk without the aid of my Valet. In fact I am in a very bad way. You may keep the Mss for a month. Make my kind Compliments to your Lady & the little Lady. You know I have her Photograph. Many thanks for your Invitation. I have this year been forced to renounce going to Norfolk or Wiltshire.

> believe me
> in haste
> Yours very sincerely
> Medwin.

In 1869, shortly before Medwin's death, Trelawny called upon him and after the meeting paid tribute to him: he decided that Medwin had been "always faithful and honest in his love" of Shelley.[77] Perhaps the two old men made up their differences finally. At this time Trelawny understood that Medwin's revised *Shelley* was in press and would be published in the autumn of the year. But in August, aged eighty-one years, occupation gentleman, Medwin died, in the Carfax, in North Horsham, and in the old part of the Denne Road cemetery he was buried.[78] His tomb faces east, toward Italy, Germany, India. On the white marble stone is inscribed,

[77] *Letters of Trelawny*, p. 221.
[78] Medwin's death certificate, in Somerset House, London.

S A C R E D

TO

THE MEMORY OF

THOMAS MEDWIN

LATE CAPTAIN IN THE 24TH LIGHT DRAGOONS,

THIRD SON OF THE LATE T. C. MEDWIN,
OF HORSHAM, SOLICITOR.

DIED 2ND. AUGUST 1869, AGED 81.

HE WAS A FRIEND AND COMPANION OF
BYRON, SHELLEY, AND TRELAWNY.

PUBLISHED WORKS OF THOMAS MEDWIN

Oswald and Edwin, An Oriental Sketch (Geneva, 1820).

"Some Account of the Cave Temples of Ellora, etc. Quelques détails sur les temples souterrains d'Ellora dans les Indes orientales, extraits d'un journal inédit, par le Capit. Medwin" [translator unknown], *Bibliothèque universelle des Sciences, Belles-Lettres, et des Arts*, XVI (April, 1821), 344–357; XVIII (September, 1821), 3–13, 111–122.

Sketches in Hindoostan with Other Poems (London, 1821).

Ahasuerus, The Wanderer: A Dramatic Legend, in Six Parts, (London, 1823).

"The Death of Mago," translated from Petrarch's *Africa*; in Ugo Foscolo, *Essays on Petrarch* (London, 1823), pp. 215, 217.

Journal of the Conversations of Lord Byron: Noted during a Residence with His Lordship at Pisa, in the Years 1821 and 1822 (London, 1824). [For translations and other editions, see the text.]

Prometheus Bound [translated from Aeschylus], Siena, 1827; London, 1832; *Fraser's Magazine*, XVI (August, 1837), 209–233.

Prometeo portatore del fuoco, translated by L. A. Damaso Pareto (Genoa, 1830) from Medwin's unpublished English, "Prometheus the Firebearer," in the Humanities Research Center of The University of Texas.

Agamemnon [translated from Aeschylus], London, 1832; *Fraser's Magazine*, XVIII (November, 1838), 505–539.

"Original Correspondence. Lord Byron, His Biography, &c.," *The Literary Gazette*, No. 785 (February 4, 1832), pp. 73–74; No. 786 (February 11, 1832), pp. 88–89.

"The Choëphori: From Aeschylus," *Fraser's Magazine*, VI (November, 1832), 511–535.

"Memoir of Shelley," *The Athenaeum*, No. 247 (July 21, 1832), pp. 472–474; No. 248 (July 28, 1832), pp. 488–489; No. 249 (August 4, 1832), pp. 502–504; No. 250 (August 11, 1832), pp. 522–524; No. 251 (August 18, 1832), pp. 535–537; No. 252 (August 25, 1832), pp. 554–555.

"Shelley Papers," contributed by Medwin to *The Athenaeum*, No. 253 (September 1, 1832), pp. 568–569; No. 254 (September 8, 1832), p. 586; No. 255 (September 15, 1832), pp. 601–602; No. 256 (September 22, 1832), pp. 617–618; No. 257 (September 29, 1832), p. 633; No. 260 (October 20, 1832), p. 680; No. 261 (October 27, 1832), pp. 698–699; No. 263 (November 10, 1832), p. 730; No. 264 (November 17, 1832), p. 746; No. 265 (November 24, 1832), pp. 761–762; No. 267 (December 8, 1832), p. 794; No. 286 (April 20, 1833), p. 250. [Sylva Norman, *Flight of the Skylark* (Norman, Oklahoma, 1954), p. 93, note 19, states that Shelley's "Lines Written During the Castlereagh

Administration," which appeared in No. 267 of *The Athenaeum,* was contributed not by Medwin but by T. F. Kelsall. Unfortunately, the 1832 volume is missing from the marked file of *The Athenaeum* in London.]

The Shelley Papers; Memoir of Percy Bysshe Shelley (London, 1833).

"*The Persians*: From Aeschylus," *Fraser's Magazine,* VII (January, 1833), 17–43.

"*The Seven Before Thebes*: From Aeschylus," *Fraser's Magazine,* VII (April, 1833), 437–458.

The New Anti-Jacobin: A Monthly Magazine of Politics, Commerce, Science, Literature, Art, Music, and the Drama, edited during its only two issues, April and May, 1833, by Medwin, who made the following contributions: for April, "A Cast of Casti," pp. 30–35; "The Diavolessa, Translated; The Origin of Lord Byron's Don Juan," pp. 35–54; "Autobiography of a Picture-Fancier," pp. 74–79; "The Drama," pp. 104–106; for May, "Horace in Parliament: Ode to William C[obbet]t," pp. 142–143; "A Scene in the Life of an Artist: Imitated from the German," pp. 166–178; "Epigram," p. 186; "Goethe and his Faust," pp. 198–204; "Specimen of a Translation of Faust," pp. 204–210; "The Connoisseur," pp. 211–213; "Bigarrures," pp. 217–218; a paragraph on the drama, p. 218; "Critical Notices," p. 220. Medwin's marked copies, identifying his own contributions, are in the University of Pennsylvania Library.

"*The Eumenides*: From Aeschylus," *Fraser's Magazine,* IX (May, 1834), 553–573.

The Angler in Wales, or Days and Nights of Sportsmen (London, 1834).

"The Duel," *Bentley's Miscellany,* II (July, 1837), 76–81.

"Mascalbruni," *Bentley's Miscellany,* II (September, 1837), 254–268.

"The Sacrifice; or, the Country, Town, and the Continent," *Fraser's Magazine,* XVI (November and December, 1837), 549–561, 696–710.

"The Last of the Bandits," *Bentley's Miscellany,* II (December, 1837), 585–590.

"The Three Sisters. A Romance of Real Life," *Bentley's Miscellany,* III (January, 1838), 66–70.

"The Inkeeper of Andermatt," *Bentley's Miscellany,* III (February, 1838), 143–148.

"The Two Sisters," *Bentley's Miscellany,* III (March, 1838), 278–284.

"The Cuisine Maigre," *Bentley's Miscellany,* III (April, 1838), 367–368.

"Pasquale: A Tale of Italy," *Bentley's Miscellany,* IV (September, 1838), 286–293.

"Hazlitt in Switzerland: A Conversation," *Fraser's Magazine,* XIX (March, 1839), 278–283.

"The Quarantine," *Bentley's Miscellany,* V (May, 1839), 502–506.

"Canova: Leaves from the Autobiography of an Amateur," *Fraser's Magazine,* XX (September, 1839), 370–375.

"Our Weekly Gossip," third paragraph only, *The Athenaeum,* No. 642 (February 15, 1840), p. 133.

"Miscellanea," paragraph from Berlin, *The Athenaeum,* No. 642 (February 15, 1840), p. 140.

"Foreign Correspondence," *The Athenaeum,* No. 643 (February 22, 1840), p. 155; No. 646 (March 14, 1840), p. 213; No. 648 (March 28, 1840), pp. 252–253; No. 653 (May 2, 1840), pp. 349–350; No. 659 (June 13, 1840), pp. 475–476.

"The Contrabandista," *Bentley's Miscellany,* VIII (July, 1840), 17–22.

"Sydney: From the Memoranda of a Physician," *Bentley's Miscellany,* IX (February, 1841), 168–179.

"Desaga: A Fantastic Tale, after the Manner of Hoffmann," *The New Monthly Magazine,* LXV (July, 1842), 387–394.

"The Two Skeletons: A Tale of Florence," *The New Monthly Magazine,* LXV (August, 1842), 484–497.

"My Moustache," *Ainsworth's Magazine,* I (1842), 52–54.

"A Short Chapter on Beards," *Ainsworth's Magazine,* I (1842), 113–114.

"The Tengin Pass," *Ainsworth's Magazine,* I (1842), 219–224.

"A Bengal Yarn," *Ainsworth's Magazine,* II (1842), 57–63.

"Doctor Crispinus," *Ainsworth's Magazine,* II (1842), 317–325.

"The Adventures of a Picture," *Ainsworth's Magazine,* III (1843), 155–160.

"A Day at Strasburg," *Ainsworth's Magazine,* III (1843), 226–229.

"A German Sunday," *Ainsworth's Magazine,* IV (1843), 317–322.

Lady Singleton; or, The World as It Is (London, 1843).

"The Sabre Duel," *Ainsworth's Magazine,* VIII (1845), 58–65.

"The Malocchio," *Ainsworth's Magazine,* VIII (1845), 217–224.

"Hermann and Regina: A True Anecdote," *Ainsworth's Magazine,* VIII (1845), 463–466.

"Adolphe Delessert: The Medical Student," *Ainsworth's Magazine,* XI (1847), 55–61.

The Life of Percy Bysshe Shelley (London, 1847).

"Black, Red, and Gold," *The New Monthly Magazine,* LXXXIV (October, 1848), 160.

"On the New Heidelberg Bastille Now Constructing," *The New Monthly Magazine* (November, 1848), 310.

"Hawking at Loo, A Palace of the King of Holland," *The New Monthly Magazine,* XCI (February, 1851), 157–167.

"Oscar and Giannetta: From the German of a Sonnetten Kranz, by Louise von Ploennies," *The New Monthly Magazine,* XCI (March, 1851), 360–361.

"To the King of Wurtemberg: From the German of Justinus Kerner," *The New Monthly Magazine,* XCII (June, 1851), 218.

"To Her Hand in Age: From the German of Justinus Kerner," *The New Monthly Magazine,* XCIII (September, 1851), 116.

"The Maiden of Rodenchild: From the German of the Late Droste Hülshof," *The New Monthly Magazine,* CII (October, 1854), 147–149.

"To Justinus Kerner: With a Painted Wreath of Bay-Leaves," *The New Monthly Magazine,* CII (October, 1854), 196.

"To the Emperor of Austria: On His Marriage," *The New Monthly Magazine,* CII (November, 1854), 340.

Nugæ (Heidelberg, 1856). Edited by Medwin with poems of his own.

"Absens-Praesens: Version of Goethe's 'Ich Denke Dein,' " *The New Monthly Magazine,* CX (July, 1857), 307.

"Renderings in Latin," *The New Monthly Magazine,* CXIII (July, 1858), 363–365; (August, 1858), 488–489.

Odds and Ends (Heidelberg, 1862).

The Life of Percy Bysshe Shelley (London, 1913). A new edition, edited by H. Buxton Forman.

DOUBTFUL, LOST, AND UNPUBLISHED WORKS

Alternate chapters, with Shelley, of "a wild and extravagant romance," *Nightmare.* Lost.

With Shelley, *The Wandering Jew,* completed 1810, first published in *The Edinburgh Literary Journal,* June 27 and July 4, 1829. The extent of Medwin's contribution is uncertain.

With Frank Mills, an unpublished satiric poem on the English in Paris, lost.

A pamphlet replying to Hobhouse's review of Medwin's *Conversations,* printed and suppressed by Henry Colburn.

Prometheus the Fire-bearer, unpublished but edited as a Master's thesis by John Pollard Guinn, Jr. The manuscript is in the Humanities Research Center of the University of Texas.

Some Rejected Stanzas of "Don Juan," with Byron's Own Curious Notes . . . From an Unpublished Manuscript in the Possession of Captain Medwin (Great Totham, Essex, 1845). These stanzas are most certainly not Byron's, and there is no evidence linking them with Medwin except the title page. See Samuel C. Chew, *Byron in England* (London, 1924), p. 61, note 1.

"On the Agamemnon of Aeschylus," *The Athenaeum,* No. 238 (May 19, 1832), pp. 320–321. The quotations from the play are identified as from Medwin's translation, and an article of the same title was recommended to the editor of *The Athenaeum* by Robert Montgomery. Probably Medwin's.

Various unpublished poems in the unique interleaved copy of Medwin's
The Shelley Papers; Memoir of Percy Bysshe Shelley, in the Humanities
Research Center of the University of Texas.

The Conspiracy of Fieschi, lost.

The Conversations of Lord Byron, revised for a new edition never
published, in the Library of Harvard University. I am now editing
this copy for publication.

An eclogue or elegy on Shelley, lost.

A "version" of the Book of Job, lost.

A translation of the *Frogs* of Aristophanes, lost.

INDEX